Myth

and

Modern Living

Myth

and

Modern Living

A PRACTICAL CAMPBELL COMPENDIUM

Stephen Gerringer

Dedicated to Becca Kitson,
Crystal Sinclair-Seay,
and Destiny Gerringer,
the Muses who have provided inspiration,
encouragement,
and support
every step of the way

Contents

INTRODUCTION

> If you do follow your bliss, you put yourself on
> a kind of track that has been there all the while
> waiting for you, and the life you ought to be liv-
> ing is the one you are living. When you can see
> that, you begin to meet people who are in the field
> of your bliss, and they open the doors to you . . .
> Doors will open where you didn't know they were
> going to be.[1]

Eighteen years ago, Robert Walter, co-founder and president of
the Joseph Campbell Foundation, held open one of those doors
when he invited me to write a series of thought pieces for JCF.

I had been teaching English and literature to minds on the
cusp of adolescence, a position filled with many challenges and
much joy—but, in the wake of 9/11, I decided to step away
from the classroom to pursue my first love: exploring creativity
through the lens of the mythic imagination.

No surprise there weren't any job openings in my chosen
field, which I wasn't really sure *was* a field. I didn't entirely
leave public education behind, subbing a few days a month
for friends and colleagues so I could count on at least a min-
imal income; meanwhile, I kept the creative juices flowing

with prolific contributions to the Joseph Campbell Mythology Group (JCMG) on Yahoo, under the nom de plume *bodhibliss*.

Coincidentally, Robert Walter had learned of JCMG when it became an Editor's Pick on Yahoo, which ballooned membership manyfold. Bob soon noticed and started keeping track of the entries by this *bodhibliss*, eventually reaching out and initiating a conversation. Skipping past details to cut to the chase, over time I was offered the opportunity to write on any subject I found relevant to Campbell's mythological perspective.

"Doors will open where you didn't know they were going to be."

The 24 essays in this collection, published on the Joseph Campbell Foundation website between 2004 and 2008 as the *Practical Campbell* essay series, are the evidence of what happened when I walked on through that door.

My experience would seem to confirm that Joseph Campbell knew whereof he spoke. I wanted to share that with others—not just fantastic tales out of dusty tomes, but what I perceived to be the practical aspect of how myth plays out in our lives today, and in the world around us.

Experience is the key word here. In my own head, I distinguish Campbell's perspective as *experiential mythology*—grounded in the human experience. More than just a relic of the past, there is a dynamic to myth that is always humming along in the background, whether we know it or not. The boon Campbell shares with us from his lifelong quest is an awareness of how those energies inform our lives, along with the tools to consciously engage and partner with the mythic imagination.

I trust that comes through in my writing.

Several of these essays started with the intention to answer common questions I've heard over the years ("What does Joseph

Campbell mean by 'follow your bliss' or 'joyful participation in the sorrow of life'?"). Others are deep dives into the multidimensional layers of a single mythological image (trickster, mask, dragon, flood). There are musings on the nature of esoteric subjects (dreams, oracles), and pieces that explore major aspects of key concepts (the symbiosis between myth and ritual, the nature of archetypes, the relationship of science to myth, the resonance between the mythologies of cultures distant from one another in time and space, and even the evolution of human consciousness). There are chapters that delve into the creative arts, from filmmaking to writing and music, and several that offer little-known biographical details illustrating how Campbell experienced these energies in his life. I even share little bits and pieces of my own adventures where relevant.

Despite the presence of "practical" in the title, I just can't help but take a sideways approach to many of these topics. There comes a point in every essay where we veer in brain-bending directions —which, for me, is when the view really gets interesting.

Along the way, I experienced an unexpected epiphany. Each essay was written as a stand-alone piece, some in response to questions posed in public forums I administered, others inspired by a current event, and most of the rest, musings on what held my fascination at that particular moment in time. There was no grand design in mind. Pulling these together for this volume is the first time I've approached them as one whole —so I'm pleasantly surprised to find that, taken together, they reflect a cohesive, comprehensive worldview, a perspective playful and, at times, profound, which still guides my life today.

I had considered grouping these selections into a few broad categories—but there's enough overlap that most could fit under several umbrellas, making that a somewhat arbitrary choice. Opting for the simplest approach, I have kept the chapters in the chronological order in which they originally appeared. Nevertheless, each essay is able to stand on its own; adventurous readers drawn to a particular title needn't feel bound by the sequence in the table of contents.

Please bear in mind these were written several years ago; a few do contain topical references to what then were current events—starting with the opening sentence of the very first essay, an anticipation of the centennial of Joseph Campbell's birth, the celebration now a distant memory; there's even a chapter ("After the Deluge") penned in the wake of Hurricane Katrina. These fleeting moments, however, shouldn't prove a distraction, but a launching point for what I trust is an enduring conversation.

That conversation continues today at the Joseph Campbell Foundation, where a diverse selection of mythologists, psychologists, writers, artists, and thinkers regularly contribute to JCF's weekly *MythBlast* essay series.

There are a few people I'd like to acknowledge. In particular, I am grateful for the support and friendship of Robert Walter for the reasons mentioned above, and far more. At the time of Campbell's passing only a few of his works were available on bookstore shelves; thanks in large part to Bob's vision and his tireless efforts, the Joseph Campbell Foundation has not only breathed life into long neglected and out-of-print works, but compiled and published a number of posthumous volumes that Campbell had planned before his death.

Which brings me to David Kudler.

For well over two decades, David put in long hours and hard work assembling and editing much of Campbell's posthumata, along with creating revised and updated editions of Campbell's most important works. David is not only a friend, mentor, and author in his own right, but for years carefully and conscientiously edited my own contributions on behalf of the Foundation.

A special thanks as well to John Bucher, JCF's Creative Director, and Managing Director Ilya Smirnoff, whose guidance and encouragement at a critical stage helped carry this ball over the finish line.

Thanks to the efforts of board members and countless colleagues past and present, *The Collected Works of Joseph Campbell* include some 18 books in print, all of which, along with a number of additional titles, are also available to the general public in e-book and audiobook formats. In addition, the Foundation has made possible multiple video lectures, including the 15 in the *Mythos* series, and a few more on the horizon. There are 70 hours of audio lectures available, and over 20 hours (so far) of previously unreleased Campbell talks accessible through JCF's *Pathways with Joseph Campbell* podcast.

This is a collective effort. Thinking back to how quickly I devoured the few Campbell titles on store shelves before I found the Foundation (or, more accurately, before the Foundation found me), this proliferation of Joseph Campbell's work warms my heart—so I would like to take this opportunity to thank JCF, as a whole, for all you do.

And finally, I would like to thank my wife, Des (yes, I literally am married to my Destiny), for, well, for everything. Your laughter, your love, and your tolerance of "the other woman" in my life (that seductive, sometimes elusive muse of myth) is priceless. You, My Love, bring the meaning and joy to my life.

— *Stephen Gerringer (bodhibliss)*

MODESTO, CALIFORNIA, NOVEMBER 21, 2021

NOTES

1   Joseph Campbell, The Power of Myth with Bill Moyers. (New York: Doubleday, 1988; New York: Anchor Books, 1991), 150. Citations refer to Anchor Books edition

ONE

/

ANSWERING THE CALL

March 26, 2004 marks the hundredth anniversary of Joseph Campbell's birth. Articles will be written, speeches will be made, and glasses will be raised in celebration of a gifted scholar and teacher who embraced life to the full. Much will be made of the breadth of his research and the depth of his knowledge, his natural charm and way with words, his contributions to the fields of literature and mythology, and his prodigious output (he authored twenty-three volumes and innumerable articles, edited 14 books, participated in countless workshops and seminars, conducted national lecture tours, and co-founded the Theater of the Open Eye with his wife, dancer Jean Erdman—not to mention his day job, serving on the faculty at Sarah Lawrence for 38 years!).

Whew . . . just reciting this list leaves me feeling the inveterate underachiever! Indeed, the all-encompassing nature of Joseph Campbell's interests provides so many openings to the world of ideas—from mythology to psychology, history, religion, spirituality, mysticism, humanism, etc.—that it's hard to know where to begin.

I'm not the only one with that problem. I regularly hear from undergraduates in classes on mythology who have been assigned to write a term paper on Professor Campbell's mythic perspective, but are having trouble getting a handle on his thoughts. There's just so much to absorb in so few weeks, particularly given the specialized vocabulary and questions favored in academic settings (e.g., is Campbell into structuralism, or perhaps reductionism? Does he favor diffusion, or parallel development? Is the man a monist, or a dualist?). Often these students are overwhelmed, reeling under the weight of trying to cram this expansive vision into a limited, linear construct—and so are left believing that only someone with a string of abbreviations after his/her name can comprehend Campbell's intellect.

Of course, this isn't a dynamic limited to discussions of Campbell. Five years ago, the principal of a local, rural high school asked me to step in for a literature teacher who had been critically injured in an automobile accident. The English department chair decided this would be the perfect time to introduce the entire student body to the poetry of Maya Angelou, but wanted to do so in a controlled setting, given troubling aspects of Ms. Angelou's life (raped at age eight, madame of a brothel at 19—the type of episodes guaranteed to alarm concerned parents).

That entire week, each period of the day, all literature classes in every grade assembled in the school's ancient, rickety auditorium. The first session began with the distribution of a packet of biographical material on Maya Angelou, along with a copy of her poem, "I Know Why the Caged Bird Sings." The department chair placed a copy of the poem on the overhead projector, and I settled into my seat, keen to observe the reaction of students to this bittersweet verse.

I'm still waiting.

The department chair circled the words, "caged bird," and instructed students to do the same and then write "metaphor" in the margin—and that's the way it went, line by line, stanza by stanza, circling words and writing definitions, followed by a discussion of the rhyme scheme—but never once did anyone read the poem complete!

Great way to teach teenagers to hate poetry! Ironically, the English teachers loved Maya Angelou, but were so intent on teaching their charges *about* "I Know Why the Caged Bird Sings," that they failed to let the students *experience* the poem. No one was allowed to hear sadness and yearning in the poem's rhythm—nor did any of these teenagers have the opportunity to relate the poignant, heartfelt emotions expressed by Ms. Angelou to their own tangled feelings. Instead, they were forced to categorize, analyze, and dissect the life right out of it.

That's a danger that exists for Campbell as well. His reputation as a scholar—and a growing body of Campbell criticism, pro and con—proves intimidating to those who have yet to actually read him, and so it's natural to assume his writing cannot be penetrated without much study and hard work—an indulgence reserved for graduate students and those with the leisure and the inclination for such pursuits, but with little or no bearing on real life.

Understanding Joseph Campbell, however, is not dependent on reading Latin and Sanskrit, or being conversant with Schopenhauer and Chuang-Tzu. Whether or not one "gets" Campbell isn't measured on the final exam. That might tell us what one knows about Campbell, but offers no insight into one's relationship to the material he presents.

As with a poem by Maya Angelou, a painting by Picasso, or a violin solo by Itzhak Perlman, the essence is encountered through experience.

What's required is an experience of myth.

> My writing is of a very different kind from anything I've heard about. All this mythological material is out there, a big gathering of stuff, and I have been reading it for some forty- or fifty-odd years. There are various ways of handling that. The most common is to put the material together and publish a scholarly book about it. But when I'm writing, I try to get a sense of an experiential relationship to the material. In fact, I can't write unless that happens . . . I don't write unless the stuff is really working on me, and my selection of material depends on what works.[1]

Clearly, Joseph Campbell was well read, articulate, a brilliant scholar. None of these descriptions, however, fully account for Campbell's impact. Why are people so hungry for his words today, 16 years after his passing? Yes, Joe's engaging manner first draws our attention—the sparkle with which he tells a story in the *Power of Myth* interviews with Bill Moyers, for example—but sooner or later, there comes a moment of clarity when we recognize the motifs and patterns he tickles out of myth as alive and active in our own lives.

Joseph Campbell remains influential today because his observations ring true to readers who experience the "power of myth" for themselves ("experiential mythology"—rooted in the human experience). However, the awareness that the same energies informing myth and dream also shape one's own life can have dramatic effects.

Christina Grof's encounter with Campbell illustrates this dynamic. Her story has been told several places, most notably in the Larsens' Campbell biography, *A Fire in the Mind*, and in Christina's own words (Stan and Christina Grof, "Spiritual Emergencies," *Yoga Journal*, July/August 1984, 40).

A housewife raising her children in the early seventies in Hawaii, Christina abruptly began to experience strange sensations and disturbing altered states, to the point that she feared she was going crazy. With her marriage on the rocks, Christina returned to New York where she turned for help to her old literature teacher from Sarah Lawrence. Hearing her plight, Joseph Campbell thought his friend Stanislav Grof, a pillar of the school of transpersonal psychology and expert on altered states, would be of help, so he arranged for Christina to visit Grof at the Esalen Institute in Big Sur, California (which led to an unanticipated, happy development as love bloomed between Stan and Christina, who soon were wed).

> "I reread my notebooks from Joe's course," Christina remembered. "I realized that I had taken intricate notes about the chakra system and the transformative power of the Kundalini, which had been so elegantly described by my teacher. I somhow missed that his description was more than a complex yogic attempt to describe spiritual development. I hadn't made the connection that Joe was describing *a real-life experience that could happen to anyone.*"[2]

Whereas in Eastern traditions the custom is to guide and nurture this process, in Western culture such spontaneous spiritual awakenings are frequently assumed to be evidence of mental illness (or the devil). Many are medicated and/or institutionalized, often against their will—which can arrest development and leave one trapped in a personal, and institutional, hell. Hence, the Grofs in 1978 founded the Spiritual Emergence Network (now the Center for Psychological and Spiritual Health, under the auspices of CIIS—the California Institute of Integral Studies), a support network of mental health professionals who help midwife this transformation, providing strategies to ease the process and explaining to family and legal authorities the dynamics involved.

Hmm . . . notes taken by a student in Campbell's upper division course on mythology lead to a breakthrough in transpersonal psychology, psychology, ultimately averting the misdiagnosis and tragically mistaken treatment of thousands: now that's what I call the power of myth!

Since this is my first column for JCF, I'll sneak in an introduction by drawing on my personal experience as a further example. Raised in Modesto, California, I earned a B.A. in history from a local campus in the state college system. Singularly unambitious, I decided I needed to "take a break" after graduation, so killed time the next few years with a series of meaningless, throwaway jobs and an active social life. When my father contracted stomach cancer, responsibility for running the family business fell to me (the only family member still at loose ends). Duty and a sense of family loyalty kept me tethered to the business after my dad's death; I now had money, success, and stability—but marketing oil and grease to farmers, truckers and loggers up and down California's Central Valley was clearly not my bliss. I found myself living the unintended life.

With my heart not in the job, I made poor choices, over time running the business into the ground, and losing everything: income, car, home, and the respect of friends and family. Naturally, after losing my insurance, my health rapidly declined. Sparing the details, I ended up in the emergency room, where I was subjected to a battery of tests. The news that I would be dead within weeks without immediate radiation or surgery was but one more in a series of surreal, seemingly random indignities.

Fortunately, I had stumbled some time before across a mention of Joseph Campbell while standing in line at a Grateful Dead concert. I purchased *Myths to Live By* and was immediately taken by the clear command of facts, the wry humor, the soaring tone; however, I thought of this work as fascinating, well-researched religious history and speculative philosophy. I collected other Campbell books, but, like Christina Grof, it never occurred to me that these mythological images were anything other than the elements of ancient, archaic beliefs or the vestiges of dream, with no relevance to mundane reality.

Still, given a choice of radiation or surgery, it was to Joseph Campbell I turned when I opted for door number three. Without telling concerned family members, I declined treatment, retreating instead to the local Best Western for three days, intent on coming to terms with certain death. I took with me Campbell's *The Hero with a Thousand Faces*, and *Creative Mythology* (Volume IV of *The Masks of God*). The first day I used a powerful entheogen as a meditation aid (I was dying, after all), and then spent all of the second and third day immersed in *Hero* . . .

Finally, the "aha" moment! I had read *The Hero with a Thousand Faces* before, but never in terms of my own life. Now I sometimes have trouble understanding how one can read it any other way.

Clearly, I had missed the call time and again, mired in the Wasteland, afraid to follow my bliss (not even aware I had the option). The Call had grown louder, more insistent, as, obstacles blocking my bliss were removed and I was gradually stripped of attachments to family and duty. The loss of health and death's approach seemed the final Call—psyche's way of slapping me silly in an attempt to get my attention. In the course of those three days, I understood that yes, I was going to die, but then, who isn't? In what little time I had left, I resolved to take Campbell's advice to heart and follow my bliss.

But just what the heck was my bliss? To discover that, I needed to know my Self, so again, I followed Joe's advice and started writing down my dreams. From there, everything snowballed. It was a few months before I fully realized all my symptoms had simply vanished. To this day I remain astounded that something so very physical and measurable in medical terms evaporated into thin air.

I spent most of the next decade on the road, hitchhiking across the United States, reading, writing, enjoying "invisible" means of support, meeting magic helpers, guides and teachers along the way, and slaying the occasional dragon. During this period, I was an active seeker, studying a variety of mythological traditions, meeting shamans and gurus of every stripe, as well as burying myself in university libraries from Missoula to

Madison, from Seattle to San Diego. I even thumbed my way to the campus of the Pacifica Graduate Institute near Santa Barbara, exactly ten years ago [1994 – SG] to check out the graduate program in mythological studies, and pay a visit to the Joseph Campbell Library and Archives.

My path led off the road and back into the classroom. I spent a few years teaching English and literature in junior high and currently teach part time, working just enough to support my writing habit (must be a twelve-step program for that some-where); and now, here I sit, at my bliss station, pursuing what I love, still living the adventure.

Of course, the point of my story is the same transform-ing power of myth Christina Grof encountered. Deep in my Wasteland experience, near to death, I discovered in Joseph Campbell's work clues that enabled me to re-imagine my story. Myth provided the tools for making sense of life in a time of utter confusion and moral uncertainty—and from there, the whole world opened up, with astounding results.

Neither Christina nor I are anomalies. The past three years I have been an active participant in the Joseph Campbell Mythology Group over on Yahoo (posting under the nom de plume, *bodhibliss*). The JCMG is a spontaneous grass roots movement—just a bunch of people who want to talk about Campbell, getting together in cyberspace—a bit unwieldy at times with 1700 members! Participants include waitresses, psy-chologists, teachers, truck drivers, students, computer techni-cians, housewives, performers, writers, and the unemployed—only a sprinkling of advanced degrees, and many members with little or no college. [JCMG is no longer active; Yahoo Groups ceased operation at the end of 2020 - SG.] Over the years I was involved, I couldn't help but notice a recurring theme: JCMG members are drawn to Campbell because they experience the myths he discusses unfolding in their individual lives. The tools Joseph Campbell presents the reader actually work.

Scholars can debate whether the man was a monist or a dualist, or if he believes myths should only be interpreted in psychological terms, or what his politics might have been—all fascinating topics that I love to explore—but I keep bumping up against the reality that I'm alive, not dead; life was meaningless, and now it isn't. For me, it's not a question of whether or not Joseph Campbell is right or wrong by some specialized academic standard.

Possession by mythic Hindu forces, spontaneous healings, discovering meaning in one's life through the discussion of ancient stories: no wonder mainstream scholars shudder—this smacks of things that go bump in the night! How do we quantify and categorize subjective experience?

Then again, how can we deny it?

Fortunately, Joseph Campbell used a different yardstick. As Bill Moyers points out in the forward to the printed version of *The Power of Myth*, Campbell...

> ...never seemed bothered by the controversy. He just kept on teaching, opening others to a new way of seeing . . . When he said that myths are clues to our deepest spiritual potential, able to lead us to delight, illumination, and even rapture, he spoke as one who had been to the places he was inviting others to visit.[3]

The last word belongs to Joseph Campbell:

> When I wrote about the Call forty years ago, I was writing out of what I had read. Now that I've lived it, I know it's correct. And that's how it turned out. I mean, it's valid. These mythic clues work.[4]

NOTES

1. Joseph Campbell, A Joseph Campbell Companion, ed. Diane K. Osbon (New York: Harper Collins, 1991), 268.
2. Stephen and Robin Larsen, A Fire in the Mind (New York: Doubleday, 1991; Rochester, Vermont: Inner Traditions International and Bear & Company, 2002), 496.
3. Campbell, The Power of Myth, op.cit. xx
4. John M. Maher and Dennie Briggs, eds., An Open Life: Joseph Campbell in Conversation with Michael Toms (New York: Harper & Row, 1989), 2.

Two

/

Discovering Bliss

> If you follow your bliss, you put yourself on a kind of
> track that has been there all the while, waiting for you,
> and the life that you ought to be living is the one you
> are living.[1]

When I read Joseph Campbell, I find two major threads braided
together: one details the broad sweep of mythology and its
development in tandem with human culture, while an accompanying theme elaborates on the harmony between myth and
"real" life—the life each of us is living, one's individual universe.
"Follow your bliss" belongs to this second category.

"Follow your bliss" is a phrase forever associated in the public consciousness with Joseph Campbell. Yet that same public consciousness remains unclear on exactly what Campbell
means by "bliss" and how one is supposed to follow it. For
some, this maxim has morphed into a warm and fuzzy, "touchy-
feely" New Age mantra, while others contend Campbell is
advocating escapist, hedonistic narcissism in the face of life's

difficulties—the height of irresponsibility.

Neither of these interpretations manages to capture Campbell's vision.

Oddly enough, the expression does not occur in work Campbell published during his lifetime. It's a theme developed by the mature Joseph Campbell, amplified in lectures, workshops, and interviews the last decade of his life. It is a small boon of wisdom, gleaned from a lifetime of studying myth, distilled into a single phrase and enunciated to the world-at-large in the *Power of Myth* interviews with Bill Moyers, which aired within months of Campbell's death.

Though this advice clearly strikes a chord in the popular imagination, many new to his work find the phrase elusive. Variations on the following questions continue to be asked by those struggling to get a handle on this key idea:

What does Campbell mean by bliss? Isn't bliss just another word for desire? Is "following one's bliss" code for doing whatever the heck you want, or some sort of Pollyanna prescription—"don't worry, be happy?" Could there be a dark side to it—after all, weren't Ted Bundy and Adolph Hitler merely following their bliss?

And if it is something more than just doing whatever you feel like, how do you go about finding that bliss?

> Eternity is a dimension of here and now. The divine lives within you. Live from your own center.
>
> Your real duty is to go away from the community to find your bliss. The society is the enemy when it imposes structures on the individual. On the dragon are many scales. Every one of them says 'Thou Shalt.'

Kill the dragon 'Thou Shalt' . . .

Breaking out is following your bliss pattern, quitting the old place, starting your hero journey, following your bliss.[2]

Bliss is born of Shadow, that chunk of the Jungian unconscious where the parts of ourselves we aren't willing to embrace are shoved away. For many, it *is* shadow—we aren't issued a particular bliss on our birth certificate. Most of us remain unconscious of our bliss, not following our passion, but following duty (what society expects of us), or following money—majoring in business or engineering, for example, not because the subject moves us, but because the career opportunities are better. Security and practicality all too often trump dreams in the waking world.

My general formula for my students is 'Follow your bliss.' Find where it is, and don't be afraid to follow it . . . If the work you are doing is the work that you chose to do because you are enjoying it, that's it. But if you think, "Oh no, I couldn't do that!" that's the dragon locking you in. "No, no, I couldn't be a writer," or "No, no, I couldn't possibly be doing what So-and-so is doing" . . .

Any world is a valid world if it's alive. The thing to do is to bring life to it, and the only way to do that is to find in your own case where the life is and become alive yourself.[3]

Not just what you want to do, or would like to do—"I want to play guitar like Hendrix," or "I'd like to be another Hemingway"—but your passion. What do you keep coming back to?

Joe is speaking of that which catches your soul and will not let you go. There is a world of difference between wanting to play the guitar like a rock star and always having a guitar in your hand, practicing six, eight hours a day, because you love making music, because this is what you would rather be doing than anything else in the world, even if there's no money in it, no fame—because you have no choice.

Campbell sometimes describes bliss as "rapture," which might be very different from one's will. You might consciously will to become a lawyer or computer programmer or news anchor, but if your bliss, your passion—your Calling—is music, or teaching, or preaching, or building, or writing, then by all means, follow the Call. This is the path out of the Wasteland . . .

Our bliss is the what, where, and when in which we feel most authentic, most ourselves.

What is your bliss? It is what you are doing when time drops away and you reside in an eternal now.

I sit down to write in the morning, stare into space, flip through the pages of books, put words on paper or screen, re-arrange those words, stare into space a bit more, craft another paragraph or two, and suddenly notice it's dark outside.

But I just had breakfast!

What happened to lunch?

Where did the day go?

You know you are in your bliss when in an eternal moment ("eternal" doesn't necessarily mean "forever." It's from the Latin: *e* = outside, *ternum* = time . . . that which is outside — or transcends — time). When you are in your bliss, ego concerns dissolve: you aren't thinking about the argument with your spouse, or how you're going to pay the light bill Tuesday, what you should do for dinner, how the boss came down on you yesterday, or what's on television tonight. When you are in your bliss, time ceases to exist (whether that bliss is sculpting clay or crunching numbers).

Professor Mihalyi Csikszentmihalyi conducted research while chairman of the department of psychology at the University of Chicago that led him to similar conclusions, independent of Campbell:

> What is common to such moments is that consciousness is full of experiences, and these experiences are in harmony with each other. Contrary to what happens all too often in everyday life, in moments such as these what we feel, what we wish, and what we think are in harmony.[4]

Csikszentmihalyi (pronounced, so he says, as "chicks-send-me-high"), interested in the psychology of happiness, focused on 90 individuals widely recognized as living creative, fulfilling lives—from author Madeline L'Engle (*A Wrinkle in Time*) to scientist Jonas Salk—in an attempt to identify attitudes and practices held in common by such a diverse group. This evolved into a second study of 2300 individuals, from mountain climbers to chess players. Csikszentmihalyi describes the data collected and conclusions reached in his groundbreaking book, *Flow*, which describes "how to live life as a work of art, rather than as a chaotic response to external events. . ."

The overlap between Campbell's concept of bliss and the state-of-being labeled "flow" is apparent. Csikszentmihalyi designates individuals who live such lives "autotelic personalities" (Latin: *auto* = self; *telos* = aim/goal), who generally "do things for their own sake, rather than in order to achieve some later external goal." Compensation is not the primary consideration for such individuals.

Compare this to Campbell:

> [Y]ou follow your bliss, you'll have your bliss, whether you have money or not. If you follow money, you may lose the money, and then you don't even have that. The secure way is really the insecure way and the way in which the richness of the quest accumulates is the right way.[5]

Csikszentmihalyi begins with the collection of raw scientific data, while Campbell starts from the mythic imagination—yet both men arrive at the same place. Even though Csikszentmihalyi seems unaware of Campbell's observations, he does acknowledge that many mythologies anticipate his own conclusions:

> Much of this has been already said, in one way or another, in the religions of the Plains Indians, the Buddhists, the Zoroastrians, and innumerable other beliefs based on a systematic observation of life. What contemporary science adds is a systematic expression of these facts in a language that has authority in our time.[6]

Determining what one's bliss might be isn't simply a matter of choosing what we want and then waiting for the universe to hand it over. We don't "will" our bliss; we "discover" our bliss. How do we make that discovery?

Socrates' dictum is relevant here: "Know thyself."

> We are having experiences all the time which may on occasion render some sense of this, a little intuition of where your bliss is. Grab it. No one can tell you what it is going to be. You have to learn to recognize your own depth . . .
>
> The way to find out about your happiness is to keep your mind on those moments when you feel most happy, when you really are happy—not excited, not just thrilled, but deeply happy. This requires a little bit of self-analysis. What is it that makes you happy? Stay with it, no matter what people tell you. This is what I call "following your bliss."[7]

Myth and dream—realms where the individual and subjective intersect the collective and transcendent—provide clues to uncovering one's bliss. My bliss is not your bliss—I have to discover my bliss on my own, by listening to myself, following clues dropped by the greater, "unconscious" part of my being (the psyche is called unconscious not because it is unconscious and without purpose, but because the waking ego—"me," "I", how I experience myself—is unconscious of psyche's workings). "Following your bliss" is metaphor for a process that begins with a journey to uncover what you find most fulfilling in your life: the quest for the Holy Grail, that which gives life meaning and purpose. This requires journeying into the dark forest, into what is Shadow and Mystery—a journey into the depths of the soul.

Finding one's bliss means meeting and engaging the shadows. When we do this, we are following the trajectory of the classic Hero's Quest—Joyce's monomyth, Campbell's cycle of Separation/Initiation/Return. Joe points out that myths won't tell you what your bliss is, but they will "tell you what happens when you begin to follow your happiness, what the obstacles are you're going to run into."

Is there a dark side to "bliss?"

Yes—the Shadow predominates when we refuse the Call and remain unconscious of the forces that move us, unaware of the patterns recurring in our lives. This is to be subject to Fate, or rather to one's inner drives—reacting, almost in victim mode—whereas finding and following your bliss is to consciously embrace and partner Fate.

Here is where critics are eager to raise an objection: Campbell advises all to "follow one's bliss"—so, is he advising Hitler to slaughter millions of unarmed, defenseless civilians, advising Ted Bundy to lure young women to their death? Weren't they just living their bliss?

They may have been elbows deep in their own Shadow stuff, yes, but that is hardly following one's bliss, as Campbell defines it. Last winter [2002 - SG] a controversial movie came out, entitled *Max*, in which John Cusack portrays a one-armed Jewish art dealer in post-World War I Vienna, who befriends a young art student named Adolf Hitler. The film hints that, had Hitler been able to follow his bliss and pursue his art, the Second World War and the Holocaust might have been avoided.

Of course, I can't speak for Joseph Campbell, but I feel I can safely infer that he did not believe Hitler was following his bliss—far from it, for following one's bliss implies consciously exploring and moving in harmony with one's psyche. You cannot know what your bliss, your passion, is—as opposed to what your ego desires—if you have only a surface understanding of who you are, no sense of your own depths. Hitler was anything but conscious, in a psychological sense; instead of exploring his shadows, bringing unconscious contents forward into the light, he repressed and denied his Shadow, projecting it outward onto the Other, the Enemy—particularly "inferior" races.

Archetypal possession is one way to explain Hitler—the exact opposite of following one's bliss. Keep in mind that following your bliss doesn't mean simply doing what you want to do: there can be plenty of pain, suffering, and delayed gratification associated with following one's bliss, whereas many who have no idea where their bliss lies fill a hole they don't know exists with what feels good, which can range from wholesome activities to perversion and violence, depending on the individual.

I do believe the psychology of a Hitler or a Bundy is worth exploring—and it is worth pondering what in our own lives could move us so far off the beam. But in terms of the hero's journey, of discovering and following one's bliss, these are not examples of a genuine response to a Call.

After stumbling across Campbell's work, I floundered for a few years, at a loss as to what my bliss might be. One night, during an extended stay in Taos, New Mexico, I chanced upon a lecture about Joseph Campbell at the historic Harwood

Library. During the question-and-answer session that followed I asked, "How do we find our bliss?"

I was expecting some degree of profundity—but all the kind yet elderly gentleman behind the lectern offered before taking the next question was, "Joseph Campbell said to write down your dreams."

Heavy sigh—somewhat anticlimactic for me. I was already compiling my dreams, and have recorded hundreds since then . . . and yes, they help me understand myself a little bit more, but how is recording my dreams my bliss?

Over time I realized that I had missed the point. Writing down my dreams was not my bliss—but exploring the dark shadows, the corners, crannies, nooks, and niches of my psyche, delving into the unconscious, slowly revealed essential elements of my bliss, a process still unfolding in my life. A fast forward button it isn't, but attending to your dreams can be a valuable step on the path to self-discovery.

Another important clue comes from listening carefully to you: notice those moments when you lose yourself, moments when you are doing something you enjoy—telling a story, painting a picture, cooking a meal, playing with children, solving a knotty mechanical problem—moments when you forget about "I," about ego. Look for those eternal moments when time is transcended and everything seems to flow effortlessly. Note what you're doing in such moments, and you should be able to detect patterns that point toward your bliss.

As awareness of bliss grows, opportunities to do whatever it is that triggers that bliss seem to present themselves of their own accord.

If you do follow your bliss, you put yourself on a track that has been there all the while, waiting for you, and the life that you ought to be living is the one you are living. When you can see that, you begin to meet people who are in the field of your bliss, and they open doors to you. I say follow your bliss and don't be afraid, and doors will open where you didn't know they were going to be.[8]

It just takes time to recognize one's bliss – a process of discovery – or a quest. A hero's quest.

It's one heck of a ride!

NOTES

1. Joseph Campbell, The Power of Myth, op.cit., 113.
2. Joseph Campbell, A Joseph Campbell Companion, op.cit., 21.
3. Joseph Campbell, The Power of Myth, op.cit., 183-184.
4. Mihalyi Csikszentmihalyi, Finding Flow: The Psychology of Engagement with Everyday Life (New York: Basic Books), 29.
5. Maher and Briggs, An Open Life, op.cit. 25.
6. Csiksentmihaly, op.cit., 141.
7. Joseph Campbell, The Power of Myth, op. cit, 147, 193
8. Joseph Campbell, The Power of Myth, op. cit. 150.

THREE

Mask and Metaphor

"Who was that Masked Man?"

A childhood memory, televised in black and white—yet I still feel chills up my spine in anticipation of the weekly revelation, followed always by the sound of thundering hooves, the strains of the William Tell Overture, and a hearty "Hi Ho, Silver! Away!"

The power of the mask!

We feel it even today, in our un-superstitious age. This ancient vehicle of identities and energies that transcend the individual is still worn among the pantheon populating contemporary childhood tales. The Lone Ranger, Zorro, Batman— each of these characters is more the mask than the man who wears it: individual identity dissolves beneath the disguise. Halloween masks play a similar role. When the doorbell rings and voices cry out "Trick or treat!" it is the monster, ghost, or witch we appease with sweet offerings. This quaint custom is more secular than religious in its observance—yet several strict, literal-minded denominations denounce Halloween for opening children to demonic influence. Ironically, even though such groups oppose the celebration of Halloween, their objections suggest they do believe the underlying myth of spirits roaming the night needing appeasement.

This seems an example of reading the myth literally—but there are certainly hooks in the practice on which these projections catch. Masks have long provided a gateway to other dimensions, other realms, beyond the senses:

> The masks that in our demythologized time are lightly assumed for the entertainment of a costume ball or Mardigras—and may actually, on such occasions, release us to activities and experiences which might otherwise have been tabooed—are vestiges of an earlier magic, in which the powers to be invoked were not simply psychological, but cosmic. For the appearances of the natural order, which are separate from each other in time and space, are in fact the manifestation of energies that inform all things and can be summoned to focus at will.[1]

The phrase "the masks of God"—the title of Joseph Campbell's exhaustive, four-volume survey of mythological development—generally refers to the deities of the various mythological systems (whether Indra, Zeus, Isis, Yahweh, or others) as local manifestations of the divine, transcendent source of being: that which is beyond thought and conception, beyond the personality of particular cultural deities. Through one or another of these local gods, individuals are able to approach the greater Mystery.

Campbell repeatedly emphasizes that a god should be "transparent to transcendence"—opening up to the radiance behind the mask. Problems arise, however, when people are caught up in one particular "mask" of God—Yahweh or Allah or Krishna, for example—believing God is that mask alone, and nothing else: the mask is seen as the final term. Not only does this approach create problems between peoples and cultures ("My Allah/Jesus/Yahweh is God; yours is not."), but it closes off those who see only the mask to the essence of God, which permeates all the various manifestations of the divine and, indeed, all that exists.

> For, indeed, in the primitive world, where most of the clues to the origin of mythology must be sought, the gods and demons are not conceived in the way of hard and fast, positive realities. A god can simultaneously be two or more places—like a melody, or like the form of a traditional mask. And whenever he comes, the impact of his presence is the same: it is not reduced through multiplication.[2]

How does Joseph Campbell arrive at this metaphor of the mask? Is it simply a clever literary device, no more than instructive analogy? Or does the mask present an embodied experience, serving as the vehicle for archetypal energies that actually transform the wearer? And when Campbell speaks of the "masks of God," is he speaking only of these local deities? Any mythic image is by nature elastic and multifaceted, so what else might "mask" conjure in the imagination, and how might that relate to the individual today?

Moreover, the mask in a primitive festival is revered and experienced as a veritable apparition of the mystical being that it represents—even though everyone knows that a man made a mask and that a man is wearing it. The one wearing it, furthermore, is identified with the god during the time of the ritual of which the mask is a part. He does not merely represent the god; he is the god.[3]

This is very much the way an actor dissolves into a role. When Meryl Streep and Johnny Depp step into character, their job is to make us forget they are Johnny Depp and Meryl Streep. The mark of a good actor is to become the character they portray.

The audience meets the actor more than halfway. When we watch a movie or attend a play, we expect to suspend our disbelief; we know that Harrison Ford really isn't a dashing and daring archaeologist, and that Nicole Kidman is no southern belle, but we go along with the pretense. If the actors are skillful and the drama well written, then we are able to enter into this "play world," experiencing the adventure and its accompanying emotion *as if* they are real.

It's not surprising to learn the earliest theatrical productions in ancient Greece evolved from sacred rituals – which brings us back to masks, for the actors in these plays wore masks. (That is not unique to Greece: the same can be said for the development of theater in many parts of Asia – even today, in Japan, masks are worn in *Noh* plays). The tragic and comic masks from that period still represent the dramatic arts today. Religious studies scholar Carl Kerenyi claims these evolved from "the mask of Dionysos," a cult object central to this god's mystery ritual.[4] Archaeologist Marija Gimbutas follows the development of these masks even further back in time, tracing them to Neolithic Europe. In northern Greece and the Balkans she finds evidence of snake masks, Gorgon masks, and death masks that are eight thousand years old.[5]

Meanwhile, in his *Historical Atlas of World Mythology*, Joseph Campbell places the first evidence of masks in the New World circa 2150–2000 BC, appearing on pottery uncovered in Ecuador[6]; Campbell also notes masked hunters on a rock wall from the Sahara Atlas Mountains in north Africa, roughly ten thousand years ago[7]; And he quotes archaeologist Andre Leroi-Gourhan identifying a possible mask on a shamanic figure among the prehistoric images in the Cave of Lascaux, painted between 12,000 and 17,000 years ago.[8]

Clearly, humankind's relationship to the mask extends back millennia.

We will never know with absolute certainty the exact significance of a mask worn four thousand years ago in Mesoamerica, or ten thousand years ago in Africa; nevertheless, the consistency of the ritual context in which masks or images of masks have been found, along with motifs recurring across centuries and even across cultures, does suggest possibilities.

For example, Gimbutas finds the Gorgon theme emerging in southeastern Europe, in a ceramic mask from the Sesklo culture, circa 6000 BC She follows this motif as it unfolds over the next five thousand-plus years in masks unearthed from Bulgaria to Greece, which brings us down to the historical period (from there, Greek texts are able to offer insight into the evolution of this image). Though the Medusa appears in her most fearsome aspect between the seventh and fifth centuries BC (fangs and lolling tongue reminiscent of the Hindu goddess Kali), the prehistoric Gorgons are terrifying as well—and, like their descendants, are ever in the company of symbols of regeneration—so it's not unreasonable to assume there is some resonance between the earlier and the later images.[9]

There is surprising unanimity of opinion among scholars about the role of ceremonial masks:

MARIJA GIMBUTAS

In contemporary cultures that still use masks in ritual, the masks serve to personify a supernatural force. The ancient Greeks employed masks in drama and in ritual for the same purpose: to embody the deities, as well as heroines and heroes.[10]

CARL KERENYI

By virtue of the mask, a being who is only seemingly remote is placed in this world. And this can be done even with the gods: a mask can place them in this world so that they may not merely appear but actually live among us, though remaining at the same time far off and never relinquishing their remoteness. . .The situation of man between an individual being and another, Protean being which assumes every shape is made visible in the mask. Hence the creative, participating ecstasy which the mask calls forth and disseminates.[11]

C.G. JUNG

Individual human expression is submerged . . . in psychological terms, the mask transforms its wearer into an archetypal image.[12]

JOSEPH CAMPBELL
The literal fact that the apparition is composed of A, a mask,
B, its reference to a mythical being, and C, a man, is dis-
missed from the mind, and the presentation is allowed to
work without correction upon the sentiments of both the
beholder and the actor. In other words, there has been a
shift of view from the logic of the normal secular sphere,
where things are understood to be distinct from one another,
to a theatrical or play sphere, where they are accepted for
what they are experienced as being and the logic is that of
"make believe"—"as if."[13]

In most cultures, wearing a mask in a sacred ceremony involves the adoption and channeling of energies that transcend the individual personality. When a Pueblo Indian puts on a Kachina mask, he becomes the deity. No longer calling him by the name he was given at birth, the other members of the tribe relate to and engage the individual as if he were the corn god, or the cloud god. For the space of the ceremony the individual disappears.

(Though this is a very powerful, very real experience in most cultures, it is not the same thing as "concretizing the myth." Campbell defines myth as metaphor, then cautions us against taking the metaphor literally and reading myth as history. A metaphor is experienced in the living present, with lots of wiggle room—"as if"—while historical facts belong to the past, and lack that element of play. There is no room for "as iffing" in the orthodox telling of Moses parting the Red Sea, or Jesus born of a Virgin.)

From the masked Kachina dancers, the Hactin of the Apache, the False Face Society of the Iroquois, or the Yu'pik of the Arctic, to the masked Duk-duk of New Guinea and the indigenous tribes in west Africa and the Sudan, the mask serves as a conduit for the community to powers which transcend the individual. But the mask is also used in many cultures as an agent of individual transformation.

Masks have the power to transform even when they are not worn. A classic (and classical) scene appears on a wall fresco preserved beneath volcanic ash in the Villa of Mysteries in Pompeii. A youth bends over and peers into a silver bowl held up by a bearded figure, generally thought to be playing the role of Silenos, the satyr who served as teacher to Dionysus. The bowl acts as a concave mirror.

Campbell describes the scene:

> The young man is being initiated. . . The initiator is on the left and his assistant is behind the groom. The youth is told to look in this metal bowl and he will see his own face, his own true face. However, the bowl is so concave inside that what he sees is not his own face but the distorted mask of old age, which the assistant holds up behind him. With a shock he is introduced to what our American Indians call the "long body"—the whole body of life from birth to death. Now suppose one of his friends, before he went in there, had said to him, "Now look, this guy in there is going to have a bowl and he is going to tell you that you're going to see your own face. You're not! He's got another fellow there

who's holding this mask thing up behind you so that what you will see is nothing more than a reflection."

If this happened, there would be no initiation. There would be no shock. This is why mysteries are kept secret. An initiation is a shock. Birth is a shock; rebirth is a shock. All that is transformative must be experienced as if for the first time.[14]

The indigenous tribes in the American Northwest, from the Kwakiutl to the Haida, are known for their Transformation Masks. This is a double (or, occasionally, triple) mask, with the outer mask usually in the form of an animal. After fasting in the woods, then dancing into a frenzy in the lodge house, the masked dancer reaches a state of ecstasy and opens the hinged outer mask to reveal the interior: the image of an ancestral spirit. The dancer experiences a double transformation, identifying not just with the Animal whose mask he wears, but also with the Ancestor. The masked dancer enters a realm that once was and yet still is, a dimension where humans and animals are able to change form, hidden behind the world of waking reality. The wearer experiences the unity of all life: hunter and hunted; animal, human, and ancestral spirit—these are but masks for the one Life that animates All.

Are such realizations possible today? After all, ceremonial masks seem somewhat archaic in this secular age—art objects to be collected, rather than tools of transformation.

And yet, the image still speaks to us on many levels. It's a vital metaphor. In fact, Campbell spins our brains further by proposing the mask as a metaphor for metaphor itself:

Deities have to become, as one great German scholar said, "transparent to the transcendent." The transcendent must show and shine through those deities. But it must shine through us, too, and through the spiritual things we are talking about.[15]

Well, what do you know! Turns out that *we* are the masks of God! Who is that Masked Man, indeed?

Notes

1. Joseph Campbell, Historical Atlas of World Mythology, Vol. 1: The Way of the Animal Powers, Part 1, Mythologies of the Primitive Hunters and Gatherers (New York: Harper & Row, 1988), 93.
2. Joseph Campbell, The Masks of God, Vol. 1: Primitive Mythology (New York: Viking Penguin, 1959; Novato: New World Library, 2022), 21. Citations refer to New World Library edition.
3. Ibid.
4. Carl Kerényi, "Man and Mask," in Spiritual Disciplines: Papers from the Eranos Yearbooks, ed. by Joseph Campbell (Princeton: Princeton University Press, 1960; Princeton: First Princeton/Bollingen paperback printing, Princeton University Press, 1985), 152.
5. Marija Gimbutas, The Living Goddesses (Berkeley and Los Angeles: University of California Press, 1999), 9.
6. Joseph Campbell, Historical Atlas of World Mythology, Vol. 2: The Way of the Seeded Earth, Part 3, Mythologies of the Primitive Planters (New York: Harper & Row, 1989), 382.
7. Joseph Campbell, "Myths from East to West, in Myths, ed. by Alexander Eliot (Maidenhead, England: McGraw Hill, 1976.
8. Joseph Campbell, Historical Atlas of World Mythology, Vol. 1: The Way of the Animal Powers, Part 1, op.cit., 65.
9. Gimbutas, op.cit. 24-25.
10. Ibid. 9.
11. Kerényi, op.cit. 158, 167.

12. C.G. Jung, Man and His Symbols (London: Aldus Books, 1964; New York: Dell Publishing, 1968), 263. Citations are from the Dell edition.
13. Joseph Campbell, Primitive Mythology, op.cit. 21.
14. Joseph Campbell, Mythos, Vol. 1, Episode 3: The Shaping of Our Mythic Tradition (London: Acorn Media, VHS March 21, 2000; London: Acorn Media, DVD August 5, 2012).
15. Maher and Briggs, ed., An Open Life, op.cit. 70.

FOUR

MYTHIC ROOTS OF MIDEAST TURMOIL

> You have the three great Western religions, Judaism,
> Christianity, and Islam—and because the three of
> them have different names for the same biblical god,
> they can't get on together. They are stuck with their
> metaphor and don't realize its reference. They haven't
> allowed the circle that surrounds them to open. It is
> a closed circle. Each group says, "We are the chosen
> group, and we have God."[1]

Joseph Campbell's remarks, a reflection on the violence that
wracked Beirut in the eighties, could easily be drawn from today's
headlines. Indeed, his focus is not so much on the details of the
situation as it is on the larger picture—a picture big enough to
encompass contemporary events in the Middle East.

In *The Power of Myth*, Campbell draws on the pyramid
depicted on the Great Seal of the United States, found on the
back of the dollar bill, as metaphor for two different perspectives of life. One is the view from the base of the pyramid: a

pyramid has four sides, and if we are at the bottom of one, we identify with the way the world looks from just that side, and no other. This is participation in life: we are fully engaged, like the player on one side of the net in a tennis match, who plays to win. This is the field of economic and political preoccupations—a far different perspective from that of the referee sitting in his/her chair above the net, remaining aloof, disengaged from the play, not cheering one side over another, silently observing the play.

Of course, each of us lives at the base of the pyramid. If we are to engage life, then on some level we must take sides. We work, sleep, eat, and make love and hate and war and peace on this plane, in the midst of life's passion play. It is on this level that complex and conflicting sets of economic, political, and sociological concerns factor into the clashes in the Middle East—and it is here that each individual determines how they will participate, which might range all the way from complete and utter apathy, to writing letters to the editor, enlisting in the Marines, or marching in a peace protest.

Yet atop that pyramid on the Great Seal rests the Eye of God, able to see what transpires simultaneously on all sides of the pyramid: the mystic perspective—aware of, yet not participating in, the play of Life. Campbell doesn't suggest we retreat from life in favor of contemplating our navels, but he does urge us to broaden our vision and embrace both perspectives: live in this world, participate in the passion play as best we can, yet at the same time see through mundane concerns and recognize the recurring archetypal patterns which shape experienced reality.

Joseph Campbell invites us to see with a mythic eye.

Hence my focus (if focus there be to this meandering

meditation) is not on questions of preemptive strikes and weapons of mass destruction, or a Palestinian homeland, suicide bombers, Iraqi oil, American security, justice for 9/11, or foreign policy. I have no simple, ready-made solution to offer, no "thus saith Campbell" able to sever that Gordian knot. The debate over these questions belongs instead at the base of the pyramid, where each individual is free to arrive at his or her own answers.

As we scale the pyramid, however, the questions change:

What are the mythic roots of the conflicts that rage from Baghdad to Bethlehem and beyond? Is Campbell's characterization correct: are Judaism, Christianity, and Islam separated by a common mythology? Could ancient traditions and archaic beliefs really be fueling bloodshed and barbarism in this dotcom era? Does any myth suggest a possible resolution? And what role, if any, might we as individuals play in healing this rift?

CHILDREN *of* ABRAHAM

Hebrews and Arabs are among the many Semitic-speaking people who erupt from the Arabian Peninsula in several waves between 2500 BC and 200 BC Both groups claim common descent from Abraham, expatriate of Ur (one of the oldest excavated cities in Mesopotamia—Iraq, wouldn't you know. Campbell suggests Abraham may have been a near contemporary of King Gudea of Lugash, c. 2000 BC, in *The Masks of God*, Volume 3: *Occidental Mythology*). Hence the character and culture of the Jews and Muslims are expressed in parallel, often overlapping myths.

As we read in Genesis, Yahweh promises his faithful servant Abraham that he will father great nations—but, as Abraham approaches the century mark it appears his wife, Sarah, only ten years younger, is barren. To provide her husband with an heir, Sarah gives her handmaiden, Hagar, to Abraham. Hagar gives birth to Ishmael (meaning, "God will hear"), who is raised as Sarah's surrogate son.

But the Lord visits Abraham and tells him Sarah will soon be with child herself. Sarah, overhearing this—approaching her ninetieth birthday, with shriveled, shrunken paps on a body bent with age—laughs at the very idea

. . . so, nine months later they name their son Isaac (meaning "laughter").

Sarah, intent on protecting Isaac's inheritance, withdraws her good will from Ishmael and Hagar. She badgers Abraham to turn Hagar and Ishmael out into the desert, where they would have perished had God (Yahweh/Allah, depending on who is telling the tale) not miraculously provided a spring. The firstborn outcast grows up to become a great hunter—but as the older son, child of a somewhat shady liaison, abandoned by his father, is Ishmael resentful of the younger brother who supplants him?

This brothers theme is a common motif in Hebrew scripture: Abel sacrificing a lamb of his flock, accepted by God over older brother Cain's offering of the harvest; Jacob scamming firstborn Esau out of his birthright; Joseph the young dreamer replacing his brothers in his father's affection. In the Old Testament, God consistently (and at times arbitrarily) sides with the youngest sibling.

Is it difficult to imagine that those who believe themselves to be Ishmael's descendants might resent the powerful and prosperous nation Israel has built on land that once was theirs? The Arabs first took control of Palestine in AD 620, while the Jewish population remained tiny into the twentieth century . . . but now, from their perspective, the Palestinian Arabs are supplanted by the descendants of the upstart who supplanted their own ancestor! Ejected from their homeland (which needn't have happened, had they accepted the very partition they now seek), they were once again wanderers cast adrift, like Ishmael. Meanwhile, the Israelis fight to protect a birthright Yahweh promised to Isaac's descendants.

This rivalry between Ishmael and Isaac stretches back nearly four thousand years, a story that has been told time and again around the desert campfire, and in temple, synagogue, and mosque. It's embedded in the collective psyches of both peoples. Imagine the depth and power of the complex thus constellated when the ancient pattern repeats itself on an international scale! The hatred from both sides billows out of proportion to the political disagreements that trigger it, with the results broadcast on the nightly news.

SACRIFICE & SUBMISSION

The climactic moment in Abraham's tale comes when God commands Abraham to sacrifice his beloved son. The patriarch, less than forthright with the lad, binds the youth and places him on the altar. At the last minute, God grants a reprieve and stays Abraham's hand. Secure in the patriarch's submission to His will, God provides a ram tangled in a nearby thicket as a substitute for Abraham's son, Ishmael.

Ishmael?

That's not the Genesis version familiar to those raised in the Judeo-Christian tradition, where it's Isaac who is under the knife. In the Q'uran, Ishmael is the one miraculously spared, while for Christians, as Campbell notes in *The Mythic Image* (207), the ram sacrificed in Isaac's stead prefigures the sacrifice of God's beloved Son, who dies in our place.

Abraham's willingness to sacrifice Isaac is central to all three religions. The overriding theme is that of surrender to God: Abraham's obedience securing God's blessings for the Israelites to come; Ishmael's acquiescence as the essence of Islam (in Arabic, i'slam means "submission"); Jesus' prayer in the Garden, before his crucifixion—"not my will, but Thine, be done." (Matthew 26:39)

> In the Levant, the stress is always on obeying. The idea is that God has given a revelation that is encompassed in a book, in a statement. This goes for Zoroastrianism, for Judaism, for Christianity, for Islam—all of the religions out of the Near East. In each case there is a book, a revealed truth, and one doesn't quibble with that. One finds out what it says, and one who does quibble with that is by definition an evil person, a person who has lost touch with the truth and is an outcast, a heretic. Whole races, whole worlds, can fall away.[2]

Many other points of correspondence can be found, from sacred sites (Abraham's sacrifice, Solomon's temple, and Muhammad's departure for heaven all overlap atop Jerusalem's temple mount—small wonder these mythologies keep bumping into one another!), to prophetic expectations (the anticipation of the Messiah in Judaism; the return of Jesus as Savior in Christianity; the Hidden Imam, or *Mahdi*, in Shi'ite Islam). Of course, these images and ideas vary enough in detail and interpretation for adherents to claim their religious expression is unique, denying similarities—but in the mythic imagination, a congruence exists between such images, much like that found in poetry or dream.

MYTHIC DISSOCIATION

Indeed, the absence of feminine symbolism for God marks Judaism, Christianity, and Islam, in marked contrast to the world's other traditions, whether in Egypt, Babylonia, Greece and Rome, or in Africa, India, and North America, which abound in feminine symbolism. Jewish, Christian, and Islamic theologians are quick to point out that God is not to be considered in sexual terms at all. Yet the actual language they use in daily worship and prayer conveys a different message: who, growing up with Jewish or Christian tradition, has escaped the distinct impression that God is masculine? And while Catholics revere Mary as the mother of Jesus, they never identify her as divine in her own right: if she is "the mother of God," she is not "God the Mother" on an equal footing with God the Father.[3]

This devaluation of the feminine, first emerging in Mesopotamia c. 2500 BC, represents a dramatic shift in mythic forms. Prior to this development, the world was thought to be the body of the goddess; hence, all nature was considered divine. This isn't to say that the ancient Sumerians or Egyptians necessarily had a concept of nature qua nature in the sense of contemporary environmentalists, but that every rock, tree, bird, or beast—and even each other—was identical to, and an expression of, Deity. However, with this shift, God is perceived as separate from nature:

> God in this system is a kind of fact somewhere, an actual personality to whom prayers can be addressed with expectation of a result. He is apart from and different from the world: in no sense identical with it, but related, as cause to effect. I call this kind of thinking "mythic dissociation." The sense of an experience of the sacred is dissociated from life, from nature, from the world, and transferred or projected somewhere else—an imagined somewhere else—while man, mere man, is accursed. "In the sweat of your face you shall eat bread till you return to the ground, for out of it you were taken; you are dust, and to dust you shall return."[4]

This separation between Creator and Created is inherited by the religions of the Book, whose beliefs are determined by God's (Yahweh's/Jesus'/Allah's) Word.

So, if these three faiths have a common origin, revere many of the same religious figures, and share the same basic worldview, why are they so often at each other's throats?

Two reasons come to mind. One is related to who is allowed to participate:

> To the formula of mythic dissociation, therefore, there must now be added that of "social identification": Identification with Israel, with the Church as the Living Body of Christ, or with the Sunna ["consensus"] of Islam—each body overinterpreted by its membership as the one and only holy thing in this world.[5]

Membership requirements are determined by revelation, on the authority of God, which doesn't allow much room for flexibility. There is no "either/or" here, no overlap: whether Jewish, Christian, or Muslim, these religions are mutually exclusive—you can't be a member of more than one faith at a time (unlike Japan, for example, where it's not unusual to practice both Shintoism and Buddhism). Hence, they can't all be the One True Faith . . .

This leads to the other major factor precipitating religious conflict: a tendency to read myth as history, rather than metaphor. If there is such a thing as sin in Campbell's world, it would have to be taking a myth literally. The danger seems clear as we watch ancient beliefs and mythic images, treated as empirical fact, fanning the flames of discontent.

Orthodox political parties in Israel, for example, pressure the government to return no land to the Palestinians, as God has promised it all to the descendants of Abraham, Isaac, and Jacob. This limits the possibilities of a negotiated compromise. Meanwhile, Osama bin Laden and his allies believe in perpetual Holy War against all infidels. The more literal and rigid their interpretation of Islamic jihad, the more rigidly this mythic image locks them into its concrete manifestation in the material world (I think of David Koresh and the Branch Dravidians, obsessed with contorting real-world events to confirm apocalyptic predictions and fears of persecution; regardless of the tragic details and who ultimately is at fault, this obsession paved the way to a tragic, self-fulfilling prophecy in Waco, Texas, in 1993).

Nor can we exempt our own culture. A literal belief in the coming apocalypse certainly shapes the attitudes and reactions of many Americans toward the situation in the Holy Land (the very fact that we consider it "the Holy Land" adds a powerful, emotional charge to the equation). Many members of the current administration [written during the presidency of George W. Bush – SG] are devout evangelical Christians who believe a global, possibly nuclear conflict will erupt in the Middle East, with Jesus returning in the nick of time, before the world is destroyed.

Of course, the president isn't bent on hastening Armageddon—but might this mythic mindset unintentionally influence the shape of some foreign policy objectives? Might the American psyche be more willing, albeit unconsciously, to take risks in that part of the world, knowing that the ultimate *deus ex machina* waits just offstage?

That alone doesn't discount the effectiveness of any particular policy directive—but there is no denying that a literal reading of cultural myths can have harmful, destructive effects. Campbell makes this point over and over—with the Inquisition, with the rise of Nazi Germany, with Catholics and Protestants in Northern Ireland, Hindus and Muslims in India and Pakistan, and Arabs and Israelis.

A NEVER-ENDING STORY

Is there no way out of this cycle?

Bill Moyers suggests to Campbell that what Islam, Christianity, and Judaism need is a new myth. Campbell, however, has a better idea:

> Each needs its own myth, all the way. Love thine enemy.
> Don't judge. All things are Buddha things. It is there in
> the myth. It is already there.[6]

Of course, this is easier said than done.

> Nevertheless, the popular orthodox expression of both
> the Mohammedan and the Christian doctrines has
> been so fierce that it requires a very sophisticated read-
> ing to discern in either mission the operation of love.[7]

We find one such sophisticated interpretation in Wolfram von Eschenbach's *Parzival*. As the epic nears its end, Parzival, before being allowed once again to gain the Grail Castle, faces a Muslim knight in armed combat, unaware his opponent is Feirefiz, the half-brother he's never met.

> And I mourn for this, for they were the two sons of one
> man. One could say that "they" were fighting if one
> wished to speak of two. Those two, however, were one:
> "My Brother and I" is one body, like good man and
> good wife. Contending here from loyalty of heart, one
> flesh, one blood, was doing itself much harm.[8]

"One flesh, one blood, was doing itself much harm."

Feirefiz and Parzival eventually recognize each other. Both knights, along with the entire company of Arthur's Round Table, are invited to the Grail Castle, where an act of compassion on Parzival's part heals the Wounded King and restores the land.

Compassion.

It's no easy task to recognize a Brother in the Other—and yet brothers are what we are talking about. In the biblical legends Isaac and Ishmael are reunited when they come together to bury Abraham; Esau and Jacob eventually make their peace; and Joseph tearfully reunites with his brothers in Egypt.

"Each needs its own myth, all the way."

This is a realization that cannot be legislated. It won't be decided by a United Nations resolution, or an act of military might, but arises out of the human heart.

Certainly, we live in perilous times. . .

What human hasn't? Campbell offers a suggestion:

> The warrior's approach is to say "yes" to life:
> "yea" to it all.
> Participate joyfully
> in the sorrows of the world.
>
> We cannot cure the world of sorrows,
> but we can choose to live in joy.
>
> When we talk about
> settling the world's problems,
> we're barking up the wrong tree.

The world is perfect. It's a mess.
It has always been a mess.

We are not going to change it.

Our job is to straighten out
our own lives.[9]

At first, this advice may sound selfish—but external and internal worlds, macrocosm and microcosm, often appear in myth as reflections of one another . . . which is why we find our dreams bear significance in the waking world.

Richard Wilhelm, best known for his exhaustive translation of the *I Ching*, told Carl Jung of an incident he witnessed in southern China, in an area suffering from a lengthy drought. Catholic processions and Protestant prayers produced no precipitation, so finally the villagers sent to northern China for a rainmaker—a Taoist adept. When this older, white-bearded man arrived, all he required was a house to stay in and food for three days.

The Taoist disappeared into his house, and was not seen for three days, at the end of which time it didn't just rain—it snowed in abundance, out of season!

When Wilhelm asked the man how he made the snow, the man denied all responsibility.

The sage pointed out that when he had arrived, after a demanding journey, he was out of harmony with the Tao. It took him three days of contemplation to place himself back in harmony with the Tao; and when one is in harmony with the Tao, so is the world around one, and when the world is in harmony, it rains when it's supposed to rain. (*Mysterium Coniunctionis,* 419)

Campbell's advice to work on oneself isn't a demand to withdraw from the world. We can still work for Oxfam, write letters to editors and congressmen, enlist in the army, lead petition drives and campaigns, join the State Department, and whatever else is appropriate to the base of the pyramid . . . but we should not delude ourselves into believing these conflicts—which are at root spiritual conflicts—can be resolved through cause-and-effect efforts, through will alone, or we will be sorely disappointed.

After all, the goal of the inward journey, according to Campbell, "is compassion. When you come past the pair of opposites, you have reached compassion. The goal is to bring the jewel back to the world . . ."[10]

Too often, we stand transfixed by the sublime horrors unfolding on our planet, horrors that have long been here, horrors to which there is no easy balm, and this fixation, this fear, despair, and woe can derail our own journey to understanding—a journey which is crucial, for the more who climb that pyramid, the more who are able to transcend the perpetual repetition of the same old story.

We must write a new story for ourselves, and trust it proves contagious.

Notes

1. Campbell, The Power of Myth, op.cit. 26.
2. Joseph Campbell, Myths of Light (Novato: New World Library, 2002), 66.

3. Elaine Pagels, The Gnostic Gospels (New York: Random House, 1979; New York: Vintage Books, 1989), 48. Citations are from the Vintage Books edition.

4. Joseph Campbell, The Flight of the Wild Gander (New York: Viking Press, 1969; Novato: New World Library, 2002), 167. Citations are from the New World Library edition.

5. Ibid. 168.

6. Campbell, The Power of Myth, op.cit. 26.

7. Joseph Campbell, The Hero with a Thousand Faces, 3rd ed. (Princeton: Bollingen/Princeton University Press, 1949; Novato: New World Library, 2008), 136. Citations are from the New World Library edition.

8. Joseph Campbell, Myths To Live By (New York: Viking Press, 1972; New York: Penguin Compass, 1993), 136.

9. Campbell, A Joseph Campbell Companion, op.cit. 17.

10. Ibid. 24.

FIVE

NOCTURNAL PASSAGES

> Since the power of nature in this dreamer, in that
> dreamer, and in the macrocosm of nature itself, are the
> same, only differently inflected, the powers personified
> in a dream are those that move the world. All the gods
> are within: within you—within the world.[1]

I would like to keep hand to plow, cutting straight rows through
the earth with the precision and focus so much admired in academic disciplines—but attention wanders, and I find myself off
chasing rainbows into landscapes unknown, daydreaming the
day away . . .

Much as I try to ignore the lure of the subject, I am captured by dream.

We all dream—each night, every night, four to seven cycles
a night—yet remember so few dreams. Why?

Carl Gustav Jung believes dreams are expressions of the
unconscious psyche (of course, it's called "the unconscious"
because it's unconscious to me, to ego—the waking me—and

not because the unconscious psyche itself is blind and deaf and dumb). Jung identifies several archetypal figures met in dream, patterns he labels the Shadow, the Persona, the Anima/Animus, the Mother, the Father, the Wise Old Man, the Hieros gamos (or sacred marriage), the Underworld, and countless others—though these don forms more familiar to us each night, whether a threatening villain, an exotic lover, Mom or Dad, a wedding, a cave, even the clothes we wear and more, in infinite variety.

Dreams though are quicksilver. Even when we wake with wisps still in our head, the traces trickle away at the slightest distraction—the sound of the alarm, a cat crying for breakfast, even an insistent bladder—and the dream dissolves. In fact, the dreams we are most likely to remember are those that contain an emotional charge high enough to propel their images across the threshold separating liminal from waking consciousness. This would have to be a dream that packs quite a wallop, most often a nightmare—though erotically charged dreams also often manage to generate the energy necessary to break through into conscious awareness.

Of course, when we practice dream work, the usual question is, "What does the dream mean?"

Interpretation is thought to aim at meaning, but no dream dictionary will capture that ethereal flow. Dreams are beyond meaning, not at all linear and literal; dreams instead suggest a holographic structure with a multitude of meanings, parallel and paradox, enfolded in each image—much the same as the imagery of music, poetry, theater, and the other arts.

What, after all, is the meaning of those first four notes of Beethoven's Fifth, or that F-sharp buried in the middle of a Tchaikovsky suite? What is the meaning of a color dancing through a Jackson Pollack painting, or the tone Jerry Garcia wrings from his guitar?

Meaning arises in subjective consciousness—but even within one individual different possibilities arise, a response to the manifold layers of association embedded in each image presented to consciousness. In inner work, multiple and sometimes contradictory interpretations serve to flesh out the vapors of dream and paint a multidimensional portrait of the polymorphic psyche.

> [Dreamtime] is the time you get into when you go to sleep and have a dream that talks about permanent conditions within your own psyche as they relate to the temporal conditions of your life right now . . .
>
> Now the level of dream of "Will I pass this exam?" or "Should I marry this girl?"—that is purely personal. But on another level, the problem of passing an exam is not simply a personal problem. Everyone has to pass a threshold of some kind. That is an archetypal thing. So there is a basic mythological theme there even though it is a personal dream. These two levels—the personal aspect and then the big general problem of which the person's problem is a local example—are found in all cultures.[2]

Some dreams do have literal components—if you dream your mother-in-law has died, and the next day she keels over, this is indeed spooky—but such instances are relatively rare, much like the Death card in a Tarot spread actually indicating a real live death. But dreams that do echo surface events also resonate at deeper octaves: my friend Crystal, crying alone at a party in my dream, may be a clue that the waking Crystal is sad and unhappy—something I might not have consciously noticed—but my psyche's choice of her image might also point to emotions repressed or depression yet unrealized, buried within me, which leads me to ponder why my soul-image weeps.

Joseph Campbell believed one should attend to dream because there, as he tells Bill Moyers, "You learn about yourself." This prompts the question of how to pay attention to our dreams:

> All you have to do is remember your dream in the first place, and write it down. Then take one little fraction of the dream, one or two images or ideas, and associate with them. Write down what comes to your mind, and again. You'll find that the dream is based on a body of experiences that have some kind of significance in your life and that you didn't know were influencing you. Soon the next dream will come along, and your interpretation will go further.[3]

Though reading other people's dreams can be tedious, I'll risk a personal example of how I've applied Campbell's advice:

Roughly ten years ago I was nearing the end of what proved to be a brief fling with "Julie," who, at twenty-three, was thirteen years my junior (relationship in lieu of a sporty red convertible?). Ours was a tenuous mismatch that could not sustain Julie's interest; however, infatuated and in denial, I was the only member in my circle of friends who did not anticipate the inevitable approaching.

Then, one night, I dreamt I was invisible, and had broken into a large warehouse, a place I did not belong. The night watchman glances inside, but cannot see me as I dash into a room off the main hall (I remain invisible even to myself). However, the watchman releases the guard dog, a large, menacing, black Doberman, to sweep the building. The dog enters the room where I hide and somehow senses me: bristling and vicious, it tries to attack—so I bludgeon the beast to death with a fire extinguisher!

(*Not* my typical behavior; as St. Augustine said, thank God we can't be held accountable for our dreams!)

I found this imagery disturbing. Here is a snarling black dog, a gatekeeper of sorts, which threatens me. I couldn't help but think of Cerberus, the sharp-fanged, triple-headed, black hound guarding the entrance to Hades.

Could it be that I can't "see myself" because of something I am unconscious of—and this content in my unconscious (clad in the skin of that vicious, snarling Doberman) appears so threatening to ego (my sense of myself) that I forcefully, violently repress it?

But I had no idea what, specifically, I could not see in waking life (I guess that's why it's called the unconscious), so I decided to sleep on it.

Two nights later I dreamt that I was at the top of a flight of stairs leading down into a dark subway tunnel—and somewhere below, loose in the tunnel, is a large, silver-gray timber wolf. I slip quietly down the steps and carefully close and latch a huge cage door at the bottom of the stairs, thinking to lock the wolf in the subway; but then, when I turn around, I realize the wolf waits for me at the top of the stairs—I have locked it out with me, in the daylight world!

Notice how the image of the black Doberman, bred to be vicious and deadly, has morphed into a silver wolf, a creature more in tune with nature—suggesting a subtle shift in accent—though what is unknown, what must emerge from below, is still threatening enough to ego that I want to keep it locked in the unconscious (the subway). However, working with the earlier dream, playing with and reflecting on its images (suggested by that hesitant descent into the subway), served to release what is repressed into the light of day.

As I pondered the second dream, I gradually realized that I had been denying the reality of my collapsing relationship. After several days of reflection, I finally opened an honest discussion with Julie, and we came to a mutual parting of the ways. Yes, it was awkward and uncomfortable—but, had I continued to ignore the relationship's trajectory, I would have felt shattered and heartbroken, perhaps reacting in blind desperation, facing far deeper, longer lasting wounds. Instead, I was surprised to feel a measure of bittersweet relief.

That night the dream series wrapped up with me walking out of Julie's shower and across the street. Though in the dream it was about 4 a.m., there were two workmen wearing overalls, on hands and knees in the gutter, clearing out the debris clogging the storm drain. A golden retriever puppy nipped playfully at their heels while they worked. The workmen found the happy pup a bit distracting, but were more amused than irritated.

Hmm . . . undertaking this interior work clears an obstruction in my psyche, and shifts my perspective, thus inaugurating a change in circumstance in waking life.

Keep in mind that I am by no means a qualified psychotherapist, but am simply speaking from my own experience.

Certainly, this dream series addresses the personal level Campbell mentions above ("Will I marry this girl?"); nevertheless, the archetypal level is represented as well. Notice how mythological themes play through the dreams, and how, though details of an image may differ from dream to dream—depending on what is being emphasized—the underlying motif remains in play: the snarling Doberman, the aloof timber wolf, and the playful golden puppy are all different inflections of the same archetypal pattern (Cerberus /Anubis; dog as psychopomp or guide of souls, etc.); similarly, the warehouse, the subway, and the storm drain all suggest the Underworld of the unconscious.

Even though the details of that brief and distant relationship have faded into memory, the recurring and enduring nature of archetypal patterns in dream *and* myth remain etched in awareness yet today.

How does this work? *Why* does it work?

Carl Jung, in the first section of *Symbols of Transformation* (the book, published in 1912, that catalyzed Jung's rupture with Freud), writes about "Two Kinds of Thinking."

One is the focused concentration that most often comes to mind when we hear the term "thinking": *directed* thinking—linear, with a specific end, a goal (solve the math problem, build the bridge), what today we call task-oriented thinking. Jung believes this to be a relatively recent development for our species.

But Jung believes there is a deeper layer of thought, far older on the evolutionary scale: *associational* thinking: drifting, daydreaming, letting the mind wander, gathering wool—which seems to be where we spend most of our time. We might concentrate on a difficult problem at length—but the solution often comes when we're singing in the shower, thinking about any and everything but . . .

In this mode, one image flows into another, like in a daydream, or when a mind just wanders—not just random thoughts, but words, ideas, and images related to one another one way or another. Dreams, even more so: no mediating ego. Subtle nuances speak volumes in dream. Pun imagery—verbal or visceral, humorous or obscure—runs rampant. Dream images, like all components of psyche, are fluid, quicksilver— and quicksilver, mercury, is ruled by Hermes, a trickster, god of communication (and *mis*communication). Wherever one thing is also another, whether symbolic ritual or trivial pun, Hermes hides in the ambiguity, cloaked in paradox, and puts the alchemical flavor into dream work.

In dream we are immersed in the stuff of poetry, images wet, electric, self-luminous, and fluid—a nighttime Sensurround theater in 3-D, in which we are sometimes audience, sometimes extra, sometimes star—at times, all three; here we dance in Elysian Fields, bathe in the wellsprings of creativity and pure imagination. Is it any wonder patterns we find there point to energies manifesting in waking realities?

Dream helps us relate to these patterns, and can bring us into a conscious harmony with the natural rhythms of life.

But what, then, is the relationship between dream and myth?

> Mythologies are in fact the public dreams that move
> and shape societies, and conversely one's own dreams
> are the little myths of the private gods, antigods, and
> guardian powers that are moving and shaping oneself:

revelations of the actual fears, desires, aims and values
by which one's life is subliminally ordered.[4]

Dreams speak to soul, and are soul (psyche) speaking to us.
Dreams are inside us—we are the source of our dreams—
and yet we experience ourselves inside the dream. Dream,
Dreaming, and Dreamer are One...

... which is a motif playing through myriad mythologies
from all eras and all parts of the planet—an observation Joseph
Campbell develops in *The Mythic Image* (the hundredth—and
final—book published by Bollingen, in 1974). Here he highlights an archetypal theme common to most cultures: that Life
itself is a Dream. We find this concept in Eastern traditions, in
Aztec beliefs, in the practices of shamanic cultures, even in the
works of Shakespeare and Calderon.

In particular, Campbell traces the evolution of this metaphor through the Hindu / Buddhist traditions. Hindu mythology portrays creation as the manifestation of Vishnu's dream
while he sleeps, afloat on the cosmic sea. We are all characters
in Vishnu's dream. From time-to-time life is so distressing that
one or another of us beseeches God for help, and so Vishnu
enters into his own dream, taking form as one or another of a
multitude of avatars (Krishna, Rama, etc.).

Buddhism takes this one step further. Again, we are all
characters in the cosmic dream, but "Buddha" means "the
Awakened One," or "He Who is Awake": Buddha achieves
enlightenment / illumination by waking up within the dream.
The Buddha responds to the situation by, in essence, withdrawing from the dream. He achieves nirvāna (from the
Sanskrit for "blowing out," like the flame of a candle), and so

is extinguished, no longer subject to the suffering inseparable from the temporal nature of life's dream.

As a character within the dream, Buddha simply ceases to be, "blowing out" the flame of ego, of "I," which seems the goal of devotees the first three centuries of Buddhist history—today referred to as Theravada or Hinayana ("lesser vehicle") Buddhism.

Eventually, Mahāyāna ("greater vehicle") Buddhism, in its many branches, enlarges the concept of the bodhisattva—one whose being (sattva) is enlightenment (bodhi). A bodhisattva stands on the cusp of Buddhahood but, rather than evaporate in nirvanic rapture, is moved by compassion to remain, awake within life's dream, "joyfully participating in the sorrows of life," until all other beings awaken to their suffering and transcend the grand illusion.

(Is it just me, or is this a theme echoed in *The Matrix* and other contemporary films?).

Of course, to be awake within a dream changes the nature of the experience. If, for example, a tiger chases me, the immediate threat to life and limb triggers extreme terror and physical distress. Powered by adrenaline, I am lost in fear (of pain, suffering, death) and desire (for safety, security, comfort), the dual dynamos driving life's suffering in the Buddhist mythos.

If, on the other hand, the "dream me" is aware that I am only dreaming that a tiger chases me, then I am released from fear and desire, no longer subject to the terror of the moment. I am free to act, rather than just re-act. It doesn't necessarily mean that "dream me" doesn't get eaten by the tiger—but there is more of a sense of play, coupled with the awareness on some level that I will survive the dream, re-absorbed into the larger, waking me.

If we realize a dream is a dream, fear disappears, and it's not such a terrible thing now to turn and confront that tiger (face our fear?), maybe even change the dream. Could such a shift in perspective effect how we engage life as well?

> You can actually guide your dreams by paying attention to them. That means you are guiding your life and shaping it into some kind of relationship to the dream force, the force of what's operating right now in the heat of your volcanic insides.[5]

Campbell notes in several places the correspondence between Vishnu, the Cosmic Dreamer, and Schopenhauer's depiction of life as a dream, dreamt by a single dreamer, in which all the characters in the dream are dreaming too, and we are characters in their dreams as they are characters in ours. This complex arabesque metaphor seems a psychedelic version of the old Morton Salts label: a girl holding a canister of Morton Salts, with a picture on the label of the same girl holding a canister of Morton Salts, with the same picture of the same girl on the label and so on, receding into infinity. Fits the prime alchemical dictum—"As above, so below; as below, so above"— and matches the holographic model of the cosmos emerging in contemporary science (as expounded by physicist David Bohm, neurologist Karl Pribram, biologists Rupert Sheldrake and Lynn Margulies, transpersonal psychologist Stanislav Grof, and others).

Why wouldn't the universe within reflect the universe without—and vice versa?

When we encounter an object in the external world, we don't observe the actual "thing in itself" (Kant's Dinge an sich), but an image formed by our senses. The rose I see is perceived differently by a dog, or a butterfly, or an amoeba encountering that same rose. Our senses, in conjunction with the mind (considered a sixth sense in Hindu / Buddhist metaphysics), in effect construct the universe out of metaphors—those subjective sensory images we perceive.

Archetypal psychologist James Hillman offers imagination as the organ through which we perceive and engage "reality"—which could be described as a projection of the interior world onto the external universe. Myth, then, becomes both the womb, and the substance, of experienced reality.

We can expand this theme and approach mundane reality as we would a dream, where everything we experience, everything we encounter, has a symbolic value that deepens and enriches life. Life as a waking dream is a perspective adopted by the many cultures (and individuals) that value oracles. Hence, everything bears significance: the appearance of a rainbow or an abrupt shift in the flight of a bird speaks volumes to an African pygmy or Australian aborigine, as does an I Ching spread to a Taoist adept. "All that exists is but a metaphor," to paraphrase Campbell's favorite quote from Goethe (*"Alles Verganglich ist nur ein Gleichnis."*). We can interpret, analyze, and engage the stuff of life just as we can the stuff of dream, if we view life with a mythic eye.

Does embracing the metaphor that consensus reality is as illusory and transitory as dream somehow negate the searing pain I feel when I touch a hot stove? Hardly. On one plane, I can recognize that I "am One with" a brick wall—but it doesn't follow that I'll decide to physically become one with that wall while zipping along the freeway at ninety miles an hour.

That would be taking the metaphor a mite literal!

The mythical perspective is in addition to that of waking consciousness—not intended to replace rational thought and ego consciousness, but to deepen and enhance our experience.

Nevertheless, this metaphor can't help but open one to metaphysical possibilities:

> When you move into the level of dream consciousness, all the laws of logic change. There, although you think you are seeing something that is not you, it is actually you that you are seeing, because the dream is simply a manifestation of your own will and energy—you created the dream and yet you are surprised by it. So the duality there is illusory. There, subject and object, though apparently separate, are the same.
>
> The realms of the gods and demons—heaven, purgatory, hell—are of the substance of dream. Myth, in this view, is the dream of the world. If we accept gods as objective realities, then they are the counterpart of your dream—this is a very important point—dream and myth are of the same logic. . . And since the subject and the object seem to be separate but are not separate in the dream, so the god that seems to be outside you in myth (or religion, if you prefer) is not different from you. You and your god are one. Now we are moving to something very interesting. All the heavens and gods are within you and are identical with aspects of your own consciousness on the dream level.[6]

And so we dream the myth onward.

NOTES

1. Joseph Campbell, The Masks of God, Vol. 4: Creative Mythology (New York, Viking Penguin, 1968; New Yor: Penguin Books, 1976), 650. Citations are from the Penguin Books edition.

2. Campbell, Power of Myth, op. cit. 47.

3. Ibid. 47-48.

4. Joseph Campbell, The Hero's Journey: Joseph Campbell on His Life and Work, ed. Phil Cousineau (New York: Harper & Row, 1990; Novato: New World Library, 2003), 187.

5. Joseph Campbell, "An Interview with Joseph Campbell," interview by Gerald McDermott, New Boston Review 2, No. 2 (Fall 1975).

6. Campbell, Myths of Light, op.cit. 70.

SIX

/

RITUAL: WHO NEEDS IT?

> Mythology and the rites through which its imagery is
> rendered open the mind . . . not only to the local social
> order, but also to the mythic dimension of being—of
> nature—which is within as well as without, and thereby
> finally at one with itself.[1]

The popular conception of ritual today borders on the ridiculous, conjuring images from B-grade movies of seemingly ignorant, half-naked savages working themselves into a frenzy, or
menacing Satanists, in robes and hoods, drawing pentagrams
and making strange hand passes over nubile, scantily clad sacrificial victims. At best, ritual has been portrayed in the popular media as a means of manipulating and controlling people
and circumstances to fulfill one's desires; at worst, onscreen
rites serve as a conduit for evil forces opposed to the rational,
honest efforts of the good and the innocent.

Hollywood caricatures aren't born in a vacuum, however;
it's not unusual today for otherwise intelligent, well-read

individuals to disparage ritual—perhaps because the rituals we're most familiar with don't speak to the soul anymore, instead falling flat and lifeless, favoring form over substance. Many of us have experienced rituals that were nothing more than obedience to rote and repetition—nothing animated, inspiring, or ensouled.

And yet there is a power latent in even the most innocuous ritual: witness the recent controversy in the United States surrounding the wording in the Pledge of Allegiance. A morning ritual repeated for decades in classrooms throughout the nation, a pro forma nod to patriotism—rarely given a second thought by those whose school days have long since passed—but vested nevertheless with enough psychological force to stir a national uproar over attempts to tamper with its symbolism.

Where do rituals come from? Aren't rituals merely the archaic vestiges of belief systems long-since vanished—or might they have some relevance for today? Do they serve any useful purpose? Do they work? Considering so many rituals seem group activities, what role might they play in an individual's life? And what rituals are appropriate to contemporary life? (Hint for the uninitiated: steer clear of human sacrifice.)

The earliest evidence of ritual surfaces in Neanderthal burial sites and the Neanderthal cave bear cults, c. 100,000 BC to 40,000 B.C; the clues are even clearer in the temple caves of the Paleolithic period (Altamira, Lascaux, and Les Trois Freres, among others), as well as the "Venus" figurines from roughly the same era, some twenty thousand years ago, unearthed across Europe in a swath stretching from Spain to Siberia. In the *Historical Atlas of World Mythology, Volume I: The Way of the Animal Powers, Part 1: Mythologies of Primitive*

Hunters and Gatherers, Joseph Campbell links the development of the mythological mindscape to these discoveries.

FUNCTIONS OF RITUAL

Joseph Campbell identifies two parallel, yet at times opposing, functions of ritual alluded to in the quote that introduces this chapter—but both functions share one dynamic:

> The characteristic of mythic themes and motifs translated into ritual, consequently, is that they link the individual to transindividual purposes.[2]

One function is to "open the mind. . .to the local social order." An example, mentioned above, is that of the Pledge of Allegiance—a shared childhood experience intended to imprint collective national values. It may seem a trivial exercise, but one sacrosanct still to a majority of the American public.

Far more intense are the initiation rites common to primal cultures around the globe, which serve to align the individual psyche with that of the group. Adolescent boys who have reached an "unruly" age are forced to endure a series of painful ordeals—tests of endurance ranging from fasting, sleep deprivation, and trance dancing to mutilation (circumcision, subincision, tattooing, knocking out of a tooth, etc.). This is not induction into the Elks or Kiwanis, but dangerous, often life-threatening events orchestrated to induce a physical and psychological crisis: these rites initiate the adolescent youth by pitching him past the narrow confines of his individual needs and desires, expanding his consciousness to embrace the needs and goals of the tribe.

Initiation rites also fulfill the second function of ritual, the one that interests Campbell most: to "open the mind to the mythic dimension of being—of nature—which is within as well as without." These coming-of-age rituals not only initiate the adolescent into the traditions and ways of the local group, but also bring him into harmony with his own nature, which includes the changes in emotional and physical make-up that accompany the dramatic transition from child into adult, and the psychological shift from a condition of dependence to that of responsibility for one's own welfare. The boy dies, and in his place is born a man, in a new role, marked by a difference in dress, duties, and, in some cultures, even a new name.

Initiation rituals enact the primary stages of the hero's journey, the "monomyth" Campbell explored in *The Hero with a Thousand Faces*: Separation (from the community); Transformation (physical and psychological); and Return (once again part of the community, but in a new role).

Myth = Ritual = Myth?

We tend to think of rites as those accompanying critical transitions—birth, coming of age, marriage, death—sacraments all . . . but there was a time when ritual permeated every aspect of life:

> [T]he archaic world knows nothing of "profane" activities: every act which has a definite meaning—hunting, fishing, agriculture, games, conflict, sexuality—in some way participates in the sacred. . . the only profane

activities are those which have no mythical meaning. . .
Thus we may say that every responsible activity in pur-
suit of a definite end is, for the archaic world, a ritual.

Every ritual has a divine model, an archetype . . .
"We must do what the gods did in the beginning."[3]

Eliade illustrates his point by providing examples of construction rituals in early cultures—required, for example,
in ancient Mesopotamia, whether laying the foundation of
temple, palace, or peasant's house. These rites replicate "the
primordial act" of the creation of the cosmos (traces of such
construction rituals echo today in the rites of the Masonic
Order). Yet other examples of "the divine model" abound
in rituals still observed, from the Judeo-Christian Sabbath
(God rested on the seventh day, after six days of creation) to
the marriage ceremony (the divine *Hierogamy* of the union of
Heaven and Earth).

Campbell arrives at a parallel conclusion:

Well, the value of mythology in the old traditions, one
of the values, was that every activity in life had been
mythologized. You saw something of its relevance to
the Great Mysteries and your own participation in
the Great Mysteries in the performance—in agriculture, in hunting, in military life and so forth. All of
these were turned into spiritual disciplines. Actually
they were. There were rituals associated with them
that let you know what spiritual powers were being
challenged, evoked, and brought into play through
this action.[4]

The relationship between ritual and myth is still a matter of debate within the fields of anthropology and mythology. There's no question, though, as to where Joseph Campbell stands:

> A ritual is the enactment of a myth. And, by partici-
> pating in the ritual, you are participating in the myth.
> And since myth is a projection of the depth wisdom of
> the psyche, by participating in a ritual, participating
> in the myth, you are being, as it were, put in accord
> with that wisdom, which is the wisdom that is inher-
> ent within you anyhow. Your consciousness is being
> re-minded of the wisdom of your own life. I think
> ritual is terribly important.[5]

Ritual takes many forms—but the point of ritual seems to be to open a portal and propel us past surface realities, into an experience of a deeper reality underlying the world we perceive with our senses. Ritual allows us an experience transcendent to, yet in harmony with, that of the physical senses.

A living ritual has a numinous, dream-like, surreal compo-nent—that sense of *participation mystique*, as Campbell labels it, using a term borrowed from French scholar Levy-Bruhl. Ego breaks down, and one's sense of self both dissolves, and expands beyond, individual identity. Like in a play (drama, come to think of it, having evolved from sacred rituals), we suspend our disbelief and participate in the myth . . . and then we return to this world, as if waking and remembering a dream, bringing with us a gift, a tiny draught of wisdom.

That whole problem of breaking out of the field of waking consciousness into a field of dream consciousness is a basic problem of ritual . . .

I would say the main function of ritual is to orient an individual to the dream consciousness level, which is the productive level . . . Dream consciousness is further in, and it's a *creative* consciousness, whereas waking consciousness is a *critical* consciousness.[6]

Campbell believes ritual is closely entwined with the realms of myth and dream, which share a common origin. He points to the example of Black Elk, the Lakota youth who is seized by a shamanic crisis, manifested through intense physical and psychological symptoms—in the process, experiencing a vision crucial to the future of his people—and who then, on emerging from the crisis, creates out of that vision corresponding rituals for his people to follow.

Does Ritual Work?

Apart from the sociological and psychological ramifications of ritual—which may or may not be the conscious intent of individual participants—do rites actually work on the physical plane? Does rain come? Are the sick healed? Or are these merely superstitious acts with no substance in reality?

Two examples from Joseph Campbell's own life come to mind.

The first is an elaborate fire ceremony Campbell witnessed during his sabbatical sojourn in Japan, in 1955, detailed in the

"Tea and Fire" chapter of *Asian Journals: India and Japan*—his personal journal of this period. A sense of wonder comes through as Joe describes the complex ritual, which includes several moments of pure spectacle—including one when Campbell is alerted to the actions of a *yamabushi* ("mountain hermit"), whose hand motions appear to be directing the smoke from the huge fire.

The ceremony culminates with a fire walk:

> The wizard was at one end of the pit conjuring a power to cure into the fire and cooling the flames; his assistant was at the other end doing the same. And so, since I had seen, through his work on smoke, that he was a true master of fire, I caught the fever and began to decide that I would walk across too.[7]

This is decades before fire walks were introduced at trendy New Age workshops in Marin and elsewhere: Campbell didn't have the assurances of friends or acquaintances who had passed through the flame unharmed. Nor was there any doubt the fire was real—sparks had already burned two holes in his suit!

Joe took off shoes and socks, but was last in line, delayed by having to unwind an Ace bandage from his right ankle (sprained over two months before at Angkor Wat, in Cambodia). His first step proved tentative.

> But then I thought, "Well now, come on!" and seeing a nice fat flame in front, I put my foot down on top of it, squarely. Crackle! The hairs on the lower part of my leg were singed and a pleasant smell of singed hair went up

all around me, but to my skin the flame was cool—actually cool. This gave me great courage, and I calmly completed my walk, strolling slowly and calmly right down the center of the road. Three more steps brought me to the end, and the hands of several yamabushi helped me off. I went back to our seats, and the two ladies in our party were gasping at what I had done. I went out to one of the water tubs to wash my feet and get into my shoes and socks—and it was only when putting on my right shoe that I noticed that the swelling in my ankle had gone down. All the pain had disappeared too. Around the remains of the fire in the center of the area a lot of the little old women were standing who had gone over to the fire, holding their hands out to the cinders and then rubbing their poor, aching backs—dear souls. It had certainly been a wondrous event.[8]

Note that Campbell originally attended the ceremony as a spectator, not a participant—nor was healing his sprained ankle his intent when he seized the opportunity to join the procession through the fire—but healing was the intent of those conducting the rite, and healing is what occurred.

Nor is Campbell writing with an audience in mind: this episode is found in his personal journal, published several years after his death.

Stan Grof, a friend and colleague of Campbell's, describes a similar incident:

[T]hose of us who have actually had first-hand experience with such rituals have been repeatedly amazed at the results. The late Joseph Campbell, a man of superior intelligence and education, often told a story about his attendance at a Native American rain ceremony in the Southwest United States. When the ceremony began, he felt amused and somewhat cynical, as the sky was clear and blue and there was not a single cloud in sight. To his amazement, during the ceremony heavy clouds covered the entire sky and the day ended with a cloudburst. The Indians did not seem at all surprised; because of their past experience with such rituals, they expected the ceremony to be successful.[9]

(An amusing version of this anecdote, drawn from Jean Erdman's account, appears in Robin and Stephen Larsen's biography of Campbell, *A Fire in the Mind,* on pages 349–350.)

How does this work?

The Navajo perform a healing ceremony, which involves the creation of a large sand painting that portrays a healing myth. The patient is placed in the center of the sand painting, where...

. . . the patient or initiate is ceremonially identified in mind and heart and costume with the mythological protagonist of the relevant legend. He or she actually enters physically into the painting, not simply as the person whose friends and neighbors have solicitously assembled, but equally as a mythic figure engaged in an archetypal adventure of which everyone present knows the design.[10]

Carl Jung refers to this as getting back into an archetypal situation:

> The old priests and medicine men understood this, not by
> knowledge, but by intuition. They tried to get a sick man
> back into an archetypal situation. . .What is the use of such
> foolishness? I assume that these people were by no means
> idiots. They knew very well what they did, they were as
> intelligent as we are, they had good results with these
> methods so they used them; it was "good medicine."[11]

Stan Grof follows his anecdote about Joseph Campbell and
the rain ceremony with a parallel experience of his own, when
the Huichol shaman Don Jose Matsuwa (whom some have
identified with the mysterious Don Juan of Carlos Casteneda's
books), during a two-year drought in California, performed
a rain ceremony at Esalen, in Big Sur. A six-hour downpour
followed the ritual! Grof then makes a point similar to Jung's:

> It is unthinkable that so many cultures would continue
> conducting rain ceremonies for centuries without some
> statistically significant success rate. It would also be dif-
> ficult for a shaman to maintain his or her reputation for
> very long against a series of failures.[12]

Do rituals work? That certainly seems the experience of participants.

However, sooner or later all rituals fade as they lose their
connection to nature and lived experience, thus becoming rigid
and set in concrete. Such has been the fate of so many collective
"living" rituals today, leaving only those that fulfill the first
function—from the Pledge of Allegiance to the black robe a

judge wears—of lifting an individual above ego concerns to identify with a social role. Few indeed "open the mind . . . to the mystery dimension of being."

RITUALS FOR TODAY

Are rituals important today? In Campbell's thinking, yes:

> The myths, when they are translated into rites, organize the field. Now you can see why the world is in trouble.[13]

But where should these rituals come from? Campbell offers a prescription reminiscent of Mircea Eliade's description of the archaic world, where every meaningful act participates in the sacred:

> The way mythology is integrated into life is by way of ritual. What has to be ritualized is essential to the life of the day. If one is to try to bring a mythological perspective into action in the modern world one has to understand the relationship of what is being done to the essentials of life, not to the superficialities of life. The essentials of life remain the same; they've been the same since the Paleolithic caves. Eating, reproduction, being a child, being mature, growing old. To realize that these things one is doing are not personally initiated acts but are functions of a biologically present world within yourself is to live in a very different way from the way one lives if one feels that one is the volitional initiator of everything going on.[14]

The stuff of ritual is the stuff of Life.

Attention and awareness can transform almost any mundane activity into a sacred act.

In my life this is best illustrated in the act of writing. I don't just grab a pencil and slap whatever comes into my head onto a piece of paper (despite all appearances to the contrary). Instead, I create a sacred space, retiring to a modest writing table in the smallest bedroom of our home (which serves as office, library, and meditation chamber). I intentionally set the atmosphere: books arranged in order on shelves (replacing them according to categories of my own at the conclusion of each project); notes handy; desk clear of clutter; a dozen or so pens in a variety of bright colors in a cylindrical pouch woven of Guatemalan yarn—a gift from dear friends—to the right of a notepad, laptop, or journal (depending on whether I'm performing research, writing an article, telling a story, or recording personal reflections); green desk lamp, candles, even incense, depending on subject and mood; significant objects (images of Buddha and wizards, crystals, stones, feathers, pictures, and other souvenirs of soul) placed on my altar and at strategic locations throughout the room; and so on. Thought and intention even determine the music, if any, playing in the background.

Anal-retentive? No buts about it, from one perspective— but the act of preparing a sacred space mirrors an interior journey as my mind shifts focus from the concerns of day-to-day reality (paying bills, changing the kitty litter, watching the news, fixing dinner, and the like) and enters into a more reflective, creative consciousness.

For me, such moments evoke numinous qualities—an encounter with the unconscious mystery—and, ultimately, that is what living ritual offers: a means to engage the Mystery that underlies Life and Being and All That Is and All That Isn't.

We each have different doors into that realm.

What moves and inspires you? What are your rituals?

NOTES

1. Campbell, The Flight of the Wild Gander (New York: Viking Press, 1969; Novato: New World Library, 2002), 86.
2. Campbell, Myths To Live By, op. cit. 57.
3. Mircea Eliade, The Myth of the Eternal Return (Princeton: Princeton University Press), 27-28, 21.
4. Joseph Campbell, The Wisdom of Joseph Campbell, audio interview by Michael Tom (Cary NC: Hayes House Productions, 1997), Tape 1 Side 1.
5. Campbell, The Wisdom of Joseph Campbell audio interview, op. cit. Tape 1 Side 2.
6. Campbell, The Hero's Journey, op. cit. 74-75, emphasis mine.
7. Joseph Campbell, Asian Journals (Novato: New World Library, 2017), 493.
8. Ibid.
9. Stanislav Grof with Hal Zina Bennett, The Holotropic Mind (San Francisco: HarperSanFrancisco, 1993), 190.
10. Joseph Campbell, The Inner Reaches of Outer Space (New York: A. van der Marck, 1986; Novato: New World Library, 2002), 63.
11. C.G. Jung, Dream Analysis: Notes of the Seminar Given in 1928-1930 (Princeton: Princeton University Press, 1984), 129.
12. Grof, The Holotropic Mind, op. cit. 190-191
13. Campbell, The Hero's Journey, op. cit. 239.
14. Ibid.. 238.

SEVEN

Heroes, One and All?

> The effect of the successful adventure of the hero is the unlocking and release again of the flow of life into the body of the world.[1]

I often hear from college students introduced to Joseph Campbell in class. The sudden immersion in a sea of ideas foreign and new leaves many struggling to grasp core concepts, preferably before the midterm. Questions they pose range from the nature of archetypes to what it means to "joyfully participate in the sorrows of life." The most common query, however, is, "Just what is Campbell's idea of the hero?"

You could write a whole book about that (come to think of it, Campbell did!).

Certainly, there are multiple facets to the image of the hero, a motif that appears across the mythological spectrum—not the only type of myth there is, but a darn persistent pattern.

Robert Segal, author of the first published critique of Campbell's body of work (*Joseph Campbell: An Introduction,*

1987), summarizes Joe's formulation of the hero thusly:

> For Campbell, the hero of a myth is heroic for two rea-
> sons. He does what no one else either will or can do, and
> he does it on behalf of everyone else as well as oneself.[2]

This includes not just the Jesus, Buddha, or Hercules of traditional myth, but also the popular conception of a hero: the
Medal of Honor winners and 9/11 firefighters who sacrifice their
lives to save individuals. The "everyone else" on whose behalf the
hero performs his or her deed might be another individual, or
one's family, the local community, the nation, or all humanity.

In fact, Joe himself often cited an account from his morning
newspaper in Hawaii, the story of a police officer who risked
his own life to save a young man intent on committing suicide. Campbell expands on this incident in conversation with
Bill Moyers, revealing a pattern underlying the hero archetype,
whether encountered in myth, or in waking reality:

> Do you realize what happened to that policeman who
> had given himself to death with that unknown youth?
> Everything else in his life had dropped off—his duty
> to his family, his duty to his job, his duty to his own
> life—all of his wishes and hopes for his lifetime had
> just disappeared. He was about to die. . .
>
> How come?
>
> Schopenhauer's answer is that such a psychologi-
> cal crisis represents the breakthrough of a metaphys-
> ical realization that you and that other are one, that
> you are two aspects of one life, and that your apparent

separateness is but an effect of the way we experience forms under the conditions of space and time. Our true reality is in our *identity and unity with all life.* This is a metaphysical realization which may become spontaneously realized under circumstances of crisis. For it is, according to Schopenhauer, the truth of your life.

The hero is the one who has given his physical life to some realization of that truth. The concept of love your neighbor is to put you in tune with this fact. But whether you love your neighbor or not, when the realization grabs you, you may risk your life . . .[3]

A hero is one who pierces the veil that separates one individual from another—in effect, a manifestation in real life of the realization that *All are One.*

On some levels this doesn't require a massive transformation of consciousness: one sees a child about to be run over by a car and spontaneously leaps into danger oneself; once the moment has passed and the danger is over, it doesn't necessarily follow that the local hero has a major metaphysical realization

But for one brief moment the strongest biological urge we know—the survival instinct—is overcome as the shock of crisis spontaneously propels one into alignment with a cosmic truth that transcends one's own life or death.

No matter how fleeting the moment, we have something here beyond mere intellectual understanding.

This local hero in Campbell's anecdote, the policeman, bestowed a boon—he gave the despairing young man his life in one swift, unpremeditated act (a gift perhaps unappreciated by the suicidal youth). On other levels, the physical and mental realization of "the truth of your life" might last longer and shape the hero's behavior throughout life. We see this with the heroes of ancient myth and recent legend, especially those who bestow boons on humanity, from a Jesus or Buddha or Prometheus, to an Albert Schweitzer or Albert Einstein, a Mother Teresa, a Dalai Lama . . . or even that dude who lives just down the block and mentors a reading program for illiterate adults, or the housewife next door who visits the blood bank every other month.

Campbell frequently speaks of the Hero acting in harmony with Nature, but he isn't necessarily touting ecology and environmentalism as the lone path to enlightenment; instead, he is talking about moving in harmony with the nature of the cosmos, the nature of depth reality (what quantum physicist David Bohm calls the *implicate order* underlying and enfolded within the *explicate order* of the perceived world). Moving in harmony with Nature has as a corollary moving in harmony with *one's own nature*—which suggests a certain sense of self-awareness.

In interviews with Michael Toms, Campbell ruminates on the hero's place today:

> There are two aspects of the hero, I think. The hero is somebody whom you can lean on and who is going to rescue you; he is also an ideal. To live the heroic life is to live the individual adventure, really. One of the problems today is that with the enormous transformations in the forms of our lives, the models for life don't exist for us. In a traditional society – the agriculturally based city – there were relatively few life roles, and the models were there; there was a hero for each life role. But look

at the past twenty years and what has come along in the way of new life possibilities and requirements. *The hero as model is one thing we lack, so each one has to be his own hero and follow the path that's no-path.* It's a very interesting situation.[4]

Campbell further asserts that "the rejuvenation of the Arthurian grail hero [is] that of recognizing God as the dynamic of your own interior"[5], restating his definition from *The Hero with a Thousand Faces*:

> [T]he hero is symbolical of that divine creative and redemptive image which is hidden within us all, only waiting to be rendered into life.[6]

. . . and *that* is the hero's journey within reach of each individual today, a quest for one's self—for the real Self, not just the mask of ego. Is it any wonder that Bill Moyers points out that Campbell believed in "the hero's journey not as a courageous act, but as a life lived in self-discovery"?

> This is what Joyce called the monomyth: an archetypal story that springs from the collective unconscious. Its motifs can appear not only in myth and literature, but, if you are sensitive to it, in the working out of the plot of your own life. The basic story of the hero journey involves giving up where you are, going into the realm of adventure, coming to some kind of symbolically rendered realization, and then returning to the field of normal life.[7]

The imagery that comprises the myriad expressions of this monomyth serves as a picture language, in symbolic form, of the crises met in our own lives.

Some critics contend that Campbell claims all myths are simply a retelling of the hero's quest—but Campbell points to the hero archetype emerging somewhere in the third millennium BC (with the Epic of Gilgamesh). This period throughout the Near East marks the appearance of a masculine solar hero, "dispelling darkness and shadow," identified with the sun. Previous traditions identify the sun as feminine and the moon as masculine, common to early Bronze Age cultures (traces of which linger in the gender of sun and moon in the German tongue—*die Sonne* and *der Mond*—or in *Amaterasu,* the sun *goddess* of the Shinto nature religion native to ancient Japan). Campbell finds this orientation differs from what he terms "heroic mythology."

The hero's journey is not the only form myths take—but Campbell finds it *is* a continuing theme from this period forward, one still relevant today:

> [T]the journey of the hero . . . I consider the pivotal myth that unites the spiritual adventure of ancient heroes with the modern search for meaning. As always, the hero must venture forth from the world of common-sense consciousness into a realm of supernatural wonder. There he encounters fabulous forces—demons and angels, dragons and helping spirits. After a fierce battle he wins a decisive victory over the powers of darkness. Then he returns from his mysterious adventure

with the gift of knowledge or of fire, which he bestows
on his fellow man.

Whenever the social structure of the unconscious
is dissolved, the individual has to take a heroic journey
within to find new forms. The biblical tradition, which
provided the structuring myth for Western culture, is
largely ineffective . . . So there must be a new quest.[8]

We are each of us an incarnation of the Hero—if we answer
the Call. The quest today is for each to find within our self the
resources to meet and embrace our individual destiny.
Myths, ancient *and* modern, point the way.

Now, all these myths that you have heard and that
resonate with you, those are the elements from round
about that you are building into a form in your life. The
thing worth considering is how they relate to each other
in your context, not how they relate to something out
there—how they were relevant on the North American
prairies or in the Asian jungles hundreds of years ago,
but how they are relevant now—unless by contemplating their former meaning you can begin to amplify your
own understanding of the role they play in your life.[9]

Why would this work? How is it possible that the deeds of
figures from stories told hundreds and thousands of years ago,
in cultures distinct and distant from my own, bear some relevance in my life today?

This is one reason why Campbell places such emphasis on
the episode of the police officer risking his own life for another

human being. The significance lies in its graphic demonstration of the recognition in one's actions of the metaphysical truth,

> . . . that you and the other are one, that you are two
> aspects of one life, and that your apparent separateness
> is but an effect of the way we experience forms under
> the conditions of time and space.

Whether an Egyptian serf hauling stone for the pyramids or Bill Gates building Microsoft, life's initiations remain the same: each is born of woman, an episode fraught with struggle and danger; each comes of age amid changes in body, emotions, and perception; each must come to terms with the dynamics of marriage and raising a family (questions which even those who choose alternative lifestyles—whether same-sex relationship, a life of contemplative celibacy, or something other—still must face); each grows old, withers, and dies. There aren't two ways of digesting food, two ways of menstruating, two ways of dying; these life moments, large and small, are remarkably constant for Hapsburg as well as Hottentot.

There are dragons to be slain and treasures to be gained in every life—these are also constants. Campbell identifies the motif of the hero's adventure as a map, an outline to follow, but every individual fills in his or her own details in the circumstances of one's own life.

Joseph Campbell challenges each of us to write our own hero's tale.

As usual, I'm only skimming the surface of a bottomless sea. My role is not to provide the final word, but to crack the door—those interested in what they see are welcome to walk on through and explore the premises for themselves. Joseph Campbell's *The Hero with a Thousand Faces*, of course, addresses this subject in great detail, focusing on the many appearances of the hero image in classical mythology.

I'd also recommend Campbell's *Pathways to Bliss*, edited by David Kudler. Compiled from hours of lectures and seminars recorded between 1968 and 1983, this delightful volume includes an accessible and refreshing amplification of the role of the hero motif in shaping a life, as well as a discussion of the role of women today in relation to the hero's journey.

Skillful editing captures Joseph Campbell's informative yet playful approach. He even answers a question I've often been asked, something along the lines of, "Does Campbell believe life consists of a single hero's journey, or do we live an endless series of such quests, wandering wastelands, slaying dragons, facing ever anew the possibility of gain, and loss?"

Joe's answer?

I guess you'll just have to read the book . . .

NOTES

1. Campbell, The Hero with a Thousand Faces, op. cit. 32.
2. Ibid. 33.
3. Campbell, The Power of Myth, op. cit. 138, emphasis mine.
4. Maher and Briggs, eds., An Open Life, op. cit. 109.
5. Ibid. 65.
6. Campbell, The Hero with a Thousand Faces, op. cit. 31.
7. Joseph Campbell, Pathways to Bliss (Novato: New World Library, 2004), 112.
8. Joseph Campbell, "Man & Myth: A Conversation with Joseph Campbell," interview by Sam Keen, Psychology Today (July, 1971), 36.
9. Campbell, Pathways to Bliss, op. cit. 132.

EIGHT

Converging Metaphors: Virgin Births and the Waxing of the Light

The real important function of the Church is to present the symbol, to perform the rite, to let you behold this divine message in such a way that you are capable of experiencing it. What the relationship of the Father and the Son and the Holy Ghost to each other might be, in technical terms, is not half as important as you, the celebrant, feeling the Virgin Birth within you, the birth of the mystic, mythic being that is your own spiritual life.[1]

Once again, the holiday season is upon us. It's a time when thoughts turn to Yuletide carols, sprigs of mistletoe, wreaths of holly, and festively wrapped packages piled at the foot of Christmas trees decorated with shiny ornaments and colored lights—a joyous time, celebrated with family and friends and parties galore. Yet Christmas is no secular holiday: whether or not one is a devout Christian, there is no denying that all the positive feelings of the season—peace on earth, good will toward men, all those glad tidings of joy, indeed, the birth of hope itself—are contained in one central religious image: the Babe in the Manger, whose birth we celebrate every December 25.

Note that when I use the term "we" above, I am identifying in the broadest sense with Western culture as a whole, and am not speaking for the significant numbers of Jews, Muslims, Wiccans, Buddhists, atheists, agnostics, indigenous peoples, and other individuals outside the Christian tradition. (And a related caveat—the term "pagan," bound to appear in the following paragraphs, is not used in any pejorative sense, but as shorthand for the generally polytheistic, nature-oriented traditions Christianity encountered in its formative years.)

This holiday so closely identified with the birth of Christianity, a religion known for insistence on the historical accuracy of its body of belief, is a treasure trove for comparative mythologists. No other day—apart from Easter—so clearly illustrates the morphing, merging and melding of mythological motifs across the porous membranes of distinct and disparate cultures.

ECHOES & AMPLITUDES

We all know the traditional story:

> In the reign of Caesar Augustus, a call goes forth for all people to return to their ancestral cities, to be counted in a census. Joseph and his wife Mary—heavy with a child that is not his—make the journey to Bethlehem, in Judea. Finding no room at the inn,

they take refuge in the stable, where Mary gives birth to Jesus, the Son of God, whose coming has been foretold. Angels announce his birth to shepherds in the field, who find Jesus in a manger and offer their adoration; meanwhile Three Magi—Wise Men from the East—follow a star to Bethlehem, bearing gifts for the Holy Infant. Though the newborn babe faces the wrath of the cruel, old tyrant whose throne is rightfully his, his family successfully flees beyond the evil Herod's reach—humble beginnings indeed for the King of Kings and Lord of Lords.

Yes, it *is* a familiar tale, one told in multiple variations over thousands of years, both before *and* after the time of Caesar Augustus, a tale that has morphed in the telling, changing names and details—but underneath, ever the same old story:

All over the world for countless millennia, people have participated in a religious ritual at the winter solstice, when the sun's downward course is arrested and it turns back, as it seems, to earth. This change of state in the bleak mid-winter of the year was experienced as the rebirth of the sun and commemorated as the birthday of the sun god, the luminous divine child. Like the heavenly sun arising from the depths of the darkness, these divine sons were born at midnight, hidden in the depths of the earth, in a cow-byre, in the reeds, in a cave, out of a rock, in a manger. The cry, "The Virgin has brought forth! The light is waxing," would have echoed in various tongues across the centuries. In Mesopotamia he

was called Tammuz and Dumuzi; in Egypt he was called
Osiris and Horus, and, later, Aion; in Greece, Dionysos,
Helios and Orpheus; in Persia and Rome, Mithras.[2]

The mythological motifs predating Christianity that have
become part of the official canon are almost too numerous to
detail: celestial signs, a virgin birth at the solstice in a cave or
similar humble shelter, shepherds in the field, adoration and
worship by heavenly beings, the massacre of innocents and
flight to safety, and a hero who is the dead- and-resurrected
god . . . all these and more are found in the Christian narrative.

ORIGINS & ANTECEDENTS

When did the celebration of the winter solstice begin?

When humans first linked the cycle of the seasons to the
heavens (indeed, the word Yule is descended from the Old
English *geol*, apparently derived from the Indo-European base
qwelo, meaning "go round" and the source of "cycle" and
"wheel"—thus denoting the turn of the year). We can follow the diffusion of myriad mythological motifs throughout
time—but observance of the winter solstice enjoys near universal distribution.

At Maeshowe in Orkney, Scotland, a stone structure dated
to 2750 BC has a long passageway through which the sun's rays
illuminate the back of the chamber on the winter solstice at
dawn. Another megalithic monument that performs the same
function has been found at a five-thousand-year-old ceremonial
site in Newgrange, Ireland. Cahokia, a complex of pyramids

outside St. Louis created by the native "mound-builder" culture almost twelve hundred years ago, includes remains of a "woodhenge"—a circle of posts that line up with the sun on the winter solstice—and similar older, more permanent ritual centers are found in the American southwest, where Pueblo tribes still observe rites marking the solstice. Even the Incas, in the southern hemisphere, celebrated the sun god, Wirachoa, in the solstice festival of Inti Raymi.

Popular Christmas traditions have unconsciously borrowed elements from these solstice celebrations. A prime example is the evergreen tree, which does not lose its leaves and so is able to withstand winter and the vanishing of the sun. Of course, it isn't difficult to distinguish the congruence between the Christmas tree and other manifestations of the archetype Jung labels the World Axis (the Tree of Life in Eden; the *djed* pillar raised to Osiris; the cross on which Christ is crucified; the Bo tree under which the Buddha attains enlightenment; *Yggdrasil*, the World Tree of north European mythology, etc.). But a more direct relationship with pre-Christian practices also exists: evergreen trees were decorated by the Greeks to celebrate Adonis; during Saturnalia (which began on December 17), the Romans adorned trees with shiny trinkets and replicas of Bacchus in his role as fertility god; the Druids tied fruit and candles to evergreen branches—the candles representing the eternal light of Baldur, the sun god—as well as representations of the sun, moon, stars, and the souls of those who had died the previous year, all as part of the *Albuan Arthuran* (Arthur's birthday, thought to be on the eve of winter solstice), also known as *Yule*.

Similarly, even though official belief pegs the origins of Santa Claus to the legend of the fourth century St. Nicholas of Bari, patron saint of sailors and children (whose historical existence remains in doubt), there are others who trace the image of the rather severe Father Christmas back to Poseidon/Neptune (also patron of sailors), the Teutonic god Hold Nickar, or even Wotan.

And then there is the Virgin Birth, long associated with solar heroes born at the winter solstice:

> The virgin birth comes into Christianity by way of the Greek tradition. When you read the four gospels, for example, the only one in which the virgin birth appears is the Gospel According to Luke, and Luke was a Greek.[3]

DOCTRINES & DATES

Did pagan traditions creep into the celebration of Christmas just because of the dates of celebration? And is it a coincidence? Then again, if no coincidence, why doesn't Christmas fall on the winter solstice instead of three days later?

On the three days following the solstice the sun appears to stand still (solstice is derived from the Latin words *sol*—sun—and *sistere*—"to cause to stand still"). Given the instruments available at the time, it wasn't until December 25 that the ancients were able to detect that the days were once more growing longer—that moment "when the light begins to increase"—hence, the birth of the sun. December 25 proved a significant date for these solar deities: among them Attis, in some traditions son of the virgin Nana, born on December 25, his cult, from Phrygia, introduced in Rome some two hundred years before Christ; Dionysus was also celebrated December

25—this son of the Greek father god, Zeus, with worshippers who consumed his flesh and blood as bread and wine; and Mithra, whose birth was witnessed by shepherds—believed to have been born roughly five centuries before Christ, on December 25.

The Magi, by the way, who worshipped the Baby Jesus and honored him with gifts of gold, frankincense, and myrrh, have their origins in the same Zoroastrian nexus that gave birth to Mithra, and are often depicted in art wearing Mithra's pointed cap. To Campbell, this element suggests a resonance with Mithraism, perhaps intended to imply that even Mithra's followers acknowledge the supremacy of the Christ.

> Mithra was the principal competitor with Christianity, in the period of the first three centuries. The Christmas date was placed on December 25, which was the solstice time, in order to compete with the Lord of Light, Mithra. No one really knows when Christ was born. It was settled on December twenty-fifth for mythological, not historical, reasons.[4]

But this does raise the question—how conscious was the adoption of December 25 as the date of Christ's birth? Was it, as is sometimes described, a bold act of hypocrisy designed solely to manipulate followers of other religions into joining the Christian faith? "Hey, you have a party on the Solstice—well, so do we. Your guy is the sun god—well our guy is the son of God. Your guy died and was resurrected? Well, ours too, so maybe they're really the same guy, and we're just using different names—not really worth losing your life over a few minor differences, is it? After all, you'll still be celebrating the way you always have—under Rome's direction, that is . . ."

Was the decision to celebrate the birth of Christ on Christmas made at the top of the Church hierarchy and sent down through the ranks?

Not exactly.

The early Church was neither well organized, nor unified behind any central authority. Diffusion—the spontaneous spread of a mythic motif from culture to culture—seems the more likely culprit, with the gradual adoption of Christmas an official recognition of processes already in progress.

No mention of the date of Christ's birth appears during the first century and a half of the Christian era. Clement of Alexandria, around AD 200, mentions that some Egyptian theologians favor a date in May, some in April, while others preferred January 6, still celebrated in some of the orthodox communions—in Alexandria this date was the birth of Aion, a syncretistic conflation of Osiris with other solar deities. There is evidence, albeit sketchy and open to question, to suggest a December Nativity is celebrated in Rome as early as AD 205, and an unsubstantiated tradition claims Christmas was observed in Rome as early as the time of Bishop Telesphoros (c. AD 139), but the Roman Catholic Church confirms neither of these dates.

However, we do know December 25 had been firmly established in Rome by AD 354, where it appears on the civil calendar and in a list of Christian martyrs. Chrysostom, in AD 386 in Syria, preached a noteworthy sermon intended to persuade the Antioch congregation to unite behind the December date, pointing out part of the community already observed this day;

he notes Christ's birthday is observed throughout the West—primarily Christianized Europe—yet he also speaks of it as a new feast.

The Irish church adopted December 25 as the Nativity in the fifth century, but the church in Jerusalem didn't accept it before the late sixth or early seventh centuries. Austria, Switzerland, and England embraced Christmas by the eighth century, but it didn't take hold in the Slavic regions before the tenth. Hardly a quickening pace—nor is this change legislated from the top down. Even though the Pope in Rome and the Eastern Churches might observe Christ's birth on December 25, conservative clergy elsewhere fought the trend, sometimes for centuries, before finally bowing to the will of the people in popular practice.

Most theologians today calculate Christ's birth as sometime in the autumn, with a minority preferring a spring date—but few, if any, clergy or theologians still believe Jesus was actually born on December 25.

However, roughly a century before Chrysostom's famous sermon in Antioch, the cult of Mithra had reached its pinnacle. During this period, all the solar deities—Apollo, Attis, Dionysus, Helios, Hercules, Horus, Mithra, Osiris, Perseus, and Theseus—were celebrated in a single, all-purpose festival called *Dies Natalis Sol Invicte*, "The Birthday of the Unconquered Sun," on December 25—and in AD 274, the Emperor Aurelian designated Mithraism the official religion of the Roman Empire.

Given the syncretism encouraged within the Roman Empire, it's not surprising that many early Christians noticed the parallels between the attributes of Christ and other solar deities. Especially during periods of persecution, rituals celebrating a god who is born to a virgin and points the way to eternal life could provide protective cover for followers of the Christ. Nor is it surprising that the differences between these various incarnations became blurred in the minds of Christians and non-Christians alike. This blurring of distinctions was so endemic that early church fathers—for example, Tertullian at the end of the second century, Augustine in the middle of the fourth century, and Pope Leo I—condemned the identification of Christ with Sol, the sun god. Others, such as Augustine's contemporary, Chrysostom, while claiming these pagan deities to be sinister counterfeits of the One True God, weren't troubled at drawing an analogy between the sun god and the Son of God:

> But our Lord, too, is born in the month of December . . .
> the eight before the calends of January [December 25] . . .
> But they call it the "Birthday of the Unconquered." Who
> indeed is so unconquered as our Lord?[5]

Ironically, the Catholic Encyclopedia entry for Christmas, which also acknowledges the solar symbolism applied to Christ in scripture and in tradition, concludes not that Christmas is borrowed from pagans, but that "the same instinct which set *Natalis Invicti* at the winter solstice will have sufficed, apart from deliberate adaptation or curious calculation, to set the Christmas feast there too"—thus affirming Campbell's observation that the date of December 25 was selected for mythological, rather than historical, reasons.

PATHS & PERSPECTIVES

This can be a damning realization for those who believe the Bible is literally true.

A memory that stands out from childhood is one of my parents listening to a radio preacher out of Pasadena, California, who offered listeners "The Plain Truth About Christmas!" Back in the fifties and sixties the idea that Christmas had pagan origins was heresy to the general public. Cognitive dissonance sometimes set in for the individual believer whose research confirmed this radical preacher's claims.

For the literalist, this essentially turns Christmas into a satanic ritual. Certain small sects today completely eschew Christmas, excommunicating members who celebrate the holiday (e.g., the Jehovah's Witnesses, and, until recently, the Worldwide Church of God). Often corollary to such beliefs is a perception that the Roman Catholic Church under the papacy consciously conspired to hoodwink the Christian world into participating in "the ancient Babylon Mystery Religion"—a reading of mythic images so literal and concrete as to create a reality infested with paranoia.

Perhaps Christians are more sophisticated today—even most fundamentalists who read scripture as literal, concrete fact, and know that Christmas is an extra-biblical celebration, still find spiritual value in the day. I suspect this is because these mythic motifs point past intellect and ring true on a deeper level—metaphors that speak to the soul of spiritual transformation. Many mainstream denominations today support such understandings.

And then there are those who have been moved to step outside the Christian paradigm and embrace one or more of the pre- or post-Christian manifestations of this archetype (which might include participation in Wicca, or other pagan, New Age, or shamanic beliefs and rituals).

Here Comes The Sun

What, then, is the significance of this solar imagery?

> The sun is our second symbol of rebirth, evoking the idea of not coming back at all, of not being reborn here but passing beyond the spheres of rebirth to a transcendent light. The typical image for this is the sun. The moon carries darkness within it, but wherever the sun goes there is no darkness. There are only the shadows of those forces that do not open themselves to its light. The image of the sun-door speaks of yet another kind of rebirth, that of the return of the lost one—that is, the one who is lost in the spheres and shadows of time, who returns to the eternal root which is his own great root.
>
> . . . That which you are was never born and will never die; that is the insight rendered in terms of the solar mystery, the solar light.[6]

The mythic images associated with the winter solstice help us shift our identification from the individual human body, which dies and is discarded, to that which is eternal, bringing us into alignment with the powers of nature that operate in the universe, and in ourselves—thus generating harmony between macrocosm and microcosm. The metaphorical reference of the image of the newborn god is to a spiritual birth.

In Heinrich Zimmer's words,

> We must effect [God's] new incarnation from within
> ourselves. Divinity must descend, somehow, into the
> matter of our own existence and participate in this
> peculiar life-process.[7]

Christians certainly experience this dynamic through the
indwelling of the Holy Spirit (or Holy Ghost—the aspect of
the triune God through which Mary conceived); nevertheless,
Christianity tends to read the birth of Jesus exclusively as a
unique historical event. An awareness of the mythic imagery
Christmas shares with the solstice celebrations of other traditions throughout the world thus expands our understanding
beyond the literal, to the realization of a metaphorical truth.
Angelus Silesius, a seventeenth century mystic, penned a cou-
plet that Campbell is fond of quoting:

> Of what use, Gabriel, your message to Marie,
> Unless you now can bring the same message to me!

THE MOTHER & CHILD REUNION
IS ONLY A MOTION AWAY

I think that one of the great calamities of contemporary life is that the religions that we have inherited have
insisted on the historical accuracy of their symbols. The
Virgin Birth, for example . . . these are symbols that

are found in the mythologies of the world. Their primary reference must be to the psyche from which they have come. They speak to us of something in ourselves. They cannot primarily refer to historical events . . . The image of the Virgin Birth: what does it refer to? A historical, biological problem? Or is it a psychological, spiritual metaphor?

. . . The child then becomes symbolic of the coordination of the opposites, male and female. Of course, this is the real meaning of the motif of the Virgin Birth.[8]

There is no denying Christianity's history of overt hostility toward those who worship the Goddess, whether in one or all of her many incarnations. Nevertheless, the union of masculine and feminine mythological systems is represented not just by the adoration of the Virgin or the birth of the Divine Child, but is embedded in the very structure of Christianity itself.

Alan Watts (who at thirteen carried the train of the Archbishop of Canterbury upon his enthronement, and subsequently served as an Episcopal priest in the United States) makes exactly this point:

In the cycle of the Christian Year the rites of the Incarnation are governed by the solar calendar, since they are connected with the Birth of the Sun, and so fall upon fixed dates. On the other hand, the rites of the Atonement, of Christ's Death, Resurrection, and Ascension, are governed by the lunar calendar, for there is a figure of Death and Resurrection in the waning and waxing of the moon.[9]

Hence Christmas always falls on December 25, in tune with solar mythology. Easter, on the other hand, floats, falling on the Sunday following the first full moon after the spring equinox, when winter turns to spring—thus linking the death and resurrection of Christ to the dead and resurrected lover of the goddess in lunar mythologies (e.g., Dumuzi and Inanna, Tammuz and Ishtar, Baal and Astarte, etc.).

This dynamic is neither haphazard coincidence, nor consciously constructed artifices seamlessly patched together by a central authority determining approved imagery. Mythology is a picture-language of the collective soul; the same archetypal patterns contionue to recur, regardless of attempts to stifle, suppress, or exploit them. The essence of wisdom and eternal truth does not seem to change over the life of our species—but to see these same detailed themes and symbols emerge where least expected does engender wonder, awe, and an appreciation for the majesty and power of myth.

Whether one prefers to observe the Winter Solstice, or Christmas, or both, or neither, there is no denying the joyous possibilities and potentialities inherent in the season's central image. And so, for the last word on the subject, Campbell takes us back to that babe born of a virgin:

> We are all born as animals and live the life that animals live: we sleep, eat, reproduce, and fight. There is, however, another order of living, which the animals do not know, that of awe before the mystery of being, the *mysterium tremendum et fascinans*, that can be the root and branch of the spiritual sense of one's days. That is

the birth—the Virgin Birth—in the heart of a properly human, spiritual life.[10]

NOTES

1. Campbell, Pathways to Bliss, op. cit. 42.
2. Anne Baring and Jules Cashford, The Myth of the Goddess: Evolution of an Image (New York: Viking, 1991; New York: Penguin Arkana, 1993), 561. Citations are from the Penguin Arkana edition.
3. Campbell, The Power of Myth, op. cit. 217.
4. Joseph Campbell, Thou Art That, ed. Eugene Kennedy, Ph.D. (Novato: New World Library, 2001), 65.
5. "Christmas," The Catholic Encyclopedia, http://www.newadvent.org/cathen/03724b.html.
6. Campbell, Thou Art That, op. cit. 89, 90.
7. Heinrich Zimmer, Philosophies of India, ed. Joseph Campbell (Princeton: Princeton University Press 1951, 1989) 2. Citations are from 1989 edition.
8. Campbell, Pathways to Bliss, op. cit. 88, 117.
9. Alan Watts, Myth and Ritual in Christianity (New York: Vanguard Press, 1953), 126.
10. Campbell, Thou Art That, op. cit. 29.

NINE

/

JOYFUL PARTICIPATION
IN THE SORROWS OF LIFE

One should know that in turmoil, loss, unhappiness,
and passion there is Brahman, no less than in peace,
victory, happiness, and repose . . . Brahman is to be
found not in one term of a dichotomy, but beyond and
within both![1]

Given the constant stimulation and steady stream of information assaulting us from all sides, it's not unusual today to
reduce the core concepts of essential thinkers into convenient,
easy-to-process sound bites (e.g., Einstein's "$E = MC^2$," Ayn
Rand's "the virtue of selfishness," or Karl Marx's "from each
according to his ability, to each according to his need"). Such
key phrases are easily remembered, each invoking and encapsu-
lating a complex structure of percepts, postulates, theories, and
observations associated with their authors. At the same time,
these phrases sometimes serve as crib notes for those who may

have read little of the thinkers in question, which can lead to misunderstanding and unfounded criticism.

Two such phrases closely identified with Joseph Campbell are open to frequent misinterpretation. The most widely recognized is the subject of "discovering bliss" (see Chapter 2).

Almost as well known is the maxim highlighted in the following passage from *The Power of Myth*:

> [A]ll life is sorrowful; there is however an escape from sorrow; the escape is *Nirvāna*—which is a state of mind or consciousness, not a place somewhere, like heaven. It is right here, in the midst of the turmoil of life. It is the state you find when you are no longer driven to live by compelling desires, fears, and social commitments, when you have found your center of freedom and can act by choice out of that. Voluntary action out of this center is the action of the bodhisattvas—*joyful participation in the sorrows of the world.*[2] (emphasis mine)

Joyful participation in the suffering of life—sounds callous and uncaring when taken out of context—but even those familiar with Campbell's body of work can find this a difficult principle to absorb, especially in light of specific and personal tragedy. Some critics believe Campbell thus encourages passive acceptance of poverty, injustice and catastrophe, even providing a perverse rationale for taking glee in the misfortunes of others.

What is the source of this phrase and the thoughts it illustrates? Are criticisms of the concept fair, or are they rooted in the literalist fallacy—misunderstanding Campbell's allusion through the concretization of a mythic image?

What does Campbell intend by this adage?

> One of the great challenges of life is to say "yea" to that
> person or that act or that condition which in your mind
> is most abominable.[3]

Shortly after the tragic loss of life in the 9/11 attacks, a friend remarked, "I just can't be as pragmatic or masochistic about it. I cannot find any way to joyfully participate in the death of thousands of people."

I too struggle in such moments with what that phrase might mean—most recently, in the wake of the killer tsunami that swamped shores ringing the Indian Ocean, causing 225,000 deaths on December 26, 2004. As an academic concept, I have no problem with "joyful participation in life's sorrows," but horrors of such magnitude task my understanding. Where the aphorism sounds jaunty and optimistic, actual experience proves wrenching and overwhelming.

But does Joseph Campbell suggest we take joy in this? That's not my understanding.

A literal reading might arrive at such a conclusion, but the concept is rooted in a mythic image that emerges within Buddhism and, like all mythic imagery, is metaphor. The form itself suggests a metaphoric reading—"joyful sorrow" (or "sorrowful joy") is an oxymoron, the language of paradox that points beyond sensate experience to the transcendent perspective shared by mystics of all traditions.

Nor is this a concept applied exclusively to the natural world—humanity itself, after all, is a part of nature. Campbell even singles out sinister examples of man's inhumanity to man—Hiroshima, Auschwitz, the firebombing of Dresden, the rape of Tibet.

"Joyful participation" is not simply adopting a Pollyanna perspective, jollying one's way through catastrophe and ruin; rather than retreating into denial, one instead fully embraces the experience. Campbell points to Victor Frankl losing his wife, and almost his own life, in a German concentration camp, and to a Buddhist monk and colleague of Campbell's who had seen family and friends slaughtered during the Chinese annexation of Tibet. These are individuals who "joyfully participated" by fully experiencing what life presented them, and who emerged from these experiences not harboring bitterness and hatred, but with compassion for all—even for those who injured them most!

Campbell isn't saying we have to acquiesce in evil, accept it as inevitable and resign ourselves to being victims. But as the Wheel turns, wherever we are—whether tasting Paradise, or enduring Hell—we are best off if we embrace each moment and experience the full range of emotions, the ecstasy *and* the agony of life. It is this that Campbell means by "joyful participation." Embracing the experience includes acknowledging the feelings that arise, which means fully experiencing negative feelings—frustration, rage and vengeance, loss, fear, the emptiness of a broken heart—as well as the positive.

Campbell refers to this concept as "the bodhisattva formula."

The bodhisattva, in Mahāyāna Buddhism, is one who is on the point of achieving Buddhahood, but instead of embracing nirvāna and ending his/her experience of suffering by simply ceasing to be—stepping off the Wheel of Death and Rebirth, to be reborn no more—the bodhisattva remains on this plane and "joyfully participates in the sorrow of the world" until all beings attain enlightenment.

This means returning to this vale of suffering lifetime after lifetime—the ultimate in compassion . . .

The sorrow and suffering come from our existing in Time and Space. We live in a temporal universe, which implies loss—this moment will pass. No one gets out of here alive, as Jim Morrison sings. "All life is suffering"—the Buddha's First Noble Truth—doesn't mean every waking moment is morose and painful and one never laughs or feels pleasure. Rather, because of the temporal nature of the experienced universe, all pleasure, all happiness, all joy, is fleeting, and all too soon mourned in their absence.

This is just the nature of life. You might have the best job in the world, feel fulfilled and respected and happy—and then the economy tanks and the firm goes bankrupt, and there you are under pressure again, scrambling to fill your belly and keep a roof over your head (even if you don't lose your job, there's always the awareness you could—pressure at odds with any pleasure you might take in your work). Or, you might have married your soul mate, the love of your life—but then, they could be hit by a passing truck, fall into an affair with the new boss, join a religious cult, or some similar shift in the status quo...

. . . and joy turns to sorrow.

We resist change—so when change (temporality) occurs, we experience loss and sorrow and suffering—yet change is the only constant in the universe. The details may differ in each individual life, but the nature of suffering remains the same.

In *Asian Journals*, Campbell's record of his sojourn in India and East Asia in 1954–55, he details his encounter with the guru, Sri Krishna Menon, in Trivandrum. This meeting is also described in *A Joseph Campbell Companion*, as follows:

> Two days later I was invited to meet with the guru. If you're on the right track, that's the way it goes: doors open miraculously. So, I went up to a lovely cottage, and at the door was an Indian with a long, white beard. He said, "The master is upstairs." I went up to an attic that was perfectly naked except for two chairs. Atmananda was seated in one, and I was to sit in the other, facing him. I mean, it was a real confrontation.
>
> He said, "Do you have a question?" I had the good fortune, I later learned, to ask exactly the question that had been his first question to his guru, so we had a very good conversation. When we'd concluded, he said he now had to go down to his class. He dismissed me, and I thanked him. Now, I had made arrangements to meet some members of his class in the coffee shop after the class was finished. When I came in, one of them said, "The master said you are on the brink of illumination." Why? Because of the question I had asked.
>
> My question was this: "'Since all is Brahman, all is the divine radiance, how can we say 'no' to ignorance or brutality or anything?" His answer was: "For you and me, we say 'yes.'"[4]

I like the way Jack Kerouac phrases it, in his classic Beat novel *On the Road*, as being "mad for life"—saying "yes!" to it all. This is the way of the artist, and not the moralizing theologian.

Does this perspective lead to passive acceptance of evil and suffering, fostering a victim mentality? Hardly.

> There are two aspects to a thing of this kind. One is your judgment in the field of time, and the other is your judgment as a metaphysical observer. You can't say there shouldn't be poisonous serpents—that's the way life is. But in the field of action, if you see a poisonous serpent about to bite somebody, you kill it. That's not saying no to the serpent, that's saying no to that situation.[5]

Campbell values fully engaging our world of *samsara*, while at the same time seeing through this passion play—embracing at once both mundane and transcendent perspectives—the paradox underlying "joyful participation in the sorrows of the world." *Samsara* is a Sanskrit term for the world of delusion—the messy, painful world in which we live; in Buddhism, *samsara* is the world of suffering from which we seek escape in *nirvāna*.

But in Mahāyāna Buddhism, *nirvāna* and *samsara* are ultimately one and the same, an understanding that provides the context for Campbell's advice:

> Participate joyfully in the sorrows of the world.
>
> We cannot cure the world of sorrows, but we can choose to live in joy. When we talk about settling the world's problems, we're barking up the wrong tree. The world is perfect. It's a mess. It's always been a mess. We are not going to change it. Our job is to straighten out our own lives.[6]

How does one do this? By "following one's bliss" and "joyfully participating . . ."

Sri Krishna Menon suggested a helpful tool:

> Then he gave me a little meditation: "Where are you between two thoughts?" That is to say, you are thinking all the time, and you have an image of yourself. Well, where are you between two thoughts? Do you ever have a glimpse beyond your thinking of that which transcends anything you can think about yourself? *That's* the source field out of which all your life energies are coming.
>
> In meditating, meditate on your own divinity. The goal of life is to be a vehicle for something higher. Keep your eyes up there between the world of opposites watching your 'play' in the world.
>
> Let the world be as it is and learn to rock with the waves.[7]

This is the essence of esoteric truth in the mystic traditions, including Hinduism, Buddhism, and Taoism.

Alan Watts describes it as if one is an actor in a play. A good actor becomes the character he plays: when on stage he isn't thinking of the bills he needs to pay or the girl he hopes to seduce or what he's having for dinner later; such thoughts distract and detract from the performance. Instead, the actor's ego-personality disappears and he *becomes* King Lear betrayed by his daughters, *feels* Hamlet's angst and the urge to seek revenge, or *experiences* Romeo's desire for Juliet.

The Universe, Watts points out, wears many masks—an Alan mask, a Tom mask, a Sally mask, a starfish mask, a tiger mask, a rodent mask and so on, ad infinitum, myriad roles in this cosmic passion play ––and when I'm playing me, I play me to the hilt, experiencing fully my loves and losses, triumphs and defeats, ecstasies and agonies . . .

This is joyful participation in life's sorrows. When my father dies of cancer, I experience terror and fear and grief and agony— saying "yes" to life, participating fully . . . and when it's a beautiful spring day and I am frolicking with my beloved in the sunshine, this too is saying "yes" to life, participating fully.

But I also know that I am more than just me ("a vehicle for something higher"), and I know that the joy and suffering of life are just play . . . which doesn't mean I experience less grief, or less pain—but grief and pain and sorrow and despair are placed in a larger context.

In other traditions, good and evil are relative to the position in which you are standing. What is good for one is evil for the other. And you play your part, not withdrawing from the world when you realize how horrible it is, but seeing that this horror is simply the foreground of a wonder: a *mysterium tremendum et fascinans.*

"All life is sorrowful" is the first Buddhist saying, and so it is. It wouldn't be life if there weren't temporality involved, which is sorrow—loss, loss, loss. You've got to say yes to life and see it as magnificent this way . . .

It is joyful just as it is. I don't believe there was anybody who intended it, but this is the way it is. James Joyce has a memorable line: "History is a nightmare from which I am trying to awake." And the way to wake from it is not to be afraid, and to recognize that all of this, as it is, is a manifestation of the horrendous power that is of all creation. The ends of things are always painful. But pain is part of there being a world at all . . . "I will participate in the game. It is a wonderful, wonderful opera—except that it hurts."[8]

I have yet to meet anyone who perfectly embodies this concept—just not that many living bodhisattvas in my neighborhood, I guess—but I do notice the more I'm able to consciously cultivate this attitude, the less likely I am to either magnify or deny the suffering I do encounter. Ironically, the conscious acknowledgment and embrace of the pain inevitable to living and dying actually dissipates much of my unnecessary, self-generated suffering, leaving me better equipped to deal with what life throws at me.

Myth thus leads us out of the realm of imagination and into the real world, offering pragmatic, practical advice. "Life will always be sorrowful. We can't change it, but we can change our attitude toward it," is how Joseph Campbell sums up this point—though he prefers the power of the poetic image:

"Joyful participation in the sorrows of the world."

More than just a sound bite!

Notes

1. Campbell, Asian Journals, op. cit. 301.
2. Campbell, Power of Myth, op. cit. 203.
3. Ibid. 42.
4. Campbell, A Joseph Campbell Companion, op. cit. 188.
5. Campbell, The Power of Myth, op. cit. 83.
6. Campbell, A Joseph Campbell Companion, op. cit. 17.
7. Ibid. 189.
8. Campbell, The Power of Myth, op. cit. 80, 81.

TEN

/

THE TUATHA DE MENEHUNE?

Living with these things all the time, I can see how
there are certain universal patterns for these manifestations. A shaman among the Navajo or in the Congo
will be saying things which sound so much like, say,
Nicholas Cusanus or Thomas Aquinas, or C.G. Jung,
that one just has to realize that those ranges of experience are common to the human race. There are some
people who close themselves away from them, some
people who open themselves to them . . .[1]

So, ever wonder what the islands of Hawaii have in common
with the Emerald Isle?

Now there's a *non sequitur* for you!

Apart from an absence of poisonous snakes, there doesn't
seem much to link the two—different oceans, different cli-
mates, and not even the wildest speculation has Finn McCool
founding Honolulu . . . but this summer, experiencing for
the first time the magic of the Hawaiian islands, I found my

thoughts wandering to the "little people," the *Sidhe* or faery folk of Ireland, often identified with the *Tuatha de Danaan*.

> NOTE: Faeries shift shape, and so do the words that refer to them. Their name can be spelled any number of ways—fairye, fayerye, fayre, faerie, faery, etc. I prefer "faery" and "faeries" to denote an entity chthonic, floral, or ethereal, and mysterious, as opposed to the more common "fairy," which calls to my mind the Disneyfied version.

The Tuatha da Danaan are legendary inhabitants of Ireland displaced by the Milesians (generally thought to be the Celts), in much the same way the Tuatha da Danaan had displaced the Firbolgs and Fomarians before them. Some scholars believe we can't be certain of their historical existence, but there is growing acceptance of this theory, based not just on archaeology, but on clues embedded in the myths themselves (For example, a common characteristic attributed to the Sidhe in story is a fear of iron—which may be significant, as the Milesians/Celts were an Iron Age people, with better arms than those whose lands they occupy).

But if this people did once exist, they have long since morphed into creatures of myth, alive today only in fairy tale and dream. Joseph Campbell mentions them in several places, particularly in *Occidental Mythology*, the third volume in *The Masks of God* tetralogy:

> [I]n the epics of ancient Ireland, the Celtic warriors and their brilliant chariot fighters move in a landscape beset

with invisible fairy forts, wherein abide a race of beings
of an earlier mythological age: the wonderful Tuatha da
Danaan, children of the Goddess Dana, who retired,
when defeated, into wizard hills of glass. And these are
the very people of the sidhe or Shee, the Fairy host, the
Fairy Cavalcade, of the Irish peasants to this day.[2]

According to some legends, the Tuatha may once have been
human in size—but as they retreat before the invading Celts
(which didn't just happen on a Thursday at 4:20 in the afternoon, but occurred in waves, a migration unfolding over
time) and shrink into the out-of-the-way places (dark woods
and "hollow hills"), they also shrink in size. Meanwhile, massive structures existing before the Celts arrived (such as the
many barrows, menhirs, and megaliths dotting the land) are
attributed to the "little people" or "ancient ones" there before
them; in legend, these structures are often built with special
powers in a single night (*á la* Merlin's raising of Stonehenge).

ECHOES

Why think of this in Hawaii?

Everywhere I walked on the islands—every beach and
inlet, every mountain stream, every mound and cliff, and even
the breeze—is the stuff of myth. Scratch beneath the restau-
rants and condos and shops, and one finds the spot where Maui
fished the islands out of the sea; or that rock poking up out of
the water just offshore is the tail of a defeated dragon; or that
cliff jutting out over the sea is where a ghost maiden lures male

travelers to their deaths (you *really don't* pick up any female hitchhikers on that stretch of road—whereas anywhere else you had better, as you're likely giving a ride to Pele herself, who will bless you if you help, and curse you if you don't).

That sense of enchantment is palpable and manifest throughout the islands.

The more I saw of their magic—the spectacular vistas, stunning waterfalls, lava landscapes, inviting valleys, and lush tropical rainforests—the more I was moved to explore the local mythology . . . but it's harder than I thought to find a bookstore in Paradise.

Eventually, tucked in between the bongs and Bob Marley CDs in a Rastafarian shop somewhere on Oahu's north shore, I uncovered a lone copy of Martha Beckwith's *Hawaiian Mythology*—published in 1940, still considered the definitive work in the field. Beckwith was a find, a welcome read on the beach in between surf and sun and snooze . . .

Tales of the *Menehune* (which literally translates to "little people"), however, are what captured my imagination. In the many descriptions and classifications of these folk I realized I'd heard this story before . . . on the far side of the world.

I couldn't help but notice certain mythic parallels between Hawaii's "little people"—the *Menehune*—and the "little people" of Ireland.

BLURRING HISTORY & MYTH

In brief, most historians, anthropologists, and even native people believe that "Menehune," as used in Hawaii, refers to the original settlers: colonists from the Marquesas who came to Hawaii in great double-hulled canoes, around AD300–400, carrying with them plants and livestock—which proved necessary baggage as, apart from fish, there were no edible plants or animals capable of sustaining a human population on the volcano-forged islands. Breadfruit, taro, sweet potato, pigs, and more came across the sea with the settlers.

Over the next seven hundred years the Marquesan voyagers and their descendants built huge *heiaus* (sacred platforms and temple structures) and extensive irrigation systems which are startling not just in size, but in scope of vision. They developed a prosperous, mostly peaceful culture—but were gradually displaced when colonists from Tahiti arrived and eventually conquered the islands.

Both the Tahitians and Marquesans come from common stock —— but the first Hawaiians, having mellowed over the centuries, had relaxed the strict *tapus* (taboos) common to Polynesian religion and drifted away from human sacrifice—in contrast to the Tahitians, who brought with them an unyielding adherence to tradition. Their fundamentalist revival included the re-institution of human sacrifice, an increase in the power of the nobility (the ali'i, or "chiefs") enhanced by a greater portion of *mana* concentrated in their person, and strict enforcement of the *tapus*, punishable by death. A rigid caste system evolved, with the original Hawaiians—now called the *Menehune*—on the bottom. Many were enslaved, and the

Menehune became the branch of society identified with the tasks no one wanted, akin to the *Dalit* (aka "untouchable") caste in India.

Much like the Tuatha da Danaan when overrun by the Celts, the Menehune retreated into the wild places—remote mountain valleys—leaving the lowlands, where the fish are jumping and the living is easy, to the dominant newcomers. Squeezed further and further north, fleeing from island to island as the newcomers expand, they are eventually confined to a remote corner of Kauai, before disappearing from history altogether.

. . . And so the Menehune receded into myth.

There was, though, a period of overlap when both peoples lived on the islands. The label of "little people" may have originally referred not to physical size, but to the fact that the early Hawaiians were considered inferior, of the lowest caste—"little people," to the great ones who came after them. True, there are physical hooks on which these projections catch: inhabitants of the Marquesas are on average of somewhat shorter, stockier build than the Tahitians, but not dramatically so. Of course, neither the Menehune who lived among and served the newcomers, nor those scrabbling out an existence in the less hospitable parts of the islands, enjoyed as rich, nourishing, and varied a diet as their new overlords—so there may indeed have been a resultant contrast in physique

But as the Menehune vanish from the physical plane, they morph into the "little people" of lore, vested, like the Sidhe, with magical powers.

(Could this be an unconscious compensation on the part of the conquering invaders, whether Celt or Tahitian, in response to the displacement and subjugation of their predecessors?)

The Menehune can be conceived as either impish prank-
sters or helpful spirits: they deliver death and disaster, or treasures beyond compare—depending on circumstance and the
attitude of the mortals they encounter. They are great builders,
erecting grand monuments in a single night (sound familiar?)
. . . and there is no mistaking the massive architectural style
of heiaus, irrigation systems, and other structures attributed
to these faery folk, compared to those built by the later
Hawaiians. Legend has local kings calling on the Menehune
to create fishponds, dig canals, and magically manifest other
engineering marvels.

Hmm . . .What kinship might there be between the *Tuatha
da Danaan* and the *Menehune*?

What intrigues me is the dynamic. The pattern seems the
same: an earlier people are overcome by a later folk and, on the
one hand, demeaned and marginalized—made "little"—but
then, as they die off, disappear, or are absorbed by their succes-
sors, become the recipients of projections of superior powers—
powers that exist in the elemental forces of nature, and in the
human psyche.

These earlier people thus become identified with the archetypal energies that inform nature—e.g., the fertile energy that
pollinates the flowers and makes green the sprout, or the siren
energy that lures men to their death (whether taking shape as
the Irish Glaistig, an alluring water fairy who dances with men
before she feeds off their blood, or the seductive, spectral hitch-
hiker who lures lusty males off that cliff on Maui).

I'm just having fun with these motifs, noting the resonance between patterns in play in island cultures eight thousand miles apart. Of course, the historical details differ, and

there is room for speculation of all sorts—myth, after all is ever shifting shape . . .

SHAPING MYTHS

How does Joseph Campbell account for the parallel motifs found in mythological belief systems widely separated in time and/or space?

> In Volume Two of the *Historical Atlas of World Mythology*, Campbell distinguishes three possible explanations of similarities in myths: "diffusion," "convergence," and "parallelism." Convergence means independent invention through similar experiences of the environment: similar environmental conditions produce similar myths. Parallelism means independent invention through similarities in the mind: the psychic unity of humanity yields similar myths. Diffusion continues to mean the spread of myth from one culture to another.
>
> Campbell accepts all three explanations . . .[3]

Segal's summary rings true, though he seems seriously perplexed by Campbell's failure to commit to and rigorously defend a single explanation. Nevertheless, while such consistency may be admired in academic circles, Campbell makes clear the real world is not so black-and-white, so either/or—especially in the field of comparative mythology. Anthropologists and mythologists have been arguing these theories for generations, with papers written and battles fought, yet rarely can the appearance of a motif recurring across cultures be attributed to just one or another of these factors. It takes the three braided together to make a myth:

> In the main, I should think that for most of the earth it can be assumed that all three of these argued forces will have operated in the formation of those widespread cultural continuities . . . each of us must decide for himself whether to believe it possible that the human mind might be programmed in such detail that through the interfacing simply of the psyche and the landscape such a multitude of correspondences could have evolved.[4]

Sometimes the tendency in the Cartesian West is to seek one explanation: to each phenomenon must be ascribed one cause, and one cause alone—and once we settle on an explanation, we stop looking. The universe, alas, is far more complex: every-thing-that-is arises from a confluence of interdependent fac-tors and interlocking events. Scratch the surface of any single individual and we find a collection of genetic codes, biolog-ical drives, chemical interactions, environmental limitations, social ties, psychological motivations, and aspirations all acting together, from which it's impossible to isolate any one feature as the direct cause of a lived life.

How might these "three argued forces"—parallelism, con-vergence, and diffusion—"operate together" to explain the con-gruencies between the "little people" of Hawaii and Ireland?

PARALLELISM

Campbell explain these forces by identifying a common ground underlying all mythology, which is then variously inflected by two "differentiating factors":

> The "common element" in mythology is, of course, the human psyche, which is a function of the human body . . .
>
> Myth, like dream, is an expression of the human imagination thus grounded in the realities of the psyche and, like dream, reflecting equally the influences of a specific social environment (nomadic hunting-and-gathering tribe; settled agricultural sib, city-state, or nation; vagrant desert horde; or militaristic empire), which, in turn, is linked to a landscape.
>
> The common ground, or element, of all mythology is consequently the biology of *Homo sapiens sapiens,* whereas the differentiating factors are (1) geography and (2) the cultural stage horizon. For it is a fact that every mythological system has taken shape within a given geographical horizon, conditioned not only by the landscape from which its imagery is derived, but also by the limits of the body of information according to which all appearances in that only known world are interpreted.[5]

Our common biology shapes our experience and our concerns. Whether aboriginal shaman, Egyptian serf, or dotcom cybernaut, life's initiations remain the same: each is born of woman, an episode fraught with pain and peril; each comes of age, making the precarious transition from child to adult; each faces the question of marriage and family; each grows old, withers, and dies. There aren't two ways of digesting food, two ways of menstruating, two ways of dying—these life moments, writ large and small, remain remarkably constant whether Hapsburg or Hottentot—and the human psyche expresses remarkable consistency in the way it engages and processes these moments. Images of birth and death, rites of initiation, sacred marriage, a "transcendental yet ubiquitously immanent sacred power (*mana, wakonda, sakti,* etc.)," survival after death, and more are, in Joseph Campbell's words, themes "conterminous with the human species."

This would be the realm of the *elementargedanken* ("elementary ideas") of Adolf Bastian, which Campbell finds cognate with Jung's archetypes of the collective unconscious. We never, however, directly experience the archetype, but instead engage the *völkgedanken* ("folk ideas"), the mythic images encountered through a specific tradition.

The Hawaiian Menehune and the Irish Sidhe would then be localized expressions of an archetypal image. We find faery folk after all in every culture, whether the dryads, satyrs and nymphs of Greek mythology, the djinn in Islam, or the nagas, devas, and apsaras of Hindu and Buddhist traditions. These beings fulfill corresponding roles. Hence some form of faery lore is bound to rise in almost every culture regardless of circumstance, given Segal's description of parallelism as "independent invention through similarities in the mind: the psychic unity of humanity yields similar myths."

But why should this pattern take the specific shape of the Menehune in Hawaii and the Tuatha da Danaan in Ireland, with their peculiar similarities? For that, we need to take a look at the other two "argued forces": convergence and diffusion.

Discussing the congruencies between the Cosmic Buffalo of the Sioux and Pawnee, and Śiva as Nandi, the white bull in Hindu mythology, Campbell contrasts one with the other:

> Who will say by what miracle—whether of history or psychology—these two homologous images came into being, the one in India and the other in North America? It is possible that one of the paths of diffusion . . . may have been followed. However, it is also possible that the two images were developed independently by some process of convergence . . . for in India, too there was a meeting of animal and plant cultures when the Aryans arrived with their flocks in the Dravidian agricultural zone. Analogous processes may have been set in play—as in two separate alchemical retorts.[6]

CONVERGING GEOGRAPHIES

These faeries of Hawaii and Ireland emerged on islands where an earlier culture is defeated, displaced, and diminished by an invading culture. Might the parallels we see be a function of a similar dynamic, arising out of the fight over turf in a contained geography, the defeated inhabitants and their deities having nowhere to retreat—except into the vast ocean of myth?

While there are a number of mythic motifs that are universal—common, that is to most cultures—the environment influences the form of the local mythology. For example, the trickster appears in all cultures—but an energy that might manifest as a leprechaun in verdant, fecund Ireland instead takes shape as Coyote in the harsh, rugged landscape of the American Southwest—different geography, different image, different accent. Conversely, similar geography would evoke similar themes—convergence. Campbell certainly admits the possibility—hence another factor in the mythic resonance between islands half a world apart.

When people come into a new land, they follow an unconscious process Campbell labels *landnáma*—a term borrowed from Icelandic scholar Einar Palsson—or "land-taking": identifying aspects of the local landscape with the deities and myths they bring with them, until these become part of the landscape itself:

> It is everywhere the same myth, but in each province the local landscape is its theater and the local animals and plants become its actors. Land-taking, then, is the act of taking spiritual possession of a newly entered land with all its elements, by assimilation to a myth already carried in one's heart in the way of a continuing culture. We are not to suppose that in every province of the cultural continuum the one same myth was separately developed.[7]

DIFFUSION: MYTH THROUGH OSMOSIS

Though Joseph Campbell is open to both parallelism and convergence as explanations for the appearance of recurring images in seemingly disparate mythologies, he provides example after example of the diffusion of mythic themes from one culture to another—particularly in his four-volume *The Masks of God*, which surveys the roots and range of human mythology, and the image-laden *Historical Atlas of World Mythology*, tragically incomplete at the time of his passing, which examines the evolution of mythological archetypes from historical and geographical perspectives.

Often Campbell is able to trace the development of a mythic image in tandem with the diffusion of a cultural innovation or technological advance—such as the spread of the domestication of the pig as primary food source and the myth of the dead-and- resurrected god slain by a boar—but more about that in a moment. Some scholars suggest diffusion is incompatible with the idea underlying parallelism, which posits the human psyche as source of mythic archetypes. Campbell rejects this mutual exclusivity:

> To speak for diffusion doesn't diminish the force of the psyche. Why does it last? It lasts because it has a symbolic meaning. It excites a resonance in the psyche, and a truth is somehow suggested . . . Now, of course, when there is an outside influence, it's developed in the receiving area and it requires stylistic inflections, as well as new things from the animal and vegetable world round about. And so there is great creative development.[8]

For a mythic motif to be transferred from one culture to another, the motif must be compatible with the traditions of those adopting the image. A myth cannot be enforced by fiat if the collective psyche is not receptive—as we see with Ikhnaton, who erased the polytheistic mythos supporting Egyptian tradition, replacing it with his own solar monotheism: theology by decree. Within eight years of his passing the worship of Aton, which never took root in the popular imagination, collapsed in the face of the resurgence of orthodox tradition. A mythic image must ring true in the collective soul if it is to be embraced by the people.

Could diffusion explain the similarities between the Tuatha da Danaan and the Menehune?

Diffusion does occur, but is Ireland the source?

Martha Beckwith (*Hawaiian Mythology*) reveals the whole weave of the mythology that blankets Oceania. Throughout Polynesia (from Tahiti to Samoa to Tonga to the Marquesas to Hawaii to Easter Island), we have recurring themes: common tales with common heroes, the same deities performing the same deeds—sometimes wearing the very same name (e.g., the goddess Hina, the demi-god Maui), sometimes with slight differences (e.g., Ku, Kane, and Lono in Hawaii, known respectively as Tu, Tane, and Ro'o on Tahiti). Campbell covers this in depth in *Primitive Mythology* (Volume I of *The Masks of God*), and in the *Historical Atlas of World Mythology*—a clear case of a diffusion of mythic themes across a wide geographical range.

Hawaii's Menehune echo a theme common throughout this zone, that of a "spirit race." In New Zealand these are called the "Patu-pairehe," but in the western Tuamotus they are the "Manahune" (the ancient people of Tahiti), and in Raratonga, they are the "Manu-une." Beckwith even claims they are known to the Maori. Clearly there is a direct diffusion across the South Pacific (though in most of these regions

Beckwith tells us they are known as giants—in contrast to the "little people" of Hawaii).

But can we identify direct links between the faery folk of Ireland and Hawaii?

Not without stretching the imagination beyond the breaking point.

The Celtic invasion of Ireland was well under way by 500 BC; roughly one thousand years later the first wave of settlers from the Marquesas arrived in the Hawaiian Islands, with the final wave of Tahitian colonists arriving to subdue their predecessors around AD 1000. It is possible that this lone mythic image percolated across time and space over fifteen hundred years—but there doesn't seem any evidence of the path this motif would have followed—and even if a Celtic ship or two somehow strayed from Belfast to the Big Island and tales of the Tuatha merged with pre-existing legends of the Menehune, more than this single motif would have been transferred; we could expect to find an entire constellation of close parallels.

BRINGING HOME THE BACON

On the other hand, Campbell points out that Ireland and Polynesia represent opposite ends of an earlier mythological stratum, a zone of diffusion associated with the spread of the domestication of the pig during the Basal Neolithic period, c. 7500 to 4500 BC (which he delineates, among other places, in *Primitive Mythology*, 406 – 408). He finds the pig in ritual and myth reigns supreme over a wide swath, reaching from

Ireland and its faery-lore in the west to the myths of southeast Asia and Oceania:

> Many of the great dying gods were killed by pigs or people associated with pigs. Osiris's brother Set was hunting a pig when he found Osiris and killed him. Adonis was slain by the boar. In Ireland, the Celtic hero Diarmid was slain by a boar, whom he slew simultaneously. In Polynesia, one of the principal deities is Kamapua'a, the youthful pig-lord, who is the lover of the volcano goddess, Madame Pele. This is a mythology that stretches all the way from Ireland across the whole tropic world, and it is the first mythology we have of spiritual rank and the surrogate death.[9]

Campbell even relates the death of the Buddha to this same mythic complex: the Buddha, at age 82, is invited to a meal where pork is served. The Awakened One anticipates what will come of this:

> "Only one who has achieved *nirvāna* has the power to eat this meat. I will eat it. It is not to be served to my disciples, and that which is left over must be buried in the earth." That is a continuation of this theme of the pig.[10]

Several aspects of both Irish and Hawaiian tradition appear to be a diffusion of a mythic complex emerging out of a mythogenetic zone congruent with the appearance of swineherding cultures in southwest Asia. Tales of the Sidhe and the Menehune are a later morphing and melding of a "spirit race" motif embedded in this complex. One is not the cause of the other any more than notes on one flute or the teats on one sow cause each other (imagery borrowed from Alan Watts, though blame for the pun remains mine alone—forgive me if I boar).

No wonder Campbell avers "that all three of these argued forces [parallelism, diffusion, and convergence] will have operated in the formation of those widespread cultural continuities." Myth cannot be traced to a single cause triggering a specific effect, but is fluid and vaporous as any image floating up out of the collective psyche. The intersection of the human imagination with the external world takes shape through the interaction of these varying forces as infracted through local geography and cultural accents. This allows for tremendous variety in the development of mythologies, while shedding light on that sense of the familiar we encounter even in traditions foreign and exotic to our own.

Neither Celtic nor Polynesian religions are widely practiced today. Is their faery lore merely a quaint artifact, and nothing more?

With cultures colliding and crashing into one another, and no clear collective mythology emerging, Campbell suggests the mythogenetic zone whence myths emerge is no longer confined to a specific geographic area, but includes the cultural horizon of all humanity past and present, which is to be found within the human heart:

> The mythogenetic zone today is the individual in contact with his own interior life, communicating through his art with those "out there."[11]

Perhaps the question should be what do these tales say to us today?

How are you getting on with the faery folk?

NOTES

1. Joseph Campbell, "Living Myths: A Conversation with Joseph Campbell," interview by Lorraine Kisley, Parabola 1 Issue 2 (Spring 1976): 70 – 81.

2. Joseph Campbell, The Masks of God, Vol. 2: Occidental Mythology (New York: Viking Penguin, 1964; Novato, New World Library, 2021), 40, 41. Citations refer to New World Library edition.

3. Robert Segal, Joseph Campbell: An Introduction (New York: Garland Publishing, 1987; New York: Penguin Books, 1997), 214. Citations are from the Penguin Books edition.

4. Joseph Campbell, Historical Atlas of World Mythology, Vol. 2: The Way of the Seeded Earth, Part 1, The Sacrifice (New York: Harper & Row, 1988), 29.

5. Ibid.

6. Joseph Campbell, The Mythic Dimension, ed. Antony Van Couvering (San Francisco: HarperSanFrancisco, 1997; Novato: New World Library, 2007), 75-76. Citations are from the New World Library edition.

7. Ibid. 74.

8. Maher and Briggs, eds., An Open Life, op. cit. 43-44.

9. Campbell, Pathways to Bliss, op. cit. 34.

10. Ibid. 33.

11. Campbell, Creative Mythology, op. cit. 93.

ELEVEN

BENEVOLENT SCOUNDRELS

Almost all non-literate mythology has a trickster-hero of some kind . . . And there's a very special property in the trickster: he always breaks in, just as the unconscious does, to trip up the rational situation. He's both a fool and someone who's beyond the system. And the trickster represents all these possibilities of life that your mind hasn't decided it wants to deal with. The mind structures a lifestyle, and the fool or trickster represents another whole range of possibilities. He doesn't respect the values you've set up for yourself, and smashes them.

. . . The fool is the breakthrough of the absolute into the field of controlled social orders.[1]

Exploring the figure of the trickster is akin to striking the mythic mother lode: a vein of lore rich, complex, snaking back into the distant past, yet with us still, as Campbell suggests— an archetype active in the individual as well as the collective unconscious. Book upon book upon book has been written without coming close to exhausting the subject, for no matter how much we analyze, categorize, and hypothesize, the trickster remains too slippery to pin down. At the same time, we never seem to tire of hearing trickster tales, from the wily Coyote of Native American cultures caught in a trap of his own making, to Wile E. Coyote of cartoon fame, flattened by the very boulder intended for his speedy prey *(beep beep!)*. Despite the trickster's seemingly flawed character, marked by lechery, deception, and a rather rubbery sense of property rights, we remain entranced.

Why the fascination?

Who—or what—is the trickster? What are the origins of this image? How does this motif manifest in myth? Has his mischief finally been laid to rest in our enlightened age? Is trickster no more than the comic relief in stories today, or might this archetype still influence our lives?

Definitive answers?

Not likely . . . but, having admitted that, we can play with these questions and stay true to the spirit of trickster.

SHADOW HEROES

Where to begin?

The trickster is an archaic archetypal pattern reflected in myths from around the world. Joseph Campbell's understanding of this motif differs somewhat from Carl Jung, who characterizes the trickster as "a collective shadow figure, an epitome of all the inferior traits of character in individuals." Though that description might well fit today, Campbell declares, "In the Paleolithic sphere from which this figure derives, he was the archetype of the hero, the giver of all great boons—the fire-bringer and the teacher of mankind." (*Primitive Mythology*, 252)

And of course, in the spirit of trickster, both are right, as Campbell acknowledges. The trickster embodies paradox; indeed, he sometimes appears in androgynous form, symbolically uniting opposites in his being.

Jung's depiction, though, is understandable, as in most trickster myths we are initially introduced to the unsavory aspects of this character. Tricksters are often either fools, liars, or thieves, driven by appetite, proudly lecherous, and full of, well . . . excrement (quite literally, in at least one widely told Coyote tale). The trickster is defiant of authority and his actions threaten to subvert the established order. No wonder Jung finds this image mirrors our shadow side . . . and yet he stresses the trickster is by no means the face of evil.

Indeed, trickster's character flaws prove essential to his role as bringer of culture and bestower of boons. Thief, yes— so Coyote in British-Columbia, Rabbit among the Creek Indians, Raven among the Chilcotin tribe, Kingfisher among the Andamanese Islanders, Maui throughout Oceania, and Prometheus in Greece—all steal without shame the secret of fire from the gods on mankind's behalf. In his role as Lord of Boundaries the trickster often serves as messenger of the gods and patron of the crossroads (e.g., Hermes), including in his sphere what grows up around the crossroads (again, in the case of Hermes, the marketplace—which fosters commerce, communication, and travel). This ability to cross boundaries often translates into the role of psychopomp, guiding departed souls into the Underworld.

Tricksters are inventive, creative. Coyote in the American Northwest and Loki in northern Europe are two examples of tricksters who are the first to weave a net to catch fish (both later caught in their own invention), while Eshu—trickster god of the African Yoruba—and Hermes are among those credited with inventing language. Tricksters are also noted for their spontaneity, as well as an intimacy with the dynamics of chance, and hence are often identified with forms of divination. Lewis Hyde describes one such ritual:

> There is a form of divination associated with Hermes called cledonomancy, derived from *cledon*, which means an accidental but portentous remark, the language version of a lucky find. Long ago Pausanius described this oracle of "Hermes-of-the-Marketplace": at dusk as the lamps are being lit the petitioner leaves a "coin of local money" at the image of Hermes, whispers the question he hopes to have answered, puts his hands over his ears, and walks away. When he takes his hands away from his ears the first words he hears contain the oracle's reply. All the better if the words are uttered by a child or a fool, someone clearly incapable of calculating an effect.[2]

I'm pleased to report this oracle still works today—though I sometimes draw strange looks wandering the aisles of my local grocery.

Beginnings

Whence the origin of the trickster? How does he enter myth—and what function does he serve?

> It is hardly proper to call such a figure a god, or even to think of him as supernatural. He is a super-shaman. And we find his counterparts in myth and legend throughout the world, wherever shamanism has left its mark: in Oceania and Africa, as well as Siberia and Europe.[3]

Bronislaw Malinowski is representative of the many anthropologists who similarly assign the trickster archetype to an era of development prior to the founding of civilization. Paul Radin, studying the trickster cycle in tales of the Winnebago (or Ho-Chunk), claims this image reflects an earlier, rudimentary stage of consciousness. Lewis Hyde reminds us that trickster tales "preserve a set of images from the days when what mattered above all else was hunting."

Jung, in his essay "On the Psychology of the Trickster Figure," in *The Archetypes and the Collective Unconscious*, declares, "All mythical figures correspond to inner psychic experiences and originally sprang from them" (256). Might the trickster's appearance in myth reflect the context out of which this image arose, a result of how the human psyche engaged the world around it?

For Joseph Campbell the social function of this trickster/shaman is "to serve as interpreter and intermediary between man and the powers behind the veil of nature" (*Primitive Mythology*, 267), which proved critical as our species made the transition from what Campbell terms "animal consciousness" to "human consciousness." But what are these "powers behind the veil of nature" the trickster shaman mediates?

> [A]s Carl Jung put it . . . trickster is "stupider than the animals." Animals at least have inborn knowledge, a way of being, and trickster doesn't. The animals know not to eat that plant that causes them to defecate mountains; the animals know which way the river is; the animals know how to hunt for their particular foods. Trickster knows none of this, and so ends up hungry, stumbling around, covered in his own mess.
>
> It seems a dangerous position for an animal to be in, stripped of instinct. What possible use could there be of having lost the mother wit to be in the world? What conceivable advantage might lie in a way of being that has no way?
>
> [W]hoever has no way but is a successful imitator will have, in the end, a repertoire of ways. If we can imitate the spider and make a net, imitate the beaver and make a lake, imitate the heron's beak and make a spear, imitate the armadillo and wear armor, imitate the leopard and wear camouflage, imitate poison ivy and produce chemical weapons, imitate the fox and hunt downwind, then we become more versatile hunters, greater hunters.
>
> Perhaps having no way also means that a creature can adapt itself to a changing world. Species well situated in a habitat are always at risk if that habitat changes.[4]

So it's a possibility that the figure of the trickster enters mythology as a reflection of human evolution. Such seems the experience of countless generations over hundreds of thousands of years: as we become aware of ourselves, human consciousness gradually differentiating itself from the relatively unconscious, instinct-driven animal state-of-being, we realize that we have "no way," and so survive by stealing the ways of others—which we then use to kill and eat our animal brothers.

We even steal from the elemental forces of nature, capturing the lightning in our hearths! These "tricks" do more than just allow us to survive: eventually, we become the dominant species on the planet—but somewhere in the recesses of our minds is the sneaking suspicion that we haven't earned and don't deserve our good fortune . . .

Out of that inner tension trickster is born.

Today we know that we do have a way: the Way of Learning. Joseph Campbell often points out that human young experience a lengthier period of dependence than any other animal. We aren't born with the instinct to know how to survive within a few hours, or even months, of our birth—but are taught how to survive while our parents care for and protect us during the first dozen years or so of our life. Hyde suggests one reason the coyote is such an attractive carrier of trickster projections is that its young similarly remain dependent on their parents for a long time, during which they are taught to adapt to change by learning new responses.

Incidentally, anthropologist Claude Lévi-Strauss, in *Structural Anthropology* (1963), offers yet another possibility why Coyote and Raven embody the trickster in so many Native American tales: *both are carrion-eaters*—which is a third way between that of carnivore and herbivore, predator and prey. Carrion-eaters graze like herbivores, but eat meat like carnivores—a synthesis of contradictions. Not all tricksters are carrion-eaters, but the preponderance is thought provoking . . . an animal with "no way" adopts a "middle way"?

EVOLUTION OF AN IMAGE

Just as a myth reflects psychic processes at work, the reverse also holds true. "Because of its numinosity the myth has a direct effect on the unconscious, no matter whether it is understood or not."[5]

How might this have worked?

Once language develops, it's possible to imagine stories being told around the fires—tales perhaps of the day's hunt—or that hunt many moons ago, when we trapped that elusive elk, or bison, or wooly mammoth—or that great hunt spoken of in our fathers' day—or even further back, in the time of the Ancestors, when Maui fashioned that first fish-hook, or Coyote wove that first net. . . . And the stories swell into myth.

Details may differ, depending on who tells the tale and where, but over tens or hundreds of thousands of years or more, this motif etches itself ever more deeply into the collective unconscious. Today, even though we no longer consciously identify ourselves with the trickster, viewing him at best as a rather coarse character, nevertheless the archetype remains embedded in our psyche.

The figure of the trickster does evolve over time—which Jung emphasizes, drawing on Radin's analysis of the development of the trickster cycle:

> As Radin points out, the civilizing process begins within the framework of the trickster cycle itself
> . . . the marks of the deepest unconsciousness fall away from him; instead of acting in a brutal, savage, stupid, and senseless fashion, the trickster's behavior toward the end of the cycle becomes quite useful and sensible.[6]

Joseph Campbell sees the overt influence of the trickster fading with the development of agriculture and the resultant shift from the rugged individualism of the shaman to that of a structured society, in harmony with the divine order of the heavens as interpreted by a rigid, hierarchical priesthood charged with reading the sky. He provides an example of this dynamic in a ritual of the Jicarilla Apache, where the Hactin priests bind the shamans, establishing the supremacy of the agricultural priesthood.

The trickster archetype continues in the historical period by evolving into mythic figures with more complex motivations, including Krishna in India, Hermes/Mercury in the Graeco-Roman world, and Loki in the Norse pantheon. Wotan/Odin, Prometheus, and other deities in some myths exhibit elements of this motif, but aren't exclusively identified as tricksters. Human tricksters in myth run the gamut from Odysseus to Robin Hood (who breaks society's rules and threatens to upset the established order in such acts as robbing from the rich and giving to the poor).

Tracing the diffusion and evolution of various manifestations of this archetype over time in itself echoes trickster's playful spirit. For example, slaves brought to America carried with them an African rabbit-hero, which bumped into Native American myths about Hare in the southeastern United States before morphing into tales of Br'er Rabbit. Factor in quick wit, a brazen tongue, colored ink, and a darkened theater, and we arrive at that quintessential American trickster: *Bugs Bunny!*

TRICKSTER TODAY

Apart from classic Warner Brothers cartoons, where are we likely to bump into trickster today?

Continuing in the spirit of play, I'll preface this section by drawing a perhaps arbitrary parallel between two tales from widely disparate cultures and times:

> When [Coyote] was one day wandering aimlessly, he heard someone say, "Anyone who chews me will defecate; he will defecate." "Well," said Trickster, "why is this person talking in this manner?" He moved in the direction from which the voice had come and then he heard it again. Looking around, he saw a bulb on a bush. "I know very well," he said to himself, "that if I chew this I will not defecate." So he took it, put it into his mouth, chewed, swallowed it, and went on.
>
> "Well," he said, "where is the bulb that talked so much? How could such an object influence me in the least? When I feel like defecating I shall do so, and no

sooner." But while he was speaking he began to break a little wind. "Well," he thought, "I guess this is what it meant. It said, though, that I would defecate and I'm just breaking a little wind. In any case, I am a great man even if I do expel a little gas." Then it happened again, and this time it was really strong. "Well indeed! How foolish I was! Perhaps this is why they call me the Fool!" It happened again, very loudly, and this time his rectum began to smart. Next time he was propelled forward. "Well, well," he thought defiantly, "it may give me a little push but it will never make me defecate." It happened again and this time the hind part of his body was lifted into the air and he landed on his knees and hands. "Well, just go ahead, do it again!" he cried. "Do it again!" It did, and he went far up into the air, landing flat on his stomach. He began to take the matter seriously. He grabbed a log, and both he and the log were sent into the air. Coming down, the log was on top, and he was nearly killed. He grabbed a poplar tree; it held, but his feet flew into the air and nearly broke his back. Next, the tree came up by the roots. He grabbed a large oak tree; this held, but again his feet flew into the air. Trickster ran to a village and contrived to have all the lodges piled on top of him, together with the people, dogs, and everything else. His explosion scattered the camp in all directions and the people, coming down, shouted angrily at each other, while the dogs howled. Trickster just laughed at them until his insides were sore. But then he began to defecate. At first it was only a little, but then a good deal, and then so much that he began climbing a tree to keep above his excrement. He went on up, higher, higher, and reached the top, where he slipped, fell, and came out of the bottom of the pile covered and blinded by his own filth.[7]

Compare the above ribald account to a memory from Carl Jung on the eve of adolescence that has become part of the origin tale behind analytical psychology:

One fine summer day that same year I came out of school at noon and went to the cathedral square. The sky was gloriously blue, the day one of radiant sunshine. The roof of the cathedral glittered, the sun sparkling from the new, brightly glazed tiles. I was overwhelmed by the beauty of the sight, and thought: "The world is beautiful and the church is beautiful, and God made all this and sits above it far away in the blue sky on a golden throne and . . ." Here came a great hole in my thoughts, and a choking sensation. I felt numbed, and knew only: "Don't go on thinking now! Something terrible is coming, something I do not want to think, something I dare not even approach. Why not? Because I would be committing the most frightful of sins . . . the sin against the Holy Ghost, which cannot be forgiven . . . All I need do is not go on thinking."

That was easier said than done. On my long walk home I tried to think about all sorts of other things, but I found my thoughts returning again and again to the beautiful cathedral which I loved so much, and to God sitting on the throne—and then my thoughts would fly off again as if they had received a powerful electric shock . . .[8]

Over the next three days young Carl wrestled with his thoughts, but the same image continued to lurk on the periphery of consciousness, ever threatening to surface. Finally, in bed one night, the torment grew too great to bear further, so the lad surrendered to the inevitable:

> I gathered all my courage, as though I were about to leap forthwith into hell-fire, and let the thought come. I saw before me the cathedral, the blue sky. God sits on his golden throne, high above the world—and from under the throne an enormous turd falls upon the sparkling new roof, shatters it, and breaks the walls of the cathedral asunder.
>
> So that was it! I felt an enormous, an indescribable relief. Instead of the expected damnation, grace had come upon me, and with it an unutterable bliss such as I had never known. I wept for happiness and gratitude.[9]

The original version is just as sacrilegious but even more graphic, as Deirdre Bair reports in her recent work, *Jung: A Biography*, written with full access to Jung's archives and the measured cooperation of his heirs. Ever the trickster, Jung emphasized the word "shit" in the original English translation. Jung's relatives, after his death, removed both that and "enormous turd" from the manuscript; Jung's translator, R.F.C. Hull, admiring Jung's "highly dramatic use of the word 'shit,'" fought to retain these terms as they "couldn't shock anyone, except the Swiss bourgeoisie." Compromise reached, the established order managed to blunt, if not completely eliminate, trickster's coarse speech.

Of course, I don't share this for the scatological titillation—in fact, I find the subject matter more than a bit gross, which speaks to my own insecurities, given the scholarly context (do I hear trickster chuckling at my discomfort?).

In the first tale, Coyote's behavior, driven by unconscious motivations, leads him to shoot himself in the foot, so to speak—a common human condition, metaphorically befouling oneself. This Coyote never seems to learn from consequences, but continues to blunder, unconscious, from one scrape to the next.

Jung, though, devoted a lifetime of reflection to the image of the cathedral besmirched, profaned, and destroyed by that divine dropping. Yes, it seems to speak of Christianity's shadow—and, indeed, Jung's exploration of that shadow breathed life into a repressed paganism, reawakening a polytheistic perspective that challenged the dominant paradigm and is still expanding today.

. . . But his vision speaks as well of a more personal shadow.

Jung spent the rest of his life wading through the filth, guiding others in the same task—what Lewis Hyde calls the "dirt-work" of depth psychology, digging around in the shadows, turning up the dank, dark matter buried in the depths of the psyche, seeking its source. Everything from personal gaffes and slips of the tongue to dreams, complexes, neuroses, self-destructive behaviors, and other psychopathologies provide the raw material—but no matter how repugnant at first, all sorts of treasures are uncovered along the way, often through serendipity common to tricksters. In fact, Jung adopted Mercurius, an alchemical descendent of Hermes, as patron of his science.

In a flash of inspiration worthy of trickster, Lewis Hyde links this development to the soul-shaping vision of God's "throne":

> If it's right to make a creation story by juxtaposing Carl Jung's fecal epiphany, his later attraction to Mercurius, and his sense that Mercurius is guide to the unconscious, then we already have a modern case in which dirt-work enables a "theft of fire," a story whose protagonist challenges a weakened spiritual system with its own exclusions and, out of that, acquires a psychological method, a new technology for the human race.[10]

Jungian, archetypal, and transpersonal psychologies embrace the trickster, encouraging us to tend to the archetype behind slips of the tongue, synchronicities, the quicksilver of dreams, and other manifestations of psyche. Similarly, in *The Hero with a Thousand Faces*, Joseph Campbell follows a parallel path, making clear that an encounter with the trickster is part of our journey.

But what happens when the trickster is denied?

> My definition of a devil is a god who has not been recognized. That is to say, it is a power in you to which you have not given expression, and you push it back. And then, like all repressed energy, it builds up and becomes completely dangerous to the position you're trying to hold.[11]

Campbell believes this to be true on both individual and collective scales. On the grand stage Christianity can't help but spring to mind. There is no playful, mischievous, impish trickster in a universe so starkly divided between good and evil, black and white. Having excluded trickster figures, Christianity subsumes those traits in the only mythic figure allowed to be shadowy and deceptive—Satan the Devil, and, by extension, his legions of demons. This is no trickster whose flaws are outweighed by redeeming qualities: Satan is the embodiment of evil—a Christian obsession, as Campbell points out.

Every act contains elements of good and evil, black and white—but where I might perceive eating a steak as a good thing, the cow undoubtedly holds a different perspective. The best we can do, in Campbell's words, is "lean toward the light."

When we repress/deny/demonize this element in our own natures and identify ourselves only with what we perceive to be all good and righteous and just, we at the same time increase the power of the shadow—patterns and dynamics of which we are unconscious that nevertheless have the power to affect our behavior. What's true for the individual applies as well to the group mind. Christianity's obsession with battling the Devil inflates the collective shadow, which then gives birth to unspeakable acts of evil. It's more than ironic that followers of a belief system rooted in the golden rule ("love your neighbor as you love yourself") could come up with the Inquisition, torturing and murdering their neighbors in the name of God's love.

This isn't true just for Christianity; in any culture where the trickster is denied or repressed an unconscious compensatory reaction takes place in the collective psyche. Turning to the playfulness of trickster, Patrick Harpur offers the appearance of crop circles, alien encounters, cattle mutilations and such as manifestations of this dynamic:

> But I suspect that the god whose hand can be found in crop circles is the god who lies behind all anomalous events . . . Hermes is especially important for our culture, which has increasingly fallen under the aegis of Apollo, the archetypal principle behind consciousness, masculine detachment, rationality, clarity, purity of purpose and so on. Apollo is the God of Science. Hermes is his brother and a thorn in his side. . . [Hermes'] deceptions can, like Art, be dressings-up which entice us into a deeper truth. He misleads us, but often for our own good, leading us out of our ideas of truth—out of literalism, for instance—and into the tricky paradoxical twilight of the daimonic realm.
>
> Like Coyote, Raven and Hare—Hermes is a Trickster. It is as difficult for us to countenance Tricksters as it is daimons: our monotheism, whether of Christianity or Science, has excluded them. So Hermes is forced to operate from the Underworld, to shadow Christianity in esoteric, "occult" Gnostic and hermetic philosophies. As his Latin counterpart, Mercurius, he is the soul of alchemy. He returns to torment science with paranormal phenomena and maddening anomalies—all daimons are tricksters, as the fairies are; all are in the pay of Hermes—Mercurius. He unsettles our lives with all manner of impish tricks and pixilations; the more we ignore him, the more he

bedevils us, until his tricks begin to look sinister. He becomes, in fact, the Devil.[12]

Harpur isn't suggesting Hermes literally walks the earth; instead, he draws on the mythic imagination—and, indeed, to embrace the trickster is to embrace metaphor and imagination in the way of Carl Jung, Heinrich Zimmer, James Hillman, and, of course, Joseph Campbell, among others. It's a way of re-imagining the world, and of understanding the dynamics and patterns at play in our own lives as well.

TRICKSTER & PSYCHE

We experience the trickster in our individual lives just when we are most unsuspecting. We meet him when we find ourselves at the mercy of the most annoying "accidents." In dreams the trickster is the one who sets obstacles in our path for his own reasons; he is the one who keeps changing shape and appearing and disappearing at the oddest moments.

The major psychological function of the trickster figure is to make possible for us to gain a sense of proportion about ourselves. This he does by testing and trying us, so that we might discover what we are made of. His motto might well be, "if the fool persists in his folly, he would become wise."[13]

At a recent wedding I attended, held in the Rockies over the spring equinox, several examples of trickster-at-play surfaced—including some of which fall into Patrick Harpur's purview of the paranormal. Less dramatic, though, was a conversation with a guest in his twenties whom I'll call Bill, accompanying his girlfriend. The night before they left for the wedding, Bill dreamt that he had defecated in his pants, with the rest of the dream spent trying to hide this condition from his lover. On waking the next morning, the couple rented a car and spent eight hours on the road, a strenuous drive through the mountains in winter conditions to a place Bill had never been, where he knew not a single soul and would be sleeping on some stranger's floor—but where he would be introduced to some of his paramour's best friends.

Sounds stress inducing to me! Poor guy was walking on eggshells when he arrived, clenching his sphincter, so to speak, in fight-or-flight mode (an instinctive reaction to stress and danger among primates). Sharing the dream, though, in combination with recounting the hectic preparations for the trip, seemed to ease the pressure as Bill settled into casual mode. He could sense a parallel between his anxiety over soiled drawers in the dream and insecurities over winning the approval of his lover's most intimate friends in waking life.

I was struck by the continuity of this motif across centuries and across continents. Does this image carry the same specific meaning in Bill's dream as it does in Coyote's tale or Jung's profane vision?

Hardly.

Nor does the young man come up with a definitive answer for what exactly the dream means, apart from some correspondence between feelings in the dream and feelings in waking life . . . but by talking about the dream, exploring these shadow concerns so well concealed from waking consciousness that psyche portrays them in a socially taboo image, Bill experienced a measure of release and relief—a dynamic similar to Jung on facing and embracing the forbidden—and a glimpse of something beyond conscious intentions at work.

THE ONCE & FUTURE TRICKSTER

Joseph Campbell seems to expect a resurgence of the trickster and his close kin, the shaman archetype—triggered by a cultural shift already in process.

> The binding of the shamans by the Hactin, by the gods and their priests, which commenced with the victory of the Neolithic over the Paleolithic way of life, may perhaps already be terminating—today—in this period of the irreversible transition from an agricultural to industrial base, when not the piety of the planter, bowing humbly before the calendar and the gods of rain and sun, but the magic of the laboratory, flying rocket ships where the gods once sat, holds the promise of boons for the future.[14]

How much more so as the industrial gives way to the information age? Interest in shamanism, polytheism and neopagan revivals, astrology and tarot and the I Ching, Jungian and archetypal psychologies and related areas, continues to surge—especially on the burgeoning Internet.

If we see with a mythic eye, trickster is everywhere we look: in the entertainment media, from the aforementioned

Bugs Bunny, to Jon Stewart's irreverent fake news program, to "Q" (the omnipotent trouble-maker from "the Continuum" who poses unsolvable riddles and plays deadly tricks on humans in episodes of *Star Trek* franchises); in science, in the central role random, spontaneous chance plays in every-thing from evolution to chaos theory to quantum physics; in politics; in paranormal phenomena, from UFO sightings to poltergeists; in art ("The telling of untrue things is the proper aim of art"—Oscar Wilde); in our dreams, and in our psyches; and, always, in the unexpected.

NOTES

1. Maher and Briggs, eds., An Open Life, op. cit. 39
2. Lewis Hyde, Trickster Makes This World (New York: Farrar, Strauss, and Giroux, 1988), 135.
3. Campbell, Primitive Mythology, op. cit. 253.
4. Hyde, op. cit. 42-43.
5. C.G. Jung, The Archetypes and the Collective Unconscious, 2nd edi-tion (Princeton: Princeton University Press, 1968), 268.
6. Ibid. 266.
7. Campbell, Primitive Mythology, op. cit. 248-249.
8. C.G. Jung, Memories, Dreams, Reflections (New York: Vintage Books / Random House, 1963), 36.
9. Ibid. 39.
10. Hyde, op. cit. 189
11. Maher and Briggs, eds. An Open Life, op. cit. 28.
12. Patrick Harpur. Daimonic Reality: A Field Guide to the Other World (New York: Viking Press, 1994; Grand Rapids: Pine Woods Press, 2003), 166. Citations are from the Pine Woods Press edition.
13. June Singer, Boundaries of the Soul (New York: Anchor Books, 1973), 289.
14. Campbell, Primitive Mythology, op. cit. 258.

TWELVE

THE MYTH OF ZIMMER & CAMPBELL

> Thank you ever so much for kindly sending me your beautiful book. I had already seen it before and have duly admired it. You are certainly shaping after my late friend Heinrich Zimmer. It is the same style and outlook . . .
>
> (Carl Jung, in a note to Joseph Campbell, on receiving an autographed copy of *The Hero with a Thousand Faces*)[1]

Joseph Campbell never lacked for friends. In fact, he displayed a knack for collecting a somewhat eclectic assortment of friends and acquaintances over the course of his life, enjoying encounters with a cast of characters that included many names we recognize today: nutritionist Adele Davis, Indian sage Krishnamurti, novelist John Steinbeck, biologist Ed Ricketts, philosopher Alan Watts, composer John Cage, and director George Lucas are some who come to mind. Others are less well known. Few people in the United States, for example, have heard of Heinrich Zimmer—and fewer still would know who he was had Heinrich Zimmer and Joseph Campbell never met.

And it's just as likely that Campbell's life would have followed a far different trajectory, absent this relationship; Zimmer exerted a profound and undeniable influence on the direction of Campbell's career, honing Joseph's realization of his own passion for comparative mythology. References to Zimmer abound throughout Campbell's books and lectures—including favorite, oft-told tales, such as "The Humbling of Indra," or the "Tiger Among the Goats." Indeed, Heinrich Zimmer was for Campbell one of those doors we come across that open "where you would not have thought there would be doors," when we follow our bliss.

. . . Which is exactly what Campbell was doing when he was one of three people to sign up for a course on Indian art and mythology at Columbia University in 1941. At 36, Joseph was already an established instructor at Sarah Lawrence, recently married and leading a busy life. One might think there's no need for a teacher to squeeze in an evening course not directly related to his/her own career advancement, but Campbell had just met Heinrich Zimmer, a noted Indologist, through Swami Nikhilananda (whom Joe was assisting in the translation of *The Gospel of Sri Ramakrishna*). Aware of Zimmer's reputation, and favorably impressed with the man's energy and enthusiasm, Campbell decided to sit in on the professor's lectures—with no inkling of the impact Zimmer would have on his life.

> Hearing Zimmer's lectures and the way in which these myths came out, not as curiosities over there somewhere, but as models for understanding your own life— this is what I felt myths to be all the time. Of course,

Jung had it, but not the way Zimmer did. Zimmer was much more in myth than Jung was. Jung tends to put forms on the myths with those archetypes; the Jungians kind of cookie-molded the thing. None of that with Zimmer. I never knew anyone who had such a gift for interpreting a symbolic image. You'd sit down at a table with him and bring up something with him—he'd talk about the symbolism of onion soup. I heard him do it! I don't remember what it was, but he went off on onion soup . . . oh God! This was a genius![2]

WHO WAS HEINRICH ZIMMER?

Joseph Campbell had long been familiar with Heinrich Zimmer—Heinrich Zimmer, Sr., that is, a renowned Celtic scholar whose untranslated body of work helped persuade young Joe, pursuing medieval studies in Paris on a Proudfit Fellowship, of the value of learning German ("all the best work is in German" remains a recurring refrain in the field yet today.) The elder Zimmer (1850–1910) is known for tracing the eponymous hero of the romance of Tristan and Isolde to the historical "Drustan son of Talorc," who reigned in southern Scotland from AD 780–785 and who becomes "Tristan son of Tallwch" in Welsh lore—with Rivalin eventually replacing Talorc/Tallwch as Tristan's sire once the legend reaches Brittany, near the end of the first millennium.

(In his footnotes to *The Masks of God* volumes, Campbell distinguishes between father and son by listing the elder as H. Zimmer, to avoid confusing readers.)

The father died before his son's career began, when the boy was barely twenty. Heinrich Zimmer, Jr., nevertheless continued in the family business, distinguishing himself as an authority on Indian culture, mythology, and art. Zimmer's command of Sanskrit, Pali, Arabic, Pahlavi, Chinese, Gaelic, Gothic, Old Norse, Greek, and Latin provided access to a range of sources beyond the reach of less formidable linguists. Zimmer became the first to translate portions of the little-known *Kalika Purana* into a European language, offering insights into the Goddess tradition often obscured in India's more familiar, orthodox texts.

In 1926, Heinrich Zimmer published *Kunstform und Yoga* (English title: *Artistic Form and Yoga in the Sacred Images of India*), which eventually caught Carl Jung's eye (and which, according to Campbell, "introduced the whole mystery of the mandala to Jung"). In his inaugural lecture to Zurich's C.G. Jung Institute in 1948, Jung credits Heinrich Zimmer and Richard Wilhelm (the noted Sinologist, whose translation of the I Ching remains the gold standard for that oracle) with opening up his thinking and leading him in new directions, into a recognition of a resonance between India's and China's mythic lore and the archetypal patterns emerging out of dreamwork in depth psychology.

Though Jung had disciples galore, Richard Wilhelm and Heinrich Zimmer are widely recognized as his only close male friends. Neither man saw Jung as his master; each enjoyed an established reputation in his respective field and had produced a body of work independent of Jung's before ever they met—yet they shared overlapping observations and arrived, by their own paths, at conclusions parallel to those of Jung. They also inspired Jung's pioneering investigation into alchemical symbolism. (Even Jung's one-time patient, colleague, and life-long soul mate, Toni Wolff, could not fathom the relevance of alchemy to depth psychology, thinking it an irrational obses-sion on Jung's part; where he went with these two men, few dared to follow). When finally they did meet, in 1932, Carl Jung invited Heinrich Zimmer to his home in Kusnacht for a weekend spent sailing, sight-seeing, and lounging about—which were all merely settings for a conversation heady, intox-icating, and just short of transcendent. Zimmer confessed to his wife the inflating effects of this experience; meanwhile Jung was so enthused he interrupted a series of his own lectures at the Psychological Club of Zurich so Zimmer could take his spot (a gesture at odds with Jung's Leo nature).

Heinrich Zimmer's friendship with Jung was no anomaly. Thomas Mann dedicated *The Transposed Heads* to Zimmer, whose telling of the tale of "The King and the Corpse" inspired the novel, and Zimmer's wife, Christianne, was the daughter of German playwright Hugo von Hofmannsthal.

Christianne was half Jewish, which added to the tensions of the Hitler years. In 1938, after Zimmer's anti-Nazi stance finally led to his dismissal from the university at Heidelberg, the family fled Germany. Jung helped Zimmer secure a position at Oxford; two years later Zimmer moved to the United States, where he was taken under the wings of Mary Mellon (yes, that Mellon—Paul and Mary Mellon, wealthy philanthropists with ties to Jung) and the omnipresent *Jungfrauen*—"the little old ladies of the Jung Foundation."

The Jungfrauen arranged the lectureship at Columbia that Campbell attended, while Mary Mellon appointed Zimmer to the Board of Directors of the Bollingen Foundation—which she had created to provide a forum for scholarly works on esoteric topics. Zimmer was hardly an unknown quantity, for the Mellons had also subsidized the annual Eranos Conference in Ascona, Switzerland, legendary in Jungian circles. Heinrich Zimmer had been invited to present the opening paper at the initial Eranos Roundtable in 1933.[3]

Opening Doors

Heinrich Zimmer and Joseph Campbell hit it off right away. Zimmer was certainly conversant with Celtic and Arthurian lore, which had been Campbell's original field of study (Joe's master's thesis addressed "the dolorous stroke" of Grail Legend – which can be found in an appendix to Campbell's *Romance of the Grail*), while Joe's work with Swami Nikhilananda on the translation of *The Gospel of Sri Ramakrishna* crystallized his interest in Zimmer's field. Both men were natural storytellers, with several of Zimmer's favorites finding a permanent home in Campbell's repertoire. Zimmer spent many an evening holding forth in the Campbells' living room, and both men enjoyed each other's companionship on outings exploring their mutual bliss.

> Joe loves to tell of an occasion when he and Heinrich Zimmer were attending a celebration of Wesak, the Buddha's birthday. A swami was explaining that so many Westerners thought of the Buddha as a weird Oriental idol with eight arms and six fingers, whereas he was in fact just a plain ordinary man like ourselves.

Zimmer leaned over and whispered to Joe, "I prefer them with six fingers."[4]

This sense of whimsy, coupled with an insistence on the primacy of the mythological image, surfaces in Campbell's own work. Zimmer's influence, however, manifests in more material ways as well.

Heinrich Zimmer's involvement proved critical to the Bollingen Foundation. He recommended Kurt Wolff, founder of Pantheon Press, to manage and publish the envisioned Bollingen Series, a perfect fit that lasted a quarter of a century. (The Bollingen Series eventually included all of Jung's *Collected Works*, Zimmer's books, Campbell's *The Hero with a Thousand Faces* and *The Masks of God* tetralogy, Wilhelm's *I Ching*, Plato's *Timaeus*, and six of the *Eranos Jahrbuchs*, reaching its conclusion with the publication of Bollingen's hundredth volume, Campbell's *The Mythic Image*, in 1974).

Campbell, in the *Parabola* interview, relates that Zimmer also recommended the first work to be published by Bollingen should focus on Native American mythology—"something of the land, thus giving respect to the land, letting the spirit of the land support us." Maude Oakes, an artist and friend of Mary Mellon, received a commission to study and record a Navajo war ritual practiced prior to battle. Zimmer suggested Joseph Campbell serve as editor, writing the introduction and scholarly commentary for what became Bollingen's first volume: *Where the Two Came to Their Father: A Navajo War Ceremonial*.

Thus began Campbell's lengthy association with the Bollingen Foundation, which published *The Hero with a Thousand Faces* when no one else would, and provided financial support during the years spent writing *The Masks of God*. In 1960, Joseph was himself appointed a trustee of the Bollingen Foundation.

Without the Zimmer connection, Campbell might never have found a publisher. I can't help but wonder, had *The Hero* not been published, would the remainder of Campbell's corpus have found the light of day?

Joseph Campbell's friendship with Zimmer lasted barely two years. In March of 1943 Zimmer contracted a cold that rapidly developed into pneumonia, and death followed within days. Joe was astonished at the suddenness with which this vital, creative force was extinguished.

> What an ebullient man! Wonderful! The first person I ever met who was way down the road that I found, interpreting symbols positively, deep in Oriental material. And if anybody should ask me who my guru was, it was Zimmer, who really just kicked it: I was just ready for the signal of that man. I was thirty-six, thirty-seven. Then, in the middle of the second year of his lectures, Heinrich Zimmer is suddenly dead. He'd been carrying pneumonia around with him and didn't know it—a big man, powerful. I and another chap would go out with him for a beer after his lecture and the next weekend we're burying him![5]

THE WRITER & THE GHOST

Before his death, Zimmer had shared with Mary Mellon his plans for several books in English to be published through Bollingen. Now she and Christianne Zimmer asked Joe to take on the job of collecting and wrestling Zimmer's notes into pub-lishable form. This task defined the next 12 years of Campbell's life. Boxes full of typewritten lecture notes, partial outlines, "scraps of paper, scribbled in German, English, Sanskrit, and French," and even notes found in the margins of books, formed the raw material.

David Kudler, editor of several volumes of Campbell's post-humous works, weighing three possible approaches to editing Campbell's words, explains in the preface to *Myths of Light* the technique that Joe applied to Zimmer's work:

> The first was to create a truly syncretic work, taking the words from various pieces, breaking apart the component ideas, and moving them into an order that suited the work as a whole. This model was the one followed by Campbell in assembling the posthumous works of Heinrich Zimmer. Unfortunately, I didn't feel quite the mastery of the mate-rial that Campbell himself possessed.[6]

Sometimes Zimmer's material wore thin, as in the final chap-ters of *Philosophies of India*, where Campbell warns that the ideas, based more on remembered conversations than on Zimmer's notes, aren't well developed and may not correctly reflect Zimmer's thought. On arriving at such an impasse the resourceful mythologist would, in essence, channel Zimmer:

> Zimmer used to give his manuscripts to his friends and students just to have them read them over and help him straighten out his prose. So when I would come to certain chapters, they wouldn't be there. There would be a gap. Some little lady would have

kept them somewhere in her memory chest. But he had a very striking and forceful presence in his presentation: in my memory I could hear him. I would get to the point where pages were missing and a break came; I'd jump the break and pick up again where the thing resumed and do a few paragraphs of that. Then I'd see what the gap was between the two and what had to be covered. I had talked with Zimmer a lot about these things and I would bridge the gap with one or two questions; I'd ask a question and listen, and he would dictate. The style was his style, more or less. Then when I got to the big book on *The Art of Indian Asia*, I could no longer hear him dictating— that was eleven or twelve years later—and I was finished. There was no way to go on.[7]

For the record, Joe didn't think of this in some sort of "spooky" New Age sense so much as a writer's device—an imaginative technique for reconstructing those missing bridges out of his recollections of Zimmer.

Myths and Symbols in Indian Art and Civilization, printed in 1946, is a fleshing out of the first course Campbell took from Zimmer in the winter of 1941. Opening with the tale of "The Humbling of Indra" (which Joseph Campbell takes great delight in relating to Bill Moyers, some four decades after he first heard it, in *The Power of Myth* interviews), Zimmer explores a variety of motifs recurring in Indian art and myth, wandering through the symbolism of water, serpents, and elephants, and examining in artistic detail a number of carvings and their related myths.

The King and the Corpse, which followed in 1948, is a delightful romp through several stories from different cultures—from "The Slippers of Abu Kasem" to the Celtic hero Conneda, from tales of Gawain and Lancelot and other Arthurian heroes to those of Vishnu, Brahma, and Shiva dancing to Maya's tune, as well as the central tale of king and corpse. This is my favorite of the Zimmer collection; as Campbell describes it, in this "comparative study of a series of Oriental and Occidental tales, there is indeed a correspondence both in incident and in sense between the adventures of Arthur's knights and those of the great and little heroes of the Orient, even of the Buddha himself . . ."[8]

Philosophies of India, published in 1951, also drawn from Zimmer's Columbia lectures, examines the differences between Indian and European culture, then follows the broad sweep of Indian philosophy through its major branches—Jainism, Sankhya and Yoga, Brahmanism and the Upanishads, Buddhism, and Tantra. This is a comprehensive work that Campbell describes as "a corker!"

The Art of Indian Asia, published in 1955, is a rare, two- volume set filled with hundreds of photographs. I've read descriptions but have never seen this expensive, hard-to-find work. [Shortly after completing this essay fifteen years ago, I was able to secure a copy. Though all photographs are in black and white, it is magnificent.] Campbell approved the final galleys and proofs during his sojourn in India in 1954, where he set a goal of visiting as many of the sites of Hinduism's monumental art as possible, bringing to a close his twelve-year commitment to the ghost of Heinrich Zimmer.

Zimmer's books are a treat for anyone who enjoys Campbell—and are, in some senses, easier to read than, say, the heavily footnoted volumes of *The Masks of God*. I think of them as "proto-Campbell"—hints of his humor and traces of Joe's voice are readily apparent, as is the appearance of a number of themes that reverberate throughout Campbell's own work. Of course, this is hardly a minority opinion:

> It should be known that the vivid and rich style of these works is more Campbell than Zimmer, notably in *The King and the Corpse* where a number of mythological tales are retold as only Joseph can tell stories.[9]

In *Asian Journals*, Joe's personal journal of his months in India and Japan, there are hints that Campbell felt a justifiable pride of ownership in his prose. When an article in India's "The Statesman" plagiarized portions of *Philosophies of India* without attribution, Campbell in one place speaks of this passage as "lifted from Zimmer-Campbell" (76–77), and in another complains that "Mr. Pyarelal Nayar steals *my* paragraphs" (88, emphasis mine). Indeed, it can be difficult to tell where Zimmer ends and Campbell begins, so seamless is the editing –– though a comparison with other Zimmer works translated from the German (such as the entries in the *Eranos Yearbooks*) suggests an extra sparkle and lilt to the Zimmer/Campbell collaborations.

FORESHADOWING CAMPBELL

A number of themes introduced by Heinrich Zimmer recur throughout Joseph Campbell's work, where they are further amplified and developed. Similarly, in Zimmer many of the ideas Campbell introduces can be glimpsed in gestation, hinting at the birth to come. And then as well, reading Zimmer as arising out of the same context from which Campbell forms his own perspective, we are sometimes able to "fill in the gaps" in areas where Campbell remains silent.

For example, many scholars are either dismissive or even openly hostile toward Campbell's work—which never seemed to bother him much. Campbell's confidence in the power of mythic symbols and the absence of a need for academic validation certainly make sense in the light of these passages from the "The Dilettante Among Symbols," the opening chapter of Zimmer's *The King and the Corpse:*

> The only difficulty is that the interpretation of the disclosed forms cannot be reduced to a dependable system. For true symbols have something illimitable about them. They are inexhaustible in their suggestive and instructive power. Hence the scientist, the scientific psychologist, feels himself on very dangerous, very uncertain and ambiguous ground when he ventures into the field of folklore interpretation
>
> . . . No systematist who greatly valued his reputation would throw himself open to the adventure.[10]
>
> The method—or rather, habit—of reducing the unfamiliar to the well-known is an old, old way to

intellectual frustration. Sterilizing dogmatism is the result, tightly enwrapped in a mental self-satisfaction, a secure conviction of superiority. Whenever we refuse to be knocked off our feet (either violently or gently) by some telling new concept precipitated from the depths of the imagination by the impact of an ageless symbol, we are cheating ourselves of the fruit of an encounter with the wisdom of the millenniums. Failing in the attitude of acceptance, we do not receive; the boon of converse with the gods is denied us. We are not to be flooded, like the soil of Egypt, by the divine, fructifying waters of the Nile.

It is because they are alive, potent to revive themselves, and capable of an ever-renewed, unpredictable yet self- consistent effectiveness in the range of human destiny, that the images of folklore and myth defy every attempt we make at systematization . . . With a sudden laugh and quick shift of place they mock the specialist who has got them pinned to his chart. What they demand of us is not the monologue of the coroner's report, but the dialogue of a living conversation.[11]

Delight, on the other hand, sets free in us the creative intuition, permits it to be stirred to life by contact with the fascinating script of the old symbolic tales and figures. Undaunted then by the criticism of the methodologists (whose censure is largely inspired by what amounts to a chronic agoraphobia: morbid dread before the virtual infinity that is continually opening out from the cryptic traits of the expressive picture writing which it is their profession to regard) we may permit ourselves to give vent to whatever series of creative reactions happen to be suggested to our imaginative understanding. We can never exhaust the depths—of that we may be certain; but then, neither can anyone else. And a cupped handful of the fresh waters of life is sweeter than a whole reservoir of dogma, piped and guaranteed.[12]

Whoa—Zimmer (through Campbell's pen) certainly pulls no punches! No wonder Campbell declares that Zimmer "gave me the courage to interpret myths out of what I knew of their common symbols." Zimmer encouraged Campbell to follow his instincts, give free rein to his imagination and actually engage the mythic archetypes, rather than analyze, categorize, and systematize them to death. This experiential mythology, with its emphasis on the numinous image and the power of myth, is guaranteed to make an academic specialist uncomfortable.

Joseph Campbell recognizes this, and is generally more genteel in the tone he takes toward the academy. Further, as he notes in his personal journal, in the course of completing Zimmer's books he found himself correcting enough mistakes to convince himself scholarship has its place: "I am now for a very meticulous checking after all the lovely intuitions: we have got to have both if we are going to have a book" (*Asian Journals*, 501); nevertheless, Campbell's confidence in the powers of the creative imagination and his own intuitive process continues to unnerve the scholastic community.

The primary theme running throughout Zimmer's books can be stated many ways—"all the gods are within you," or "the world outside lies within"—but I prefer the following description:

Everything outside ourselves, whether we know it in its proper relationship to us, or whether it remains for us apparently without significance and unrelated to our mind and heart, actually reflects and mirrors our inner selves. This we are meant to learn. And we are meant to approach through this way of learning to the last and highest possible realization . . . that of our own divine identity with the substance, the consciousness, and the bliss that we know as "God." This is the realization of the absolute nature of the Self. This is the discovery of the jewel at the core. This is the last experience in the long course of initiation-integration. And with it comes the immediate knowledge that we—not only we, but all the "thou's," also, of our surrounding night and day—are so many avatars, disguises, masks, and playful self-duplications of the Self of the world.[13]

"Thou art That"—*tat tvam asi*—is a succinct phrase Campbell uses that echoes the above.
Other major themes resounding throughout both Zimmer and Campbell include, but are not limited to:

- the power of symbol—and of myth—to shape life

- the shamanic role of the artist in a world devoid of living myth (e.g., "Those who have ceased to belong to a religious community endowed with rite and myth are guided by the poets"—Zimmer in "The Significance of Tantric Yoga," in *Spiritual Disciplines*, ed. Joseph Campbell, 23)

- the transcendent as beyond thought and speech ("the best things cannot be spoken, the second best are misunderstood, and the third best are everyday conversation. . .")

- and the value of depth psychology in exploring the inner world of symbols and the outer world of myth

Indeed, in regards to the latter, Zimmer suggests Jungian psychology is not only a science, but a myth for our time, especially in the absence of a valid cultural myth:

> The merit of the new depth psychology is that it unearths that which is timeless in us, in a form appropriate to our time, so that we can comprehend it and live by it. This psychology and the analytic method by which it operates constitute no more than a symbolic and visual means of obtaining knowledge about our being; it is a science born of our time and our predicament with which it will also pass away, but for that reason it is more intelligible than any other set of symbols; precisely because it is the only form in which we can validly explain to ourselves how we live, it puts us into relationship with the very same reality that speaks through the fading hieroglyphic system of other ages.[14]

Just as important as Zimmer's individual contribution was how his material corroborated the insights gleaned from the many other projects in which Campbell was involved. At the same time that Joseph was poring over Zimmer's collection of Celtic tales, Arthurian lore, and Hindu/Buddhist myths, he was also composing the commentary for Maud Oakes's book on the

Navajo war ceremonial, helping Swami Nikhilananda trans-late *The Gospel of Sri Ramakrishna*, and writing, with novelist Henry Morton Robinson, *A Skeleton Key to Finnegans Wake*. Campbell couldn't help but notice how the mythic material from these many separate sources dovetail together: "My dis-tinct impression throughout those years was that I was at work only on separate chapters of a single mythological epic of the human imagination."

> It was a real season of writing, and very, very exciting, and wonderful, wonderful material. And whether it was *Finnegans Wake* or the Navajo material, or the Hindu material, or Heinrich Zimmer's, it was all the same material. That was when I realized—and nobody can tell me anything differently—that there's one mythology in this world. It has been inflected in various cultures in terms of their historical circumstances and needs and particular local ethic systems, but it's one mythology.[15]

INITIATION & REBIRTH

On August 25, 1954, Joseph Campbell embarked on a year-long sabbatical—six months in India, then on to Japan. This trip marked a major life transition, the time in India providing closure, serving as a *coda* to the Zimmer years. With work on the fourth and final volume complete, Campbell was now free to chart his own course.

The question before Campbell, however, was just what that course might be—his journal of that trip reflects "the need now to find a point of view of my own with respect to the relationship of my Indian studies to the whole field of my science" (*Asian Journals*, 177). Ironically, though it seems clear to us in retrospect, Campbell, at fifty years of age, is still trying to define exactly what it is he does:

> The name that best suits my field is *Comparative Mythology:* it is a study of symbols, in relation, primarily, to the fields of art, literature, philosophy, and religion . . .
>
> [M]y own [preference] is for . . . the symbolism that seeks—and here, I believe I am in accord with Zimmer. This interest in the active questing attitude toward symbols has led me to give considerable stress, in my studies and my writings, to the work of the psychoanalysts, Freud, Jung, Roheim and the rest, since there one can see the process of symbol formation and interpretation from within . . . I am also interested in modern art and literature, as controlled renditions of the symbolic themes of contemporary significance, and my chief masters in this field have been Joyce and Mann, Klee and Picasso, with Jean and her associates as my immediate guides and examples.
>
> [. . .]
>
> Resolution: *Comparative mythology* (philology, in the German sense), is indeed my field—and the method is indeed to be first of all philological (*The Basic Mythologies of Mankind*) and secondly, that of the Jungian amplification (example: *The King and the Corpse*).[16]

This clarity of resolve marks the end of what Campbell termed his "Graduation Tour"—the point at which his path and Zimmer's diverge—for from here Campbell expands his focus beyond Indian mythology to embrace themes universal to all myths. Joseph devotes many pages of his travel journal to fleshing out ideas for a comprehensive work—*The Basic Mythologies of Mankind*—that provides the impulse for what eventually becomes the multi-volume *The Masks of God*. With this project, Campbell recovers his own voice.

> The work of Joseph Campbell has long been hiding under the name of his former mentor and teacher, the great German orientalist Heinrich Zimmer. With this labor of love now completed, Mr. Campbell is now coming out on his own with a series of titles comprising the result of many years' devotion to the study of mythology. The appearance of a magnum opus on this scale is much to the credit of a commercial publisher, though it must be said that Mr. Campbell is one of the (sadly) few scholars who combine vast learning with a literary style that is highly readable and often vigorously poetic. (Alan Watts, Saturday Review, June 2, 1962).[17]

It's no surprise that Campbell discovers many of the themes Zimmer found in Indian culture present in all mythologies, to varying degrees—indeed, this realization was dawning for Campbell years before they met. Nevertheless, even as he stepped outside the shadow cast by his mentor, Campbell never forgot the man who touched his life the way Campbell himself has touched so many.

So what *is* the secret to interpreting myths, the secret into which Zimmer initiated Campbell and Campbell initiates us, the secret that sets the teeth of mythologists, anthropologists, and other specialized methodologists so on edge?

> I learned this from him, that one should not be afraid of one's own interpretation of a symbol. It will come to you as a message, and it will open out . . .
> If you live with the myths in your mind, you will find yourself always in mythological situations. They cover everything that can happen to you. And that enables you to interpret the myth in relation to life, as well as life in relation to myth.[18]

Myths aren't dead. They are alive, in us. *We* are the figures of myth.

Notes

1. Joseph Campbell, Correspondence: 1927 – 1987, eds. Evans Lansing Smith, Ph.D. and Dennis Patrick Slattery, Ph.D. (Novato: New World Library, 2019), 141.
2. Joseph Campbell, "Elders and Guides," interview by Michael McKnight, Parabola 5 No. 1 (February 1980): 57 – 65.
3. Heinrich Zimmer, "On the Significance of the Indian Tantric Yoga," in Spiritual Disciplines: Papers from the Eranos Yearbooks, ed. Joseph Campbell (Princeton: Princeton University Press, 1960; 1985), 3- 58. Citations are from the 1985 printing.
4. Alan Watts, In My Own Way (New York: Pantheon Books, 1973; New York: Vintage, 1973), 266. Citation is from the Vintage edition.
5. Joseph Campbell, "The Professor with a Thousand Faces," interview by Donald Newlove, Esquire Magazine 88 No. 3 (September 1977).

6. Joseph Campbell, Myths of Light (Novato: New World Library, 2002), xiv.
7. Campbell, "Elders and Guides" interview, op. cit. 62.
8. Campbell, Creative Mythology, op. cit. 47.
9. Watts, In My Own Way, op. cit. 264.
10. Heinrich Zimmer, The King and the Corpse, ed. Joseph Campbell (Princeton: Bollingen Foundation / Princeton University Press, 1958; 2nd edition Princeton: Princeton University Press, 1956) 1. Citations are from the 2nd edition.
11. Ibid. 3.
12. Ibid. 5.
13. Ibid. 234.
14. Zimmer, "Indian Tantric Yoga," op. cit. 28-29.
15. Campbell, The Hero's Journey, op. cit. 126.
16. Campbell, Asian Journals, op. cit. 175, 595.
17. Larsens, A Fire in the Mind, op. cit. 450.
18. Campbell, "Elders and Guides," op. cit. 60, 64.

THIRTEEN

SMOKE OR MIRRORS?

We are now observing through our cultural world a
resurgence of the cult of the immanence of the occult,
within ourselves and within nature. The old Bronze Age
realization of a micro-macrocosmic unity is returning,
and everywhere all the old arts that were banished are
coming back.[1]

"The occult"—an emotionally charged term evoking sinister
associations, everything from fraudulent and greedy fortune
tellers to satanic rituals—imagery reinforced on movie screens
and in pulpits across the country . . . but is this the reality,
or merely projections of the public imagination? Is the practice of occult arts—particularly popular forms of divination,
including astrology, tarot, and the I Ching—simply ignorant
superstition? Do such represent at best an exercise in futility, an
abdication of responsibility for one's own life?

Or do they really work?

And, if oracles do speak true, is it because they work evil, in league with the devil? Or might there be other, more benign, natural forces in play? Is there anything to be gained from consulting oracles in today's high-tech information age, or would we be opening the door to malevolent supernatural beings intent on wreaking havoc in our lives?

Can we make use of these forms of divination without feeling like we've been cast in a really bad, low-budget horror flick?

THE NATURE OF NATURE

> To receive an oracle is to receive guidance, knowledge, illumination from a numinous source beyond the personal self. From the earliest times, humanity has sought counsel from the voices of nature, messages of dreams, divine arts of divination, and words of inspired mediums. Oracular knowing is the ability to receive and understand such messages. It draws upon intuitive and imaginal processes which are archetypal in the human psyche.[2]

Forms of divination have been practiced in all cultures—whether a Roman augur examining the liver and entrails of a sacrificial ox, a Chaldean priest charting the stars, an Iroquois shaman taking note of a sudden shift in the flight of a bird, or Delphi's Pythia inhaling the fumes emanating from a cleft in the earth—all seek information from Elsewhere, a realm beyond the confines of limited, waking consciousness. When the way is not clear, oracles offer wise counsel over a decision to be made, insight into the motivations of others, or a glimpse of futures likely to unfold from specific courses of action.

Oracles differ in many ways from the prophetic pronouncements of biblical traditions. They are often ambiguous—no clear direction in the "this is the way, walk ye therefore in it" sense of scripture. Nor does the outcome hinge on obedience or disobedience to the decrees of a specific deity.

> I'll never forget the experience of going to Delphi in Greece . . . That is where the oracle, the prophetess, received inspiration in the fumes, the smoke coming up from the abyss, and she prophesied and gave statements of destiny.[3]

Not jeremiads delivered on behalf of a wrathful god, but "statements of destiny." The future so conceived is not then determined by some external agency, but arises out of one's own inner nature, a reflection of the larger patterns present in Nature itself. The word "occult" means "hidden" (sharing the same root as "occluded"); from this perspective oracles open a window on the "hidden unity beyond or informing the world of multiplicity and its phenomena" (*The Mythic Dimension,* 262). They require not blind obedience, but open-minded reflection.

This "hidden unity" is depicted differently depending on the form the oracle takes: at Delphi, it emerges from the chthonic Underworld in the form of fumes unfurling from cracks in the Earth; in ancient Sumer this "hidden unity" manifests in the heavens, in the regular movement of Sun and Moon and planets through the constellations (source of the alchemical adage, "As above, so below"). These are but two metaphors for the experience of what is "hidden" (or "occult"), yet "immanent within ourselves and within nature."

But in neither instance is this a causal relationship.

Still, there remains a persistent impression that the stars determine our fate.

MYTHIC RESIDUES

Do popular forms of divination today employ active, effective symbols, or are they merely the traces of fading myths mistakenly read literally, taken as concrete fact?

> Even today, people who still believe in astrology fall almost without exception for the old superstitious assumption of the influence of the stars. And yet anyone who can calculate a horoscope should know that, since the days of Hipparchus of Alexandria, the springpoint has been fixed on 0 degrees Aries, and therefore the zodiac on which every horoscope is based is therefore quite arbitrary, the spring-point having gradually advanced, since then, into the first degrees of Pisces, owing to the precession of the equinoxes.[4]

What was commonly thought in Carl Jung's day is not nearly so universal today, thanks no doubt to these observations, widely shared by Campbell and a number of contemporary astrologists. (In fact, the anticipation of "the dawning of the Age of Aquarius," celebrated in a sixties rock opera anthem, is rooted in this awareness of the precession of the equinoxes). And yet Jung by no means discounts astrology, but suggests moving beyond a literal reading of the stars as determinants—recognizing in the archetypes of the constellations a resonance between inner and outer worlds, rather than any causal relationship.

The zodiac in one sense seems an accumulation of thousands of generations of collective patterns.

The *Enuma Elish*, for example, discovered in the library at Nineveh, records how Ishtar—the planet we call Venus, the Morning and Evening Star—guides passion and love. This is a powerful mythic image.

Does that mean the planet (Ishtar/Venus) causes love?

Not necessarily—but there are times of the year when this planet appears in the evening sky: lovers have met and embraced beneath her light since time immemorial—part of the collective human experience across countless generations— so it's no anomaly that this planet, the target of thousands of years of archetypal projections, is associated with love.

Similarly, for millennia people have been noting traits shared by those born at certain times of the year—and when we look at how the winter can affect the growth of a tree or the thickness of an egg's shell, or how the menstrual cycle parallels the lunar cycle, it's not a far stretch of the imagination to conceive an association between time of year and the development of a child born during that season.

I'm not stating a scientific fact, but am offering possibilities suggesting how certain traits and patterns may have been projected into the images of the zodiac.

Projection, here, is the key term. It is projection—projection of my unconscious—that makes astrology, or any oracle, work for me.

THE PRIMACY OF IMAGINATION

Humans are pattern-seeking creatures. It's part of our nature, easy enough to confirm through personal experience. Even stuck in the bathroom a bit long with no diversion, some people find themselves picking out patterns and images, mentally connecting the dots on the stucco wall . . . which provides a clue to how oracles like the Tarot, the I Ching, dream interpretation, or even the daily newspaper horoscope, work. They are intentionally vague, the vaguer, the better—the better to receive our projections.

Imagination mediates our perception of reality.

Everything that comes to us comes through our senses: we perceive a sensory image of the universe ("image" need not be limited to the visual field). The image I have of the table where I sit is of a solid, material object. Contemporary science reveals this table to be over 99% empty space—inner space just as empty as the vast reaches of outer space—yet if I slam my hand down on the table (ouch!), I perceive no empty space.

Similarly, the rose I see is different from the same rose as experienced by a dog, a bee, an owl, an aphid, or an amoeba swimming in a dewdrop on one of its petals. Our perception of reality could thus be described as a function of image—so we engage the universe through image . . . and imagination. All we perceive, all we experience, is a metaphor that mediates between the individual subject (thee, or me) and the vast "Ground of Being" (Brahman, the Infinite, the Voidless Void, the Transcendent, etc.) that underlies consensus reality. Whether we know it or not, we live in a mythic world.

People say that what we're all seeking is a meaning for life. I don't think that's what we're really seeking. I think that what we're seeking is an experience of being alive, so that our life experiences on the purely physical plane will have resonances within our own innermost being and reality, so that we actually feel the rapture of being alive. That's what it's all finally about, and that's what these clues help us to find within ourselves . . . Experience of life. The mind has to do with meaning.

What's the meaning of a flower? . . . There's no meaning. What's the meaning of the universe? What's the meaning of a flea? It's just there. That's it. And your own meaning is that you're there. We're so engaged in doing things to achieve purposes of outer value that we forget that the inner value, the rapture associated with being alive, is what it's all about.[5]

Life could certainly be described as a series of largely random, chance encounters and meaningless events. And yet, in the same way we connect the dots on a stucco wall, see a unicorn in the formless vapors of a cloud, or pick constellations out of the stars, so we create patterns out of the random events of our own lives.

What is the meaning of life?

"What's the meaning of a flower?" asks Campbell. It has no meaning—it just is.

Unless we give it meaning.

We bring the significance into our own life.

For example, 17 years ago, had I walked into Miss Marple's Tea Room just five minutes later, I would have missed bumping into Eugene, who noticed I was reading Alan Watts's *Tao:*

The Watercourse Way—and I then would never have been introduced to Eugene's daughter, Cassandra, an artist in Taos, through whom I've met many of my closest friends. In memory, this chance meeting has a fated feel to it, having played a pivotal role in shaping my life, and so is imbued with meaning—meaning for me, that is.

MIRRORS OF THE SOUL

The pattern I see in these seemingly random occurrences I recognize as . . . *me!* They form the fabric of my life —— imagination spinning the yarn, weaving the strands together into the plush, colorfully embroidered tapestry that is my life story. The same imagination that thus structures life will discover in a tarot spread, an I Ching throw, or a natal chart, motifs that echo that same structure, clarifying the larger patterns not immediately apparent to the waking ego.

> The seeker is supposed to look for some sort of correspondence between all this and his own case, the method of thought throughout being that of a broadly flung association of ideas. One has to feel, not think one's way into these secrets, letting each symbol grow into a cosmos of associated themes
>
> . . .
>
> The Book of Changes [*I Ching*], in a word, is a kind of geometry of mythology, referring particularly to the immediate present—the moment of the casting of the yarrow stalks. It tells of the readiness of time and the

art of moving with its tides, rocking with the waves, and is the most important statement remaining to us of that aspect of ancient Chinese thought which relates the individual to the order of the outer world.[6]

Though Campbell's remarks are focused here on the I Ching, they nevertheless apply to all forms of divination. Indeed, in Stephen and Robin Larsen's biography, *A Fire in the Mind*, Campbell is portrayed as interested in horoscopes "as a kind of mythological Rorschach (a projective technique from psychology)"; Joe even finds that his and Jean's charts complement one another, which "worked out beautifully" for their marriage.

(Campbell eventually gives up casting horoscopes because he didn't really want to know the future before it unfolded, and because "they gave me a feeling I knew too much about people; you know you get these intimate things. . .")

Two people look at the same cloud, but see different images, depending on how their individual imaginations engage that cloud; you see a unicorn, I see Mr. Magoo. Neither is more right than the other—underneath it's still a cloud, after all. Similarly, in a Rorschach inkblot you may see a butterfly where I see a bat—again, no right or wrong answer, but the image one perceives offers clues as to how each might engage reality.

This especially holds for oracles. I can read the same horoscope as two other Geminis: I might interpret "difficulties in communication" as related to a snafu at work, while another could read the same line as referring to a romance in jeopardy, while a third might recognize a recurring personal pattern that blocks self-expression—one cloud, three different pictures. The circumstances of each life are different, so each brings their own experience and imagination to bear on the oracle, which serves as mirror to our inner worlds.

There is no independent, objective meaning to a horoscope, or a tarot spread, or an I Ching reading, apart from the individual. To borrow an insight from physicist Werner Heisenberg, "the act of observation determines what is observed." Rather than supply a rigid, unyielding rule that applies equally across the board, oracles remain fluid, inviting self-reflection.

> Oracles serve psychological life in profound ways. They bring us into contact with numinous "otherness," thereby penetrating the ego's felt sense of separation. Consciousness is lifted into timeless realms where past, present, and future offer up their images. Since oracles reveal the broader spiritual meaning of human experience, they help realign personal identity with the larger matrix of all-that-is.[7]

Most forms of divination practiced today—whether consulting the stars, the tarot, or the I Ching—offer a series of mythic images (e.g., Mars, the Moon, Mercury, the Water Bearer, the Twins, the Lovers, the Fool, Death, dualities of Heaven/Earth, Masculine/Feminine, etc.) in combinations that mirror the present moment and correspond to those patterns in the human psyche that Jung terms "archetypes of the collective unconscious." These motifs are symbolic of experiences common to all humanity (birth, love, death, etc.).

At their best, methods of divination provide a portal into the mythic imagination. In the words of Novalis, "The seat of the soul is there, where the outer and the inner worlds meet." As with any mythological system, we are presented with metaphor—but remember, metaphor does not mean false; myth as metaphor is a set of living symbols that propel the individual beyond the confines of the personal ego into an experience of the transcendent.

Read literally, such oracles smack of the "Ms. Cleo Knows All" variety . . . but when approached as sacred ritual, as an expression of cosmic harmony, they present a powerful, numinous experience indeed.

DYNAMICS OF THE DIABOLIC

Oracles have not fared well in the contemporary era. With the adoption of Christianity as the state religion, the might of the Roman Empire descended on those who practiced other beliefs. Delphi, site of an oracle sacred in the Mediterranean world for over a thousand years, shared the fate of so many other pagan temples and shrines, and was razed to the ground.

> In this mythological context, the idea of the occult, as black magic, becomes associated with all of the religious arts of the traditional pagan world . . . Moreover, there now begins to become associated with the occult a new tone, one of fearful danger, diabolical possession, and so forth . . . a new mythology of warlocks and witches, pacts with the devil, and so forth, comes into being. But there is an earlier mythological law that tells that when a deity is suppressed and misinterpreted in this way, not recognized as a deity, he indeed may become a devil.[8]

For almost two thousand years those who practice the occult arts have been portrayed as dabbling in the demonic. We all know the story from countless variations in books and films: even those who merely display an innocent curiosity about such subjects are depicted as flirting with disaster, opening themselves to satanic influences—and pacts with the devil, while providing immediate gratification and short-term gains, maybe even granting supernatural powers such as the ability to foresee the future, nevertheless always end badly, in needless anguish, death, even eternal torment in hellfire.

This attitude is typified today in broadsides from fundamentalist televangelists warning of the dangers of letting children read J.K. Rowling's *Harry Potter* novels.

It's not just Christianity, though, that consigns occult practices to the shadows in this secular age. Even though most people might not believe reading tarot cards is a burn-at-the-stake offense, the common perception seems that those who approach astrology or tarot with an open mind are automatically suspect—either a bit shady, with questionable motives, or, at best, flaky and naive.

These aren't satanic projections so much as shadows cast by the Enlightenment.

Empirical science has never been enamored of things that go bump in the night. One of the surest ways to destroy one's scientific reputation is to propose a balanced, objective study of paranormal phenomena, whether of ghosts and poltergeists, telepathy, or the predictive aspects of astrology, tarot, or other means of divination.

Ironically, the scientific establishment is so adamantly opposed to "primitive superstition" that it at times falls victim to the same sloppy techniques it so rigorously condemns.

One notorious example is a 1959 survey by French psychologist and statistician Michel Gauquelin, who found Mars prominent in the birth charts of athletes and military leaders—at odds of 500,000 to 1 over pure chance! Saturn surfaced in the charts of professors of medicine at odds of 10,000,000 to 1, while Jupiter appeared to play an active role in the horoscopes of politicians. Subsequent studies, while failing to document Gauquelin's observations regarding Saturn and Jupiter, have nevertheless consistently replicated the prominence of Mars in athletes' horoscopes. This has become known as the controversial "Mars effect," a thorn in the side to skeptics.

In fact, CSICOP (Committee for the Scientific Investigation of Claims of the Paranormal), which prints *The Skeptical Inquirer* and is the leading organization of scientists leery of "psi phenomena," added fuel to the fire in 1981 by publishing a study that claimed to debunk Gauquelin's observations. Alas, this led to a fracture within the organization when one of the participants in the project, astronomer Dennis Rawlins, a member of CSICOP's executive committee, charged the research was fundamentally flawed, with data intentionally skewed to ignore findings confirming Gauquelin's results. Rawlins, responsible for the calculations and data analysis on the CSICOP project, was surprised to find results actually supported the Mars effect! This led to behind-the-scenes conflict and the departure of several members of the committee who resigned, seeing in these biased results the same type of pseudo-science the group had been created to combat. CSICOP, while standing by its published interpretation, has since adopted a policy against performing research itself.

These studies by no means provide empirical proof that astrology or any other method of divination actually works, even if some correlation is suggested (though what is meant by "works" is somewhat nebulous, given the role psychological projections play in oracular interpretation). In fact, the Mars effect remains a point of contention. However, most practitioners of the occult arts don't seem to need "objectively replicated" confirmation of their experience of the hidden unity to which oracles point—and it's unlikely empirical science will ever provide such clear cut evidence.

It's easy to see why. As but one of dozens of personal examples, I think of a conversation I had over a decade ago with an executive of a company based in the Seattle area. He was in the midst of a major life transition, having recently separated from his wife, given up cocaine, and now about to see his only child off to college. Though I knew he was conservative by nature and thought tarot, astrology, ritual, and myth foolish pre-occupations for a grown man, I happened to be playing with my deck while we talked—so I handed him my tarot cards and suggested he shuffle the deck and pull a card at random, which might offer a glimpse of what quality or characteristic life called for in this moment.

The gentleman good-naturedly decided to humor me. He shuffled the cards once, then drew the Seven of Wands: Courage. He admitted this card was indeed relevant, given his inner turmoil, his fear and feelings of abandonment—but then, he wondered if any card drawn might prove just as relevant.

Well, maybe . . . of course, it might have been a bit of a stretch applying, say, "The Lovers," or "The Magician" to his circumstances, but I'm sure it could be done, with a little song and dance; "Courage," on the other hand, seemed to speak directly to his soul, with no need for clarification from me.

Nevertheless, given his skepticism, I suggested he might be happier with another card—so he replaced the Seven of Wands, shuffled the deck a bit more thoroughly...

... and drew the Seven of Wands.

He was surprised at the coincidence, but considered it just that—coincidence, nothing more. Bound and determined to draw something else, he replaced the card in the deck once more, shuffled several times, cut the deck into three piles, and fanned the cards out face down in front of him. Closing his eyes, he reached over and selected, at random...

...Courage—the Seven of Wands.

This completely threw the dude! He suspected some trick—but considering he was the only one to shuffle the deck or touch any of the cards, he just couldn't figure out how I pulled that off . . . and neither could I. Of course, I was just as amazed, though hardly surprised.

The repetition underscored his own concerns, and we fell into a discussion of ways to foster the courage he would need to transit this difficult passage in his life. It wasn't even a full spread, just a single card—but what a chord it struck.

This is an example of anecdotal evidence. Science simply cannot replicate such a moment—not without "fixing" the deck—but neither is an "objective" scientist likely to just take my word for it, and understandably so. However, all James Randi (the one-time professional magician best identified in the public mind as the face of CSICOP) need do to "disprove" my experience is demonstrate that it's possible for a magician to manipulate a deck so that "the mark" draws the same card three times over. If such a possibility exists, then Occam's razor kicks in; the simplest rational explanation obviously isn't an esoteric concept like Jung's synchronicity—so there must be a scam in progress.

That argument might "debunk" my account in a skeptic's mind, but does nothing to change my own. I know my heart, I know my intentions, and I know my limitations when it comes to sleight- of-hand. The episode I describe was an act of friendship, not a commercial transaction, with nothing to be gained (nor have I ever charged for a tarot reading). That a professional magician can achieve the same result is fascinating, a trick I appreciate—especially since I know there's no way I could intentionally pick the same card out of a deck three times in a row—but it hardly contradicts my own experience . . .

Nevertheless, no matter how sincere and sure personal accounts may be, they do not constitute scientific proof of anything. (Nor do I mean to disparage CSICOP or its periodical, *The Skeptical Inquirer*, which do perform a valuable service.)

In recent decades though, several scientists have advanced models of the universe that parallel Campbell's mythological observation of that "hidden unity beyond or informing the world of multiplicity and its phenomena." Pioneer psychologist Carl Jung's concept of *synchronicity* ("an acausal connecting principle" explaining "meaningful" coincidence), physicist David Bohm's hypothesis of a holographic structure to the universe (an *implicit order* underlying the *explicit order* of our perceived reality), and biologist Rupert Sheldrake's theory of *morphic resonance* (similar forms in nature linked through "a subtle web of relationships," which Sheldrake terms "morphogenetic fields," acting on each other not through cause-and- effect but by "a process of similarity or resonance" limited by neither time nor distance), are all contemporary paradigms which re-frame our conceptions of consensus

reality in ways that make room for oracles and related phenomena. We see similar stirrings in the fields of quantum physics,
chaos theory, fractal geometry, and the study of complexity.

Over time, these and related advances may help initiate a
dialogue between modern and arcane sciences (we are seeing
this happen already in modern medicine, in the growing acceptance of the efficacy of acupuncture, and in an increasing number of doctors—and even some HMOs—willing to embrace
Eastern as well as Western techniques).

APPROACHING THE ORACLE

> The creative man is often *as playful as a child* . . .
> These periods of idleness are the really fruitful ones.
> Undeterred by any will, purpose, or aim, these ideas,
> prescriptions, intuitions, images can emerge that wish
> to, that are ripe. The unconscious can move freely. This
> was known to man in the remotest past, and he made
> full use of it. *For this is the attitude of the man who ques-
> tions the oracle.*[9] (emphasis mine)

Such rituals are best approached in a spirit of play—acting
"as if," suspending our sense of disbelief just like the audience
in any theatrical production (which appropriately enough are
called "plays"). Engaging the metaphors "as if" they are real creates a sense of *participation mystique*, opening us to the magic
and power of the mythic imagination. When approached with
this sense of the sacred, this sense of ritual, then laying out a
tarot spread or casting a personal horoscope serves to place the

individual into an archetypal situation, and can even trigger personal transformation.

> Belief, or at least a game of belief, is the first step toward such a divine seizure.[10]

This attitude of play does not mean we treat the oracle as a joke—indeed, just the opposite, as we act "as if" it were so. Consulting the I Ching in the dining room of a fast-food restaurant during the midday rush generally doesn't carry the same spiritual, emotional, or psychological weight as arriving at the identical hexagram in a quiet room lit with candles, in front of a low altar on which sits a small vase holding a spray of fresh-cut flowers, a petite porcelain cup brimming with hot green tea, and a stick of fragrant incense.

Nor does this mean one need follow a prescribed, stereotyped behavior—there is always room for creativity and flexibility—but acting "as if" is to enter wholeheartedly into the ritual, even if it's a ritual you create yourself.

THE INWARD QUEST

When addressing an oracle, it is the question that counts. Recall the ill-fated Croesus, King of Lydia, who asked the Oracle at Delphi what would happen if his army attacked Cyrus the Great. Herodotus tells us the pythoness assured Croesus that "if he should march against the Persians, he would destroy a great empire"—and sure enough, he did—just not the Persian empire . . . whoops!

Note that "quest" is what gives "question" its meaning. Parzival completes his quest for the Grail not by finding the answer, but in asking the question—the right question from the heart, the question he poses to Amfortas, the wounded Grail King, in Wolfram von Eschenbach's account:

"What ails thee, Uncle?"

Wanting to know the future is a concern of ego, driven by fear and desire, seeking to avoid danger and improve one's advantage—whereas wanting to know one's Self is a concern of soul. Ideally, to consult an oracle is to venture into one's own inner world on a quest for that selfsame Grail—the source that sustains each, and all.

The questions posed in divination offer a window into a supplicant's inner orientation. Some questions are ego questions: does he love me? will I win the lottery?, etc. In fact, most questions once solicited by "The Psychic Friends Network" seem to relate to affairs of heart or wallet—love or success—superficial questions that elicit the least worthwhile responses.

Questions of soul, on the other hand, evoke uncannily accurate insights and realizations. The best seem variations on Parzival's theme—those motivated by compassion.

For example, one evening in Santa Rosa, California, I laid out a tarot spread for a young man suffering from an affair of the heart. Tall, good-looking, nearing 30, Dave had noticed a cashier at the local supermarket. He joked and flirted, made a few unnecessary trips, bought some extra groceries—and finally summoned the courage to ask her out . . .

The lass, alas, had a lad. With his chiseled good looks, Dave was a babe magnet—but his heart had been captured, and he continued to charm the girl at the cash register. Two months later, boyfriend out of the picture, the young lady looked more favorably on Dave's suit. Their third date, they spent a week together at the Grand Canyon.

By the time they returned, Dave had learned she was not the woman of his dreams. Anticipating another broken romance, he asked me for a reading.

I expected his question to be along the lines of "should I stay or should I go?" or maybe "how do I find the right woman?"

He surprised me.

Dave asked the cards, "Why—what is it in me that, once a woman I've been pursuing finally returns my feelings, leads me to do an about-face and lose all interest in her?"

Whoa—what a wonderfully rich, self-revealing question!

Dave wasn't trying to predict his future; he wanted to know himself, penetrate his own heart. The question proved telling: David had discovered a pattern to his behavior, something of which he had previously been unaware, something over which the well-intentioned, waking Dave seemed to have no control, but which nevertheless shaped both present and future.

He had only just tumbled to this, and so sought insight.

When mind and soul are open to reflection, the clarity and focus of what is revealed is a function of the clarity and focus of the question asked. So well-articulated was Dave's query that almost any spread would do.

It all starts with the question.

PORTENTS

I myself have been traveling around quite a bit these years, from one college campus to another, and everywhere the first question asked me is, "Under what sign were you born?" The mysteries of the Tarot pack, the *I Ching*, and Transcendental Meditation . . . Well, all this is just the beginning, the first signaling of a dawning realization of the immanence of the occult, and of this as something important for our living.[11]

Regardless of whether or not one is drawn to one or another of the many colorful forms of divination still practiced today, Joseph Campbell suggests the recent dramatic increase of interest in the oracular arts points to a growing recognition of the relationship between one's own inner, hidden, "occult" nature, and the world of nature outside oneself.

Who knows where this subtle shift in the collective imagination might lead?

Apart from the broad sweep of mythos, Campbell also suggests this is "something important for our living" on a personal level. I suspect the real value of the experience—like with dream—lies not so much in eerie, uncanny coincidence, as in the opportunity afforded to mythologize one's life. We live in a storied universe and are, indeed, figures of myth.

Joseph Campbell isn't proselytizing for "the occult," nor is he recommending we surrender reason and base all decision-making on tarot and tea leaves—but he does note that these means of divination can be valuable tools, much like meditation, like dream work, like myth itself, in determining what Campbell and Jung believe is a question central to every life:

What myth are you living?

Notes

1. Campbell, The Mythic Dimension, op. cit. 260.
2. Diane Skafte, Ph.D., "The Sibyls," in Saga: Best New Writings on Mythology, Vol. 2, ed. Jonathan Young (Ashland: White Cloud Press, 2001), 186.
3. Campbell, The Hero's Journey, op. cit. 12.
4. Jung, The Archetypes and the Collective Unconscious, op. cit. 6.
5. Campbell, The Power of Myth, op. cit. 4, 5.
6. Joseph Campbell, The Masks of God, Vol. 2: Oriental Mythology (New York: Viking Penguin, Inc., 1962; Novato: New World Library, 2021), 394. Citations are from the New World Library edition.
7. Skafte, "The Sibyls," op. cit. 186.
8. Campbell, The Mythic Dimension, op. cit. 258.
9. M.C. Cammerloher, "The Position of Art in the Psychology of Our Time," in Spiritual Disciplines: Papers from the Eranos Yearbooks, ed. Joseph Campbell (Princeton: Bollingen Foundation / Princeton University Press 1960; Princeton: Princeton University Press 1985), 430. Citations are from the 1985 edition.
10. Campbell, Primitive Mythology, op. cit. 24.
11. Campbell, The Mythic Dimension, op. cit. 260.

FOURTEEN

AFTER THE DELUGE

Then by the will of Hurakan, the Heart of Heaven, the
waters were swollen, and a great flood came upon the
mannikins of wood. They were drowned and a thick resin
fell from heaven . . .

Because they had not thought on Hurakan, therefore the face of the earth grew dark, and a pouring rain
commenced, raining by day and by night . . .

Then ran the mannikins hither and thither in
despair. They climbed to the roofs of the houses, but the
houses crumbled under their feet; they tried to mount
to the tops of the trees, but the trees hurled them from
them; they sought refuge in the caverns, but the caverns
closed before them. Thus was accomplished the ruin of
this race, destined to be overthrown.[1]

I pen these words barely a week after Hurricane Katrina
slammed into the Gulf Coast, uprooting over a million people, leaving hundreds of thousands homeless, tens of thousands

stranded, and unknown hundreds dead. Most Americans, cast involuntarily in the role of passive participants, watched this tragedy unfold with the same sense of slow-mo horror, helplessness, and fatalistic fascination we experience in that instant before cars collide, transfixed by the seemingly endless stream of devastation, suffering, and death broadcast 24 hours a day.

For those of us outside the affected area, the images of anguish, grief, and loss are surreal and almost unfathomable in their magnitude, evoking empathy, compassion, and grief of our own.

But for those in Katrina's path, particularly residents of New Orleans and the Mississippi delta, those who have lost family, friends, homes, and livelihood, it's the apocalypse.

> The only word I have to describe this is biblical.
>
> (Unidentified rescue worker, CNN, August 30, 2005)

No need to rehash this recent sequence of events, the details and images of which remain fresh in our minds. We are still trying to process the who, what, where, when, and why of it all—but I do notice that when words fail to convey the impact and aftermath of a violent manifestation of nature, we tend to turn to myth. Not just reporters, in print and on the air, but also friends, neighbors, and relatives have echoed the reaction of the relief worker in the CNN sound bite above: this is a catastrophe of biblical proportions!

Though we have weather charts, satellite photos, and 24-hour televised images unfolding in real time, myth still speaks to us, compressing the near-total, destructive power of this elemental force of nature into one motif, out of the distant past, an image embedded in the human psyche: the Great Flood.

Yes, it's a metaphor—which doesn't mean it didn't happen—or rather, that it doesn't keep happening. While waiting for the waters to relinquish their grip on New Orleans, I find my thoughts turning again and again to this mytheme.

Whence the origin of the flood motif? Is it local history misremembered, a tale that grew in the telling? Is one flood myth the same as the next? Or is the flood merely an archetype, metaphor for movement in the individual psyche? What, in myth, is the purpose of the deluge—and what insight, if any, might such myths offer in the wake of Hurricane Katrina?

THE STUFF OF MYTH

The motif of a universal deluge enjoys near universal distribution., rare only in Africa —— and even on that dry continent are found notable exceptions, such as an Efik Ibibio tale from Nigeria of the Sun and Moon, living as man and wife on earth, inviting their friend, Flood, into their house—then having to retreat to the attic, then the roof, as the waters rise higher and higher—until eventually they reach the place in the heavens where we find them today.

The Old Testament story of Noah in the ark, escaping the flood a vengeful God sends upon the world, shares the same roots as an earlier version of the Mesopotamian Utnapishtim who, in a similar vessel, escapes a worldwide flood sent by the angry Enlil, as recounted in the *Epic of Gilgamesh*. Greco-Roman mythology describes Deucalion and Pyrrha, their children, and the animals they've gathered aboard a box-shaped boat, as all that are saved alive in the flood; on the Aztec Calendar Stone, the last of four prehistoric ages ends with a flood that lingers 52 years; in China, the tenth and last of the prehistoric emperors, the Great Yu, battles the flood waters; the natives of Papua New Guinea believe there was once a global deluge when only the peak of Mount Tauga breached the surface of the water; the Blackfoot Indians of North America tell of Old Man, in a boat on the waters, sending down two or three animals—only the last of which succeeds—to bring up a bit of mud, from which he creates the earth.

Given the worldwide proliferation of flood myths, it's no surprise some wonder if they might have a common source. Those who believe in the inerrancy of scripture claim that God really did send a flood that covered the earth, nearly wiping out all life; the deluge stories of other cultures are then merely corruptions of the Genesis account. This literal interpretation, however, is not borne out by the geological record.

Others suggest the story of Noah's ark is but one echo of a vast flood that covered the plain stretching between the Tigris and Euphrates rivers, inundating cities throughout the heart of the Fertile Crescent, affecting the entire region long recognized as the cradle of civilization. The devastation, displacement, and disruption experienced throughout the region is remembered in local myths of a universal flood (Abraham, the father of the Hebrew peoples, in the biblical tradition claims the city of Ur, along the course of the Euphrates, as his birthplace—which hints at a possible path through which memories of the great Tigris/Euphrates flood entered the Bible). This memory is then thought to have survived as part of the intricate mythological complex that accompanied the diffusion of civilization from the Fertile Crescent throughout Egypt, India, China, and across Oceania into the Americas.

Joseph Campbell takes issue with the initial assumption:

> A number of scholars have thought that actually there may have been some devastating flood that all but annihilated civilization in the area of the early cities, and some have even thought that in their excavations they had discovered the evidence. However, the flood strata unearthed in the various Mesopotamian city sites do not correspond to one another in date. Those at Shuruppuk and Uruk were laid down at the close of the Jemdet Nasr period, c. 3000 BC, while that of Ur occurred at the close of the Obeid period, half a millennium before, and that of Kish two or three centuries later; so that each can be interpreted only as a local, not as a general Mesopotamian (let alone universal) catastrophe. It is of course possible that in each little city state itself the local flood was overinterpreted as a cosmic event, rendering present the mythological Deluge. However, as modern students of this subject, we cannot allow ourselves to go along with such obvious misjudgments, crying like the little hen when the pea fell on her tail, "Run, run, the sky is falling!"[2]

No region-wide flood, true—but, much as I appreciate Campbell's caution against conflating a variety of devastating local floods occurring centuries apart into the one cosmic flood of myth, after watching the coverage of Katrina's effect on those living in New Orleans and elsewhere along the Gulf

Coast I can't help but wonder if there wasn't some blurring of myth and experience in the perceptions of those residents of Sumer and Akkad who did suffer through floods.

Nevertheless, we can't trace the origin of the biblical flood back to a specific occurrence.

Or can we?

ICE AGE RESIDUES

Two Columbia University geologists, William Ryan and Walter Pittman, have proposed a novel theory, first published in 1998 in *Noah's Flood: The New Scientific Discoveries About the Event That Changed History*—a provocative title, but one complemented by sound science. An outline of their argument is as follows:

Between 120,000 BC and 18,000 BC sheets of ice up to two miles thick blanketed much of the Northern Hemisphere, locking up so much water that sea levels were roughly 400 feet lower than they are today. This was followed by a period of rising temperatures, from 18,000 BC to 13,000 BC, which triggered the glacial retreat. Melting ice fed what is now called the New Euxine Lake, a freshwater body located within the bed of today's Black Sea. Starting around 9400 BC the Near East experienced a lengthy period of drought, which would have drawn a variety of peoples to the shore of this huge lake over the next few millennia.

By 6200 BC another "mini" ice age had kicked in, followed by a significant drop in rainfall throughout the region— again motivating people to locate near a reliable freshwater source—hence another surge in population along the shores of the New Euxine Lake.

The final act of this geological drama occurred between 5650 and 5500 BC, as temperatures rose and rains increased once more. During this period the level of the Mediterranean Sea (and the adjacent Sea of Marmara) rose to a height of 426 feet above that of the New Euxine Lake, finally spilling over a small barrier of land near what is now the Bosporus Strait. The coursing water slashed a channel direct to the lake in short order. Ryan and Pittman point out the daily rate of flow down this flume would have quickly reached 200 times that of Niagara Falls, moving at a speed of 50 miles an hour, generating a roar heard over a hundred miles away! This surge would have continued at least 300 days, the shoreline expanding roughly a mile a day, ultimately swallowing over 60,000 square miles of land! Villages and fields along the lakeshore would have turned to sea bottom as peoples from a variety of cultures and language groups scattered in all directions.

In 1999 (AD, that is), following up on Pittman and Ryan's research, a National Geographic team, led by undersea explorer Robert Ballard, located the shoreline of the New Euxine Lake; surveys of the Black Sea's floor show that the beds of the Danube, Dnieper, Dniester, Don, Volga, and other rivers extend along the sea bottom as far as a hundred miles beyond the Black Sea's current shore, all ending at the coast of the New Euxine Lake. A number of what appear to be *tells* (which often mark the site of buried ruins) have been observed along the ancient shoreline, along with well-preserved, recoverable artifacts, including stone tools and carved beams. Archaeological excavations at nearby sites show an abrupt change in pottery patterns about 5500 BC, indicating the collision of cultures that would be expected as refugees fled the advancing water.

Pittman and Ryan suggest that this major geological event pushed the ancestors of the Sumerians, as well as proto-Semitic speakers, to the south, proto-Indo-European speakers to the north, and so on. They speculate the drowning of the New Euxine Lake might well be the source of cataclysmic flood stories that stretch in a swath from India to Greece.

Could be—certainly, the expansion of the New Euxine Lake into the Black Sea is a geological fact, and further exploration is expected to uncover ancient communities long consigned to a watery tomb—but the extent of that expansion remains in dispute. Nevertheless, even if confirmed in most particulars, this event hardly accounts for flood cycles in Mesoamerican cultures, or among the tribes of the Great Plains.

I wonder if the flood motif might be a universal archetype because floods are essentially a universal experience?

The recent catastrophe in New Orleans provides some insight. Whether we are talking Cahokia (outside present day St. Louis, near the confluence of the Ohio and Mississippi rivers), or the town of Ur in ancient Mesopotamia, the immediate experience wouldn't be all that different from that of those who stayed in the Big Easy as Katrina passed over: raging winds; rising waters; collapsed homes; drowned, injured, hungry friends, relatives, and neighbors; widespread panic; threat of contagion; loss of cropland; and surreal chaos and uncertainty replacing the order and routine of daily life.

Of course, the residents of Ur did not have the weather bureau to track the storm with Doppler radar, no hotels and motels to evacuate to outside the area, no sports stadiums to shelter in, no advance warning, no heavy equipment to repair levees and pump out flood waters, no National Guard or FEMA to supply aid and manage the crisis. Most people of the period would have traveled their entire life no farther than a five-to-ten-mile radius beyond their birthplace; as far as they were concerned, a major flood would indeed be the end of the whole world—of *their* whole world. In an age where everything, from birth to planting, irrigating, harvesting, dying, and everything in between, echoes a mythological event, would it be so unusual to experience this crisis as a manifestation of myth? We can observe this happening today, when individuals vested in a literal interpretation of scripture see in current events the end of the world—so, Campbell's caution notwithstanding, a devastating local flood might well become identified with the cosmic myth.

But even were that so, mythologizing an event moves it from the literal to a liminal ("in-between") realm. Stepping beyond history into myth, I have to ask what purpose, in mythological terms, the deluge serves, and what associations and projections of the individual and collective psyche have become attached to this image?

FLOOD STAGES

Two mythologies are found in the story of the Flood. One is that of the planting culture, the old city-mythology of cyclic karma -- of the ages of gold, silver, bronze, and iron. The Flood then came and wiped it out to bring about a fresh start. India abounds in stories of this kind, for the flood is a basic story associated with this cyclic experience through what we might term a year of years.

The second mythology is that of a God who created people, some of whom misbehave. He then said,
"I regret that I have created these people. Look at what
I've done! I am going to wipe them all out." That is
another God, and certainly not the same God as in the
first mythology. I emphasize this observation because
two totally different ideas of God are involved in the
word "God."

The latter God is one who creates. One thinks of
that God as a fact. That we say, is the Creator. We con-
ceptualize that God as IT. On the other hand, in the
impersonal dynamism of the cycles of time the gods are
simply the agents of the cycle. The Hindu gods are not,
therefore, creators in the way that Yahweh is a creator.
This Yahweh creator is, one might say, a metaphysical
fact. When he makes up his mind to do something, it is
promptly accomplished.[3]

Often the flood represents the gulf between the vague, dream-
like mythic age situated somewhere in a dim and distant prehistoric past, and that of the current historic age—times that
are better known and better recorded. This is suggested by the
unrealistic ages in the Bible of the patriarchs before the flood,
who live for centuries—which parallels the mythic lengths of
the reigns of the ten pre-flood Mesopotamian monarchs in the
king lists of the Babylonian priest, Berossos, that together total
432,000 years. And then the 52-year flood depicted on the
Great Calendar Stone of the Aztecs, c. AD 1479, marks the
end of four prehistoric ages of descending duration ("4 Jaguar,"
"4 Wind," "4 Rain," and "4 Water") that precede the dawn of

our own world age. These waters serve to divide a dreamlike, imaginal, mythic reality from the day-to-day waking world.

Campbell notes a shift in roles, from the flood marking the end of an age, into the flood as an instrument of divine retribution, already apparent in the tale of King Ziusudra of Shuruppak, the tenth king of that ancient city-state, who plays the local Noah in a version recorded c. 1750 BC:

> [W]e cannot rule out the probability that in our tale of the Deluge of Ziusudra, Semitic influences already were at work. The sudden stress given to the role of Utu, Sumerian counterpart of the great Semitic sun-god Shumash, points to a bit of such doctoring as priestly hands always allow themselves. And the whole idea of the Flood as the work of a god of wrath than as the natural punctuation of an eon of say 432,000 years seems, indeed, to be an effect of later, secondary, comparatively simple cerebration.[4]

This marks the transition noted in *Thou Art That*, from the gods as agents of a cosmic order that is reflected in the regular movements of the celestial bodies, to God as an active, creative personality, one who travels with—and is in relationship to—His people. We observe this change most clearly in the encounter between the invading, Semitic-speaking nomads, and the agricultural Sumerian civilization long settled in the Fertile Crescent.

As an aside, in this context, the term Semitic refers to a language group; Campbell is referring to Semitic speakers, which include a number of different peoples, mostly polytheistic nomads with a primary tribal deity—a sky god—who emerge from the deserts of Arabia over a period stretching from the Akkadians, in the third millennium BC, to the Arabs, circa 200 BC In common with other scholars of his day—Toynbee, for instance—even when speaking of the Hebrews Campbell generally isn't referring exclusively to the twelve tribes of Israel, but also to the Ammonites, Edomites, Midianites, Moabites, and to the Canaanites already parked in Palestine before the Exodus. Campbell observes the same dynamic among the nomadic Indo-Europeans, who invaded the Balkans under the aegis of their patriarchal sky-god, in what are called the Kurgan (or barrow-people) incursions, and who then also settled along the shores of the Aegean, overwhelming the agrarian, goddess-oriented cultures already in place.

The passage from the *Popol Vuh* quoted earlier blends both types of flood myths together: Hurakan and his colleagues are disappointed in their creation and so wipe away this failed version of humanity, replacing them with us—marking the end of the mythic age and the dawn of our current era.

Ironically, some of those who declare Noah's flood to be concrete, historical fact are already claiming Katrina is the punishment of a vengeful god. An "analysis" on the website of the Restored Church of God, a strict fringe sect of a few thousand, declares the following:

As residents and tourists sought shelter or fled the city, a giant hand-painted sign was left behind, which read, "Please Pray for New Orleans." Praying for New Orleans—"The Big Easy," known around the world for its "anything goes" party atmosphere, and countless stories of debauchery and lewdness—to be spared means that a God must exist to answer. How would the God of the Bible answer such a prayer—what would be His reaction? Would He turn a blind eye to the indescribable excesses that have run rampant throughout New Orleans' history? There is a reason why "The Big Easy" was struck—and why the rest of the United States will feel its rippling effects.

(www.realtruthmag.org/articles/0305- wawucgu.html)

This isn't just a right-wing phenomenon: some ecological activists hurry to suggest a perceived increase in the frequency and intensity of hurricanes is due to global warming, implying New Orleans's destruction is the penalty exacted for environmental misdeeds—reaping the results of our collective sins against the Earth. I'm not arguing that no scientific correlation will be found—and proponents of the Gaia hypothesis do seem more willing to embrace metaphor than literal-minded fundamentalists—but the parallels do intrigue me. Perhaps myths reflect the patterns of the universe we perceive, the shape of our thoughts—a pre-conscious context not easy to transcend?

"Natural disasters" never seem quite natural to the people who must undergo them. Numberless myths explain such happenings as being chastisements for human impiety or disobedience.[5]

Storm Surge

What might this archetype signify in the human psyche?

> [W]e know that there was no Universal Flood. So we
> have to ask . . . [w]hat is the spiritual meaning of the
> Flood? Interpreting Biblical texts literally reduces their
> value; it turns them into newspaper reports. So there was
> a flood thousands of years ago. So what? But if you can
> understand what the Flood means in terms of a reference
> to spiritual circumstances—the coming of chaos, the loss
> of balance, the end of an age, the end of a psychological
> posture—then it begins to talk to you again.[6]

The coming of chaos, the loss of balance—no great mystery
that this dynamic is associated in the human psyche with the
image of a flood, for that is exactly what we've witnessed in New
Orleans in recent days. The psyche doesn't arbitrarily construct
abstract symbols that can be understood only through the study
of elaborate, arcane, esoteric traditions; rather it uses images that
convey a powerful and appropriate emotional charge.

In *The Hero with a Thousand Faces* (29), Campbell points
out, "This circular adventure of the hero appears in negative
form in stories of the deluge type, where it is not the hero that
goes to the power, but the power that rises against the hero, and
again subsides." Often, in dream, this motif assumes a seemingly mundane form. How many of us, for example, have had
dreams where there is flooding, whether rising water in a dark

cave, or some unstoppable, overflowing toilet—without having ever been through an actual flood ourselves?

> Here is the deluge motif: annihilation of the ego system. His conscious programs are breaking up. He is being overwhelmed by the surges of his own nature, which does not run in the channels designated by his strongly disciplinary society.[7]

Of course, the best we can do is paint with a broad brush, for there is no universal key, no rigid definition that can be assigned to a specific dream image. The significance of a dream motif is a function of that image in relation to the circumstances and psychology of the individual dreamer. Generally, though, floodwaters in dream can symbolize undifferentiated emotions and passions—everything from anxiety to lust to anger to grief—unconscious aspects of our psyche that can no longer be suppressed or denied, so threaten to swamp our conscious awareness.

Again, it's not difficult to understand why the psyche provides such associations to this image, given the raw emotions erupting from thousands of New Orleans residents—and officials—at the height of the flooding.

THE WAKE OF THE FLOOD

Interiorizing and psychologizing the Flood, while a valuable exercise, does nothing to address the suffering and loss experienced by the victims of Katrina, who lived through a real flood, and have real and immediate needs. What comfort, if any, might flood myths offer in the current moment?

One thought that comes to mind is our human resilience. The myths tell us this has happened before, and it will happen again—but we will endure. The cycle endlessly repeats itself, or some remnant survives to repopulate the world. Yes, there is death and destruction, chaos and confusion—but this, too, shall pass.

Joe shares an image with Bill Moyers that seems relevant:

> I think of grass—you know, every two weeks a chap comes out with a lawnmower and cuts it down. Suppose the grass were to say, "Well, for Pete's sake, what's the use if you keep getting cut down this way?" Instead, it keeps growing.[8]

The flood myths that appear over and over document the power of the human spirit to persist in the face of adversity. This same drive is already apparent among those who have survived Katrina, whether deciding to start a new life elsewhere, or focused on returning to and rebuilding New Orleans.

A related theme is the end of one age, and the creation of something new. A sense of renewal and rebirth always follows in the wake of the flood.

Campbell speaks of "the end of an age, the end of a psychological posture"—and we see this too, as the aftermath of Katrina sparks a nationwide discussion of issues largely ignored before—discussions of everything from our collective responsibilities to those trapped on the bottom rungs of the socioeconomic ladder, to the realities of race, the value of ecological

restoration and preservation of wetlands, the role and responsibilities of federal, state, and local governments, and a host
of other concerns brought into focus by catastrophic forces of
nature.

Where this will lead, I cannot say—but it's difficult to deny
we live in a different world than existed before Katrina. As the
floodwaters subside, a new world emerges.

> The deluge hero is a symbol of the germinal vitality of
> man surviving even the worst tides of catastrophe . . .[9]

After the Deluge comes optimism, and hope.

NOTES

1. Lewis Spence, tr. The Popol Vuh: The Mythic and Heroic Saga of the
   Kiches of Central America (London: David Nutt, 1908).
2. Campbell, Oriental Mythology, op. cit. 116.
3. Campbell, Thou Art That, op. cit. 43-44.
4. Campbell, Oriental Mythology, op. cit. 121.
5. Alexander Eliot, with Joseph Campbell and Mircea Eliade, Myths
   (Maidenhead: McGraw Hill, 1976), 284.
6. Maher and Briggs, eds. An Open Life, op. cit. 67.
7. Joseph Campbell, Mythic Worlds, Modern Words, ed. Edmund L.
   Epstein, Ph.D. (New York: Harper Collins, 1993; Novato: New World
   Library, 2003), 33.
8. Campbell, The Power of Myth, op. cit. 274.
9. Campbell, The Hero with a Thousand faces, op. cit. 29.

FIFTEEN

INTELLIGIBLE DESIGN

For nature, as we know, is at once without and within
us. Art is the mirror at the interface. So too is ritual;
so also myth. These, too, "bring out the grand lines of
nature," and in doing so, re-establish us in our own
deep truth, which is one with that of all being.[1]

Nature plays a vital role in Joseph Campbell's approach to
mythology. Nature has long supplied the raw material: the sun
and moon and stars, wind and clouds, storms and rain, rivers
and springs, mountains and valleys, cycles of night and day
and of the seasons, the flora, the fauna, the earth itself—these
elements form the bedrock imagery of myth.

For Campbell, though, mythology is not just an abstract
by-product of the human imagination, but part and parcel of a
larger picture. He speaks, for example, of mythology as "nature
talking," or as an "expression in personified images" of the
energies of nature.

What, though, does he mean by "nature"?

Is Campbell speaking here in the voice of the Romantic poets? Is his a nature tinted in sepia tones, awash in touchy-feely New Age sentimentalities?

Or are Campbell's views grounded in scientific observation of the natural world? Could it be a little of both?

Joseph Campbell is the only comparative mythologist I know to ponder the biological implications of myth in the evolution of our species. Such speculation naturally unnerves those scholars who confine their inquiries to the narrow focus of a specialized field. Of course, in Campbell's day mythology wasn't exactly a specialized field. No institution offered a degree in the subject; indeed, the study of myth cut across a variety of fields, with literature, folklore, history, anthropology, psychology, and other disciplines all contributing colorful fragments to an expanding mythic mosaic.

But where do biology and the natural sciences enter the mix?

Is there a common framework underlying the worlds of mythology and the world of nature? What might this mean in an individual life? Has science superseded mythology, or are there points where the two intersect today—and, if so, where might that dance take us in the future?

Perhaps we can flesh out the context by tracing the origin of Campbell's thought back to his own formative encounters with the natural world.

COMING OF AGE

Over the winter of 1918 Joseph Campbell, not quite 14, lay in bed nearly two months fighting fever, bronchitis, and pneumonia, while enduring treatments that ranged from calomel and creosote to mustard plaster and morphine injections. He eventually recovered—but a lengthy convalescence meant long days alone while everyone else attended school. According to Campbell biographers Stephen and Robin Larsen, Joe filled the hours by immersing himself in the study of Native American culture. Campbell notes in his journal working his way through the many volumes of the Bureau of American Ethnology, as well as *The Handbook of American Indians*.

> While most of his friends remained fascinated by guns and cowboys, young Joe was preoccupied now not only with the romantic image of the bow-and-arrow wielding Indian but with the details of the Indian experience: The actualities of their way of life; their relation to the animals, plants, and all of nature; and, of course, their mythology—the wonderful trickster demiurges, the clever foxes and ravens, the vision-seeking heroes, and the deep mystical contemplation of Wakan Tanka, the Great Spirit whose living spirit pervades the world.[2]

Ever curious, the recuperating youth also focused his attention on the heavens, building his own telescope—and learning in the process how to identify stars, planets, and the constellations. By April he was well enough to continue his recovery at the family bungalow in rustic Pike County, Pennsylvania. Joseph spent many evenings at the camp of friend and neighbor Dan Beard, founder of the Boy Scouts of America; most of his summer, though, was spent in the company of Elmer Gregor, a naturalist and author of adventure books for children, who lived near the Campbell spread. Gregor took Campbell fishing, taught him the names, properties, and lore of the local flora and fauna (the Larsons note one excited entry in Joe's journal where he details identifying 43 different species of birds in a single day!), and allowed the boy free run of "his good-sized library of adventure stories, nature books, Indian tales, [and] animal stories."

By the end of a summer spent tracking animals, classifying species of plants and birds, studying the stars, visiting petroglyphs and the remains of an Indian sweat lodge, fishing, hiking, and more, Joe had regained his naturally robust health; meanwhile, his relationships with Beard and Gregor reinforced a connection already established in Campbell's mind between the world of nature and that of Native American myths.

HIGHER EDUCATION

This fascination remained in force three years later when Joe entered Dartmouth, where he majored in science, with a concentration in biology. A year of botany and zoology triggered profound religious doubts; partly due to this crisis in faith, partly due to general dissatisfaction with the party atmosphere on campus, Joe transferred to Columbia his sophomore year, where he leaned toward anthropology before settling on a degree in English and comparative literature.

After attaining his Master's degree, Campbell studied in Europe on a Proudfit Fellowship. While in Paris he was admitted to the inner circle surrounding master sculptor Antoine Bourdelle, who had once been Rodin's student. From Bourdelle he learned what was to be one of the guiding themes of his life: *"L'art fait ressortir les grandes lignes de la nature."*

> Antoine Bourdelle: "Art brings out the grand lines of nature." And this is what myths are also about.[3]

Elsewhere Campbell expands on this thought, drawing on other artists (e.g., Cezanne: "Art is a harmony parallel to nature."). In this period, we see Campbell first growing conscious of the resonance between art and myth. Both, he comes to believe, are expressions of nature.

At the same time, Campbell discovered the work of Freud and Jung. Jung, in particular, intimates a biological ground to the human psyche, apparent in the congruence between human instincts and the archetypes of the collective unconscious (which closely parallel universal mythological archetypes).

These ideas simmered in Campbell's psyche the next several years, brewing and bubbling beneath the surface—but it took a return to the laboratory of nature, in collaboration with another pioneering mind, for the brew to reach critical mass.

The Alchemist Of Cannery Row

> I was five years without a job. I went out to California looking for one and settled down in Carmel, where I met John Steinbeck, who was also broke. That was an important moment for me, especially getting to know his collaborator, Ed Ricketts, who's the doctor in his novels.

> Ricketts was an intertidal biologist and I had been
> interested in biology from my school days. Talking with
> Ricketts, I realized that between myth and biology there
> is a very close association. I think of mythology as a func-
> tion of biology . . .[4]

Eric Enno Tamm, reporting on a symposium on Ed Ricketts for the *San Francisco Chronicle* (October 16, 2005), describes Ricketts as "the Jerry Garcia of American science—a beer-drinking, bearded guru who ignored the social and scientific orthodoxies of his time, a progenitor of the counterculture, an enigmatic ecologist whose pioneering work was initially rejected by the scientific establishment."

Ed Ricketts cut a figure larger than life—a Renaissance man with a passion for biology, drawn to explore the margins, whether the elegant, unique, complex forms of life in the tidal zones along the Pacific coast where sea and earth collide, or the writers, prostitutes, artists, bohemians, and bums inhabiting the dark corners and jagged edges of civilized society.

Ricketts' writings are few, with little apart from *The Sea of Cortez*, his collaboration with Steinbeck, reaching beyond a limited scientific audience; nevertheless, we hear his voice in both Steinbeck and Campbell. Steinbeck mythologizes the biologist in *Cannery Row, Tortilla Flats, Sweet Thursday, In Dubious Battle,* and *The Grapes of Wrath*—generally a persona equal parts sinner and saint.

And notice the resonance between the following quotes, from Campbell and from Ricketts, both addressing "the meaning of life."

People say that what we're all seeking is a meaning for life. I don't think that's what we're really seeking. I think that what we're seeking is an experience of being alive, so that our experiences on the purely physical plane will have resonances with our own innermost being and reality, so that we actually feel the rapture of being alive ... Experience of life. The mind has to do with meaning. What's the meaning of a flower? ... There's no meaning. What's the meaning of a flea? It's just there. That's it. And your own meaning is that you're there.[5]

The truest reason for anything's being so is that it is. This is actually and truly a reason, more valid and clear than all the other separate reasons, or than any group of them short of the whole. Anything less than the whole forms part of the picture only, and the infinite whole is unknowable except by being it, by living into it.[6]

This mutual emphasis on seeking *experience*—the living of life—over the search for a nebulous *meaning* of life, is an example of *non-teleological thinking*, a phrase Ricketts employs to describe a concept he and Steinbeck present in *Log from The Sea of Cortez*, but an idea Ricketts and Campbell had fleshed out on a collecting expedition over the summer of 1932.

Ed Ricketts established Pacific Biological Laboratories in 1923, at the age of 25. Despite the prestigious name the lab was a mostly ramshackle affair on Monterey's Cannery Row; nevertheless, over the next quarter-century Ricketts' lab developed a sterling reputation as a supplier of prepared slides and preserved specimens for high schools, universities, and other research facilities. Ricketts, a recognized expert on the Pacific coast, compiled an index of every form of sea life from the Gulf of California to the Alaskan coast. Fifteen different species discovered by Ricketts bear his name, and his definitive volume on life in the coastal zone, *Between Pacific Tides*—published by Stanford University Press in 1939—remains "the bible of marine biology." Ricketts' detailed and comprehensive study of the life cycle and migratory habits of the sardine predicted the collapse of the sardine industry in Monterey, absent steps to reverse the trend.

(To no one's surprise, Ricketts' predictions were ignored— and the once-thriving canneries and fishing fleet simply faded away.)

Joseph Campbell, without a job at the height of the Great Depression, wandered out to California the fall of 1931; a twist of fate brought him together with John Steinbeck and Ed Ricketts in Monterey. This proved a creative encounter for all three men. Apocryphal tales proliferate: Ricketts appears to have played Dionysus, treating young Campbell to his first bender; a spontaneous gathering on Joe's birthday may well have provided the prototype for the legendary party at "Doc's" lab in Cannery Row; and, of course, what idyllic interlude would be complete without affairs of the heart? Alas, following these and other tangents would take us too far afield . . . many amusing anecdotes, however, can be found in the Larsens' bio of Campbell, *A Fire in the Mind*, or Eric Enno Tamm's study of Ricketts, *Beyond the Outer Shores*.

Campbell's collaboration with Ricketts proved more than just boisterous parties and bohemian rap sessions. In the summer of 1932 Ricketts had an order to fill for 15,000 specimens

of *gonionemus vertens*—"a little pink jellyfish"—which supplied
the funding for an expedition to study marine life in the Pacific
Northwest. Ed persuaded Joe to sign on, and the two young men
(Campbell at age 28, and Ricketts, 34) spent the next ten weeks
together, sailing with writer Jack Calvin and his wife aboard
a 33-foot one-time naval launch, re-christened *The Grampus*,
exploring tide pools from Puget Sound to Sitka, Alaska.

Though Ed, seven years older, was in many ways a mentor to
Joe, Tamm makes the case that Campbell influenced Ricketts
as much as the other way around. Ricketts, for example,
acknowledges Campbell's help in crafting the 43-page research
paper recording their findings ("Notes and Observations,
Mostly Ecological, Resulting from Northern Pacific Collecting
Trips Chiefly in Southeasterly Alaska with Especial Reference
to Wave Shock as a Factor in Littoral Ecology"—has to be scientific with a title that dry!), thanking his "constant and interested companion, for outlining in some detail certain conclusions attained en route." (Tamm, 228)

Ed and Joe had no contact the next seven years, each caught
up living the adventure of his own life, until an exchange of
letters in 1939 following the publication of Ricketts' *Between
Pacific Tides* renewed their friendship. Thereafter they maintained close ties until Ricketts' untimely death in 1948.

Joseph Campbell, on the occasion of Steinbeck's and
Ricketts' publication of *The Sea of Cortez*, remarks on one of the
mythic realizations to emerge from the *Grampus* expedition.

> These little intertidal societies and the great human
> societies are manifestations of common principles; more
> than that: We understand that the little and the great

societies are themselves units in a sublime, all-inclusive organism, which breathes and goes on, in dream-like half-consciousness of its own life-processes, oxidizing its own substance yet sustaining its wonderful form . . .[7]

Given the seven-year hiatus, Campbell expresses pleasant surprise at the parallels between his and Ricketts' thought, which had developed independently, in seemingly separate fields, during that time. Journal entries and the correspondence of both men illustrate the creative cross-fertilization that characterized their relationship.

NON-TELEOLOGICAL THINKING

In the letter cited above, Campbell mentions another major consequence of the *Grampus* expedition.

. . . and then, emerging out of all of this, the great, solid realization of 'non-teleological thinking.'

Non-teleological thinking steps outside the western tradition, looking on causal explanations as linear and limited. Rickets and Steinbeck offer the analogy of a foreman who blows a warning whistle just before a charge is set off, and the effect that repeated routine might have on those living within earshot.

Having experienced this many times without closer contact, a naïve and unthinking person might justly conclude not only that there was a cause-effect relation, but that the whistle actually caused the explosion. A slightly wiser person would insist that the explosion caused the whistle, but would be hard put to explain the transposed time element. The normal adult would recognize that the whistle no more caused the explosion than the explosion caused the whistle, but that both were parts of a larger pattern out of which a why could be postulated for both . . .Determined to chase the thing down in a cause-and-effect sense, an observer would have to be very wise indeed who could follow the intricacies of cause through more fundamental cause to primary cause, even in this largely man-made series about which we presumably know most of the motives, causes, and ramifications. He would eventually find himself in a welter of thoughts on production, and ownership of the means of production, and economic whys and wherefores about which there is little agreement.

The example quoted is obvious and simple. Most things are far more subtle than that, and have many of their relations and most of their origins far back in things more difficult of access than the tooting of a whistle calculated to warn bystanders away from an explosion. We know little enough of a manmade series like this—how much less of purely natural phenomena about which there is apt to be teleological pontificating.[8]

Intelligent design is irrelevant; Aquinas' teleological argument of God as First Cause, to which all can be traced, no more than wishful thinking. Non-teleological thinking does not deny the existence of causal connections, but examines them within the framework of the larger picture. The Larsens expand on this insight:

> Ricketts' approach is a deliberate attempt at non-Aristotelian thinking. One can only understand a situation or process in terms of its context. The whole of something is 'greater than the sum of its parts.' Campbell and Ricketts were in fact reading Einstein, Heisenberg, and other works on the New Physics during this journey.[9]

This holistic approach had far-reaching consequences for the relatively new science of ecology. According to Tamm, "Ricketts classified an organism not based on its inner structure, but rather on its relations to the outer world, its biotic and physical environment, on its *ecology*. In effect, he turned on its head the idea of a taxonomic pyramid built on the species-unit with *Homo sapiens* at its glorious pinnacle."[10]

Ricketts accepts that his ecological model cannot "achieve the finality so characteristic of the taxonomic order [where] an animal belongs irrevocably in the one place finally assigned to it . . ."[11] Grouping species by habitat and ecological niche, emphasizing their interactions with other species and their environment, is certainly more flexible than the traditional taxonomic model, and no doubt easier for the layman to understand—and yet it is at times admittedly vague, for a species might thrive naturally in more than one environment. As Tamm points out, "[T]he new science tried to paint a holistic picture, which was a bit blurry, like Renoir's paintings, but nevertheless a more illuminating and accurate reflection of nature."[12] Hence the academic establishment initially resisted Ricketts' approach, labeling it populist science (a charge sometimes leveled at Campbell, for similar reasons).

This shift in perspective, however, from viewing the particular only in terms of its placement on a taxonomic family tree (a member of a specific *species*, which belongs to a particular *genus* grouped with others into one *family*, which belongs to an order that is part of a class in a certain *phylum* within a broad *kingdom*), to seeing the whole in the particular and the particular in the whole, secured Ricketts' reputation as "patron saint of deep ecology."

> If one observes in this relational sense, it seems apparent that species are only commas in a sentence, that each species is at once the point and the base of the pyramid, that all life is relational to the point where an Einsteinian relativity seems to emerge. And then not only the meaning but the feeling about species grow misty. One merges into another, groups melt into ecological groups until the time when what we know as life meets and enters what we think of as non-life: barnacle and rock, rock and earth, earth and tree, tree and rain and air. And the units nestle into the whole and are inseparable from it . . . all things are one thing and that one thing is all things—plankton, a shimmering phosphorescence on the sea and the spinning planets and an expanding universe, all bound together by the elastic string of time.
>
> It is advisable to look from the tide pool to the stars and then back to the tide pool again.[13]

I am reminded of Campbell's many references to the vision of Black Elk, Keeper of the Sacred Pipe of his people, who describes being in trance atop Harney Peak, South Dakota— "the central mountain of the world"—yet then declares, "But anywhere is the center of the world," a realization Campbell suggests corresponds to a maxim from the twelfth century *Book of the Twenty-four Philosophers* (*Liber XXIV philosophorum*):

> God is an intelligible sphere, whose center is every-where, and circumference nowhere.

"Intelligible," Campbell points out, means, "known to the mind." Hmm . . . *intelligible* design?

Joseph Campbell was not surprised to find the observations of the natural world he and Ricketts shared aboard the *Grampus* embedded in mythologies throughout the world. In a lecture included as an appendix to *Asian Journals*, Campbell finds a parallel in a Buddhist image:

> Usually the progression of causality is reckoned as coming from past to present, in our direction, as it were. But since, according to the doctrine of the Yonder Shore, the nondualistic Prajnaparamita doctrine, "past" and "present" are not to be regarded as two separate things, the chain of causality must also be reckoned as proceeding from the future to present. Furthermore, since "here" and "there" are not to be regarded as two completely separate things, the influence of causality moves from there to here as much as it does from the other way, so that all things contribute to the causality

of any given situation at any moment—all things past, future, and to the sides.

Another name for this doctrine is the Doctrine of the Net of Gems, in which the world is regarded as a net of gems, each gem reflecting perfectly all the others. It is also called the Doctrine of Mutual Arising . . . Everything creates everything else. The doctrine works, furthermore, on all levels.[14]

Particle physicists, from Neils Bohr to David Bohm, have borrowed this imagery to portray the relationships and interactions of matter at the quantum level—relationships and interactions which give rise to the physical universe we perceive.

Clearly myth mirrors nature, whether on the level of the Aborigines of Australia or Pueblo tribes of the American Southwest, whose myths revolve around the local landscape, or in the complex, exquisite imagery of Kegon Buddhism cited above.

How, though, does myth mediate nature in an individual life?

MYTH AND THE TIDES OF LIFE

Talking with Ricketts, I realized that between myth and biology there is a very close association. I think of mythology as a function of biology; it's a production of the human imagination, which is moved by the energies of the organs of the body operating against each other. These are the same in human beings all over the world and this is the basis for the archetypology of myth. So I've thought of myself as a kind of marginal scientist studying the phenomenology of the human body, you might say.[15]

Early anthropologists assumed that myths and rites were attempts to control nature on the part of primitive and superstitious people. Campbell points out the opposite is true: "in the long view of mankind," myths and rites evolved to help place us—individuals and society—in accord with nature. For example, building on Geza Roheim's observation that humans have the longest period of childhood dependency of any species—at least 12 years—he finds that "rites, together with the mythologies that support them, constitute the second womb, the matrix of the postnatal gestation of the placental Homo sapiens."[16]

This is most clearly observed at adolescence, as hormones kick in, genitalia awaken, and thoughts turn to yearnings and imaginings that no six-year-old would ever entertain. I have taught junior high for years and regularly bear witness to this massive paradigm shift as childhood gives way to something foreign and new. Not only does the body change, but a confused tangle of strange, unfamiliar motivations and intense emotions are suddenly fueling behavior.

This isn't a conscious choice—it happens, ready or not.

In primal cultures, myths and rituals of initiation midwife this transition. Mythology provides a context within which to assort and assimilate these new energies without destroying the individual or endangering society.

Campbell points out that we can see what happens in the absence of an active mythological tradition of initiation simply by looking out the window, so to speak, viewing the chaos and disruption in our own culture.

Ironically, in the violent initiations and rituals associated with gang life we recognize the spontaneous emergence of mythic forms from the unconscious psyche—even unbidden, they come . . . but in the absence of elders to serve as guides, working within a mythological tradition that supports this transition and grounds potentially destructive energies, there is no authentic initiation.

Myths and rites of initiation that mark the coming of age are but one example of how mythology places the individual in accord with nature.

Campbell, in *Mythic Worlds, Modern Words,* is struck by psychologist John Weir Perry's description of "mythological images as affect images, images that evoke in the observer equivalent sentiments and emotional responses," for, as Joe says, "my own definition of an effective mythological symbol has been 'an energy-releasing and -directing sign.'"

> The energies that move the body are the energies that move the imagination. These energies, then, are the source of mythological imagery; in a mythological organization of symbols, the conflicts between the different organic impulses within the body are resolved and harmonized. You might say *a mythology is a formula for the harmonization of the energies of life.* (emphasis mine)[17]

"Mythology is a formula for the harmonization of the energies of life"—that's my favorite answer to the question "What is myth?" Not that difficult to understand, even on the most mundane level: my stomach has one impulse to action, my genitals another—and there are times when the two are very much in conflict . . . But the argument isn't just between the reproductive system and the digestive tract, for we also have the brain entering into the fray, and the heart, and even more abstract "organs."

This thought can be troubling to those who can't fathom heart or stomach or any organ as more than a machine, or who see nature itself as composed of only inert, soulless matter—which is not how we experience either the world around us, or the world within. When Campbell speaks of the "organs of the body" he isn't describing cuts of meat on the butcher's slab, but the miracle and mystery of the organizing principle of life. There is a distinct resonance between *organ* and *orga-nization* here . . .

Individual cells grouped together form an organ, a whole that is greater than the sum of its parts—and these organs and related bodily processes working in concert also form a whole greater than the sum of its parts, a synergy we call the individual (and this metaphor can be extended from individuals to a society, and indeed to humanity as a whole).

The coordination and organization of the billions of individual impulses within the human body that, taken together, add up to a human life is a mystery, one which we continue to explore from a variety of different angles, from biology and psychology to philosophy and theology—all of which can't help but overlap and/or bump into one another at times.

Mythology both reflects this elusive organizing principle, and serves as guide when consciousness is at odds with one or another of the elements of our being.

I think Carl Jung's term "archetypes of the unconscious" is fundamental and appropriate here. The archetypes of myth are manifestations of the nature of man in accord with the nature of the universe. Interpose, before these, ideas derived from man's limited knowledge of the world, and we have then a system of rational thought. In dream the rational mind becomes aware of impulses of the larger nature, of which it is itself but one organ. Impose the will of that one organ upon the whole, and the imposition has to be by violence.[18]

Note that Campbell refers to the rational mind as one of the "organs" whose impulses are at odds with those of other organs of the body. Mind—and even imagination—can fit the metaphorical usage of the term.

If my head is exclusively running the show, then heart is neglected—and if belly is in charge, or phallus always gets its way, ignoring cautions of head and heart, then the whole is imperiled. Of course, no one "organ," no one system, is supreme. One just has to fall in love, for example, to realize how little control conscious rational intention exerts . . . and then even sex addicts have to stop and order a pizza now and then.

I used to teach literature in junior high (still do, on occasion). The key to plot in every story is conflict. No matter how poetic the imagery, how precise the characterizations, there is no story without conflict.

But conflict is not something new, something foreign to nature that enters the scene only with the emergence of the human ego.

Spengler reminds us that the natural state of the animal world is characterized by polarity—whether an amoeba floating in a drop of dew on a blade of grass, a hawk soaring through the sky, or a commuter stuck in traffic, the individual exists as foreground against the background of everything else—and this contrast gives rise to a natural state of tension, a state which, at least for vertebrates, is only relaxed when fatigue sets in and one falls asleep, slipping into dream (a state of consciousness where the separation between oneself and other objects is fuzzy at best), eventually waking once more to that state of separation and conflict.

> I can remember when I spent a long time with intertidal biologist Ed Ricketts, in that area between low and high tide [1931–32]. All those strange forms, cormorants and little worms of different kinds and all. You'd hear, my gosh, this generation of life was a great battle going on, life consuming life, everything learning how to eat the other one, the whole mystery, and then from there they crawl up on land . . .[19]

Humans are by no means exempt. We do not stand outside biology, outside nature, immune to the principles of evolution. Conflict is inherent to life—a concept my inner hippie resists . . . but then, that inner hippie takes the word a mite literal at times. Conflict does not automatically translate into fighting and violence. Whenever and wherever there is a choice to be made, there is conflict.

It shouldn't be a surprise when Campbell speaks of the structure out of which myths come as "the structure of the human body and of the relationships to each other of the energies of the organs of the body as impulse-givers . . ." The body, after all, is the organ through which we mediate reality. All we perceive is filtered through the sense organs of our body, and we interact with the universe on the basis of those perceptions, which are very different from the way the universe is perceived and experienced by, say, a dog—or a butterfly, or an amoeba, or a rock, or a photon (not sure to what extent the latter two phenomena can perceive and experience—but clearly a photon occupies a very different universe than the one constructed by my senses).

Yet, though mythology's structure is related to the body, it is not "caused" by the body . . . a subtle difference, I know.

> How mythology functions, why it is generated and required by the human species, why it is everywhere essentially the same, and why the rational destruction of it conduces to puerility, become known the moment one abandons the historical method of tracing secondary origins and adopts the biological view . . . which considers the primary organism itself, this universal carrier and fashioner of history, the human body.[20]

In the absence of an effective, contemporary, collective mythology, Campbell offers a clue to uncovering a personal mythology that will place one in accord with nature:

> Your biology is related to the biology of plants and animals: they too share the life energies—what we might term "body wisdom," in contrast to mental wisdom.

> When you move deeper in dream, when you move into
> the sphere of the permanent energies of your body, your
> mental wisdom is gradually extinguished, body wis-
> dom (as it were) rises, and you experience the collective
> order of dream, where the imagery is identical to the
> imagery of myth. And since some of these images have
> not been allowed to play a role in your life, you come
> into relation to them with surprise.[21]

We aren't automatons, abdicating our decision-making powers
to some sort of uniform biological code. We don't all take Betty
to the dance—some choose Veronica, some prefer Archie, and
a few remain celibate. Every individual is unique, facing different circumstances, with differing priorities—and so makes
different choices. Myths (and dreams) don't tell us what to
choose, but provide guidance on how to make choices in harmony with our own nature—especially when the conflict is
unbearable and one is unable to make a choice, or has no sense
of one's own nature.

NATURAL HARMONY

Critics have sometimes characterized Joseph Campbell as hostile to Judaism and Christianity, despite often elegant, insightful
renderings of mythemes playing through both these religions.
(For example, Campbell's positive reading of the children of
Israel—the Chosen People—as a collective Hero who wanders the Wasteland and emerges transformed from the exodus
out of Egypt into the Promised Land—a theme developed in

Occidental Mythology). These criticisms are often unfair, ignoring the context—but I can see where there are hooks on which such projections might catch.

Campbell's primary objection to the Judeo-Christian mythos (equally true of Islam and Zoroastrianism, though without generating the same hue and cry among critics) is that, when read literally, these religions, though more or less accurately reflecting the harsh realities of the unforgiving environment in which they were born, are nevertheless incongruent with the world around us.

They are out of sync with both science and nature.

A flood of technological advances have allowed us to see beyond once-limited horizons into the farthest reaches of outer space, the microcosmic depths of the quantum universe, even the interior of the human psyche—and the picture we arrive at is nearer in harmony to the imagery of nature-oriented mythologies, whether shamanism, goddess-oriented cultures, Buddhism, Taoism, or even neo-pagan revivals like Wicca, than to the prevailing religious paradigm in the West which sees nature as fallen and corrupt.

> These stories represent a tension between two totally different mythologies. One is the goodness of nature with which individuals try to harmonize themselves. That is considered a virtuous and healthy and humanly sustaining act. The other sees nature negatively and the person's choice is to say "no" to it and to pull away from it.
>
> I deem this distinction of mythologies very important. We have the nature mythologies, which put us in touch with our own nature. But there also exist

antinature mythologies. These are the mythologies of the nomadic people.

> When you live in the desert, you cannot depend on Mother Nature . . .[22]

This doesn't mean that polytheism or Buddhism or New Age thought is "true" and that Judaism and Christianity are "false"—but the metaphors common to nature-oriented mythologies are rapidly becoming the metaphors of science. The traditional image of God as a watchmaker who designs the universe and sets it in motion does not fit a quantum reality where time flows in more than one direction and the laws of causality are ignored . . .

A literal reading of scripture enshrines a worldview no longer relevant—a rigid, inflexible concretization of mythic imagery that desacralizes nature, with devastating consequences:

> When you are in accord with nature, nature will yield its bounty. This is something that is coming up in our own consciousness now, with the ecology movement, recognizing that by violating the environment in which we are living, we are really cutting off the energy and source of our own living. And it's this sense of accord, so that living properly in relation to what has to be done in this world one fosters the vitality of the environment.[23]

Campbell's words remain relevant to contemporary discussions regarding global warming, the exploitation of natural resources, even the debate over teaching intelligent design (the epitome of teleological thinking) as science. Even more so Ed Ricketts' research and observations, grounded in his understanding of the concept of nonteleological thinking: ecologists and biologists are turning to Ricketts to provide the crucial framework that will allow us to understand and address the major planetary crises we face today—ironically, a framework resonant with almost all mythologies (even the Old Testament contains the traces of earlier, nature-oriented myths).

THE COMING MYTH

Joseph Campbell argues that an active, effective mythology would need to be in harmony with the science of AD 2000, rather than that of 2000 BC—but cautions that we can't predict what form that might take any more than we can predict what we will dream tonight.

Nevertheless, it is tempting to speculate. What can we expect from an emerging mythology?

It should provide a lens through which we perceive the universe and ourselves. Though differing in details, any new mythology would express the motifs basic to previous mythologies, interpreting them in ways that match our experience of the universe (no Hairy Thunderer hurling lightning bolts from the peak of Olympus or Sinai—just doesn't jive with "the facts" as we know them).

Perhaps most significant, an emerging "universal" mythology would not be perceived as "myth," but simply as what is. All earlier mythologies, as they developed, were recognized as part of the warp and woof of that culture. Myth explains what is, who we are, and how we (and everything) came to be. Hence, though one culture might recognize another culture's myths as myth, it rarely perceives its own as such.

There are multiple candidates for the role, but most carry baggage heavy enough to make them unacceptable to the multitudes without some sort of miraculous, mass "road to Damascus" conversion—possible, albeit unlikely in this skeptical age.

Many who have discovered Campbell's work are led in the direction of Eastern traditions, but it's hard to imagine a majority of U.S. citizens flocking to a Zen temple or adopting various "New Age" practices.

Campbell awakes in others a renewed interest and enthusiasm in their birth religion, helping them see through external trappings to the essence of true faith and divine being at its core—but contemporary Christianity, as mentioned above, especially the influential fundamentalist wing, often projects an exclusive orientation ("there is but one path to God") and reads its myths literally, contrary to current scientific awareness, making it an unlikely carrier of a "new" mythology.

A living, working mythology would be in harmony with the science of the day. So what might fill the bill?

Can there be a secular mythology? Do we find such elements of a new paradigm, not at odds with personal religious experience and expression, on the horizon?

Hmm . . . images related to science and psychology come to mind.

Ecology isn't the only science to stumble upon non-teleological thinking. Examples abound:

In particular, advances within the field of physics and

biology, the development of depth and transpersonal psychologies, and the emergence of consciousness research (cognitive
science and artificial intelligence) and information technologies—particularly the internet—provide a medium through
which the collective imagination recasts the universe and our
role in it. The same archetypal energies and forces of nature
personified in gods, demons, and myth remain in play, but the
dynamics are depicted in terms and imagery more befitting
Star Trek than Homer's *Odyssey* or the *Bhagavad Gītā*.

Each of these elements, however depersonalized, contains echoes of earlier myths—the same patterns, the same
motifs—". . . in new relationships indeed, but ever the same
motifs" (Campbell). Science, psychology, and information
technology are providing new myths to replace the old—but
we read them as fact alone, taking no account of how they act
on the Imagination.

Discoveries this past century in the field of quantum physics, particularly regarding the relationship of matter to energy
and the central role of perceiver/observer in determining what
is observed (Heisenberg, 1934), serve as metaphors as elegant
as the Buddhist image of the spontaneous mutual arising of
all things. Physicist David Bohm's theory of an implicit order
underlying/enfolded into the explicit order of the phenomenal
universe suggests the metaphysics of an invisible world behind
the visible, fundamental to the mystical traditions of every faith.

Bohm's holographic model of the universe, Karl Pribram's
exploration of the holographic nature of memory and the brain,
and Stanislav Grof's observations regarding the holographic
structure of the human psyche, conjure a realization similar to
the alchemical dictum so succinctly inscribed on the legendary

Emerald Tablet—"As above, so below; as below, so above." Any fragment of a holographic image contains within it an image of the whole—which can't help but evoke the Buddhist metaphor of the Net of Gems.

The nonlinear dynamics of chaos theory and fractal science, which find exquisite beauty and complex order hidden within chaotic systems, impact fields ranging from meteorology to marketing. Is it a surprise that most ancient myths begin with order emerging out of chaos—from the face of God moving across the void (*tehom*) in Genesis, or the Babylonian Marduk fashioning the world from the vanquished corpse of Tiamat, dragon goddess of chaos, to Chaos as origin of Eros, first of the gods, in Ovid's *Metamorphosis*?

Similarly, depth psychology, beginning with Freud's *Interpretation of Dreams* in 1899, has opened the interior world of the psyche. Jung's work delves into the archetypal patterns fueling psychological drives and behaviors, which on the one hand can be linked to instincts and biological imperatives, and on the other appear to be a source of dream and myth. Neumann, Jung, Adler, Assagioli and others have mapped portions of the inner world. Indeed, the path to psychological wholeness and self-realization often mirrors the quest for enlightenment and illumination common to traditions from Taoism and Buddhism to ancient mystery rites (those of Isis, Dionysus, Orpheus, Eleusis, etc.) and shamanic vision quests.

. . . Yet the discoveries of depth psychology have influenced individuals and institutions not always partial to spiritual experience (Jung's role in the formation of Alcoholics Anonymous comes to mind).

Scientists, such as James Lovelock and Lynn Margulies

(first wife of Carl Sagan, a respected research biologist in her own right), studying the biology and geology of Earth as a series of integrated, interdependent systems working in harmony and following patterns consistent with those of a self-regulating organism, term their theory, "the Gaia hypothesis." This doesn't mean they "worship" the goddess Gaia . . . but there is a resonance between the ancient conception of Earth as a living goddess and what we are discovering about the interdependence of life and the mechanisms that regulate the planet.

Scientific foundations, academic institutions, and government agencies aren't in the habit of awarding grants to study the role of ancient goddesses in the contemporary universe; investigating the workings of "dynamic systems," on the other hand, seems to deserve funding. One doesn't have to have a vested interest in mythology, or any spiritual belief system, to find value in these fields.

And then there's the internet, which also displays holographic properties—again bringing to mind the Net of Gems. Some consciousness researchers see in the internet a model of the way the brain has developed—links "spontaneously" established between disparate groups of cells, creating neural networks that perform specific functions (for example, clusters of cells throughout the brain related to hearing or to memory hook up and establish a network, in the same way those reading these words are linked by an interest in the ideas of Joseph Campbell, and how we relate those ideas to our individual lives and to society as a whole). The internet can also be perceived as a manifestation of Teilhard de Chardin's *noosphere*, the realm of consciousness, envisioned as a slender skin that floats upon the *biosphere*.

These are but bits and pieces—fragments of a yet

unrecognized myth?

Many more parts to the puzzle seem to be falling into place, too many to cover here—from Rupert Sheldrake's theories of morphic resonance, to HMO's accepting acupuncture and other alternative therapies, to the post-Darwinian concept of punctuated equilibrium in evolution, and, in particular, the gradually dawning awareness of environmental concerns in the public mind.

Of course, one could look ridiculous trying to stitch together an all-purpose mythology from these elements, none of which automatically posit a spiritual aspect to existence. We can't stage manage a myth—but taken together, they suggest the emergence of a new worldview that unconsciously shapes the way we relate to nature, and to each other, while at the same time accommodating personal spiritual beliefs (or the lack thereof—one doesn't have to be a Druid to protest clear cutting the forests or damming a river).

Secular disciplines, yes. I'm not suggesting science is the same as myth—but the mythic images science employs to express metaphorical relationships underlying the world around us can't help but evoke a sense of wonder and mystery that is religious in the deepest sense.

Any future, living myth must do the same.

Time alone will tell. Joseph Campbell provides a clue when he suggests any effective mythology will have to be a "mythology of this earth as of one harmonious being."

> [W]e are the children of this beautiful planet that we
> have lately seen photographed from the moon. We are
> not delivered into it by some god, but have come forth

from it. We are its eyes and mind, its seeing and its thinking. And the earth, together, with its sun, this light around which it flies like a moth, came forth, we are told, from a nebula; and that nebula, in turn, from space. So that we are the mind, ultimately, of space.

No wonder, then, if its laws and ours are the same! Likewise our depths are the depths of space, whence all those gods sprang that men's minds in the past projected onto animals and plants, onto hills and streams, the planets in their courses, and their own peculiar social observances.[24]

And so we come full circle—back to bedrock.

NOTES

1. Campbell, Inner Reaches of Outer Space, op. cit. 101.
2. Larsens, A Fire in the Mind, op. cit. 16.
3. Campbell, The Hero's Journey, op. cit. 42.
4. Joseph Campbell, "Seventy Years of Making Connections," interview by D.J.R. Bruckner, New York Times Book Review (December 18, 1983).
5. Campbell, Power of Myth, op. cit. 4, 5.
6. John Steinbeck, The Log from the Sea of Cortez (New York: Viking Press, 1951; New York: Penguin Classics, 1995), 123.
7. Campbell, Correspondence, op. cit. 48.
8. Steinbeck, op. cit. 116-117.
9. Larsens, A Fire in the Mind, op. cit. 204.
10. Eric Enno Tamm, Beyond the Outer Shores (New York: Four Walls Eight Windows, 2004), 91.
11. Ibid. 92.
12. Ibid. 93.
13. Steinbeck, op. cit. 178.
14. Campbell, Asian Journals, op. cit. 657.

15. Campbell, "Seventy Years of Making Connections," op. cit.

16. Campbell, Flight of the Wild Gander, op. cit. 37.

17. Joseph Campbell, "The Mythic Journey," interview by Joan Marler, The Yoga Journal (Nov./Dec. 1987).

18. Unpublished interview with Joseph Campbell by Costis Ballos (9-27-85), Box 93,, Folder 24, Joseph Campbell Papers, Manuscripts and Archives Division, The New York Public Library.

19. Campbell, Hero's Journey, op. cit. 15.

20. Campbell, Flight of the Wild Gander, op. cit. 35.

21. Campbell, Mythic Worlds, Modern Words, op. cit. 98.

22. Campbell, Thou Art That, op. cit. 47.

23. Campbell, Hero's Journey, op. cit. 22.

24. Campbell, Myths To Live By, op. cit. 266.

SIXTEEN

MOVIES:
THE MEDIUM FOR MYTH?

The modern myth has to do with machines, airshots, the size of the universe, it's got to deal with what we're living with.

Star Wars deals with the essential problem: Is the machine going to control humanity, or is the machine going to serve humanity? Darth Vader is a man taken over by a machine, he becomes a machine, and the state itself is a machine. There is no humanity in the state. What runs the world is economics and politics, and they have nothing to do with the spiritual life.

So we are left with this void. It's the job of the artist to create the new myths. Myths come from the artists.[1]

In the absence of a dynamic, contemporary mythology that supports the spiritual life, Joseph Campbell notes the creative artist is left holding the shaman's torch, illuminating the dark passages and sacred shadows for those who seek to experience the mysteries of myth. Campbell draws on the giants of twentieth century art and literature as examples of this principle in play—James Joyce, Thomas Mann, Paul Klee, and Pablo Picasso, among others. It's not difficult to equate Joe's conception of the artist with genius, particularly given a circle of friends and acquaintances that over his lifetime included sculptor Antoine Bourdelle, novelist John Steinbeck, dancer/choreographer Martha Graham, avante-garde musician John Cage, director George Lucas, and the Grateful Dead.

There has been a tendency to assume that the artist-as-shaman speaks only to an elite, as if there exists an unbridgeable divide between art and popular culture. Comic books, movies, television, video games, and such are considered merely the trappings of pop culture, the profit-oriented mass media mass-producing entertainment that serves primarily as an escape—bread and circuses to placate the restless mob.

But do films and other popular media play a role in creating and conveying mythologies? Does Hollywood merely borrow a mythic theme here and there, or might the movies serve as a vehicle for myth?

There are moments when Campbell wonders if Hollywood is up to the challenge:

> I never really caught on to the talkie as an interesting art. Too naturalistic, you know? Naturalism is the death of art. And that's one of the big problems in our American arts, I think—they don't understand the metaphor. It's all naturalism.[2]

and

I've never seen anything in movies that seemed to be myth-directed.[3]

In the wake of *Star Wars*, however, Campbell was willing to entertain previously unacknowledged possibilities . . . though not without some reservations.

LUCAS AN ANOMALY?

The motion picture as an art form held little appeal for the mature Joseph Campbell. He points out that he rarely went to the movies, as he was "deep into my scholarship"—and then Joe and his wife, noted dancer Jean Erdman, lived on the edge of Greenwich Village. Leisure time was more likely to be spent attending the theater—whether plays, dance, or other performance art—or in small, intimate, gatherings with close friends, many of whom were artists, both starving and established.

Jean eventually formed her own dance company and, with Joe's active participation, founded the influential Theater of the Open Eye. Jean and Joe lived, worked, and played in a creative setting their whole life together; immersed in the lively arts, they had little time to waste on seemingly frivolous fare.

Hence, they really weren't paying attention in the late seventies when the *Star Wars* phenomenon swept the country. According to Campbell, it had been at least 15 years since he had seen a movie—which indicates how little the film industry factored into Campbell's thought.

It's not that he didn't consider film an art form—in fact, in the sixties, Joseph Campbell served as president of the Creative

Film Foundation, a Maya Deren project designed to encourage and reward young artists; however, these student art films weren't designed with the general public in mind.

Joe later expressed his surprise on viewing Lucas's student effort, *THX 1138*, which paralleled themes and techniques common to submissions Campbell reviewed for the film foundation: "We had these by the dozen every year! It was very thrilling to see that this man had started out where they all start, you might say, and then in two enormous leaps made these grand strides . . ." (*The Hero's Journey*, 220).

Of course, you'd think Joe might have suspected something more than synchronicity when the one commercial film he does remember seeing in the sixties—Stanley Kubrick's production of Arthur C. Clarke's science fiction masterpiece, *2001: A Space Odyssey*—opened with a scene right out of *Primitive Mythology* (the first of Campbell's four volumes in *The Masks of God*)!

Fifteen years later Joseph experienced a major epiphany when, seemingly out of the blue, George Lucas flew Jean and Joe to San Rafael to view the first three episodes of the *Star Wars* saga (Episodes IV—VI), all in one day:

> I saw the *Star Wars* movies recently . . . And I could see my own stuff up there, no doubt about that. I ended up a fan, in great admiration of that young man. He has an artist's imagination and a great sense of responsibility to his public that what he is rendering must have value. And with all the galaxies out there to work with, he's got the kind of open field the early poets used to have. For example, when the Greek Argonauts go up into the Black Sea, where nobody had been, they could meet all kinds

of strange monsters and strange people—Amazons and such. It's a blank sheet for the play of the imagination.

As I watched these movies, I realized that he is systematically using the archetypes that he learned about from my books.[4]

But is George Lucas an anomaly? Is he the exception, or the rule? Are movies and other popular media proper vehicles for myth, or merely bromide for the masses? Are we in danger of revealing priceless secrets, harnessing mythic motifs in the service of mammon? Or might movies reflect the emerging cultural mythos?

PEARLS BEFORE SWINE?

Joseph Campbell seems of two minds at times. He might never have given the subject much thought had not Lucas' acknowledgement of Campbell's influence brought the matter to his attention. Campbell's views appear to evolve over time; while he is clearly fascinated by the possibilities of the medium, he's at the same time hesitant to trust an industry that favors the profit motive over artistic vision:

> [Movies] might be our counterpart to mythological re-enactments—except that we don't have the same kind of thinking going into the production of a movie that goes into the production of an initiation ritual . . . What is unfortunate for us is that a lot of the people who write these stories do not have the sense of their responsibility.

> These stories are making and breaking lives. But the
> movies are made to simply make money. The kind of
> responsibility that goes into a priesthood with a ritual is
> not there. That is one of our problems today.[5]

Money certainly drives the industry—but studios are unable
to completely ignore substance. Despite a tendency to appeal
to the lowest common denominator, only so many sequels to
Porky's and *Friday the 13th* suffice before a significant portion
of the audience develops a craving for greater depth and creativity. The film industry would stagnate were it to divorce
completely from the creative artist—those writers, directors,
and actors with vision.

Both Carl Jung and Joseph Campbell suggest the creative
imagination is formed of the same substance as myth and
dream—so the surprise would be if mythic themes and the
hero's journey were not represented in movies, as in the other
arts. Indeed, despite Campbell's concerns, several significant
films—such as the *Lord of the Rings* trilogy, *The Matrix*, *The
Chronicles of Narnia*, *The Passion of the Christ*, or the recent
Brokeback Mountain—are described by participants on all levels, from directors and writers to cast and crew, with a level of
passion, awe and commitment rivaling that of religious devotees—which suggests there are movies produced with the same
kind of attention to symbol and presentation that attends religious rites.

Campbell believes myths arise from the visionary experience of exceptional individuals, and offers examples of shamans
who translate the images of their visions into ritual and myth
(e.g., the Lakota shaman Black Elk, Keeper of the Sacred Pipe,

or Australian Aborigine shamans). These mythic images speak not to the head, but directly to the heart—and so a myth strikes a corresponding chord in the interior of those for whom it is meant, evoking a sense of *participation mystique.* Myths then continue to evolve as they are passed down from one generation to the next around communal fires, during sacred celebrations, or in transmission from one culture to another.

Unfortunately, myths and ritual tend to grow stagnant and rigid in the hands of an entrenched priesthood.

> The priest presents for consideration a compound of inherited forms with the expectation (or, at times, even requirement) that one should interpret and experience them in a certain authorized way, whereas the artist first has an experience of his own, which he then seeks to interpret and communicate through effective forms. *Not the forms first and then the experience, but the experience first and then the forms.*
>
> Who, however, will be touched by these forms and be moved by them to an experience of his own? By what magic can a personal experience be communicated to another? And who is going to listen?[6]

Today it is the artist who has an inward visionary experience and then gives it life, re-presenting the creative vision in a chosen medium. As to who "will be touched by these forms and be moved by them to an experience of his own," Campbell recognizes this as a possibility inherent in film. Asked whether people get any value from the mythic content of movies like *Star Wars* and *Excalibur*, he responds:

Well, I'm told they do, but I haven't seen a movie for something like fifteen years, and I can't speak from my own experience or judgment, but I think that the movie is the perfect medium for mythological messages. The medium is so plastic and pliable and magic things can happen. And then the combination, you know, of fantastic landscape and possible modes of action and voyaging that we can hardly conceive of in good solid terms . . . That's a mythological realm, and movies could handle this kind of thing.[7]

In *The Power of Myth*, Joe offers a specific example: "I've heard youngsters use some of George Lucas' terms—'the Force' and 'the dark side.' So it must be hitting somewhere. It's a good sound teaching, I would say."[8]

Michael Toms, citing Robert Bly, wonders if the cinematic presentation of mythological themes might be giving away the store to the uninitiated, revealing sacred mysteries better left secret. Campbell acknowledges Bly's concern, and points out that just presenting a mythological image is ineffective if it does not work on a level beyond rational consciousness:

You have to participate in it. That's the sense of the ritual—it's an enactment of a myth, and by participating in a myth you're participating in the mythic message. And myths don't count if they're just hitting your rational faculties; they have to hit the heart and then be absorbed, and you have to absorb them and adjust to them and make them your own life, and perhaps going from one movie to another like that, the thing's just passing too fast. People in a religious tradition live with that myth from infancy, and it builds in, builds in builds in . . . and one mustn't mistake just picking up a story, playing a role, for absorbing a myth and making it the structuring form of your life.[9]

And yet I'd argue that movies do that—not just an individual movie, in isolation, even one with the impact of *Star Wars*, but the sum of all movies the last century present a fluid medium on which is projected an ever-evolving cultural mythos—conscious or no, these images do reflect the structuring forms of our lives.

Joseph Campbell wasn't keeping track—but, had he the time to focus on the field of popular film over the decades, he might have noted a mythic tapestry as rich and vibrant as that underlying the other arts. Given that cinema evolved from theater, and the dramatic arts have their origin in the performance of sacred rites—and also considering that ritual, theater, and film all foster a suspension of disbelief, coupled with a sense of *participation mystique* known to trigger cathartic release— there should be little surprise that movies present a platform for myth.

Mythic Resonance

A common perception today seems to be that the novel has written "The End" to myth: an author may well weave archetypal images and mythic concerns into story, but no room is left for motifs to morph around the campfire as myths take on a life of their own; instead, each tale is etched in marble the moment the book rolls off the press. Novels remain individual efforts, intended for individuals, rather than elements of a dynamic, changing, living mythology . . . or, might that be a "myth"-conception?

Stories have a history of leaping from printed page to silver screen, whether we begin with classical literature or comic books. The classic tales are told and retold around our culture's version of the collective campfire, changing from year to year and generation to generation, in cast and presentation, if not in plot. Whether it's Alistair Sims, George C. Scott, or even Bill Murray who growls "Bah! Humbug!" we are still visited by the Spirits of Christmas, Past, Present, and Future, experiencing ever anew Scrooge's epiphany.

In fact, in my own experience, Christmas provides a textbook example of how the movies can support a mythic structure.

Christmas is my favorite holiday. The irony is that I am not able to draw on childhood memories or a strong family tradition; my siblings and I were the third generation in a strict fundamentalist cult that eschewed Christmas, Easter, and Halloween as pagan celebrations, observing instead the more biblical Hebrew festivals.

Our church's stance towards Christmas and similar "worldly" holidays was complete and total nonparticipation. I could not sing Christmas songs with my class, and had to leave school early the afternoons of the annual Halloween, Christmas, and Valentine's Day parties to avoid contamination—so no Easter Egg hunts, no trick-or-treat, no presents under the tree. Relatives who made the mistake of sending Christmas or birthday gifts had their packages returned unopened. I even recall church pastors railing from the pulpit that "Santa" is an anagram for "Satan"; a cheerful "Merry

Christmas!" from a helpful salesclerk was taken as a slap in the face and an insult to God.

Once off to college, however, I evolved beyond that mind-set (which only confirms what adherents of so many strict, literalist sects believe, whether Christian, Islamic, or other: a little education can be a dangerous thing).

Celebrating Christmas for the first time in my early twenties proved only slightly awkward: my first tree had bright lights and shiny, brand new Christmas ornaments, and looked no doubt a little like a superficial re-creation of a "real" Christmas tree. Took a few years to collect ornaments and trinkets imbued with personal *mana* (memories and recollections of significant moments and people in my life), and to learn the art of placing lights and ornaments deep within the interior of the tree, spontaneously creating dozens of warm, inviting, mysterious tableaus amid shifting shadows and light—but, nevertheless, Christmas came easy for me.

Why is that? In the absence of tradition and experience, how did the practice take root so well?

Even though my family never celebrated Christmas, we grew up in the womb of our culture. The mythology supporting that culture is woven into the fabric of our lives, whether we recognize it or not. We may have shied away from all things Christmas, but we could not shut out every image—and the mythic images we did see spoke a story to the heart at odds with the one the preachers directed to our heads.

Cary Grant, David Niven, and Loretta Young in *The Bishop's Wife*, O. Henry's altruistic lovers in "The Gift of the Magi," the longsuffering Jimmy Stewart in *It's a Wonderful Life*, the sweetly dysfunctional middle-America family of *A*

Christmas Story, the Christmas-stealing Grinch, or that magical *Polar Express*, all present bits and pieces of the Christmas mythos. . . which suggests how literature and movies reflect and even shape a culture's mythology.

Images from and references to the films and stories mentioned above permeate American culture, presenting themes picked up via osmosis; few films bludgeon the viewer with Christian doctrine. In fact, apart from Linus's recitation from the Gospel of Luke in *A Charlie Brown Christmas*, even the image of the Christ child in the manger floats, at best, somewhere in the distant background of most productions, while in the forefront compassion, joy, celebration, and renewal are emphasized—traits characteristic of all celebrations of the winter solstice regardless of culture.

Movies reflect myth, not dogma—they are better at conveying an experience of the heart than a detailed theology. Despite the childhood gap, I found myself firmly rooted in a tradition on which to draw as I embraced Christmas.

However, I didn't recognize the power of myth in the movies until I saw Christopher Reeves in *Superman*, in the late seventies.

Hard to miss the Messianic overtones: a baby not of this Earth, displaying supernatural powers, born of a heavenly father yet raised by surrogate human parents, comes of age, retreats into a desolate wilderness (the Arctic Circle) for a period of instruction and preparation, then returns to the world, sacrifices personal desires and relationships, and employs his power to benefit mankind.

Now where have we heard that story before?

We are compelled to keep telling each other the same

tales—comes with being human.

King Kong's legend, for example, has been told in 1933, 1976, and again in 2005—and that's not counting the various, inane *Son of Kong* sequels, knockoffs (like *Mighty Joe Young)* and innumerable guest appearances battling Godzilla and the other screen monsters who apparently regularly menace the Japanese archipelago.

The mythic resonance rings clear:

> It's really "Beauty and the Beast." It is a fairy story. Fairy stories are open to any number of interpretations. There's one for each member of the audience. And it's the same with this. (Documentary filmmaker Kevin Brownlow, commenting on Peter Jackson's *King Kong*, on *CBS Sunday Morning*, December 2006)

Even political pundits recognize mythic themes. PBS's John McLaughlin and conservative commentator Pat Buchanan saw in that last *King Kong* a reflection of an emerging "environmental religion," positing a Nature that has been defiled by civilization—an observation which, alas, would take us off course on a delicious, albeit distracting, tangent into the cosmic and cultural orientation of works ranging from *Dances with Wolves* to *Lord of the Rings* and *Avatar*—but the media's "talking heads" may be on to something.

Just as myths dream themselves onward around the communal campfire, so too do today's corresponding enchantments, shifting shape in the flickering light projected from Hollywood dream factories. Batman, sporting day-glo colors and campy plots in the sixties, turns dark and conflicted on the big screen, struggling with his own shadow, film after film. Peter Pan, too, appears in many guises, each of which further fleshes out this character: in a Disney cartoon; or, in the skin of Mary Martin or Cathy Rigby as the playful, somewhat androgynous *puer aeternus*; in the historical encounter that ignited author J. M. Barrie's imagination in Neverland; or in the middle-aged, world weary figure of Robin Williams, who has lost touch with the magic and creativity of childhood, in *Hook* . . . all riffs on a common motif—and so the myth dreams itself onward once more.

THE HERO IN A THOUSAND PICTURES

The pattern of the hero's quest did not originate with Joseph Campbell. Joe merely identified a motif long present in myth, fairy tale, legend, and literature of every type. This holds for film as well. Movies—yet another form of the storyteller's art—have spontaneously followed this same archetypal structure since well before Campbell wrote word one of *The Hero with a Thousand Faces* (1949).

At roughly the same time that Lucas introduced audiences to Darth Vader and Obi Wan Kenobi, Christopher Vogler—a story analyst for Disney—penned a seven-page memo entitled "A Practical Guide to The Hero with a Thousand Faces." Vogler cited examples in movies ranging from *The Wizard of Oz* and *High Noon* to *East of Eden* and *Annie Hall*.

The memo circulated throughout Disney before leaking out to the rest of the industry. Several studios consciously adapted "the Hero's Journey" as a screenwriting formula, a number that swelled after Lucas publicly acknowledged his debt to Campbell. *The Little Mermaid, Beauty and the Beast, The Lion King,* and *Shrek* are among the many productions crafted with Campbell's model in mind.

Vogler, in fact, was story consultant on the first two mentioned. His original memo has since been expanded into book form as *The Writer's Journey: Mythic Structure for Writers*—a surprisingly useful resource, offering a perceptive analysis of how Campbell's observations can be applied to the cinematic arts.

As wonderful a tribute as it is to acknowledge Campbell's influence, I doubt he'd be comfortable with a legacy of formulaic films tending towards uniformity and mediocrity, which is not to say that *The Lion King* and *Shrek* aren't brilliant and creative—I loved them—but they do spawn a slew of dull and predictable second- and third-rate efforts that follow the map yet manage to miss the sparkle. Vogler does attempt to inoculate his readers against this approach, but there have been Hollywood hacks—shades of Procrustes—who wield this design in cookie-cutter fashion, sacrificing substance in the process.

The mythic form Campbell identifies as "the hero's journey" tends to emerge *spontaneously* from the creative imagination: familiarity with Campbell's work can certainly inspire, as with Lucas and Spielberg, helping an artist recognize what it is that bubbles up from the depths of their own soul—but the hero's journey is no substitute for artistic vision. You can't just plug it in and get a masterpiece.

Indeed, one of the most elegant cinematic evocations of the hero's journey since Campbell's passing appears in the screen translation of *The Lord of the Rings.* Director Peter Jackson might be familiar with Campbell's work, but Tolkien's novels owe nothing to Joe's writing, except insofar as they both spring from a thorough grounding in the same source material. The trilogy is richly layered throughout with complex archetypal iconography, every image dense with mythic associations. Multiple elements of the hero's quest play out on myriad levels in combinations fresh and unique, yet ever echoing the common theme.

The correspondence between the trilogy (whether book or film) and Campbell's template is clear—a correspondence noted by scholars decades ago, later spelled out in Randall Helms' *Tolkien's World* (1974), and Anne Petty's *One Ring to Bind Them All: Tolkien's Mythology* (1979)—but its power resides in the fact that this correspondence is spontaneous, rather than derived.

In *The Hero with a Thousand Faces* (1949), Joseph Campbell identifies a trajectory common to most myths and hero tales, consisting of three major movements—*Separation, Initiation, Return*: A hero is called out of the ordinary, everyday world; undergoes trials and ordeals that culminate in initiation into a greater reality, one that transcends the individual; and then returns to the everyday world to share with others the boons that have been won.

> [Campbell] found that all storytelling, consciously or not, follows the ancient patterns of myth and that all stories, from the crudest jokes to the highest flights of literature, can be understood in terms of the Hero's Journey . . .
>
> The pattern of the Hero's Journey is universal, occurring in every culture, every time. It is as infinitely varied as the human race itself and yet its basic form

remains constant. The Hero's Journey is an incredibly
tenacious set of elements that springs endlessly from the
deepest reaches of the human mind; different in details
for every culture, but fundamentally the same.[10]

Of course, each movement of this arc is formed of a number
of related elements. No myth exhibits a one-to-one correspondence to every single element Campbell identifies in the hero's
adventure. Each myth unfolds its own twists and turns, its elements arranged in a configuration unique to itself, yet revealing
on examination an inherent organic structure that Campbell,
following Joyce, labels the *monomyth*.

Campbell's overarching monomyth thus recognizes
the different forks the road might take. (Hence no surprise
to find that many creators of interactive video games know
Campbell's work.)

For example, the Hero, living in the ordinary world,
hears a Call to Adventure, which inspires him to set out
on his journey—but this Call could take any of several different forms. It might be a clear invitation (e.g., Yahweh
instructing Moses through the burning bush to return to
Egypt and confront Pharaoh; Trinity's first contact with Neo
in *The Matrix*), or completely unconscious (a hunter, separated from his companions, pursuing a hart deep into a
dark, unknown part of the woods in Celtic legend; Richard
Dreyfus sculpting the Devil's Tower out of mashed potatoes
in *Close Encounters of the Third Kind*; Kevin Costner puz-
zling over a cryptic, disembodied voice in an Iowa cornfield
in *Field of Dreams*), or there might well be a Refusal of the
Call (Jonah fleeing by boat to avoid God's command to go

to Nineveh; Luke Skywalker initially declining Ben Kenobi's invitation to help him rescue Princess Leia).

Similarly, there is the meeting with the Mentor, which Campbell places near the beginning of the hero's journey. This movement in the cycle consists of a period of apprenticeship; the Mentor traditionally provides the Hero with the gifts necessary to face the ordeals he'll meet on his quest (Parzival's time with Gurnemanz, the veteran knight who trains him in the ways of chivalry, in Arthurian lore; Wesley's offscreen apprenticeship to the Dread Pirate Roberts in *The Princess Bride*; and, of course, Luke Skywalker's instruction from Obi-Wan Kenobi, and then Yoda, in *Star Wars*).

Eventually, after a series of tests and ordeals, the Hero arrives at the climax—the moment of initiation. And what is the initiation?

> Heroes must die so they can be reborn. The dramatic movement that audiences enjoy more than any other is death and rebirth. In some way in every story, heroes face death or something like it: their greatest fears, the failure of an enterprise, the end of a relationship, the death of an old personality. Most of the time, they magically survive this death and are literally or symbolically reborn to reap the consequences of having survived death. They have passed the main test of being a hero.[11]

No need to recall in detail the entire cycle: these are but a few of the elements of the Hero's Journey motif we find in so many movies, even those that are not overtly mythic—no gods and goddesses and such in *Casablanca* or the James Bond franchise, yet they too fit the classic pattern.

CORRESPONDING FUNCTIONS

> A mythological order is a system of images that gives consciousness a sense of meaning in existence, which my dear friend, has no meaning—it simply is. But the mind goes asking for meanings; it can't play unless it knows (or makes up) some system of rules.
>
> Mythologies present games to play: how to make believe you're doing thus and so. Ultimately, through the game, you experience that positive thing which is the experience of being- in-being, living meaningfully.[12]

Campbell speaks of four functions a mythology performs (which does not mean every myth in a mythological tradition speaks to all four functions). In brief, Campbell identifies these functions as follows:

> The Metaphysical (or Mystical) Function—"to evoke in the individual a sense of grateful, affirmative awe before the monstrous mystery that is existence."
>
> The Cosmological Function—"to present an image of the cosmos, of the universe round about, that will maintain and elicit this experience of awe."
>
> The Sociological Function —"to validate and maintain a certain sociological system: a shared set of rights and wrongs, proprieties or improprieties, on which

one's particular social unit depends for its existence."

The Psychological (or "Pedagogical") Function—
"to carry the individual through the stages of one's life,
from birth through maturity through senility to death."

The mythological orientation of Western culture remains in
flux (reflected in the much touted "culture wars" dividing the
United States), which, as Campbell points out, leaves the second and third functions in disarray, as the cosmology of the
Old Testament does not correspond to our experience and
understanding of the universe around us, nor can it be claimed
the laws that regulate a twenty-first century society are divinely
ordained; indeed, the bulk of our laws are at odds with the religious, civil, and dietary code enumerated by Moses in scripture
(for example, contemporary collective attitudes toward slavery
and polygamy have clearly evolved beyond what Yahweh com-
manded three thousand years ago.)

These functions now are more likely to fall under the purview of secular institutions—science, law, etc.

However, today we find the first and the fourth functions
addressed by creative artists, who effectively employ mythological imagery from a variety of traditions, ancient and modern,
corresponding to images and insights emerging from their own
depth experience.

> We don't have much in the way of myth today to
> help us through these transitions. We can turn to the
> leftover shards of the old myths, or we can try to turn
> to art.[13]

Joseph Campbell is referring to the life stages that the psychological function of mythology addresses—and immediately follows this observation with an analysis of how George Lucas does exactly that. Nor is Lucas alone. The common structure of the Hero's Journey, as delineated by Campbell, serves as a template for life's major initiations: birth, coming of age, finding a partner and raising a family, growing old and dying, can all be seen as variations on the hero's path.

No end of movies addresses this function—whether *Zorba the Greek, Field of Dreams, The Philadelphia Story, The Graduate, Gone with the Wind, The Unforgiven, The Notebook, Gandhi,* the list of films that offer wisdom and guidance through life's transitions is endless—and that's not even counting those with overtly mythic content.

We also find aspects of the cosmological and sociological functions of myth playing out onscreen, revealing a possible shift in the cultural perspective. For example, in 1953's *Thunder Bay*, James Stewart plays an oil company engineer whose mission is to convince Cajun shrimp fisherman that drilling for oil in their waters will not harm the shrimp (petroleum is *good* for the environment!). The archetype of Engineer-as-Hero—a movie staple throughout the first half of the twentieth century—bringing prosperity to the locals by building a dam, digging a canal, drilling for oil, all while battling irrational fears of economic and ecological devastation, nears its final hurrah with this film.

The shift in the collective mythos away from that mindset is in full swing by the last decades of the century as a more holistic, ecological notion of nature as sacred and inviolable appears—not only in "high concept" films such as *Koyaanisqatsi* (1983) and *Mindwalk* (1990), but filtering on down to B-grade action flicks (e.g., *On Deadly Ground,* 1994: Steven Segal wreaks vengeance on corporate villain Michael Caine, whose oil refinery has been raping both the environment and the native peoples of Alaska—maybe somebody had been lying about the shrimp?).

Similarly, in the film version of *The Lord of the Rings,* the evil wizard Saruman's industrial Orcs lay waste to the forest in order to build their war machines, thus calling down the wrath of Nature's peaceful, tree-herding Ents (who almost seem old-growth trees come-to-life themselves) . . . and, as mentioned above, even political pundits see this same environmental mythos reflected in *King Kong.*

Do films drive this shift in perspective?

Probably not directly—but a survey of film history suggests movies mirror the culture-at-large, so perhaps we are seeing hints of an emerging mythos that addresses the cosmological and sociological functions of myth in imagery more consistent with our own experience of the world around us. Though it's too early to tell if this shift in perspective is permanent—so much, after all, remains in flux—nevertheless, the multiplex at the local mall may offer better clues to the shape of the myth-to-come than does the neighborhood church.

HOLDING TO THE IMAGE

The magic of film is that it's formed of the same polymorphic fabric as myth and dream, woven from imagination—and image. The power and beauty of symbol lies in the complex associations, personal and mythic, embedded in each image.

These reach far beyond the conscious intent of any author, expanding the dimensions of a story, yet personalizing the experience for each hearer, reader, or member of the audience. Borrowing a term from Dr. John Weir Perry, Joseph Campbell described mythological archetypes as "affect-images," which speak to heart, not head.

> What Campbell did was to think in images. That's something different than thinking scientistically or logically. And Campbell opened this up—this question of images. I think that's the most important thing he did. That's why there are so many images in his books. Not only visual images of cave paintings or of statues or of goddesses and gods and so on, but poetic images, and if there had been a chance, probably musical images as well.[14]

Hillman also approves of Campbell's ability to relate his work to popular culture. Mythology is not reserved for the halls of academia alone. A myth is nothing more than a quaint, disembodied abstraction locked away in a book in the absence of people to partake of its magic; myths need people if they are to come to life.

By paying attention to all levels of culture, Campbell is able to chart changes in the creative imagination. For example, the appearance of the novel, a literary innovation often traced to Lady Murasaki Shikibu's *The Tale of Genji* in eleventh century Japan, paralleled broad changes in cultures throughout the world.

Campbell wonders if modern movies might signal a further evolution of forms:

> I see Lucas continuing a major concern of modern life
> and shifting from the world of literate minds to the
> popular masses who seem to me to be running the
> world. It's [as] though the spark had left the easel and
> writer's pen and jumped into the camera.[15]

But Campbell's influence does not stop at the popcorn counter. James Hillman takes the discussion of images past the marquee and out into the future:

> This movement to thinking in images is part of the
> movement of our times, because we are going to stop
> reading linear sentences—one that follows another,
> and will be watching video screens with three or four
> images in them, juxtaposing images. Kids are already
> doing that. Therefore the value of Campbell's work is
> his laying out the richness of images that people will
> need to use for truly deep images rather than Nintendo
> games. We'll have an information highway where you
> sit at your own monitor and you will be able to create a
> whole world of imagery—paintings and architecture,
> symbols, ruins. All the museums will be available. A
> kind of pioneer nucleus of that is the great intellec-
> tual and educational value of Campbell's work and
> his collection.[16]

Hillman offered these remarks in 1995, before the nascent internet experienced the explosive growth that has brought us to where we are today—and Campbell lived his entire life without ever receiving an email or venturing into cyberspace—yet

Hillman's observations ring eerily prophetic. Even surfing the web at random it's not unusual to stumble across evidence of Campbell's influence in the most unlikely of places.

Movies, video games, computers, and the internet all rely on image—which has ever been the basic construct of myth. We find the same mythological motifs surfacing in these developing technologies as in ancient mythologies, albeit in fresh configurations and novel relationships—nor should it be surprising that we also find many of the creative talents involved in these fields conceding Campbell's influence.

And so, poised on the edge of the future, we return to the original question: Are the movies—and other elements of popular culture—a proper medium for myth?

> So you see, it's one thing to get the old structure of the hero myth, but now they are pitching it out into the void, where it's possible to let the imagination go.[17]

The answer is likely yes—but it's not your grandfather's idea of myth anymore . . .

NOTES

1. Joseph Campbell, "PW Interviews: Joseph Campbell," interview by Chris Goodrich, Publishers Weekly Review (8-23-85).
2. Campbell, Hero's Journey, op. cit. 214.
3. Joseph Campbell, "Mythic Reflections," interview by Tom Collins, In Context: A Quarterly of Humane Sustainable Culture No. 12 (Winter 1985/1986): 52.
4. Campbell, Pathways to Bliss, op. cit. 131.
5. Campbell, Power of Myth, op. cit. 102.

6. Campbell, Mythic Dimension, op. cit. 226.
7. Campbell, The Wisdom of Joseph Campbell, op. cit. Tape 3 Side 1.
8. Campbell, Power of Myth, op. cit. 177.
9. Campbell, The Wisdom of Joseph Campbell, op. cit.
10. Chris Vogler, The Writer's Journey: Mythic Structure for Writers, 3rd edition (Studio City: Michael Wiese Productions, 2007; 25th Anniversary edition, 2020), 4. Reprinted with permission from Michael Wiese Productions. Citations from 3rd edition.
11. Ibid. 155.
12. Campbell, Pathways to Bliss, op. cit. 6.
13. Ibid. 17.
14. Jams Hillman, "This Question of Images," in Saga: Best New Writings on Mythology, Vol. 1, ed. Jonathan Young (Ashland: White Cloud Press, 1996), 17.
15. Campbell, "Seventy Years of Making Connections," op. cit.
16. Hillman, ibid.
17. Joseph Campbell, "An Interview with the Master of Mythology," interview by Joe Nigg, The Bloomsbury Review (April/May 1984): 21-23.

SEVENTEEN

THE MYTHOLOGY OF ARCHETYPES

> The archetypes to be discovered and assimilated are precisely those that have inspired, throughout the annals of human culture, the basic images of ritual, mythology, and vision.[1]

The concept of the archetype is central to Joseph Campbell's understanding of mythology. Cross out every instance of "archetype," "primordial images," "mythic motifs," "archetypal images," "symbol," and related terms that appear in his work, and we have major holes and unreadable books.

And yet pinning down an archetype is as easy as stapling your shadow to the wall. Like so many concepts associated with mythology and depth psychology, archetypes are quicksilver by nature—indeed, that shape-shifting quality is responsible for their effectiveness, and their allure.

What, then, does Campbell mean by the term? What role do archetypes play in myth and psychology? What is their source? Are archetypes gods, metaphors, or simply convenient designations? Or might they merely be insubstantial products of the imagination with little bearing on reality? Apart from the specialized vocabulary of literature, art, psychology, and myth, have archetypes any practical application in our lives today?

"Elementary, My Dear Watson"

Joseph Campbell finds variations on the same basic motifs universally occurring throughout the myths and rituals of all cultures. Many of these images precede the written word— whether painted on pottery, shaped into figurines, or even etched on stones and bones, stretching tens of thousands of years into the past.

Campbell isn't the first to discover these patterns. The pioneering anthropologist Adolf Bastian, in the nineteenth century, refers to these motifs as *Elementargedanken*—"elementary ideas." However, we never meet these mythic structures in their raw form, but rather cloaked in raiment peculiar to each culture, which Bastian calls the *Völkgedanken*—"folk (or ethnic) ideas."

> [O]ne of the ways we realize an image is archetypal is because we see it turning up in different cultures and different times: we see a pattern, as well as the particular local instance. Studying a mythic image over thousands of years, there gradually emerges a pattern of constancy and variation that allows an evaluation of how these ideas are expressed, sometimes finely, sometimes crudely, sometimes only partially . . .[2]

The *axis mundi*, for example, or world axis—that still point around which the universe revolves—is a pattern evoked through archetypal imagery found in all mythologies: the Tree of Life, inscribed on cylinder seals from ancient Sumer over four thousand years ago, and again in the Garden of Eden creation story; the *djed* pillar, raised during rites sacred to Osiris, the dead-and-resurrected god of ancient Egypt; the serpent-entwined *caduceus* of Hermes, in Greece; the spinal column, up which the *kundalini* serpent rises in the yogic traditions of India; the Bo tree, under which the Buddha achieves illumination; the cross, to which Christ is nailed; *Yggsdrasil*, the World Tree of Nordic mythology, on which Odin crucifies himself; and the totem pole, common to the coastal peoples of the Pacific Northwest—all variations on one underlying theme . . . and yet, despite obvious congruencies, these variations are often distinct and dramatic, reflecting differences in cultures and beliefs.

Though Campbell wholeheartedly supports the study of the differences between cultures — those unique expressions of Bastian's *Völkgedanken*, which he believes more the province of historians and ethnologists—he nevertheless is drawn to the parallels, focusing on the universal aspects of these images, individual and collective. Because of that focus, some critics automatically assume Campbell believes a psychological reading of myth the only interpretation possible—an assumption that suggests a lack of familiarity with the man's work.

Joseph Campbell, however, cannot ignore the grounding of universal themes in the human psyche:

> For example, the idea of survival after death is about conterminous with the human species; so also that of

the sacred area (sanctuary), that of the efficacy of ritual, of ceremonial decorations, sacrifice, and of magic,
that of supernal agencies, that of a transcendental yet
ubiquitously immanent sacred power (*mana, wakonda,
sakti*, etc.), that of a relationship between dream and the
mythological realm, that of initiation, that of the initiate (shaman, priest, seer, etc.), and so on, for pages. No
amount of learned hair-splitting about the differences
between Egyptian, Aztec, Hottentot, and Cherokee
monster-killers can obscure the fact that the primary
problem here is not historical or ethnological but psychological—even biological; that is to say, antecedent
to the phenomenology of the culture styles . . .[3]

To that list of mythological patterns, I would add time, space,
the cosmic sea, the great goddess, the tree of life, the serpent,
virgin birth, the hero, sacrifice, the mandala, illumination, and
a host of other images culled from Campbell's writings.

THE INHERITED PATTERN

In "Psyche & Symbol," the opening lecture in the *Mythos*
DVD series, Joseph Campbell identifies Carl Jung as the twen-
tieth-century psychologist whose work says the most to him.

> Now I don't present Jung as a final, definitive theorist.
> His work is suggestive—this is an enormous subject full
> of mystery still. I want to begin . . . by reviewing Jung's
> approach to the problem of [Bastian's] Elementary

Ideas, which he calls "archetypes of the collective unconscious." Now that immediately gives us a psychological ground on which to build—that these are, in some way, features in the unconscious of the human animal, and that experiences that come in through the nervous system are assimilated and interpreted in terms of the psychological ground, archetypes.[4]

Jung borrowed the term archetype from Plato, Pliny, Cicero, St. Augustine, the *Corpus Hermeticum,* and other classical sources, re-defining it for the purposes of depth psychology. He describes archetypes as "Forms or images of a collective nature which occur practically all over the earth as constituents of myths and at the same time as autochthonous, individual products of unconscious origin." (note 17, *The Hero with a Thousand Faces,* 342)

It is necessary to point out once more that archetypes are not determined as regards their content, but only as regards their form and then only to a very limited degree . . . The representations themselves are not inherited, only the forms, and in that respect they correspond in every way to the instincts, which are also determined in form only. The existence of the instincts can no more be proved than the existence of the archetypes, so long as they do not manifest themselves concretely.[5]

Jung distinguishes between archetypes—which are unknown and unknowable to waking consciousness, any more than we can directly apprehend a raw instinct (which we identify by its effect in our lives)—and archetypal images. In the phenomenal world—which is where we all live—what we encounter and engage are those archetypal expressions, rather than the archetype itself.

Both Jung and Campbell speak of archetypes as structuring patterns of the human psyche. Our imprinted experiences, collective and individual, fill out and take the shape of these inherited forms in much the same way a crystal's shape follows the parameters of a basic, recurring pattern (which doesn't mean all crystals look the same and are identical—plenty of room for variation and individuality—and yet we all recognize the pattern).

Each human, for example, has ten fingers—the collective inheritance of our species—so it's no surprise that "base ten" is a numerical system common to most cultures—an archetypal numbering, so to speak. Critics might argue that humans are not born with base ten in their head, and they would be right— but that's not necessarily what Campbell and Jung are claiming when they speak of "archetypes of the collective unconscious." One needn't automatically assume that there's some sort of mystic, esoteric transmission of information wafting across the ether from one generation to the next, or, conversely, that base ten is embedded in our DNA.

On the other hand (pun intended), our inherited biology—the structure of our body—shapes our experience of reality. We can fairly easily tick ten items off on our fingers—but after that, we need to borrow someone else's hand. Hence, base ten becomes the default numbering system in many cultures.

Perhaps, if we had only eight fingers, base ten would just be a difficult concept in grade school arithmetic, rather than the context within which we experience the world around us.

ARCHETYPE AND INSTINCT

Jung does suggest that archetypes are related to the instincts, which leads to a school of thought that archetypes are the same as instincts—a far cry from gods! Marie-Louise von Franz and Emma Jung (Carl's wife) clarify Jung's remarks in their work on the Grail: "As inborn possibilities of forms of behavior and comprehension, the archetypes are connected with the instincts, *with which they have a reciprocal relationship*" (*The Grail Legend*, 37, emphasis mine).

The same mistake is made by those who read the first hundred pages of *Primitive Mythology* and think Campbell is arguing that only biology—genes and instinct—drive myth and archetype, ignoring the context of the rest of his work. Campbell certainly believes that myth, like dream, has a biological basis—but he doesn't cling to a causal relationship, instead revealing a correspondence between biological, biographical, mythological, mystical, psychological, and cosmic perspectives. As suggested in the myths of many cultures, these are all different layers, different dimensions, of oneself: no single one causes the other—they just all go together, like the notes of one chord.

I see a pretty girl whose qualities seem to match my *anima* image (in brief—and barely scratching the surface—"the personification of the feminine nature of a man's unconscious," sometimes inadequately described as one's inner female ideal) and heart starts to flutter, pheromones are released, and the dance begins. The eternal mating ritual unfolds—clearly, a biological impulse at work—yet that's not what I experience! I live a passion play, experience the consequence of individual choices, endure agonies and ecstasies in the loving and living of life—an experience rich, complex, and far more fulfilling than suggested by any sterile, clinical term like instinct!

Our DNA plays a role in providing the context for, if not the specifics of, individual experience—but the fact that I fall in love with Amy rather than Betty or Cindy is not genetically predetermined. My anima image is shaped by several factors, including proximity, influence, and impact of my mother and other female figures in early childhood (teachers, relatives, etc.), as well as contemporary cultural ideals (e.g., Rubenesque figures of centuries past vs. the slender models that serve as today's yardstick). Nevertheless, what is biologically based is the drive to mate, to unite with some other, and procreate. How this need is met is individually determined and takes a variety of forms, from sheer lust and physical sex, to intimacy, love, marriage, platonic friendship, religious celibacy (union with God), etc.

The Autonomous Archetype

But there seems more to it than what's been said so far. It feels as if we're circling something unseen, rather than directly addressing the question.

What is an archetype?

The short answer is you just can't put it into words.

Jung, in *Structure and Dynamics of the Psyche* (*Collected Works*, Vol. VIII), speculates that "the real nature of the archetype is not capable of being made conscious . . ."

Archetypes are examples of what Campbell, quoting Heinrich Zimmer, calls "the best things, which cannot be told." The second best things are conversations about those "best things, which cannot be told," and so are often misunderstood. A discussion of the archetypes falls into Zimmer's "second best" category—difficult to comprehend, for we are using words to describe what is beyond words.

Hence, though Jung often relates archetypes to instincts (which arise from the physical body), elsewhere (*Structure and Dynamics of the Psyche*, as well as his essay, "On Synchronicity"), he conceives archetypes as existing outside space and time, believing them responsible for the "meaningful coincidences" we experience (for which he coined the term synchronicity). It's difficult to empirically locate archetypes both in the body, and floating somewhere outside time and space in the same instant . . . unless we realize that instincts and inherited structuring principle and gods and even archetype are all metaphors— yes, metaphors—for that which cannot be precisely defined, labeled, analyzed, or categorized.

How any of us interpret archetype may depend on where we're standing at the time. It's a slippery, shape-shifting term, and Jung and Campbell seem to prefer it slippery and shape-shifty.

> Even the best attempts at explanation are only more
> or less successful translations into another metaphori-
> cal language (Indeed, language itself is only an image.).

> The most we can do is to dream the myth onwards and
> give it a modern dress . . . The archetype—let us never
> forget—is a psychic organ present in all of us.[6]

Though we risk losing ourselves in Zimmer's realm of the
"second best things," there is a longer answer to the question,
"What is an archetype?"

A working definition can be found in *Jung for Beginners*:

> Universal patterns or motifs which come from the col-
> lective unconscious and are the basic content of reli-
> gions, mythologies, legends, and fairy tales; emerging
> in individuals in the form of dreams, visions and fanta-
> sies. The archetype carries specific energy and is capable
> of acting upon the world.[7]

The author, Jungian analyst Jon Platania, directs the reader's
attention again to that last sentence: *"The archetype carries specific energy and is capable of acting upon the world."*

Clearly, as used by Jung and Campbell and company,
an archetype is far more than an abstract pattern. In Jung's
words, "The archetype is a phenomena of *'numinous'* or 'God-
like' dimensions. The archetype is in a very real sense alive and
functioning in the world. The archetypes thus have their own
initiative and their own specific energy. These powers enable
them both to produce a meaningful interpretation and to
interfere in a given situation."

In the Jungian model of the psyche, archetypes are unable
to directly access, or to be directly perceived within, mundane
reality—but when patterns that evoke the archetype arise in an

individual's life, a "complex" set of behaviors are constellated, in effect adding flesh to the archetype as it comes to life in the individual. This complex is often projected unconsciously out onto others who have hooks in their own personalities on which those projections can catch (e.g., the shadow complex—"lazy hippies," "fascist cops," etc.) and can even "possess" an individual if the underlying archetypal energy has been neglected in one's life.

How does Jung arrive at this understanding?

COMPLEX PSYCHOLOGY

I have met many who believe Jung's concept of the collective unconscious is the result of an intuitive leap—vague, touchy-feely, New Agey wishful thinking. True, Jung does have a reputation as an imaginative theorist—however, a closer study reveals that many of his "intellectual abstractions" are grounded in empirical science—indeed, his reputation and stringent research methods are what brought him to Freud's attention, providing validation for some of Freud's observations in the eyes of the greater scientific community.

Ironically, it is this same clinical research that led Jung to his theory of archetypes almost a century ago.

Jung came to Freud's attention in 1905 with the publication of the results of his pivotal word association experiments (conducted from 1901–1904). At this point in time Freud's star seemed to be fading, with few in the psychiatric community taking either his theories or his drawing room practice very seriously. Carl Jung, on the other hand, was widely respected as a researcher in the medical profession despite his youth. In his position as senior physician at the Burgholzli clinic (the psychiatric facility associated with the University of Zurich) he was on the front lines in the field of experimental psychology.

Many of the patients confined to Burgholzli suffered from *dementia praecox* (schizophrenia) and other debilitating psychiatric disorders. At the time, many doctors thought these disorders might be the result of brain lesions, which, alas, could only be discovered through the process of autopsy—just a little late to help the patient.

Carl Jung and his colleague, Dr. Franz Riklin, Sr., sought to explore the possibility that word association tests could point to the presence of brain lesions. Jung was not looking for the existence of unconscious, semi-autonomous complexes in the human psyche that interfere with conscious processes—but that's what he found.

Word association tests evoke in the popular conception an image of a psychiatrist giving a patient a word and noting the response. Most people assume there are right answers and wrong answers, and hence the psychiatrist must be looking for the right answer . . . and if we get the wrong answer, then there's something wrong with us. However, it's a bit more complex than that (pun again intended).

At first, they followed a format similar to Freud's practice of free association, but dropped that technique in favor of a more rigorous, scientific approach. Each subject was administered a list of one hundred words chosen for the rich associations possible (for example, "king" or "mother" inspire a greater variety of immediate, spontaneous associations than, say, "is").

Jung and Riklin and their colleagues weren't testing for

the "correct" answer. They early on noticed that most words on the list evoked an immediate, impromptu reply . . . but for each subject a handful of words triggered a disruption in the patient's response—hesitations, stuttering, asking to repeat the word, etc. These words tended to group together in related clusters (or complexes) that reflected unconscious disturbances within the individual's psyche.

> Jung found that his patients differed in the amount of time they took to formulate responses to the stimulus-words, usually hesitating before those that had something to do with distressing personal information. Together with Riklin, he coined the term "complex" to stand for "personal matter" that was "always a collection of various ideas, held together by an emotional tone common to all."
>
> The investigators measured precisely the amount of time it took the subject to answer, which they believed determined the underlying complex, or the root cause of the patient's distress . . . Words such as "marriage" or "mother," for example, often provided striking insights into the subject's mind.
>
> Besides the actual time it took the subject to answer, they measured other factors, which included prolonged delay or an outright inability to respond. They sought reasons that might underlie superficial or spurious reactions and paid careful attention to the reasons that the subject expressed some responses in highly charged and emotional language. Jung adapted and encapsulated Theodore Ziehen's term *gefuhlsbetonter*

Vorstellungcomplex (usually translated and explained as an emotionally charged complex of representations, of which the patient was probably unaware) into the single word: "complex."

In his terminology, he used the word to designate detached fragments of personality that maintained an independent, autonomous function within the unconscious, and from which they (i.e., one or more complexes) were capable of exerting an influence on the conscious mind. Jung described the complex as an "agglomeration of associations" that were "rather difficult to handle."[8]

Jung and Riklin and their colleagues (Drs. Frederick W. Peterson, Charles Ricker, J.B. Lang, Emma Furst, and Ludwig Binswanger, among other doctors in France, England, and America), upon noting the unconscious interference with conscious, spontaneous associations, thus designed the experiment to test for these interruptions.

Jung started with 38 normal subjects as a control group (which led him to conclude "the concept of normality must be very elastic," as complexes were found to be active in "normal" people as well), before expanding the testing to those suffering from hysteria, schizophrenia, and other pathologies. Over the four years the experiments ran, the list of words administered grew to four hundred—and clear patterns emerged in terms of the cluster of words that evoked an interrupted response. For example, "father," "police," "king," and "sun" might be part of a cluster suggesting a father complex—an authority complex—but rarely "sun" and "womb," or "father" and "cave."

Could these hesitations be conscious?

Well, out of a list of four hundred words, try for example to consciously not respond to just those words that evoke, say, authority, while spontaneously replying to the rest . . . just not possible—especially not for those suffering from psychological disturbances. Many times even "normal" subjects were flustered and seemed at a loss as to why they responded as they did, as they weren't always conscious of the disturbing personal contents contained within these complex clusters.

Just in case there might be some sort of unconscious distortion or bias in the way the researchers measured responses, Jung eventually employed a psychogalvanometer—measuring breath rate, perspiration, pulse, and skin conductivity—to record the physiological response to stimulus-words. Whatever dynamic interrupted the subject's verbal response to the stimulus-word turned out to also affect unconscious physical reactions—which suggests a degree of recognition and autonomy distinct from conscious intent.

The cluster of words to which subjects reacted—Jung's "feeling-toned complexes"—while related to the personal circumstances of each subject, provided evidence of unconscious structure underlying the human psyche. Jung's work was thus the first to experimentally confirm the existence of the unconscious, and so rescued Freud's reputation. Ironically, Jung's research provided the ground for a much broader view of unconscious processes than that espoused by Freud, though it took a few years for those possibilities to gel in Jung's mind. By 1911, Jung had noticed that each complex uncovered in his patients, though weighted with personal content, revolved around themes congruent with motifs echoing throughout mythologies from all eras and cultures—suggesting a collective core that serves as a magnet round which these personal contents cluster—an unseen structuring agent that Jung labeled the archetype.

The concept of the collective unconscious is thus rooted in empirical data collection. Jung didn't start with the theory of archetypes and work backwards from there . . .

(*Psychology Today*, without mentioning Jung, printed a blurb in 2005 criticizing "word association experiments," but the column was a bit vague itself, and the flaws detailed describe a fuzzy, sloppy approach closer to the free association of Freudian psychology—assuming, for example, that results are a subjective call of the researcher rather than measured physiological responses outside the administrator's control—very different from the rigorous standards applied by Jung. These justifiable complaints about sloppy performance seem nevertheless projected backwards in many people's minds to include Jung's research—guilt by association?)

Archetypes are not how we hope to act—but are very real energies that exert considerable power in an individual's life. We feel the influence of archetypes in our various complexes and neuroses, relationships, and patterns of behavior. It's as if these archetypes are driven to live life—to take on flesh, so to speak, and engage the world of external phenomenal reality. Generally, this drive is satisfied through us, via complexes constellated within us acting as agents or manifestations of specific archetypes, moving us, for example, to fall in love, or raise a family. When we resist or repress these impulses the back flow builds, until the dam bursts. The archetype often then "takes possession"—think of Hitchcock's *Psycho* as an extreme cinematic example—talk about a mother complex!

Jung identifies a number of figures one meets in dream—the archetypal images of the Shadow, Anima and Animus, Wise Old Man, Wise Old Crone, and other figures populating the pantheon of the individual psyche. My anima, for example may appear in dream tonight as maybe Betty, or Susan, or some other woman to whom I am drawn—but neither Betty nor Sue is my idealized anima image, which is a product of my interior world. However, this archetypal figure is often projected onto real flesh-and-blood women, and so I find myself married to Betty or Sue . . .

Archetypes thus shape and mediate our experience of the exterior world.

The same is true at the collective level. Myths are expressions of the archetypal dynamics of the collective psyche; these myths often collect around specific historical figures and events (e.g., there really was a Troy, at conflict with various Greek city-states off and on for generations), but it is those mythic patterns which fuel history, not the other way around. (For example, we don't know if there ever was an Achilles, but we do know that the frenzied battle rage that possessed him reflects an experience common in battle, reminiscent of the Viking *berserkers*—and excavations of Troy's ruins hint of this spirit animating conflicts between Trojan and Greek . . .)

On the other hand, from the individual perspective, these myths ring true only if they are rooted in history—personal history. The labors of Hercules, the wanderings of Ulysses, Parzival's quest for the Grail, all harmonize with my personal experience. I recognize the same stirrings, the same feelings, and the same energies unfolding in my life.

Are Archetypes The Same As Gods?

Yes – and no . . .

Jung clearly finds some overlap between gods and goddesses and archetypes.

> Today, we call the gods "factors," which comes from
> "*facere*"—"to make." The makers stand behind the
> wings of the world-theater . . . This is a new problem.
> All ages before us have believed in gods in some form
> or other. Only an unparalleled impoverishment of sym-
> bolism could enable us to rediscover the gods as psychic
> factors, that is, as archetypes of the unconscious . . .
> All this would be superfluous in an age or culture that
> possessed symbols.[9]

Here Jung boldly asserts a parallel between gods and archetypes. He also occasionally refers to individual deities and
myths as archetypes. Campbell does much the same; for
example, in an interview with Michael Toms, he describes
Quetzalcoatl as "an equivalent archetype" to Christ. (*An
Open Life*, 47)

So Jung, who coined the term as it's used today, and
Campbell, who constructs his life work around the archetypal
elements of myth, at times use the terms interchangeably, which
does unnerve some orthodox Jungians that tend to concretize
the archetype, using it to refer only to "a specific organizing
principle in the psyche."

Unlike his disciples, Jung is fluid and expansive, and
not so rigid in his use of the term (which brings to mind

an apocryphal saying attributed to C.G. himself: "Thank God I am Jung and not a Jungian!"). We can, of course, count on Jung to be confusing if we expect one precise, specific answer. What we actually get are a number of precise, specific, and seemingly contradictory answers—but then, in the realm of myth and dream we should be used to paradox by now.

Elsewhere, Jung uses "archetypal images" or "archetypal expressions" to refer to gods and goddesses and figures in dream and imagination, distinguishing between these personages and the archetype—which bolsters the argument of those who claim that the gods are not archetypes.

Are gods and archetypes identical?

Not quite—there is overlap there, but they aren't always the same thing.

Those who rigorously profess all archetypes are gods, and/or vice versa, risk falling into the same trap as those who claim no overlap—thus concretizing the metaphor. This is why I prefer to say that gods/goddesses and archetypes are *congruent*—a word that does not mean identical, equal, or exactly the same, but corresponding—or, as in math, "coinciding when superimposed."

Archetypes are so much more than gods and goddesses, so much more than the traditional inner pantheon of archetypal Mother, Father, Anima, Wise Old Man, Self, and the other denizens of psyche. Ultimately an archetype—like gods and other mythic metaphors—points to what is transcendent, what is beyond thought and word.

The Numinous

The essence of archetype for me is found, among other places, in Jung's *Man and His Symbols*, a work unfinished at the time of his death. Jung describes how

> . . . archetypes appear in practical experience: They are, at the same time, both images and emotions. One can speak of an archetype only when these two aspects are simultaneous. When there is merely the image, then there is simply a word-picture of little consequence. But by being charged with emotion, the image gains numinosity (or psychic energy); it becomes dynamic, and consequences of some sort must flow from it.[10]

Powerful language!

We can talk about love, or we can talk about Cupid—yet these are not in themselves archetypes.

Feel the sting, though, of Eros's shaft as it pierces your heart, the burn of desire that consumes you, the rapture that seizes you as you are overwhelmed by love for some other, and you know you are in the presence of something greater than yourself, something greater than all the world.

Archetype? God? Does it really matter what we call it?

Jung continues:

> I am aware that it is difficult to grasp this concept, because I am trying to use words to describe something whose very nature is incapable of precise definition. But

since so many people have chosen to treat archetypes as part of a mechanical system that can be learned by rote, it is essential to insist that they are not mere names, or even philosophical concepts. They are pieces of life itself—images that are integrally connected to the individual by the bridge of the emotions. That is why it is impossible to give an arbitrary (or universal) interpretation of any archetype . . .

The mere use of words is futile when you do not know what they stand for. This is particularly true in psychology, where we speak of archetypes like the anima and animus, the wise man, the great mother, and so on. You can know all about the saints, sages, prophets, and other godly men, and all the great mothers of the world. But if they are mere images whose numinosity you have never experienced, it will be as if you were talking in a dream, for you will not know what you are talking about. The mere words you use will be empty and valueless. They gain life and meaning only when you try to take into account their numinosity—i.e., their relationship to the living individual . . .[11]

But, unfortunately, those rare people who do not deny the very existence of the archetypes almost invariably treat them as mere words and forget their living reality. When their numinosity has thus (illegitimately) been banished, the process of limitless substitution begins—in other words, they glide from archetype to archetype, with everything meaning everything. It is true enough that the forms of the archetypes are to a

considerable extent interchangeable. But their numinosity is and remains a fact, and represents the value of an
archetypal event.[12]

Jung doesn't mince words. An archetype is "a living reality,"
charged with numinosity—a sacred experience, fully engaging one's emotions. We can speak of Artemis, see a picture
of Shiva, or hear a sermon about Jesus—yet these are not
archetypes. If, however, you pray to Artemis, if you feel her
breath on your neck in the woods beneath the full moon,
or if you dance with Shiva, let your ego, your soul, your
being, dissolve into nothingness, dissolve into the dance,
or you experience the transformative power of sacrifice and
resurrection as you eat the flesh and drink the blood in communion with Christ, you are living/experiencing/engaging
an archetype.

> Though it is true that such living ideas become mani-
> fest only in terms of some specific historical moment,
> their force nevertheless lies not in what meets the eye
> but in what dilates the heart, and this force, precisely, is
> their essential trait.[13]

PRACTICAL ASPECTS:
ENGAGING THE ARCHETYPE

Psychologists Carl Jung and James Hillman, philosopher James Ogilvie, mythologist Joseph Campbell
and others have explored the polytheism of human

nature, showing that our inner life is many-dimensional, multilayered, and teeming with presences of various kinds. This rich complexity, they have argued, is inescapable. If we do not accommodate the many powers in which we are secretly rooted, they come to us anyway, as physical sickness, depression, obsession, or unexpected epiphanies that disrupt our everyday functioning. We are led, gradually or suddenly, sometimes successfully and sometimes not, to live in many dimensions at once.[14]

"Vocatus atque non vocatus deus aderit," reads the inscription carved above the door to Carl Jung's home—"Called or not called, the god will be present."

We ignore the power of the archetype at our peril, as Murphy points out above. But if the archetype is inescapable, aren't we then consigned to always playing the victim?

Jung offers a warning, and a clue: "When an inner situation is not made conscious, it appears outside as fate."

But can we consciously call forth what is unconscious within us?

Archetypes have little to do with consciousness. As we become conscious of the archetypes active in our lives, those archetypes tend to lose much of their power over us—but the more unconscious we are of a working archetype, the more it shapes and controls our behavior. We do not choose an archetype—the archetype chooses us. Often, a complex constellation of events and experiences will activate an archetype (for example, after years of fitful slumber, the resurgence of Ares/Mars in the national psyche in the wake of 9/11). The most common triggers are basic life initiations—coming of age, intimate relationships, bearing and raising children, etc.

Archetypes are primary.

If we allow the archetypes a life, provide a conscious conduit for these energies to express themselves and engage the outer world, then all is well

. . . but if we don't acknowledge these forces, deny them a life, they will take over ours, even at the expense of life itself.

We open such channels by tending to ritual, myth, and dream—the practical aspect of archetypes.

> We carry all potentialities within us. It is not by reason and conscious will that we can rouse them from their slumber when the need arises. But the symbolic, revealed again and again in myth, practiced forever anew in the rite, has this magical conjuring power over our unconscious . . .
>
> The archetypes or variants of archetypes in myths and rites speak to the unconscious, which no rational admonition or consolation can reach; in the unconscious they encounter something that is related to them at work in its depths, which they awaken and make into an instrument of the regent within us, a guiding image which can gain power over our individuality and adapt its behavior to that of the archetype.
>
> Thus such archetypes, awakened from their slumber within us, become visible images and effect transformations in us; when called forth by kindred archetypes in myth and observance, they rise up within us and become our guides. Our conscious will cannot

create such guides . . . and this archetype summoned
from our depths preserves us; it prevents our formless
forces from tearing our personality apart or driving it
to madness under the pressure of the eternal contents
of life, of the destiny that oppresses and threatens to
crush us.[15]

Campbell illustrates this dynamic in action (but one of multiple examples of this process found throughout his work):

The Navajo perform a healing ceremony, which involves
the creation of a large sand painting that portrays a
healing myth. The patient is placed in the center of the
sand painting, where the patient or initiate is ceremonially identified in mind and heart and costume with
the mythological protagonist of the relevant legend. He
or she actually enters physically into the painting, not
simply as the person whose friends and neighbors have
solicitously assembled, but equally as a mythic figure
engaged in an archetypal adventure of which everyone
present knows the design.[16]

Carl Jung refers to this as getting back into an archetypal
situation:

The old priests and medicine men understood this, not by
knowledge, but by intuition. They tried to get a sick man
back into an archetypal situation . . . What is the use of
such foolishness? I assume that these people were by no
means idiots. They knew very well what they did, they
were as intelligent as we are, they had good results with

these methods so they used them; it was "good medicine."[17]

How is this possible? Why does it work?

> A mythological image is one that evokes and directs psychological energy. It is an energy-evoking and energy- directing sign. A mythology is a system of affect or emotional images; these representations themselves produce this emotion or affect.[18]

Rather than either fighting fate, or resigning ourselves to playing the victim's role, we can symbolically align our self with the archetypal patterns in play, thus moving on a level beyond that of the conscious ego, restoring the harmony between our inner worlds and the universe that produced us.

The numinosity of the archetype can swamp or shatter our surprisingly limited egos. Indeed, in many cultures to look directly on a god is to die (Moses, unable to gaze on Yahweh's face; Semele, incinerated when Zeus appears to her in all his glory; the New Testament disciples, knowing the Father "who no man can see" not directly, but through Christ, as the image of God; etc.).

Ritual, however, provides a sacred space in which to confront these energies, and myth presents archetypal images we can safely engage in that sacred space.

There are many ways to do this, from following traditional paths, participating in ancient ceremonies, to tending to dream (indeed, in Jungian psychology the meeting between analyst and analysand presents a ritual setting for dream work, where one engages the archetypal figures active in one's own psyche).

Art also provides a portal into archetypal realms.

Given the lack of an active, effective mythic tradition in contemporary Western culture, Campbell advises we discover our own myth in the images that speak to us, drawn from the myths of all time:

> There are mythologies that are scattered, broken up, all around us. We stand on what I call the terminal moraine of shattered mythic systems that once structured society. They can be detected all around us. You can select any of these fragments that activate your imagination for your own use. Let it help shape your own relationship to the unconscious system out of which these symbols have come.[19]

Into The Mystic

Archetypes may indeed be projections of our psyche, or our being, but we (and our psyches) emerge from nature, both as individuals, and as a species.

Joseph Campbell makes a good case for mythology being rooted in our biology—and follows that back into the material, or manifest, universe, which today is thought to be the result of insubstantial quanta of particles (the apparent ground of matter that many physicists characterize as simply "tendencies to exist") interacting with each other, flashing into and out of existence billions of times each second, emerging from some sort of voidless void (for lack of any more precise designation, mathematical or otherwise) that transcends time and space, a universe that does not exist until it is observed (much like the gods)…

…and suddenly here we are, sailing "into the mystic."

I don't think that somewhere before the foundations of the earth Thor and Kali and Yahweh and Raven and Isis and Jesus and Coyote and Wakan-tanka and Brigid and Hermes and Vishnu and Legbe and Kuan-yin were all sitting around in the Great Hall of Archetypes somewhere, poring over blueprints of the world-to be, divvying up the map.

("Coyote, you get everything west of the Mississippi; Vishnu, since you do well in a humid climate you might as well settle in India; meanwhile Lono says he'll ride his cosmic surfboard to Hawaii . . .")

. . . but certainly the elemental forces which have everywhere been identified as gods—the sun, the moon, the earth, gravity, space, stars, night, day, the wind, a spring or river that makes green the land, the energy that opens the blossoms and unfurls the leaves, the design inherent in DNA, and the transcendent realms out of which the material universe appears to have emerged—all these existed long before humanity branched off from other primates, long before human consciousness differentiated itself from the unconscious.

Perhaps the gods are the way humans engage and experience these pre-existent patterns and energies. Maybe the gods are embedded in our DNA, or inhabit an electro-chemical impulse in the brain—which might suggest they don't exist, from one perspective—but if we look beyond the personification to the dynamic at work, one could say the gods were here before us, and may indeed be in one sense responsible for our creation, as these forces of nature have helped shape who and what we are.

In *The Hero's Journey*, Joseph Campbell captures the infinite permutations of our subject in one final image:

> [T]he implication of the mythic images . . . is that deities are symbolic personifications of the very images that are of yourself. And these energies that are of yourself are the energies of the universe. And so the god is out there and the god is in here. The kingdom of heaven is within you, yes, but it's also everywhere.[20]

NOTES

1. Campbell, Hero with a Thousand Faces, op. cit. 14.
2. Baring and Cashford, The Myth of the Goddess, op. cit. 556.
3. Campbell, Flight of the Wild Gander, op. cit. 31.
4. Joseph Campbell, Mythos, Vol.1 The Shaping of Our Mythic Tradition, Episode 1: Psyche & Symbol (New York: Unapix, 1999; London: Acorn Media, 2007).
5. C.G. Jung, Archetypes and the Collective Unconscious, op. cit. 79.
6. Ibid. 160.
7. Jon Platania, Ph.D., Jung for Beginners (New York: Writers and Readers Publishing, 1997), 58.
8. Deirdre Bare, Jung: A Biography (Boston: Little, Brown, and Company, 2002), 65-66.
9. Jung, Archetypes and the Collective Unconscious, op. cit. 23.
10. Jung, Man and His Symbols, op. cit. 87.
11. Ibid. 87-88.
12. Ibid. 90.
13. Campbell, Flight of the Wild Gander, op. cit. 32.
14. Michael Murphy, The Future of the Human Body: Explorations into the Further Evolution of Human Nature (Los Angeles: Jeremy P. Tarcher, Inc., 1992), 559.
15. Zimmer, "Tantric Yoga," op. cit. 7.

16. Campbell, Inner Reaches of Outer Space, op. cit. 93.
17. Jung, Dream Analysis, op. cit. 129.
18. Campbell, Thou Art That, op. cit. 86.
19. Ibid.
20. Hero's Journey, op. cit. 151.

EIGHTEEN

/

"THE TIMES, THEY ARE A-CHANGIN'"

> When you see the earth from the moon, you don't see
> any divisions there of nations or states. This might be
> the symbol, really, for the new mythology to come.
> That is the country that we are going to be celebrating.
> And those are the people we are one with.[1]

In the nearly 20 years since Joseph Campbell's death [this essay
was written in 2006], the world has witnessed innumerable
horrific episodes of collective violence: the slaughter of almost
a million Tutsis by Hutus in Rwanda; years of armed struggle between contending warlords in Liberia, Somalia, and the
Sudan; ethnic and religious wars in Bosnia, Serbia and Kosovo;
blood shed between Basque separatists and the government
of Spain, between Hindu Tamils and Sinhalese Buddhists in
Sri Lanka, between Palestinians and Israelis, between Irish
Protestants and Catholics, and between Hindu India and
Muslim Pakistan; al Qaeda's attack on the U.S. on September
11, 2001; and the shock-and- awe invasion and occupation of

Iraq, followed by a brutal insurgency and sectarian violence . . .

A list that barely scratches the surface.

Arbitrary geopolitical boundaries may indeed appear invisible to anyone standing on the moon, but for those who live on earth these lines are all too often traced in blood. One can't help but wonder if Campbell's confidence in the future isn't misplaced—the blind optimism that comes from wishful thinking.

And yet there does seem to be a sense that we are in the midst of a period of massive, almost unfathomable change. We no longer inhabit our grandparents' world—nor, given the accelerating pace of change, will our grandchildren live in ours.

Was Joseph Campbell wearing rose-colored glasses? Did he fail to anticipate the religious and ethnic violence that we're experiencing today? Or is this all part of a natural process as humanity gropes its way toward that inevitable "change of vision" that Campbell foresaw—and, if so, is there any way to hasten the process? What vision guides us now, and how do we get from here to there? Is Utopia unattainable, Armageddon unavoidable—or might there be some third path open to us? Does the imagery of myth offer clues to what lies ahead?

To answer these questions, we step briefly away from myth—or, perhaps, better put, we step inside the myths, go deeper, to the primary images that form the core of a mythology, in search of that vision that is "nothing new nor unnatural." But we'll take a curious path to reach the future, backtracking more than three decades into the past, to the halls of a prestigious California think tank, before returning to the now—along the way disturbing conspiracy theorists and dodging shrapnel in the thick of the culture wars.

FIXING THE WORLD

When we talk about settling the world's problems, we're barking up the wrong tree. The world is perfect. It's a mess. It has always been a mess. We are not going to change it.[2]

The above reflection seems to imply the opposite of the quote that opens this essay. In fact, some have taken it as a prescription for narcissistic withdrawal from the world . . . But nonparticipation is not what Campbell counsels here.

He's actually referring to what he terms the Bodhisattva formula—"joyful participation in the sorrows of the world"— embracing life in all its agony and ecstasy and willingly throwing oneself into the fray, so to speak.

Recognizing that the world will always be troubled doesn't mean that we don't work to end world hunger, abolish poverty, promote peace, or support political goals to which we might be committed, any more than accepting death as an inevitable part of life means we shouldn't render first aid to accident victims.

What Campbell recommended was simply a shift of perspective, so that we "say yea" to it all.

Joseph Campbell's own example is hardly one of withdrawal and nonparticipation. Throughout the 1950s and '60s, intent on increasing awareness and understanding of "foreign" peoples, he lectured regularly at the State Department's Foreign Service Institute, offering diplomats, military officers, and CIA officials insight into the complex cultures of countries to which they had been assigned.

Campbell's 1957 address before UNESCO, entitled "Asia and the United States: What the American Citizen Can Do to Promote Mutual Understanding and Cooperation," offered practical applications of the same theme.

Even more intriguing is Campbell's contribution to a detailed report, prepared for the Stanford Research Institute, designed—in the words of the report's editors—to explore:

> a plausible vision of the future in which democratic methods survive, major problems are managed success-fully if not resolved, and the unfolding of the human potential continues to expand . . . including plausible steps to its realization . . .[3]

SHAPING THE FUTURE

SRI International (formerly the Stanford Research Institute) is a nonprofit scientific research organization dedicated to an inter-disciplinary approach. SRI's mission statement declares, "We are committed to discovery and to the application of science and technology for knowledge, commerce, prosperity, and peace."

Plans to form such an institute were first discussed by Stanford's faculty committee in a 1939 meeting at the Bohemian Grove, a privately owned redwood forest located along the Russian River in California's Sonoma County, site of a legendary annual conclave of the rich and powerful. The attack on Pearl Harbor placed the program in limbo until after the end of World War II; in 1946 the Stanford Research Institute was officially born, offspring of a partnership between Stanford University and the industrial community. (SRI International ended formal ties to the university in the 1970s—hence the name change).

Over the past sixty years the Stanford Research Institute has been responsible for technological and cultural innovations that have literally transformed society—including electronic banking (1955), the computer mouse (1964), windows, hypertext, and video conferencing (1968), the liquid crystal technology used in today's flat panel displays (1963–1968), high definition television and the stealth technology used by the military (both developed in the eighties), as well as ultrasound and GPS technologies.

In 1969 SRI received the first logon to ARPANET, precursor to the internet, and in 1977 SRI sent the first internet transmission from Menlo Park to a computer at the University of Southern California—via London, England.

The Stanford Research Institute participated in site selection and design decisions for Disneyland and the John F. Kennedy Center for the Performing Arts. SRI conducted the first national evaluation of charter schools, and has constructed models for monitoring the long-term growth and planning of specific industries. In 1949 the Stanford Research Institute facilitated the first national symposium on air pollution, and today maintains a polar station that conducts atmospheric research. And SRI has worked off and on since 1979 with the Chinese government (depending on who holds the reins) to help

re-envision that country's political, academic, and business environments in ways that foster a more open, prosperous society.

While this partial inventory of accomplishments reads like a commercial (small wonder—it's gleaned from the institute's own publications), it does establish SRI's active role in imagining and shaping the future . . .

Which brings us to Research Report No. 4—*Changing Images of Man*, prepared in May 1974 by the Center for the Study of Social Policy at SRI International.

TEAM WORK

The SRI report, which was commissioned by the Kettering Foundation in order to examine the ways in which humanity's perception of itself might in fact evolve, circulated over the course of the next decade through government, business, and academic circles, but wasn't made available to the general public until 1982, when it was published by Pergamon Press. Card catalogs and bibliographies often appear to list Joseph Campbell as the primary author—an accident of alphabet. Campbell is but one of eight co-authors representing fields as diverse as physics, the social sciences, engineering, and the humanities. Two members of the team, O.W. Markley, Project Director, and Willis W. Harman, Project Supervisor, served as editors. Most Campbell bibliographies fail to list *Changing Images of Man*—and *A Fire in the Mind*, Robin and Stephen Larsen's heavily footnoted biography of Campbell, makes no mention of this episode.

Campbell's role remained significant nonetheless: anyone familiar with Joe's work will recognize his ideas and even his wording throughout the book's eight chapters; the first two, however, are the most thoroughly "Campbellian" in content and tone.

Though part of the original draft, Campbell's examination of "the role of myth in society" didn't appear in the 1974 report; the Pergamon edition corrects this omission, restoring the section in the opening chapter. The second chapter focuses on a variety of "images of man" dominant in different periods and different societies—reflected in the mythology, philosophy, science, and psychology of a culture—and how these images not only reflect a given culture, but also help shape and define that culture.

In addition to authoring a significant portion of the text, Campbell is also listed as one of a panel of 23 experts who reviewed the final draft (other notable reviewers include Yale physicist Henry Morgenau, psychologists B.F. Skinner and Carl Rogers, and anthropologists Anthony F.C. Wallace, Luther Gerlach, and Margaret Meade, among others—many of whose comments and criticisms appear as footnotes).

The research team at times ventures in unconventional directions—for example, referencing investigations of telepathy, clairvoyance, precognition, psychokinesis, and hypnosis when examining contemporary scientific perspectives—but their credentials and their approach make clear this is a serious study.

CHANGING IMAGES OF MAN

The co-authors define *image of man* as the "set of assumptions held about the human being's origin, nature, characteristics, relationships with others, and place in the universe."

> An "image of (the nature of) man" is thus a Gestalt perception of humankind, both individual and collective, in relation to the self, others, society, and the cosmos.

It may contain many levels and face contradictions and paradoxes—as does the living human being—and still be experienced as an organic whole.[4]

The report focuses on three primary tasks:

> We have attempted in this study to:
>
> Illuminate ways our present society, its citizens, and institutions have been shaped by the underlying myths and images of the past and present.
>
> Explore the deficiencies of currently held images of humankind and to identify needed characteristics of future images.
>
> Identify high-leverage activities that could facilitate the emergence of new images and new policy approaches to the resolution of key problems in our society.[5]

The first two areas are thoroughly and thoughtfully addressed. The report is weakest where it approaches task three—but then, this section is essentially brainstorming, reaching for specific policies and programs. Campbell's presence is less apparent here, and no wonder—he believed we can't stage-manage a myth any more than we can predict what we'll dream tonight.

> [M]yths don't come into being like that. You have to wait for them to appear.[6]

Campbell nevertheless clearly identifies collective universal themes found in myth that are essential to the development of any future "self-image" of humanity consonant with the realities of the universe in which we live—as opposed to those images limited in scope to local cultures and specific times and places.

The latter, especially when read literally, hinder the development of a more discerning image of reality, engendering collective perspectives ultimately ill-suited to human life and the health of the planet as a whole.

The Power of Image

But don't such images have their source in the human imagination? If they are, in essence, imaginary, then how can an image wield such power?

The world comes to us through our senses. Each sense, however, presents an *image* (in this case a term not limited to the visual) that is not reality, but how we *experience* reality.

Imagination mediates our experience of reality.

We know the desk at which I sit is over ninety-five percent empty space (to err on the conservative side), the intermolecular inner space as empty as the vast void of outer space—and what matter there is in this desk consists, at the subatomic level, of mesons, muons, pions, and a host of other particles that physicists have described as mere "tendencies to exist," each blinking into and out of and back into existence billions of times each second.

And yet I experience the desk as solid.

Images don't shape merely what we experience, but what we do. Every human undertaking begins in the imagination. I can't even make a peanut butter sandwich without first imagining it, holding an image of the sandwich in my head—an awareness which keeps me from whipping up a batch of onion and ammonia soup by mistake.

Image—imagination—draws me into the future.

It should be no surprise that what is true for the individual holds true at the cultural level as well, given that culture itself is a product of the human imagination.

Fred Polak, director of the Netherlands' Central Planning Bureau in the post-World War II period and generally credited as one of the fathers of futurist studies, addressed this question in a pioneering two-volume work that adds flesh to the following observation:

> Any student of the rise and fall of cultures cannot fail to be impressed by the role played in historical succession by the image of the future. The rise and fall of images precedes or accompanies the rise and fall of cultures. As long as a society's image is positive and flourishing, the flower of culture is in full bloom. Once the image begins to decay and lose its vitality, however, the culture does not long survive.[7]

The authors of the SRI report offer several examples of the power of a cultural image, which I'll briefly paraphrase:

> If a culture's dominant perception is of man as separate from nature (as in Judeo-Christian mythology), then an exploitation ethic is more likely, with nature considered merely a resource—whereas the perception of humanity

as part of or one with nature is more conducive to the development of an ecological ethic; similarly, if we see humans as "animated machines of physical parts" (as in Cartesian science), then the interior life is ignored and, again, our relationship to nature tends toward exploitation—and yet, if we imagine ourselves as solely spiritual, rather than physical, beings (as in some schools of Gnosticism, Hinduism, Buddhism, and other mystic traditions), then factors affecting the material health and well-being of society are often ignored.

In *Changing Images of Man,* Campbell and company identify nineteen distinct images from thirteen past cultures that remain active and influential, and where they can be found today. The authors also examine the relevance of these cultural images to our post-industrial era—which they recognize as a period of transitional crisis—determining the images most likely to help, or hinder, successful societal transformation.

For example, the image of man created from clay by a god separate from nature—which first appears in Mesopotamia, c. 2350 BC, in the myths of the Semitic Akkadians—coupled with the sense of a "chosen people" (whether by birth or conversion), a concept key to Judeo-Christian-Islamic traditions today, "stands in its present form as an obstacle to emergence of new ecological understandings."

Similarly, the Zoroastrian image of man, emerging c. 1200 BC, views humans as endowed with free will but forced to choose between absolute good or absolute evil; this view also posits time as linear rather than cyclical, leading up to a cataclysmic "End of Days" when good will triumph and evil will be forever abolished. Both concepts play into the Judeo-Christian-Islamic emphasis on a rigid, divinely ordained moral code, as well as the Christian expectation of a coming apocalypse, after which the deity will restore nature's balance. Taken literally, this worldview does not easily adapt to advances in science, philosophy, human rights, and other fields of knowledge.

On the other hand, the totemism apparent in the Upper Paleolithic from roughly 30,000 to 15,000 BC—still evident in Native American and other shamanic traditions that accent the kinship between man and animal—has much in common with the image of the mutual interdependence of all nature found in some Buddhist traditions, and with what Campbell followed Aldous Huxley in calling "the perennial philosophy" (the "view of man and the universe as essentially consciousness in manifest form") underlying the mystic traditions within almost all mythologies. The authors find elements of this mythic imagery surfacing today in our expanding ecological awareness, which they believe vital to humanity's survival.

The research team responsible for *Changing Images of Man* recognized some 50 "possible futures" that stretch before us—but only a handful of those alternate paths are at all desirable. All of the undesirable paths (those involving population upheavals, major conflict, environmental disaster, etc.) are associated with views of ourselves that are limited, inadequate, and out of touch with the world in which we live.

"IT'S THE ECONOMY . . ."

The SRI study devotes an entire chapter to the image of

"economic man" that evolved in tandem with the industrial age. This perception of humans as individual, fundamentally rational beings living in a material, mechanistic universe in which "objective" knowledge and utilitarianism are the highest values, was certainly appropriate to its time—and is responsible for the high standard of living in the United States and other developed countries.

(The authors are careful to point out that no culture's image of man is "wrong," making the case that each image they examine is appropriate to the age and culture where first found).

However, this image—basic to all industrialized nations in the "First World" (as opposed to "Third World" countries)—spawns a number of unintended consequences. It views people as "'cogs in the industrial machine,' valued chiefly for their role as producers and consumers, and motivated primarily by those roles." It, too, fosters a perception of humankind as separate from nature, and values perpetual progress and growth, thus nurturing the insatiable collective appetite that drives consumer culture. Conservative in nature (in the classical, rather than political, sense), this image that defines our times is slow to adapt to change.

Where this image dominates, decisions are made on the basis of economic efficiency rather than "what ought to be."

> We are in the old age of our culture. It's in a dissolving, disintegrating period . . .
>
> There's an awful saying of Spengler that I ran into in a book of his, *Jahre der Entsheidung (Years of Decision)*, which are the years we live in now. He said, "As for America, it's a congeries of dollar trappers, no past, no future." When I read that back in the thirties, I

took it as an insult. But what is anybody interested in? .
. . It's a terrible lack of anything but economic concerns
that we're facing, and that is old age and death, and that
is the end. That's as I see it. I have nothing but negative
judgments in respect to that.[8]

Campbell's frustration rings true today when decisions impacting the quality and even the existence of life on this planet are based on the narrow, short-term economic concerns of a relatively limited number of people, neglecting long-term implications and the big picture (e.g., withdrawing from and declining to re-negotiate the Kyoto Accords because of the cost to industry of higher emission standards; ironically, global warming will have a more drastic, devastating effect on the economy in the long run than retooling our factories).

Of course, the authors are painting with broad strokes—the study is informed speculation, not inerrant prophecy. Nevertheless, from a vantage point 30 years down the road, much of what they anticipated if this image were to remain in force bears an uncanny resemblance to current realities.

For example, given the value the economic model of man places on linear progress and unlimited growth (values which generally trump integrity, vision, and ethics in our world), they see a concentration of power and of wealth in mega-corporations:

No longer are [multi-national corporations] simply subject
to market forces; in an important sense they exert control
over the market. No longer are they simply subject to controls imposed by national governments; in an important
sense they exert control over national governments.[9]

It's hard to deny that dynamic when the people who make one's cell phones are often the same as the people who provide one's home phone, and the same as the people who provide one's cable service and internet connection, and who also own the news network and produce the television programs one watches, not to mention owning the studio that makes the movies that play at the corner cineplex—and who knows what else?

This concentration of wealth and power inevitably leads to behavior bold, brash, and so abusive that consumers, according to the authors, are bound to demand accountability.

Do we see this in the recent manipulation of energy resources to create an artificial crisis and drive prices up in California? Are trials of executives of Enron, WorldCom, and other corporations involved in multi-billion dollar scams the beginning of this backlash?

Certainly, despite its benefits, the dominant image of man as primarily an economic factor helps construct the environment in which such abuses thrive.

The researchers also see this model—driven by a technological imperative—generating a system so complex as to be extremely vulnerable to disruption from terrorist attack or natural catastrophe, which strikes me as a particularly apt insight, considering its origin in the pre-9/11, pre-Katrina world.

The authors don't claim the image of man as an economic being has no value, but stress the wisdom of integrating it with other images (such as that of the mutual interdependence of all life) that support the restoration of the balance in nature (both outer and inner natures) and a more holistic, global perspective.

Twelve years after the original report was issued, Campbell

felt this integration in full swing, with the interdependence of the global economy actually contributing to the development of a unifying image of mankind:

> Well, the cultural crises—and this is certainly a period of great crisis—is primarily caused by the very recent coming together and collision of culture forms, culture ideals, that were in total ignorance of each other one hundred years ago. I think this unification of the planet is now indeed a fact and becoming apparent to everyone—as an economic fact also; and when it is an economic fact, then it is a fact indeed, at least as far as the public mind is concerned.[10]

Unfortunately, political leaders all too often fall behind the curve, remaining locked into stale, destructive patterns. Even some who pay lip service to the value and power of the global economy seem to expect to dominate that economy.

> And when you think of this! The number of men who are in fact responsible for the condition of the world right now—I mean in its political life! They could all be contained in this room, and they are acting as if there were no way of common understanding . . . They are all men of intelligence, but so linked to this system of now archaic fears and desires that the world is in chaos simply as a function of their inability to assume the middle position in a conversation.
>
> They are thinking of themselves and their local careers—rather in terms of the past than of the future;

rather in terms of a system of conflicting communities, than as a leader of different groups within a single community . . . They are a lag, they are a drag. I think the people of the world are way ahead of them here.

But this is just my personal opinion. I'm no sociologist.[11]

Two decades later, we have a new generation of leaders—but Campbell's comments remain relevant.

Still, we've caught glimpses here and there of leaders who transcend ethnic and national loyalties: Anwar Sadat, whose concessions in the cause of peace marked him for assassination; Nelson Mandela, who ended apartheid yet eschewed revenge on the white minority for decades of oppression and his own imprisonment, instead advocating "truth and reconciliation" between black and white; Mikhail Gorbachev, who relaxed the iron fist of the Soviet Union, surrendering its power in the interests of peace, prosperity, and human rights; Vaclav Havel, who presided over the peaceful dissolution of Czechoslovakia, avoiding ethnic strife at the same time Serbs, Croats, and Muslims were slugging it out in the former Yugoslavia; and the Dalai Lama, who advocates peaceful resolution to conflict and counsels understanding and compassion toward the Chinese, despite their occupation of Tibet resulting in the death of hundreds of thousands of his countrymen.

Are these leaders anomalies—or the tip of an iceberg, harbingers of what may yet come?

THE CONSTRAINTS OF SCIENCE

The SRI report also examines the symbiotic relationship between a culture's image of humanity, and its science.

Scientific discovery regularly spawns major revolutions in belief and understanding: Copernicus and Galileo moved the earth from the center of the universe into orbit around the sun; the observations of Darwin and Mendel shattered long held certainties about the origins of life; the exploration of the quantum universe deconstructed Newton's clockwork cosmos—all examples that have led (or are leading) to massive changes in the way we conceive ourselves and our universe.

But just as science shapes our perception of reality, so too do society's perceptions shape the direction science takes:

> Science deals with a selected set of metaphors; other possible metaphors have in the past been excluded, whether because of reductionist bias or commitment to a particular concept of objectivity. The prevailing "image of man" intervenes in the scientific process by shaping the definition of both the research territory and interpretations of the results of scientific investigation . . .
>
> As we examine some of the contemporary scientific developments that challenge old scientific paradigms, it must be from the standpoint of this two-way interaction between the changing scientific paradigm and the societal image of man. It is not that either causes the other, but rather that they tend to move together.[12]

The authors offer the amusing example of the Royal Academy of Sciences under Antoine Lavoisier—considered the father of modern chemistry—which, in 1790, determined that meteorites couldn't exist, as rocks just   don't fall down out of the sky—this, despite innumerable eyewitness accounts. "Since they were no longer real," museums and universities throughout Europe tossed their meteorite collections (save for one massive meteor too heavy to move). Another 50 years passed before the scientific establishment accepted growing evidence and began rebuilding their collections.

> The goals of society, influenced by the culture image of man-in-the-universe, help to define the research territory of science. Thus the content of science is affected by the prevailing image of man . . .
>
> The myths and images of the culture influence what seems possible in the universe and is therefore acceptable, scientific or otherwise.[13]

Dreams, hypnosis, death, suicide, homosexuality, parapsychology, subliminal perception, and psychedelic drugs are some of the areas the research team identifies as taboo under the Cartesian/Newtonian paradigm that guides orthodox science. Thirty years later this paradigm shows signs of giving ground, but a serious scientist can still damage her or his reputation by announcing an investigation into some of these taboo areas.

Science, like economics, exhibits "an exclusive orientation toward the analytic/rational mode of problem-solving in the West"—which automatically assumes any other approach is illogical and irrational, and thus devalues intuition (though the authors of the SRI report remind us that innumerable scientists credit intuition as the source of their greatest achievements).

The tendency toward specialization—a response to ever-greater complexity—is another trait scientific and economic models share. In the field of science this can lead to an over-re-liance on the reductionist method, with whole systems stud-ied only in terms of their component parts—an approach that can't help but limit scientific understanding.

In ecology, however, the SRI team finds evidence of a mounting countertrend that they believe will eventually sup-plant the previous paradigm:

> There is, however, another class of systems involv-ing rich interactions between the component parts. Biological and ecological systems are good examples. In these, synergy or the properties of the whole system created by the interaction of the parts operate to such an extent that reductionist analysis cannot achieve a theory capable of extension and prediction.[14]

Three decades later, other sciences besides deep ecology are now embracing a more holistic, interdependent image of the natural world. In particular, advances within the field of phys-ics and biology, the development of depth and transpersonal psychologies, and the emergence of consciousness research (cognitive science and artificial intelligence) and information technologies, provide a medium through which the collective imagination re-casts the universe and our role in it.

There's also the development of chaos theory and fractal

geometry, which today impacts everything from meteorology to the stock market. As a result, chemists, economists, physicists, neurophysiologists, mathematicians, computer scientists, and biologists—including a number of Nobel laureates—are together exploring the science of complexity at the cutting-edge Santa Fe Institute.

Physicist David Bohm's holographic model of the universe, neurophysiologist Karl Pribram's discovery of the holographic nature of memory and the brain, Stanislav Grof's research into the human psyche's holographic structure, biologist Rupert Sheldrake's theories of morphic resonance, anthropologist Jeremy Narby's studies into the relationship between mythic images, psychotropic-induced visions of tribal shamans, and the DNA molecule, are a few of the many new, exciting avenues of exploration opening up in science.

Ironically, nonscientists—who often value the metaphors more than the hard science behind them—have also embraced this imagery, which helps support and shape an emerging belief system. Are we glimpsing glimmers of a new "image of man" on the horizon?

OBSTACLES AND OPPORTUNITIES

Changing Images of Man presents a strong case, past and present, regarding the power of a culture's self-image to shape the future, and is clear on what the future requires of us. The essential question, though, remains: "Is it possible?"

The authors see several possible barriers to positive image-formation.

The least likely obstacle is the absence of crisis—an unanticipated ability to indefinitely maintain the status quo.

Riiiiiiiight! That will happen . . .

A second, overwhelming obstacle is a media-supported consumption culture—which seems to be where we are today. It is indeed difficult to contemplate giving up those golden handcuffs—trading in the SUV for the environment, recycling our discards, reining in planned obsolescence. Even some who pay lip service to these ideas (including, at times, myself) are seduced by the luxury and ease of the path of least resistance.

Campbell and his colleagues mention a third obstacle to image-formation: terrorism. They don't dwell on this as much as we might today in the era of 9/11 and a seemingly perpetual "War on Terrorism."

A final major block to image-formation is described as "religious stasis"—the clash of cultures, whether between Judaism and Islam in the Near East, Islamic extremists and the West, or within the United States itself.

> All popular thinking is in terms of loyalties to the local communities to which all, severally, are members; and such thinking is now out of date. What we face is a challenge to recognize one community on this earth, and what we find in the face of this challenge is everybody pulling back into his own in-group. I don't want to name the in-groups, but we all know pretty well what they are.
>
> They are racial groups, class groups, religious groups, economic groups: religious conflict, regional conflict,

linguistic conflict! And this is just one example of what is going on all over the place.

Then we have a new kind of *tetraktys* here in action, whereby one tendency pulls towards more sectarian, and another one towards more universality. The one towards more universality is the trend of the century, and the sectarian is the pull of people who are afraid of what is before us.[15]

Conversely, the research team also presents two powerful catalysts likely to accelerate acceptance of a more holistic, global image of humanity. (Please bear in mind that I'm just skimming the surface of the report and its conclusions—there is far greater depth to the "desirable image of man" the authors propose than my adjectives suggest.)

Those catalysts are technological breakthroughs, and global crises—especially ecological crises. Examples of both are full upon us.

Breakthroughs in information technology—particularly communications technology and the internet—affirm the truth of a Disney refrain: it is a small world, after all. The younger generation today is linked up around the globe in ways that my Baby Boomer generation barely comprehends, in essence creating their own fusion culture. It's by no means Utopia—but the evolution of the World Wide Web suggests that the boundaries separating us are more porous than we imagined.

Global warming looms as an even more compelling catalyst.

Changing Images of Man suggests impending ecological crises may be what finally break the logjam—an evaluation echoed by Campbell in *The Hero's Journey* (published four years after his death). Climate change, shifting weather patterns, melting icecaps, the increasing intensity of seasonal storms, even shifts in the spread of contagious diseases, can all be related to humanity's effect on our environment. Even those with contrary political and/or religious beliefs are finding it increasingly difficult to deny the abundance of evidence that, "Man did not weave the web of life, he is merely a strand in it. Whatever he does to the web, he does to himself . . ."

CONSPIRACY THEORIES AND CULTURE WARS

Even though most people have never heard of the Stanford Research Institute or *Changing Images of Man*, there are a few paranoid individuals and organizations who see Joseph Campbell's participation in this study as evidence of his influence in a vast conspiracy aimed at destroying Christianity and imposing a one-world dictatorship on the United States. One pre-Y2K broadside characterized the SRI project as part of an initiative funded by the Tavistock Institute, and so somehow controlled by the Illuminati.

(The project's director and the team supervisor more accurately identify the Charles F. Kettering Foundation, seeking "possibly risky approaches to social policy research and development in which a relatively small amount of support might, if successful, lead to a beneficial effect on society that is relatively large," as providing the impetus for the SRI study.)

Meanwhile, an article offered through evangelical Christian television apologist John Ankerberg claims the Stanford Research Institute study team conducted its research with the intent of determining how "Western man could be deliberately turned into an Eastern mystic/psychic" (excerpted by Ankerberg from the book *Occult Invasion*, by David Hunt).

There are, of course, hooks on which such projections catch—such as the Stanford Research Institute's origins in discussions at the Bohemian Grove—notorious in conspiracy circles as the gathering place for members of the elite cabal that controls the world, be they Illuminati, Jews, Satanists, or all of the above (depending on who is telling the story).

Then there's the close relationship that SRI International maintains with powerful corporations, not to mention an abundance of government and military contracts, and SRI's pivotal role in the development of information technology and the internet.

Another hook hangs on a perceived arrogance in the report, a blueprint for consciously fostering a cultural image that intends a specific effect—certainly sounds like manipulation, even if it isn't. The authors walk cautiously through that minefield, anticipating resistance from the significant segment of the public vested in their religion. It's true that this study proved influential. However, the authors aren't predicting, or dictating, but merely analyzing what paths lie open to us given the information available. They do identify what they see as the most desirable and fortuitous outcome, and offer several possible alternatives on how to move in that direction—but events of the last 30 years demonstrate no coordinated efforts to implement the tentative programs and policies discussed.

Still, the observation that a literal reading of Judeo-Christian-Islamic scripture is mythology, more metaphor than history, just isn't well received even by the majority in each religion who live far from the lunatic fringe. The editors of the Permagon edition

of *Changing Images* acknowledge that later works widely identified with the New Age movement—specifically Dave Satin's
New Age Politics (1978) and Marilyn Ferguson's *The Aquarian
Conspiracy* (1980)—draw on some of the observations and implications of the original report; it should be no surprise that some
strict religionists who already feel their beliefs under siege consider this study the original salvo in the lengthy culture war that
continues to fragment our society.

The original researchers reviewed the 1974 report before
Pergamon published the expanded version; the editors sum up
their consensus thus:

> Although the authors are still in fundamental agreement
> with what we wrote almost a decade ago, there are sev-
> eral ways that in retrospect we would like to have done it
> differently. One change would be to present our findings
> in a more objective way. Although we continue to believe
> that inquiries of this sort should avoid the appearance of
> "value neutrality," much of the study has a certain tone of
> preaching that although representative of the earnestness
> in which the research was undertaken, we now find less
> than desirable in a research report.[16]

Campbell also criticizes the report's lack of recognition of the
artist "not simply as agents 'depicting a positive future,'" . .
. but "in the structuring of any future civilization." If a culture is to change its guiding image, then the image-makers,
the artists—particularly those with their finger on the pulse of
popular culture, such as the musician-poets, the novelists, the
filmmakers, etc.—will play a leading role, their work shaping

and reflecting the public imagination far more than any esoteric study issued by an eclectic think tank.

This may be why most strict religionists in the culture wars
blame rock-and-roll and Hollywood, rather than SRI (which
most have never heard of) for the disintegration of our culture.

The wing-nut factor will always be with us—but the larger
culture wars will ultimately resolve themselves, regardless of
what *Changing Images of Man* might recommend.

After thousands of years as accepted fact, the geocentric
world of scripture was destroyed by the ultimately undeniable
discoveries of Copernicus and Galileo. At the time, the pope
and Martin Luther alike considered such talk heresy, designed
to destroy Christianity.

And yet Christianity adapted.

Over time, theologians re-interpreted and re-envisioned
scripture, bringing belief into harmony with the science of the
day, much as the Catholic Church and several mainstream
Protestant denominations are doing today with evolution.
Adopting a more holistic, global image of humanity will not
mean the end of Christianity or Islam, though it might well
mean the end of some of the more extreme forms of those
religions.

And those will not go gentle into that good night . . .

THE EVIDENCE OF THINGS HOPED FOR
BUT NOT YET SEEN

Joseph Campbell's study of myth convinces him that there is a
natural dynamic to the process of image-formation, a pattern

we see recur time and again across cultures. Despite offering tentative suggestions on how to ease the transition, SRI's research team ultimately arrives at Campbell's position:

> But there exists little evidence to suggest that a change in the dominant image could be accomplished by rational deliberation, planning, and organized activity—or that the results of such manipulative rationality would necessarily be benign. On the other hand, whether by fortunate circumstances or creative unconscious process, an emerging image with many of the needed characteristics does seem to have made its (re) appearance.[17]

You can't force change. Fortunately, however, it's already on the way. What hints do we see of a cultural change of perspective? One unexpected place to find such evidence is in the field of market research.

Sociologist Paul Ray identifies three broad subcultures within the American public: Traditionals, Moderns, and Cultural Creatives—terms coined to sidestep assumed religious and political polarities. Culture, income, education, interests, hobbies, and other elements beyond the typical help define each subculture.

Moderns—mainstream Americans—represent 48% of the adult population, or roughly 93 million people; Traditionals—many of whom espouse conservative religious values—comprise 24.5%, which works out to some 48 million people; while Cultural Creatives—who embrace a holistic, global perspective akin to that suggested in the SRI study—form another 26% of the public, or 50 million adults.

That last group didn't exist 60 years ago, yet is roughly a quarter of the population today—this alone suggests a significant shift in the collective perspective—and it's a shift Madison Avenue has noted. Magazines, books, movies, cars, clothes, music, food, cable television channels, and travel destinations are being marketed with this demographic in mind. Whole Foods owes much of its success to Cultural Creatives, as does the annual Burning Man festival—and many of the creative and technical talents driving the expansion of cyberspace are members of this subculture, whether they know it or not. Paul Ray and psychologist Sherry Ruth Anderson mine survey data to examine this trend in detail in their volume, *Cultural Creatives* (Random House).

We also see this in the growth and interaction of NGOs (non-governmental organizations), especially in response to environmental imperatives. Transparency International, the World Resources Institute, and the Coalition for Environmentally Responsible Economies (CERES—now there's an apt mythic acronym!) assist businesses in developing environmentally sound policies and practices without sacrificing the bottom line.

Communication, travel, the internet—all are positive signs of what appears to be emerging, as are the new understandings in science. Of course, it might take 50 years before folks admit that rocks do indeed fall from the sky, but there is change in the air.

Nevertheless, there are tough times ahead.

IMAGINE

Anything from the past like an idea of what man of this or that culture might or should have been is now archaic, and the transformation we are experiencing is really of the whole sense of humanity; what it means to be a cultured and world- related human being. This is a whole new thing. And so we have all of us to leave our little provincial stories behind. They may guide us as far as structuring our lives for the moment, but we must always be ready to drop them and to grasp the new experience as it comes along and interpret it.[18]

\Not an easy task. Responding to a question posed by Cate Miodini, Campbell pooh-poohs the prospect of an Aquarian utopia in our future, drawing a clear distinction between warm and fuzzy "New Age" optimism, and the realities of any new age portrayed in history and myth:

Certainly there is a new age coming, and it will be a planetary age. But the beginnings of ages are usually terrible, with great violence, yang in a most brutal way. New ages don't come softly; they are times of aggression and smashing. I see no sign of anything gentle happening.[19]

Wars and rumors of wars—Bosnia and Serbia, Osama bin Ladin and 9/11, and all the rest—are the panicked struggles of those who see their world disintegrating . . . "times of aggression and smashing." I fear we will see more of the same in the years ahead.

Joseph Campbell, though, takes the long view:

> Well, personally I am an optimist with respect to
> the ability of life to survive. And I think the means
> are bound to appear for the resolution of the tension.
> Actually the tension is hardly more than a century old,
> and that the answer will come seems to me inevitable.
> Up to the present, however, one can only be terribly
> pessimistic. Pessimistic with respect to the present day,
> or the day after tomorrow, but optimistic with respect
> to, let's say, fifty odd years from now.[20]

In the meantime, what's an individual to do?

Joyfully participate—keep putting one foot in front of
another, keep living life.

And keep in mind that cultures arise out of the imagination
of generations of individuals—and hence a culture's self-image
consists of myriad individual images layered over and merging
into one another.

So, the more individuals there are who experience the shift
of perspective that Campbell describes, the closer a culture
comes to reaching critical mass.

> I think that in one's political action and influences, if one
> can think of oneself as part of a world community without
> betraying the legitimate interests of one's local neighbor-
> hood, one would be helping the world forward.
> That is all I can say to this.[21]

Sage advice.

NOTES

1. Campbell, Power of Myth, op. cit. 41.
2. Campbell, A Joseph Campbell Companion, op. cit. 17.
3. O.W. Markley and Willis Harman, eds., Changing Images of Man: Prepared by the Center for the Study of Social Policy/SRI International (Oxford: Pergamon Press, 1982), xviii.
4. Ibid. 3.
5. Ibid. xxii.
6. Joseph Campbell, "Mythic Reflections," op. cit.
7. Fred Polak, The Image of the Future, tr. Elise Boulding (Amsterdam, London, New York: Elsevier Scientific Publishing Company, 1973) 19.
8. Joseph Campbell, "Living Myths: A Conversation with Joseph Campbell," interview by Lorraine Kisly, Parabola 1 No. 2 (Spring 1976): 70-81.
9. Markley and Harman, eds., Changing Images, op. cit. 194.
10. Unpublished interview with Joseph Campbell by Emilios Bourantinos (9-30-85), Box 93, Folder 25, Manuscripts and Archives Division, The New York Public Library.
11. Ibid.
12. Markley and Harman, eds., Changing Images, op. cit. 75.
13. Ibid. 69.
14. Ibid. 74.
15. Campbell, Man and Myth Symposium, op. cit.
16. Markley and Harman, eds., Changing Images, op. cit. xix.
17. Ibid. 203.
18. Joseph Campbell, "Out of Our Own Center," interview by Michael Toms, Sunrise (Aug-Sept. 1979).
19. Joseph Campbell, "Myths of the Universe and the Coming of the New Age: An Interview with Joseph Campbell," interview by Cate Miodini, Anima: An Experiential Journal 13 No. 1 (Fall 1986): 29-36.
20. Campbell, Man and Myth Symposium, op. cit.
21. Ibid.

NINETEEN

THE KING AND "I"

> The appearance, c. 4500 – 2500 BC of an unprece-
> dented constellation of *sacra*—sacred acts and sacred
> things—points not to a new theory about how to make
> the beans grow, but to an actual experience in depth of
> that *Mysterium tremendum* that would break upon us
> all even now were it not so wonderfully masked.[1]

Human sacrifice a sacred act?

That's a concept difficult to absorb . . .

We're all familiar with the typical Hollywood scenario:
either a band of primitive, bloodthirsty, drum-pounding savages bearing a fair, unspoiled maiden, sometimes drugged,
sometimes bound, to the edge of a volcano, her sacrifice a
means of appeasing an angry god—or a variation of the same
powerless victim lashed to an altar in some sort of wild, orgias-
tic, black magic ritual.

Of course, our sympathies lie with the hero, who inevitably
rescues the maiden from her fate and condemns the collective

celebrants to theirs. We're on his team, for his character reflects our own cultural perspective. I've yet to find myself rooting for the sinister, knife-wielding, maniacal fanatic usually depicted in the role of the officiating priest . . .

. . . but then, it's just a movie—a far cry from reality.

Popular belief often assumes those sacrificed were either bred to the role and kept ignorant of their fate, or were slaves, criminals, or captives of war forced to the altar. There is certainly evidence of this in several cultures (e.g., the "Flower Wars" between Mayan cities to secure captives for sacrifice).

However, in the period that marks the birth of civilization—focusing on the two thousand years between 4500 and 2500 BC—the sacrificial ritual claimed not the dregs, but the cream of society: the best the community had to offer.

Nor were members of these societies "primitive" savages barely removed from the beasts. Joseph Campbell points out that the practice of human sacrifice is found in the early stages of every literate high culture.

Why would a people do this? *What* could they be thinking—or were they thinking at all? Does our automatic condemnation of ritual murder preclude all possibility of comprehending their mindset?

> [W]e should certainly not think of the mental state and experience of these individuals after any model of our own more or less imaginable reactions to such a fate. For these sacrifices were not properly, in fact, individuals at all; that is to say, they were not particularly beings, distinguished from a class or group by virtue of any sense or realization of a personal, individual destiny

and responsibility to be worked out in the way of an individual life. They were parts, only, of a larger whole; and it was only by virtue of their absolute submission to that in its unalterable categorical imperative that they were anything at all.[2]

While decrying the brutality and loss of life, Campbell nevertheless uncovers the elaborate and often elegant mythological themes that structured these rites. Those participating in lethal rituals in fact surrendered themselves completely to myth, acting out a cosmic realization on the physical plane—with the usual bloody consequences that come of reading a myth literally.

It's no simple task to fathom the mindset of entire cultures centered on human sacrifice—and even harder to accept that our own ancestors indulged in such rites. (This is somewhat ironic, given that such a sacrifice remains central to the prevailing religious tradition in the West—though fortunately, for us, the act has become spiritualized in modern practice.)

Is it coincidence that the development of this mythological motif parallels the evolution of human consciousness? Indeed, changes in one specific form of human sacrifice, that of ritual regicide, echo changes in human consciousness—changes that birth the self-aware, self-directed waking ego through which we filter our experience of the universe.

Though we no longer kill our kings, the forces that compelled this archaic ritual move us still—and so the myth remains relevant today. Exploring this archetype opens a window on ways to effectively engage this omnipresent pattern without shattering one's life in the process.

ANIMAL OR VEGETABLE?

Joseph Campbell identifies two orders of sacrifice in the prehistoric world. The hunting cultures of Paleolithic and Neolithic eras centered around a shamanic "master animal"—the primary food animal—who is hunted and killed, but then reborn through rites the hunters perform. Life lives off life—"first you eat me, then I eat you"—a mythological pattern still alive in the Lakota, Dakota and Blackfoot tribes hunting buffalo on the North American plains in the late nineteenth century.

It's as if there's an uneasy, unspoken sense of guilt that accompanies taking a life for personal gain, so that guilt is assuaged by participating in the animal's rebirth.

Campbell contrasts this with the tropics, where the mythos is rooted in the life that springs from what is rotting and dying. Given the relentless humid heat, decay occurs rapidly—but out of the dark, dank, rotting and decaying vegetation sprouts new life. Life comes from death—so, to propagate life, ensure this renewal, comes the oddly perverse idea of increasing death—a concept that triggers "a frenzy of sacrifice."

In planting cultures what develops is the myth of the dead-and-resurrected god: a man (or sometimes a woman) is told to kill the god and bury his corpse, out of which grows the primary food plant that feeds the region—from the coconut in the South Pacific, to the corn in Longfellow's treatment of a Native American version of this myth in *The Song of Hiawatha*—and we find echoes sounding through the myths of Osiris, Attis, and the Christ, among others: Osiris, the sprout springing from the grain when the seed germinates and dies, or Jesus, the fruit of the vine, *à la* Dionysus, etc.

There is much overlap between the two approaches, but with a significant difference in perspective:

For the hunters, the accent is on atoning for a regrettable yet necessary death by participating in bringing about the victim's rebirth (who voluntarily submits to death, a sacrifice to feed the tribe). The offering is generally an animal, sacrificed to a deity (the "Animal Master"), and the sense is what Campbell calls, from the Latin, *do ut des*: "I give that thou mayest give."

> In the hunting cultures, when a sacrifice is made, it is, as it were, a gift or bribe to the deity that is being invited to do something for us or to give us something. But when a figure is sacrificed in the planting cultures, that figure itself is the god. The person who dies is buried and becomes the food.[3]

In the planting cultures the emphasis is on taking life—no reluctance here, but human sacrifice—with the added strange twist that increasing this ritual dealing of death ensures and enhances life for the entire community. The one who is killed gives life to the community, and, indeed, to all Creation—and the sense is what Campbell terms *tat tvam asi*—"Thou art that."

> [T]he dominating idea of the sacrifice is that already noted, of a reciprocal dual offering: an eternal being is given life in this world, and temporal lives are returned to an eternal being. Through various modulations it is thereby suggested that an original downcoming or self-emptying of this kind produced the universe and

that through properly conducted ceremonials repro-
ducing that original act, life in this world is renewed.

. . .[I]n every sacrifice of this kind, the *victim is
understood to be an incarnation of the God*, transubstan-
tiation having taken place when the ceremonial costume was assumed. Furthermore, as in every celebration of the mass the sacrifice of Calvary is not simply
symbolized but repeated, so likewise in all sacrifices of
this order, both space and time are annihilated in an
eviternal act.[4]

Sacrifice is metaphor for the nature of the cosmos in which
we live: transcendent eternity, pouring into the field of time
and space (which can be represented as a cross). This eternity
(which is itself a metaphor) is thus immanent in all of creation—fragmented into the multitude of forms that comprise
the material universe, with each of us one of those fragments,
containing our own little drop of eternity. Life lives off life, a
dynamic portrayed by the deity sacrificing him/herself to feed
us and give us life. This is an image that recurs throughout the
world, particularly in planting cultures—but the reference of
the myth is to our experience in the here and now: life does
live off life, and out of death comes new life. We live the myth
every day of our lives, and so, for example, partake of the holy
communion, eat the divine flesh, every time we sit at table and
sup—a sacred act.

The mistake of many cultures is a literal rendering of the
myth, which creates a bloody mess.

"The King Is Dead . . ."

As early as 7500 BC the agricultural centers of the Near East gave rise to our first cities—and by the middle of the third millennium BC, literate civilizations had materialized in Mesopotamia and then in Egypt, each retaining many mythological forms that carried over from the earlier planting cultures.

With the emergence of civilization, attention turned from the earth to the heavens. Priestly observers, charting the regular movement of celestial bodies in the night sky, noted pattern and order above—a pattern and order they attempted to replicate here on earth. Civilization was thus structured in imitation of this perceived cosmic order—which included everything from the physical configuration of temples and cities, to assigned social roles and supporting myths.

It's not unusual for us today to project our concept of kingship backwards in time and so automatically assume early kings "ruled" the realm, imposing their whims upon their subjects with the autocratic caprice of an Alexander or a Nero, backed up at spear point, if needed. It does not occur to us that early kings and queens were locked into playing their prescribed part, as much prisoners of their role as the lowliest slave.

These were not autonomous, independent individuals bending the world to their will, but agents of the divine order, as were the gods themselves. Early rulers were god-kings incarnate—more on the order of the Dalai Lama than Henry VIII—and, like the Dalai Lama, merely the outward manifestation of an eternal being.

Campbell speaks of the king as representing "the central coordinating factor of a differentiated society" (or, as Julian

Jaynes might say, the voice of God). As such, the king personified either the lunar or solar deity, depending on the local mythology—and just as the king personified a heavenly god, so did his court:

> The king and his queen or queens, as well as the members of his high council, were identified with the sun, moon, and one or another of the planets: Mercury, Venus, Mars, Jupiter, and Saturn—the names of which suggest to this day some of the roles that they may already have represented: as Treasurer, Queen Consort, Troop Commander, Civil Magistrate, and Executioner. The comings and goings of the king and his queens, in particular, were regulated by the movements, appearances, and disappearances, of the celestial spheres to which they were assigned, so that at certain critical junctures, interpreted as representing the termination of an eon, *the king and his entire court were killed.*
>
> This was the form of sacrifice known as "Sacred Regicide."
>
> . . . It is a form of total sacrifice that can be identified in modified forms in evidences from every one of the archaic high civilizations, all of which had already received seminal influences from Sumerian Mesopotamia; namely Egypt, Crete and early Greece, India and China—with an extension to Mesoamerica.[5]

Talk about strict term limits!

Of course, the king-priest is in the ritual role of the deity—ego's interest in its own self-preservation wields little power here. Sacrifice at the end of a reign of set span was no secret—each god-king knew how his story would end, and willingly subsumed his identity in that of the deity. Hardly ego run amok—a trait more common to Caesars, kaisers, and czars (and the occasional elected official). In fact, there may be a question as to whether ego is present at all in this period—at least in the form we know it today.

Campbell offers example after example of ritual regicide, even finding lingering traces in recent centuries—from mass royal burials in ancient Sumer and Nubia, or its depiction on two Sumerian seals c. 2300 BC, to Malabar, in the sixteenth century, where a king was observed on a platform slicing away bits of flesh and body parts before finally slitting his own throat, or Zimbabwe, as recently as 1810, where priests ordered the strangulation of the king every four years.

Usually, the king's sacrifice was linked to the orbit of the planets—often Venus, which returns to the same spot every eight years, or Jupiter, following a twelve-year cycle. Stargazing priests set the date for this morbid ritual. In surviving historical records, the king was dispatched by either a trusted member of his council, or a close relative. For example, among the Shilluk in the Sudan the priests notified the nobles, who then notified the king. The act, performed by the chief noble, had to fall on a dark night between the last and first quarter of the moon in the dry season before first sowing and first rain; in Rhodesia, the king's chief wife strangled him, on the night of the new moon, with a cord made of the foot-sinew of a bull.

Nor did these god-kings enter death alone:

The astounding burials discovered by Sir Leonard

Woolley at Ur, the Sumerian city sacred to the moon god, Nanna, have left an image of a Bronze Age ritual in all its splendour and barbarity. Here lay the bodies of priest-kings, or their substitutes, together with those of priestess-queens and many court or temple servants, including charioteers, musicians, and soldiers. In the most elaborate of these graves the king, whose name was A-bar-gi, had sixty-five people who died with, or soon after, him, and the queen, whose name was Shub-ad, had twenty-five . . .

Woolley writes that human sacrifice was confined to the funerals of royal personages. There was no sign of anything similar in the graves of commoners, however rich. Neither the kings, queens nor the courtiers appear to have suffered in these royal graves, or have gone unwillingly to their death. They must have been given a soporific drink before being buried alive.[6]

The burials of 16 distinct royal courts that Woolley found at Ur mirror the royal burials of groups of up to five hundred individuals, all buried on one day, excavated in numerous mass entombments spread over several centuries (c. 2000–1700 BC) in a Nubian necropolis at Kerma, by Professor George Reisner.

As in India to this day, therefore, so also in the deep Egyptian past, we find this appalling, apparently senseless, certainly very cruel, rite of suttee—and we shall discover it again in earliest China. The royal tombs of Ur show it in Mesopotamia and there is evidence in Europe as well. What can it mean, that man, precisely at the moment of the first flowering of his greatest civilizations, should have offered his humanity and common sense (even, indeed, one can say, his fundamental biological will to live) on the altar of a dream?

Were these willing victims, or were they forced, whom we have broken in upon in the cities of their sleep?[7]

Campbell answers these questions with pages of physical, circumstantial, and historical evidence supporting the claim that the participants voluntarily embraced their sacrifice.

It seems inconceivable to us today that a human could willingly consent to such a fate—but again, that is projecting our twenty-first century mindset, shaped by a sharply defined ego, into people who appear to have experienced the world far differently than we do today.

THE EMERGENCE OF EGO & THE SELF-CONSCIOUS HERO

Ultimately, we're talking about mythology, which operates out of a dynamic more of dream than of logic. Often our behaviors in dream are very much at odds with what we expect of ourselves when awake and rational—and myth is of the same order as dream.

As Campbell points out in *The Hero with a Thousand Faces*, dreams are private myths, and myths are public (collective) dreams . . . so a culture's mythology of sacrifice offers a window into the collective psyche of that culture.

On the other hand, the analogy of dream logic might be

more than mere metaphor. This play-world/dream-world is very real for the participants—all the more so because the elements of an effective, living ritual mirror the world in which one lives—and these were indeed, for a span, effective rituals.

The rational, differentiated ego is a relatively recent development among humans. That self-conscious sense appears to distinguish us from our animal cousins. A primary question—unless one believes man was created complete, conscious and self-aware from day one—is *when* in our past did ego consciousness arise from the unconscious psyche?

Jamake Highwater points out that Campbell "thought that very early on humankind was actually in a perpetual dream state," before the ego emerged. This needn't mean that we were once pre-historic zombies, but that our sense of individuality and of a separate, distinct consciousness proved porous and diffuse—just as it does for the dream ego in our nocturnal dramas.

Even today, members of the few primal cultures still active on the planet exhibit a far less sharply differentiated ego-consciousness than in the West, along with greater openness and receptivity to the group mind (evident even among the Aborigines in Australia, who always seem to have part of their consciousness back in "Dreamtime," the mythic *alcheringa* of the ancestors that permeates and supports the physical, waking world).

The late Harvard psychologist Julian Jaynes, in his classic study, *The Origins of Consciousness in the Breakdown of the Bi-cameral Mind*, draws on myth, archaeology, and linguistic, literary, and historical evidence to argue that humanity was largely "pre-conscious" into the early years of the high cultures, with the subjective ego taking shape somewhere between 2500 BC and 700 BC (of course, this wouldn't have happened overnight, but might have taken centuries to unfold).

Jaynes isn't suggesting that the people who built Catalhoyuk nine thousand years ago were mindless automatons; he does, though, make a strong case that they did not own their own thoughts, but heard in those thoughts the voices of the gods.

Jaynes attributes this to a dissociation between the right and left hemispheres of the brain (specifically, thoughts originating in "Wernicke's area" in the right hemisphere of the brain, "heard" in the auditory areas of the left temporal lobe), a consequence of the development of language. Originally images would have formed the content of thought, but, with the advent of language, humans started thinking in words.

I experience the "voices" in my head as my own thoughts, originating within my own mind—a recognition that makes modern consciousness possible. Archaic man, however, did not experience an internal monologue, but rather took divine dictation. What we might experience as a creative inspiration, he took as direction from the gods.

Julian Jaynes even finds traces of this perspective in Homer's *Iliad*, and in the biblical prophets—late examples of a fading mode of consciousness that "heard" the voices of the gods. This theory, while controversial, is nevertheless fascinating and not easily dismissed.

What isn't controversial is Jaynes's recognition that the beginnings of a major change are apparent by the end of the third millennium BC—in tandem with the shift from hieratic city-states to dynastic kingdoms.

Independent of Jaynes and his bicameral theory, Baring

and Cashford note evidence of this same change in the archaeological record:

> In the Bronze Age, for the first time, we learn the
> names of individual men and women, what they say
> and do . . . all these differentiations reflect the grow-
> ing awareness of the individual's power to shape events.
> The challenges of many different kinds of activity give
> rise to the myth of the "hero"—the person of greater
> wisdom, power, or strength who will be able to respond
> to a whole new dimension of endeavor, and who offers
> a model for the rest of the tribe to emulate: how, for
> example, to stop a mighty river flooding the land, how
> to govern a city with many thousands of people, how to
> defend against a barbarous enemy.[8]

Baring and Cashford locate the origins of the hero's quest in the
sun's transit of the heavens. Similarly, Joseph Campbell notes
"heroic mythology" appearing by 2500 B.C, with the Fifth
Dynasty in Egypt—a "solar" Bronze Age mythology replacing
the "lunar" mythology of the earlier tradition. (Ritual regicide is
attuned to lunar mythology as, in Campbell's words, "the moon,
symbol of life's death and resurrection, carries its own shadow
within itself—as we all do." We find traces of this lunar motif
in the celebration of the death-and-resurrection of Christ—"the
King of Kings"—with the date of Easter pegged to the Sunday
following the first full moon after the spring equinox.)

The motif of the hero is closely allied to the experience of
waking consciousness—James Hillman, among others, refers
to the "heroic ego"—so it's no surprise this mytheme surfaces

at such a critical juncture.

Jaynes attributes the breakdown of the bicameral mind and the emergence of a dynamic, self-conscious ego to a variety of factors, including trade, technological innovation, and, in particular, the development of writing. Other scholars as well tie writing to an emerging reflexive consciousness:

> The scribe, or author, could now begin to dialogue with his own visible inscriptions, viewing and responding to his own words even as he wrote them down. *A new power of reflexivity was thus coming into existence, borne by the relation between the scribe and his scripted text.*[9]

As intriguing as is Jaynes's theory of the bicameral brain or Campbell's discussion of the hero quest, it's impossible to isolate any specific trigger for this change in perception; nevertheless, the myth of the hero's quest, the art of writing, and a number of other cultural markers clearly accompany this shift in human consciousness.

One such significant marker is the near universal re-visioning of ritual regicide that occurs over this period.

"... LONG LIVE THE KING!"

As humanity made the transition from tribalism to civilization, Campbell describes the figure of the king as representing the central coordinating principle for that society—in essence, functioning as the ego for the group mind. No surprise, then, that kings were among the earliest to display a sense of individuality—and that stronger sense of ego moved them to step outside their assigned role, consciously tweaking the ritual and re-interpreting the myth of the royal sacrifice.

As the self-conscious ego evolved (perhaps as recently as three thousand years ago), we find these god-kings waking up to their sacrifice as at odds with their ego's sense of self-preservation—so ceremonies were adopted that substituted a ritual re-enactment for the actual sacrifice of the ruler—ceremonies that symbolically represented the death-and-rebirth of the king and yet managed to keep those mythological term limits from being strictly and literally enforced.

> In the earliest centuries of the prehistoric hieratic city-states—for which we have ample circumstantial evidence, and which I am dating c. 3500–2500 BC—the kings in their mythic identification are to such an extent "open behind" (to use the apt phrase of Thomas Mann) that they gave their bodies to be slain or even slew themselves in the festival mime: as, indeed, kings in India continued to be slain as late as the sixteenth century and in Africa into the twentieth. In Egypt, however, already in the period of the Narmer palette (c. 2850 BC), their individualities had to a certain extent "closed," so that the holy death-and-resurrection scenes were no longer being played with all the empathy of yore—at least by the players of the leading part . . . Somewhere, some time, at some point on the prehistoric map not yet brought into focus by research, the king had taken *maat* [right order] unto himself . . .

Instead of that old, dark, terrible drama of the king's death, which had formerly been played to the hilt, the audience now watched a symbolic mime, the *Sed* festival, in which the king renewed his pharaonic warrant without submitting to the personal inconvenience of a literal death . . . the real hero of the great occasion was no longer the timeless Pharaoh (capital P) who puts on pharaohs, like clothes, and puts them off, but the living garment of flesh and bone, this particular Pharaoh So-and-so, who, instead of giving himself to the part, had found a way to keep the part to himself. And this he did by stepping down the mythological image one degree. Instead of Pharaoh changing pharaohs, it was the pharaoh who changed costumes.[10]

This transition is subtle yet effective. In some cultures, an animal is offered in sacrifice as substitute for the king (as is the Apis bull in Egypt), while elsewhere a human substitute is found. In most instances, mass suttee burials still marked the treasure tombs of these demoted deities (Jaynes notes that in Sumer the kings were now designated "the tenant-farmers of the gods").

Campbell terms the "mock-holiness" of the worshipped kings in these later dynastic states *mythic inflation* ("the god absorbed and lost in ego"), as opposed to "the actual holiness of the sacrificed kings of the earlier hieratic city-states," which he labels *mythic identification* ("ego absorbed and lost in god").

Such obsequies cannot be interpreted, like those of the archaic ritual regicide, as giving evidence of any quenching of ego in the godly role of king. Indeed, on

---

---

one level—let us say the merely personal—they would have been celebrated adequately and nobly enough in Tennyson's unexciting last stanza of *Enoch Arden:*

"So passed the strong heroic soul away. / And when they buried him the little port / Had seldom seen a costlier funeral."[11]

Nevertheless, the *Sed* festival and other such substitution rituals, while removing risk to the central player, still managed to convey the mythic impact of the original rite.

How? Why would this work? Why would the people accept this significant rewrite?

One can't simply change a myth by fiat—not even the pharaoh. Ikhnaton's revolution, replacing the gods of Egypt with monotheism, lasted but one generation before the people reverted to the old ways. Were the collective culture ready for this change, the priests of the old order would not have found it so easy to restore Amun-re and the rest of the ancient pantheon. A mythology established by the point of a sword is bound to fail—unless the new myth strikes a receptive chord in the collective psyche, sounding familiar themes. A mythology must ring true in actual experience if it is to seize one's heart.

This is a fact universally recognized among peoples familiar with the service of myth to meditation. The verbal discourse, the explanatory legend, is functionally a lure to conduct the mind to, and to prepare it for, an experience of the image as an archetype of some aspect of one's own mystery. The image comes to one as though from afar, yet from within, as an opener of the way to release from the tension of separateness in space and time, the anguish of temporality, and one goes to it as a bridegroom to his bride or an infant to the breast.[12]

Campbell suggests that both the *Sed* festival and the sacrifice of the Apis bull fulfill this function—as does another variation on this motif, a further morphing of the mytheme common today:

> The question is appropriate and was, of course, to be expected. It brings up the delicate problem as to whether in a mythic image there may be an implicit meaning, for the mythological image that is rendered in this shocking rite is the same as that of the sacrifice of the mass. The archetype or elementary idea *(Elementargedanke)* is in both ceremonials the same: the sacrifice of an incarnate divinity and a communion meal of its flesh *(Hoc est enim corpus meum)*. The secondary, local settings and interpretations *(Völkergedanken)* differ, but the psychological impact and therefore the transformative power of a myth derive from its image, not its explanation.[13]

It is, however, ironic that the end of ritual regicide coincided with the inauguration of bloodshed on a massive scale. Prior to the middle of the third millennium, conflict had been mostly limited to local affairs as one community bumped into another—but Sargon of Agade's invasion of Sumer, in 2350 BC, marks the beginning of wars of conquest and total subjugation—the world in which we live yet today. The blood shed since far outweighs that lost through human sacrifice.

In *Primitive Mythology,* Campbell puts this ritual in perspective by pointing out that "the number of lives offered up in such rites is far less, proportionately to the population, than that sacrificed in our cities in traffic accidents. However, among ourselves such deaths are thought of and experienced generally as a consequence of human fallibility, even though their incidence is statistically predictable. In the primitive ritual, on the other hand, which is based on the viewpoint of the species rather than the individual, what for us is 'accident' is placed at the center of the system—namely, sudden, monstrous death—and this becomes therewith a revelation of the inhumanity of the order of the universe."[14]

Odd that, as one form of ritual murder faded, a far more lethal form arose.

MYSTERY RITES AND MYSTIC TRADITIONS

Substitution became the order of the day as lesser humans and/ or sacred animals filled in for the king. In most high civilizations animals eventually replaced humans on the altar, though some forms of human sacrifice continued into the twentieth century, and traces occasionally surface today in isolated acts, such as the practice of *sati*—ritual suicide—in India or Japan.

Sacrifice of any sort is rare today, thanks to the next great movement in this dance—the interiorization of the myth. Again, the *Sed* festival of ancient Egypt points the way:

Such then, or somewhat such, was the rite by which the literal killing of the old king and the transfer of power to the new had been transformed into an allegory. The king died not literally, but symbolically, in the earliest passion play of which we have record. And the plot of the sacred mime was the old, yet ever new formula of the Adventure of the Hero, which is known to the later arts and literatures all over the world . . .

Thus in a marvelously subtle way the work commenced of Art, which in the course of the following long, cruel centuries was gradually to alleviate the force of the earlier, literally enacted mythic seizures, releasing man thereby from their inhumanity, while opening through the figures of their inspiration new ways to an understanding of humanity itself.[15]

And so we come to two of Joseph Campbell's major themes: the centrality of both the Hero's Journey, and the Way of Art, to the human experience. Art—in this instance, through the medium of myth and ritual drama—presents an image that conveys to those assembled a sense of *participation mystique*— an experience with all the emotional impact and transformative power of the act portrayed. This dramatic dimension is an essential element of ritual—even in the Christian mass.

One of the wonderful things in the Catholic ritual is going to communion. There you are taught this *is* the body and blood of the Savior. And you take it to you, and you turn inward, and there Christ is working within you. This is a way of inspiring a meditation on experiencing the spirit in you. You see people coming back from communion, and they are inward-turned, they really are.[16]

I imagine the real surprise would be if the sacrificial motif were missing from Christian mythology—but that is clearly not the case. There is no denying the transformative power of the experience. The only caveat is that the Christian revelation is understood to be historical and unique, and so engenders the usual complications that accompany a literal reading of any myth. Christianity, though, is not alone in rendering this theme. The mystery religions of ancient Greece and Asia Minor, those of Attis, of Orpheus or Dionysus, of Demeter and Persephone at Eleusis, and others, were influenced by ancient Egypt's mysteries of Isis and Osiris. They presented a passion play that places the initiate in the role of the dead-and-resurrected god, thus interiorizing the sacrifice.

> The fundamental experience of their Mysteries, enacted in an initiation ceremony that involved the "death" of the initiate, may have been that death was an illusion, and the soul immortal. The inner and symbolic "sacrifice" of the fear of death releases the initiate from the conception of life and death as irreconcilable opposites, and opened his or her consciousness to the wonder of being. Here *bios*, the individual life in time, was reunited with *zoe*, the ground of all life, and the finite experience was transcended in a living experience.[17]

A parallel realization appears in the *Upaniṣads*:

Brahman [the Being of beings] is the act of the offering.
Brahman is the oblation poured by *Brahman* into the
fire, which is *Brahman*. By anyone thus recognizing in
all action only *Brahman, Brahman* is attained.[18]

The sense I get is that when we read any of these myths metaphorically, surrendering to the power of the symbols rather
than acting them out in literal, graphic and bloody detail, each
of us, then, is the sacrifice (from the Latin *sacer facere*—"to
make whole or sacred").

What I "make sacred," through sacrifice, is me.

Or, in the words Campbell borrows from the Indian tradition, *tat tvam asi* – "Thou Art That."

That seems to be the crux of the matter . . .

MAKING SACRED

I am glad most of these horrendous practices are in the past;
though the symbolism remains sublime, the literal rendering
of the myth is an example of old-time religion we could all
probably do without.

Nevertheless, the symbolism of sacrifice retains its power to
effect personal transformation.

These symbols can be explored in greater detail in Joseph
Campbell's *The Hero with a Thousand Faces*, which follows
the many variations on the motif of the hero's adventure, and
relates the elements of this quest to our own life's journey.

The rendering of those symbols in art, and how they
might be drawn upon to develop one's personal mythology,

are investigated in *Creative Mythology*, the fourth and final volume of Campbell's *The Masks of God* tetralogy. And both the hero quest and the role of art are examined in several other Campbell books, particularly *Pathways to Bliss* and *The Inner Reaches of Outer Space*.

Of course, sacrifice is in itself a virtually inexhaustible topic. I'm walking through but one door here, royal sacrifice my portal into the subject. There are, though, many other doors to be opened, multiple levels of access and understanding. Campbell enjoys exploring these many layers; on the practical level, however, he arrives at the following insight:

> Why go to the Brahmans? You've got it in yourself. Turn in. All those gods that you are invited to worship through the public sacrifice are projections of the fire of your own energy . . .
>
> Deities are symbolic personifications of the very energies that are of yourself. These energies that are of yourself are the energies of the universe. And so the god out there is the god in here. The kingdom of heaven is within you, but it's also everywhere. This is perennial philosophy stuff.
>
> So with that we come to the business of finding the fire in yourself. It's a psychological act of discrimination; discriminating between the physical, transforming aspect of your entity and that enduring flame of which youth and age, birth and death are but the inflections.[19]

James Hillman depicts ego as thinking it is "the king of the soul"—so, in one sense, we do sacrifice the king—not by destroying the ego, but by relativizing it, placing it in context, in relationship to the whole. In Hillman's formulation, my ego is not the king of my psyche so much as the janitor of my soul: ego gets me from point A to point B, makes a peanut butter sandwich when I'm hungry, and tends to my being—but it's not the whole of my being. I need my ego—"me," "I," "myself," the me I think myself to be—and its "reality function" to survive—but I cannot experience the sacred and transcendent without to some extent surrendering ego (i.e., transcending "me").

It does seem ironic that ego, which in its current form coincided with the survival instinct of kings determined to escape the ritual knife, must be eclipsed if we intend to realize the transformation symbolized in that sacrifice.

So what form does sacrifice take today? We needn't act it out in the literal fashion of millennia past—instead, we participate in this act whenever we experience the transcendent pouring into the world of phenomenal forms.

Every act we do with intention and ritual—"making sacred"—achieves the same end. Gathering with friends and eating a meal is then experienced as a communion—indeed, every act becomes sacred with proper attention.

I can only speak for myself, for each is on her or his own path, and what works for me may not work for you.

When I carve space out of my busy day, take time away from ego pursuits—from working or eating or sleeping or playing or relaxing or watching TV—and spend that time meditating in front of an altar, I am sacrificing myself to my Self—"self" to "Self"—thus allowing the eternal portion of my being to live and breathe and be. This is true of prayer, of a walk in the woods, or time for reflection, or journaling, or participating in any ritual, personal or collective, that speaks to soul.

At first, it certainly feels a sacrifice (in the popular sense of the word).

I noticed this when I first started meditating, and first started keeping a journal, and first began recording my dreams. It took effort and intention to resist the thought that there were other things I could be, and probably should be, doing with this time being frittered away on a task without obvious utilitarian value . . . but, over time, I found I had no choice.

To skip meditation, fail to write, or not tend to dream seems a violation of my being—it's no longer a chore, but who I am.

. . . who *"I Am"* . . . self sacrificed to Self, god sacrificed to God—and so I am made sacred and enlarged through a sacred re-apportionment—not the "I," the ego of the little self, but an identification with the larger Self.

> This is an essential experience of any mystical realization. You die to your flesh and are born into your spirit. You identify yourself with the consciousness and life of which your body is but the vehicle. You die to the vehicle and become identified in your consciousness with that of which the vehicle is but the carrier. That is the God.
>
> . . . Behind all these manifestations is the one radiance, which shines through all things.[20]

Meditation, music, ritual, art, and comparable activities offer portals into that realm. We experience the sacrifice whenever that one radiance shines through what we do in the here and now.

That's a sacrifice I can embrace.

Notes

1. Campbell, Oriental Mythology, op. cit. 46.
2. Ibid. 62.
3. Campbell, Power of Myth op. cit. 132.
4. Joseph Campbell, Historical Atlas of World Mythology Vol.2.: The Way of the Seeded Earth, Part 1: The Sacrifice (New York: Harper & Row, 1988), 75-76.
5. Ibid. 78.
6. Baring and Cashford, The Myth of the Goddess, op. cit. 166, 167.
7. Campbell, Oriental Mythology, op. cit. 61.
8. Baring and Cashford, op. cit. 154.
9. David Abram, The Spell of the Sensuous: Perception and Language in a More-Than-Human World (New York: Pantheon Books, 1996), 107.
10. Campbell, Oriental Mythology, op. cit. 69, 74.
11. Ibid. 75.
12. Ibid. 73.
13. Ibid.
14. Campbell, Primitive Mythology, op. cit. 167.
15. Campbell, Oriental Mythology, op. cit. 73.
16. Campbell, Power of Myth, op. cit. 74.
17. Baring and Cashford, op. cit. 414.
18. Campbell, The Sacrifice, op. cit. 52.
19. Joseph Campbell, Mythos, Vol.2: The Shaping of the Eastern Tradition, Episode 1: The Inward Path (New York: Unapix, 2000; London: Acorn Media, 2008).
20. Campbell, The Power of Myth, op. cit. 134.

TWENTY

ORIGINAL CAMPBELL

> A kind of chain reaction comes from his discoveries
> that have reverberated out into writing novels, into psy-
> chiatry, into anthropology, into mythology, into film-
> making, into creative work, and apart from that, he's a
> damn nice guy. . . . It's hard to believe that Shakespeare
> didn't read Joseph Campbell. (Richard Adams, author
> of *Watership Down*, *Shardik*, and *Plague Dogs*, at the
> National Arts Club, 1985)[1]

I've been on the road most of the past six weeks, starting with
the Mythic Journeys Conference and Performance Arts Festival
in Atlanta in early June [2006], so this month's "Practical
Campbell" will be an abbreviated version of the usual lum-
bering essay—no doubt a relief to many, given my inclination
towards excessive verbosity.

Mercury remains in retrograde as I write, almost guaran-
teeing thoughts a-tangle (if you believe that sort of thing), so
I thought to sidestep the cosmic trickster by switching tactics;

instead of delving deep into just one subject, we'll sample a potpourri of topics, skimming the surface of concepts whose only common characteristic is that they originated with Joseph Campbell.

This cluster-shot approach is triggered by a contemporary criticism that Campbell, though skilled at collecting and communicating the thoughts of others, had no original ideas of his own. Campbell's work is thus characterized as bringing together material already in existence and making it available to the broader public (e.g., Adolf Bastian's classification of elementary and ethnic ideas, or Jung's conceptualization of the collective unconscious).

Joseph Campbell's words do indeed appeal to a popular audience, turning them on to what turned him on. Many are the individuals who'll admit they first encountered Joyce, Mann, Spengler, Nietzsche, Jung, and others in the pages of Campbell's books. Nor does Joe fail to acknowledge the influence of those who have gone before—but this need not mean his work is derivative.

On the other hand, Campbell toiled in the field of mythology; his source material has indeed been in existence for millennia (e.g., the motif of the virgin birth, a pattern the ancients recognized long before the Christian nativity in a multitude of myths from different cultures—a recognition so entrenched that early Christian fathers warned of counterfeit myths devised by the devil to duplicate the Savior's feats *before* the fact—so Joseph's identification of this recurring motif is hardly unique).

At the same time, I can't think of many people, even Einstein and Picasso and Joyce, whose work doesn't "bring together material already in existence." Originality lies in the creative way one arranges this already existing material in a novel expression that changes the way others view what's been in front of them all along.

As I wandered the high plains, deserts and mountains that define the American West this past month, I found myself pondering what I find original in Joseph Campbell's work—novel formulations and key concepts he introduced into the study of mythology. Rather than a comprehensive compilation, the following list tends to reflect my own interests, and so barely scratches the surface—but some topics may provide a point of departure for those interested in exploring further on their own.

MYTHOLOGY A FUNCTION OF BIOLOGY

I think of mythology as a function of biology; the energies of the body are the energies that move the imagination. These energies are the source, then, of mythological imagery; in a mythological organization of symbols, the conflicts between the different organic impulses within the body are resolved and harmonized. You might say mythology is a formula for the harmonization of the energies of life.[2]

Campbell covers this in depth in the first one hundred pages of *Primitive Mythology* (Volume I of *The Masks of God*), and also discusses aspects of this correspondence in the essay "Bios and Mythos," in *The Flight of the Wild Gander*. These insights have roots in Campbell's education at Dartmouth, where he majored in biology before transferring to Columbia, and his association with biologist Ed Ricketts—in particular a summer expedition to Alaska collecting marine specimens. (Campbell's friendship with Ricketts and the insights sparked by their collaboration are discussed in Chapter 15, "Intelligible Design.")

To the best of my knowledge, Joseph Campbell is the first mythologist to ground mythology in the human body. Others, particularly in the field of psychology, suggested particular myths have their origin in a common biological experience (Otto Rank comes to mind), but Campbell is the first to offer a complete theory. That framework makes it easier, for example, to comprehend the role that the length of childhood dependency and the female menstrual cycle play in the development of initiation rites and accompanying myths.

Mythology thus places the individual—and the society—in accord with nature.

IMAGE IS PRIMARY

> For me, myth is primarily visual, not linguistic. It comes from visions and cuts across linguistic provinces. Language is secondary. It has to do with the communication of myth.[3]

Campbell speaks of vision as coming first in the creation/ formulation of a myth—both the individual vision (of, say, a shaman), and in terms of the mythic image. He thus rejects the structuralism of Claude Levy-Strauss:

My idea is that the basic thing about myth is that it is visionary. A mythology is a system of 'affect-symbols,' signs evoking and directing psychic energies. Levy-Strauss is saying something like verbal grammar is the structuring form of myth, and this seems to me just wrong, that's all. The logic of image-thinking and of verbal thinking are two very different logics.[4]

In myth, whether in written stories or earlier images on wall-friezes or pottery, Campbell sticks with the image (much as James Hillman advises when working with a dream). This concept also prompts Campbell's confidence in the artist—today's image-makers, the musicians, poets, painters, filmmakers and such—as keeper of the mythic flame.

PUBLIC DREAMS AND PRIVATE MYTHS

The association between myth and dream has long been recognized in traditional cultures, from the *alcheringa* ("Dreamtime") of the Australian Aborigines or "Distant Time" of Alaska's Koyukon peoples, to Vishnu dreaming the dream of the world in Hindu myth—but Joseph Campbell is the first mythologist to assert this association isn't simply a figment of the primitive imagination.

True, Campbell builds on the foundation of Carl Jung, who noted parallels between dream-imagery and the images of myth—but Joe boldly states the case when he tells Bill Moyers, "the myth is the public dream and the dream is the private myth." Myth, Joe avers, is of the same order as dream: both are productions of the human imagination:

> [Myth] is dreamlike and, like dream, a spontaneous
> product of the psyche; like dream, revelatory of the psy-
> che and hence of the whole nature and destiny of man;
> like dream—like life—enigmatic to the uninitiated
> ego; and, like dream, protective of that ego.[5]

That assertion leads some to assume Campbell thus interprets myths exclusively in psychological terms. He certainly leans toward the psychological, but the first chapter of Campbell's *The Mythic Image*, "The World as Dream," embraces a more playful, even lyrical approach to this concept.

THE FOUR FUNCTIONS OF MYTH

Campbell identifies four functions a mythology performs (which does not mean every myth in a mythological tradition addresses all four functions. In brief, he identifies these functions as follows (excerpted from *Pathways to Bliss*, but multiple versions appear throughout Campbell's work):

> The Metaphysical (or Mystical) Function—"to evoke in
> the individual a sense of grateful, affirmative awe before
> the monstrous mystery that is existence."
> The Cosmological Function—"to present an image
> of the cosmos, of the universe round about, that will
> maintain and elicit this experience of awe."
> The Sociological Function —"to validate and
> maintain a certain sociological system: a shared set of
> right and wrongs, proprieties or improprieties, on which

one's particular social unit depends for its existence."

The Psychological (or "Pedagogical") Function—
"to carry the individual through the stages of one's life,
from birth through maturity through senility to death."

These classifications present a useful framework for studying
mythology. However, this framework is not meant to be rigid
and unyielding. Campbell played with other possible functions
of myth as well, including an "editorial function," a "magical" function, even a "political" function (see Campbell, et. al.,
Changing Images of Man), but found these generally fit comfortably into one or another of the categories above.

THE EMERGENCE OF THE MANDALA

This is an obscure yet little-noticed observation worth a little extra ink. Both Joseph Campbell and Carl Jung relate the
symbol of the mandala to a thirst for wholeness in the human
psyche — but where Jung generally encounters the mandala
in a dream-image and thus relates it to the individual psyche,
Campbell charts its earliest appearance as an expression of the
collective psyche.

Campbell delves into the origin and development of the
mandala in "The Symbol Without Meaning," delivered at the
Eranos Roundtable in Ascona, Switzerland, in 1957, and published as the next-to-last section in *The Flight of the Wild Gander*.
He points out that symmetry and geometrical organization are
not features of the cave art or figurines found in Europe stretching from 30,000 to 9,000 BC; however, after this period this

motif surfaces in primitive mandalas, such as the swastikas etched on ivory bird figurines in Old Europe. The theme eventually appears as detailed, full-fledged mandalas on pottery from the Halaf and Samarra cultures, c. 4000 BC, in Iraq.

Why does this image emerge in this period?

Campbell notes the mandala appears concurrent with the development of agriculture—and a consequence of agriculture is specialization.

Previously most members of a tribe or village or community had access to the whole range of technology available to that people (which doesn't mean no one specialized in making arrowheads or weaving baskets, but that knowledge of the necessary technology was within reach of all, with what specialization there was often gender-based).

Agriculture creates a surplus of food, which makes civilization possible (even necessary). Different members of the society now possess only parts of the whole, specialists in one often narrow task, whether farmer, priest, soldier, nursemaid, weaver, sacred harlot (or priestess), toolmaker, scribe, or king. Campbell theorizes it's more than coincidence that this period marks the appearance of the circular form as a recurring motif in myth, art, or even city planning (e.g., compare the beehive cluster of *Catalhoyuk* in Anatolia—the oldest known city on the planet, founded some eight to ten thousand years ago—with the geometrical layout of the cities of Sumer, which could be described as urban mandalas).

The collective unconscious thus presents the mandala as an image compensatory to the fragmentation of society—a symbol of the whole—a mythic means of restoring the balance and finding one's place.

The problem of existing as a mere fraction instead of as a whole imposes certain stresses on the psyche which no primitive hunter ever had to endure, and consequently the symbols giving structure and support to the development of the primitive hunter's psychological balance were different from those that arose in the settled villages, in the Basal and the High Neolithic, and which have been inherited from that age and continued into the present by all the high civilizations of the world.[6]

This is an excellent example of one of Campbell's unique contributions to human knowledge. Jung was among the first to find this image recurring in the dreams of individual subjects, but Campbell charts its appearance in human art and offers this novel theory of the image representing an unconscious compensation for the fragmentation of the collective psyche—a theory that, to the best of my knowledge, remains unchallenged.

"432" – THE FOOTPRINT OF THE ETERNAL ROUND

This is an obscure observation as well, one that is just plain fun to investigate (especially for those with a numerological bent), so I'll indulge myself here as well.

Joseph Campbell points out that the number 432, along with its products and factors, appears too often in distinct mythologies of distant cultures to be chance; and, where it does appear, we find traces of goddess mythology and of cultures that perceive time as cyclical and recurring—the Eternal Round.

Joe explores this phenomenon in *The Inner Reaches of Outer Space,* and in even greater detail in "The Mystery Number of the Goddess," a 55-page essay reprinted in *The Mythic Dimension*:

> As prophesied in The Poetic Edda:
> "Five hundred and forty doors there are
>> I ween, in Valhall's walls,
>> Eight hundred fighters through each door fare
>> When to war with the Wolf they go."
>
> 540 x 800 = 432,000, which in the Hindu Puranas is the number of years reckoned to the Kali Yuga, the present cycle of time, which is to be the last and shortest of four cycles that comprise a 'Great Cycle' or Mahayuga of 4,320,000 years, which is to end in a universal flood.
>
> The Puranas date from c. AD 400 to 1000; the Eddic verses from c. AD 900 to 1100. The obvious question to be asked, therefore, is, By what coincidence can this number have appeared both in India and in Iceland in association with a mythology of recurrent cycles of time?[7]

Joseph then turns to the king list of Berossos, a priest of Marduk, c. 285 BC, who presents a synopsis of Babylonian history. Berossos compiled a list of ten kings who ruled Sumer up to the time of the mythological flood (floods generally marking the end of an age), for a period totaling 432,000 years. . .

There's that 432 again—and it's even concealed in the Genesis account, in the 1,656 years that pass from the first patriarch, Adam, to the tenth, Noah (who is 600 years old at the time of the age-ending Great Flood). Campbell points to a paper presented before the Royal Society for Sciences in Gottingen by Assyriologist Jules Oppert, which notes there are 86,400 seven-day weeks in 1656 years (the seven-day week, denoted by the term "sabbath," particularly significant in Hebrew culture)— and 86,400 divided by 2 is, of course, 43,200.

Campbell finds yet another correspondence in the work of Icelandic scholar Einar Palsson, who describes the two original settlements in Iceland as intentionally aligned along an axis exactly 432,000 Roman feet in length (roughly 80 miles). Other nearby sacred sites, positions determined by the summer and winter solstice, are exactly 216,000 Roman feet (half of 432,000) from the nearest settlement.

The mythology of cyclical time and recurring ages first emerged in Mesopotamia when humans turned their eyes skyward and discovered a detailed order in the heavens, where celestial bodies follow a recurring cycle. It takes 25,920 years for the circle of the Zodiac to complete one full revolution and return each constellation to its starting point in the night sky. This is known as a "great" or "Platonic" year. Campbell does the math for us:

> If we divide 25,920 by 60 (which is the ancient Mesopotamian *soss,* or basic sexagesimal unit of astronomical measurement, still used in the measurement of circles, whether of time or of space), the quotient is 432.[8]

The number 432 is thus one-sixtieth—or one "minute"—of the cosmic clock of the Zodiac, which was central to Sumer and later cultures that based their structure on the structure in the heavens—and so kept detailed records on hundreds of thousands of cuneiform tablets of the round of the constellations. The number is even buried in the New Testament, in the description of the heavenly Jerusalem that will descend at the end of time to replace the worldly city:

> The city lies foursquare, its length the same as its breadth, and he measured the city with his rod, twelve thousand stadia; its length and breadth and height are equal.
>
> (Revelations 21:16)

A perfect cube, 12,000 stadia on a side: 12,000 x 12,000 x 12,000 = 1,728 billion cubic stadia—which, when divided by four (the foursquare city), equals 432 billion cubic stadia . . . hmmm. (Lingering traces of such concepts in the Bible shouldn't be surprising, given the birth of Judean-Christian mythology out of the womb of the Fertile Crescent.)

Joe even offers a passage from Kenneth Cooper's groundbreaking 1928 work, *Aerobics*:

> A conditioned man, who exercises regularly, will have a resting heart rate of about sixty beats per minute or less . . . Sixty per minute, times sixty minutes, equals 3600 beats an hour. Times 24 hours, equals 86,400 beats a day.[9]

I'm sure that last number looks familiar (43,200 heartbeats every twelve hours). Campbell suggests the ancient Sumerians tuned their mythology to the cosmic clock of the outer world, possibly even finding a relationship with the inner clock of the human body—and, indeed, the thrust of their mythology is that of a harmony between macro-cosm (the outer universe), mesocosm (the social order), and microcosm (the individual).

It may seem like a stretch at first, grasping at every factor of 432 we can find—but Joe does a good job of demonstrating these aren't just random values. Campbell's genius, however, lies in how he strings these disparate beads of information together, based on his knowledge of multiple mythologies. The number 432 appears in Mesopotamian mythology marking the end of an age (the Deluge), in Hindu mythology marking the length of an age (the Kali Yuga), in Norse mythology at the end of an age (the number of warriors from Valhalla who come forth to fight at the end of the world), and even in the New Testament at the end of the age (the measurements of the heavenly Jerusalem, descending to earth).

Coincidence?

Possibly—but Campbell assembles mounds of evidence and makes a cogent case . . . definitely worth pursuing for those who are interested.

THE HERO'S JOURNEY AS A TEMPLATE FOR LIFE

Joseph Campbell is closely identified with the motif of the hero's journey, largely due to the success of *A Hero with a Thousand Faces*—long recognized as a classic within the field of mythology—and yet, in many ways there is nothing unique about his interest in the hero. Other mythologists before Campbell studied the hero's role in myth—Lord Raglan in particular—and the movements of the monomyth

Campbell identifies as key to the hero's journey—those of separation, initiation, and return—had earlier been isolated by Arnold van Gennep as the essential elements underlying initiation rites (van Gennep's work, *Les rites de passage,* also influenced anthropologist Victor Turner, whose work bears parallels to Campbell's).

Psychologist Otto Rank was also drawn to hero myths, but he interprets them primarily in terms of the birth trauma and a child's relationship to their parents:

> Otto Rank in his important little book *The Myth of the Birth of the Hero* declares that everyone is a hero in birth, where he undergoes a tremendous psychological as well as physical transformation, from the condition of a little water creature living in a realm of amniotic fluid into an air- breathing mammal which ultimately will be standing. That's an enormous transformation, and had it been consciously undertaken it would have been, indeed, a heroic act.[10]

Frazer, Raglan, Tylor, van Gennep, and all the greats in the field prior to Campbell studied myth to understand other cultures, to add to our knowledge, and to get a sense of the scope of the human imagination—which is much of what Campbell did as well—but no mythologist before appears to have grasped the vast body of mythology might be applicable to contemporary life.

Campbell acknowledges the influence of his predecessors, but goes beyond them by asserting the motif of the hero's journey *can* be consciously adopted as a model for the living of life (which itself is a series of initiations).

Campbell's understanding of this aspect of the hero quest thus reflects the fourth function of mythology (the "psychological" or "pedagogical" function) noted above—"to carry the individual through the stages of one's life."

Much has been written on this subject so I won't belabor the point. Some readers grasp this immediately, and some don't (I didn't recognize any relevance to my own life until my second reading of *The Hero with a Thousand Faces*, at a time when I was deeply mired in "the Wasteland"). Campbell goes into greater detail regarding "practical" aspects of the hero's quest in *Pathways to Bliss* and *A Joseph Campbell Companion*.

FOLLOW YOUR BLISS

I have a firm belief in this now, not only in terms of my own experience, but in knowing the experience of other people. When you follow your bliss, and by bliss I mean the deep sense of being in it, and doing what the push is out of your own existence—it may not be fun, but it's your bliss and there's bliss behind pain too.

You follow that and doors will open where there were no doors before, where you would not have thought there'd be doors, and where there wouldn't be a door for anybody else.

. . . And so I think the best thing I can say is to follow your bliss. If your bliss is just your fun and your excitement, you're on the wrong track. I mean, you need instruction. Know where your bliss is. And that involves coming down to a deep place in yourself.[11]

Joseph Campbell's formulation of "Follow your bliss" is so novel and unique that it has become almost a de facto trademark. Over decades of studying mythology, Joe noticed this subtext echoing through myths from disparate times and cultures.

Of course, there are those who believe Campbell is advocating unbridled hedonism (ignoring all the instances where Campbell points out that following one's bliss leads to crucifixion or burning at the stake), mistaking this axiom for Aleister Crowley's "Do what thou wilt shall be the whole of the law"— which is very different indeed!

This adage clearly resonates with some theosophical and New Age concepts, but in Campbell's day such ideas were vague at best and hazily expressed. Campbell's axiom, though, is firmly rooted in the body of myth. He traces his initial insight to the Buddhist concept of *satcitananda* (*sat* = being, *cit* = consciousness, and *ananda* = bliss), and to the "Five Sheaths" of Hinduism's *anandamaya* culture, which influenced the *Vedanta* tradition.

Campbell and others have discussed this principle at length, so I'll move on.

EARTH – THE CENTER OF ANY COMING MYTHOOGY

> I do think we are at the end of a civilization. And I do think we're at the beginning of a global age. That is to say, it's once more a globe. No longer do you have different cultures within their bounded horizons, ignorant

of each other and indifferent to each other. All horizons are broken.[12]

In the *Power of Myth* interviews with Bill Moyers, Campbell makes clear that any future myth, to be effective, must transcend provincial forms and take into account the reality in which we live. We're experiencing the birth pangs of that process right now as cultures-in-collision are loathe to let go of their own bounded horizons—but ultimately, any living myth will be a myth of Earth as one whole:

> You can't predict what a myth is going to be any more than you can predict what you're going to dream tonight. Myths and dream come from the same place. They come from realizations of some kind that have then to find expression in symbolic form. And the only myth that is going to be worth thinking about in the immediate future is one that is talking about the planet, not the city, not these people, but the planet and everybody on it. That's my main thought for what the future of myth is going to be.
>
> And what it will have to deal with will be exactly what all myths have dealt with—the maturation of the individual, from dependency through adulthood, through maturity, and then to exit; and then how to relate to this society and how to relate this society to the world of nature and the cosmos. That's what the myths have all talked about, and what this one's got to talk about. But the society that it's got to talk about is the society of the planet. And until that gets going, you don't have anything.

> . . .When you see the earth from the moon, you
> don't see any divisions of nations or states. This might
> be the symbol, really, for the new mythology to come.
> That is the country we are celebrating. And those are
> the people we are one with.[13]

Hints and foreshadowing abound, from growing evidence for the Gaia hypothesis (advanced by biologists James Lovelock and Lynn Margolies, among others, positing that the earth's processes correspond to the actions of a self-regulating organism), to ecumenical movements, and even our current environmental crisis (in the film *An Inconvenient Truth*, Al Gore employs one of Campbell's favorite images—"Earthrise," the best-known picture of earth taken from space).

Campbell acknowledges that the beginning of every age is painful, and predicts plenty of chaos and violence before the image of One Earth can be realized—but he's confident the patterns of myth, conscious or not, will ultimately reassert themselves on the world stage. This isn't a question of faith, but of an understanding of the dynamics of myth.

This is a thumbnail sketch of but a handful of innovative insights and conclusions, major and minor, that set Joseph Campbell apart in my mind. Again, I'm just scratching the surface—I've skipped as much as I've covered, neglecting to mention anything about Joe's insights into the nature of consciousness; or his observation of an association between the diffusion of mythic motifs and the spread of technologies (e.g., flint points, pottery styles, etc.) along with the domestication of particular plants and animals; or the parallels he finds in the sudden interest in love (in the sense of "amor") that spontaneously springs up in the tenth and eleventh centuries in the myth and literature of widely separated cultures, from the troubadours and minnesingers of Europe to the Sufis of the Islamic world, the Hindus of India, and even the nobility of Japan; or Campbell's tracing a source of the legends of King Arthur (whose name means "bear" and has been linked to the motif of the Green Man, among others) back through a Celtic deity (Ardehe) to the cult of Artemis, for whom the bear is sacred, and on to the bear cults of the dim and distant prehistoric past.

So many paths to explore . . . and I'm sure I've missed far more than I know.

Which brings me to a question:

What do you find unique in the work of Joseph Campbell? What other novel concepts and constructions did Campbell pioneer?

NOTES

1. Campbell, Hero's Journey, op. cit. 210.
2. Campbell, "The Mythic Journey," op. cit.
3. Campbell, "Myths of the Universe," op. cit.
4. Campbell, "Liviing Myths," op. cit.
5. Campbell, Flight of the Gander, op. cit. 34.
6. Ibid. 114.
7. Campbell, Mythic Dimension, op. cit. 115.
8. Campbell, Inner Reaches of Outer Space, op. cit. 12.
9. Cooper, Kenneth H. Aerobics (New York: Bantam Books, 1969), 101.
10. Campbell, Power of Myth, op. cit. 152-153.
11. Campbell, Hero's Journey, op. cit. 253.
12. Ibid. 247-248.
13. Campbell, Power of Myth, op. cit. 41.

TWENTY-ONE

HERE BE DRAGONS!

> But are we justified in making such cross-cultural references? Or let us put the case another way. Is it reasonable to maintain, in cases where identical motifs appear in identically structured compositions—with, in many instances, analogous myths and legends to support them—that the informing ideas must not be assumed to have been pretty much the same as well?
>
> What, however, about that serpent of Eden, who was not worshipped as the lord of life, but humbled, cursed, and rejected?[1]

Joseph Campbell sees myth as a language of sorts, a picture-language of the soul. Myth, like art, presents images that convey what Campbell refers to as a "feeling-tone," thus evoking experiences and responses far beyond a limited, literal dictionary definition, offering glimpses of that which lies beneath the reality we experience.

Symbols can be interpreted and explained, but those explanations come *after* the fact (true for this essay as well). The immediate impact of a myth, especially when enacted in ritual, bypasses intellect; it's felt in the heart and in the gut, not in the head. The difference between the impact of a mythic image and its secondary theological interpretation, no matter how relevant, matches the gap between getting a joke, and having it explained.

Every myth contains multiple layers of embedded, often conflicting ideas and concepts, which is why these images and metaphors are so valuable—they add depth and dimension to flat, linear language. The literalness of an engineer's vocabulary is welcome when hammering nails into wood or measuring angles for a bridge's truss—but the rich, complex, often paradoxical picture-language of poetry speaks louder on questions of life and love and substance and soul.

As a result, we aren't dealing here with an Aristotelian, "A is not not-A" world. The ability to embrace paradox is then essential to Campbell's understanding of mythology, for in myth, like in dream, time and space prove fluid and images flow one into another. A certainly can be not-A: Man can walk on water, Coyote walks upright, Jesus is both God and Man, and the Triple Goddess is Mother, Maiden, and Crone at once.

Dragon is one such resplendent image, reaching back through faery tale and myth into the distant and barely discernable past. From the "lion-birds" at the portals of a shrine to the serpent-god, Ningishzida, engraved on the libation vase of King Gudea of Lagash in ancient Sumer, c. 2000 BC, to Bilbo Baggins's theft of the Arkenstone from the dragon Smaug in Tolkien's *The Hobbit* (published four thousand years later), the dragon guards the way to otherworldly realms.

A dragon's presence in a tale promises high adventure—but is this image ultimately malignant, or benign? Good, or evil? Does the dragon nurture, or destroy? Does it only lay waste, or might it inspire creativity and strength?

Where does this image come from? What are its origins, and what its ends? What role does the dragon play in the evolution of human civilization, and in our own personal evolution?

Definitive answers risk snares woven from the rigid meaning and dogmatic interpretation that come of concretizing a metaphor. Instead, we'll embrace paradox and flow with the image, following the dragon back to its earliest appearance in myth, and even further, watching as it emerges from its constituent parts, before returning to the present to find the dragon's lair hidden within ourselves.

These ruminations, while grounded in what is known, are not however to be mistaken for a set of Cartesian facts, nailed down and indisputable; instead, they echo the fluid, polymorphous multidimensionality of the mythic imagination, perhaps revealing more about ourselves than what we study.

SLAYING THE DRAGON

Slaying the dragon describes the ubiquitous hero's task. In Egypt, Apophis – the snake enemy of the sun—and the Sun-God Ra stain the sky red with blood as they battle every dusk and dawn; in Greece, Zeus defeats the Titan Typhon, a hundred-headed dragon who is son of Gaia (the Earth goddess), Apollo slays the sacred Python at Delphi, and Perseus rescues Andromeda from the sea dragon; in India, Indra impales the serpent-monster Vitra with a thunderbolt; in Christian tradition the archangel Michael casts down "the Dragon" from heaven; and Europe must have long suffered from a draconian epidemic as heroes from Siegfried to Tristan to St. George seem to bump into the beasts at every turn of the corner.

Mircea Eliade points out that even historical figures are credited with such deeds. For example, Diedonne de Gozon, third Grand Master of the Knights of St. John at Rhodes, is famous for slaying the dragon of Malpasso (of course no mention in contemporary records—this feat only surfaced centuries later):

> In other words, by the simple fact that he was a hero, de Gozon was identified with a category, an archetype, which, entirely disregarding his real exploits, equipped him with a mythical biography from which it was impossible to omit combat with a reptilian monster.[2]

Is it coincidence that this motif appears independently in so many different times and places?

Or might Campbell be right—isn't it at least reasonable to wonder if these expressions aren't variations on an underlying theme? If so, where does this image first appear, and what might it convey?

Eliade claims the image of this mythical beast is most often associated with what is "latent, preformal, undifferentiated":

> [T]he dragon is the paradigmatic figure of the marine monster, of the primordial snake, symbol of the cosmic waters, of darkness, night, death—in short, of the

amorphous and virtual, of everything that has not yet acquired a "form." The dragon must be conquered and cut to pieces by the gods, so that the cosmos may come to birth.[3]

One of the earliest sources of this image is *Tiamat*, the dragon goddess of chaos (the primal condition of the universe). *Marduk*, a sky-god of the Babylonian Amorites (one of the Semitic-speaking tribes who burst out of the southern deserts into the Fertile Crescent, overpowering the goddess-oriented Sumerian culture that formed humanity's earliest civilization), slays his great grandmother, the dragon Tiamat, and fashions all that exists in the created universe—including humans—from her flesh and blood and bone.

Tiamat is the Babylonian version of *Nammu*, the Sumerian serpent goddess of the primordial ocean—the primal goddess of undifferentiated nature whose substance infuses all creation—with all that exists sharing, as its core essence, the substance of the goddess. (Many scholars compare Nammu to *Ananta*, the cosmic serpent in Hindu myth, on whose back Vishnu sleeps, dreaming the dream of the universe).

The Amorites, on the other hand, fear in Tiamat the perils of an arbitrary, savage, cruel nature, and welcome Marduk's violent but necessary imposition of organization and order on this threatening, formless chaos. Such masculine, patriarchal deities acting *on* nature, rather than as agents *of* nature, mirror the trajectory of the developing ego-consciousness in humanity as it differentiates itself from the amorphous, mysterious workings of the unconscious psyche.

Indeed, many creation myths, including that of the Judeo-Christian tradition, open with a divine being creating order out of chaos.

Historically, the birth of this image reflects the collision of two radically different cultures, as nomadic herding peoples (Indo-European speaking cattle herders from the north, and Semitic speaking sheep and goat herders from the south) sweep into "the old cult sites of the ancient world." There, in Campbell's words, they encounter...

> . . . an essentially organic, vegetal, non-heroic view of the nature and necessities of life that was completely repugnant to those lion hearts for whom not the patient toil of the earth but the battle spear and its plunder were the source of both wealth and joy. In the older mother myths and rites the light and dark aspects of the mixed thing that is life had been honored equally and together, whereas in the later, male-oriented, patriarchal myths, all that is good and noble was attributed to the new, heroic, master gods, leaving to the native nature powers the character only of darkness—to which, also, a negative moral judgment was now added. For, as a great body of evidence shows, the social as well as mythic orders of the two contrasting ways of life were opposed . . .
>
> Hence the early Iron Age literatures of both Aryan Greece and Rome and of the neighboring Semitic Levant are alive with variants of the conquest by a shining hero of the dark and—for one reason or another—disparaged monster of the earlier order of godhood,

from whose coils some treasure was to be won: a fair
land, a maid, a boon of gold, or simply freedom from
the tyranny of the impugned monster itself.[4]

Campbell accurately observes that the Semitic and the Indo-
European peoples, pouring from the steppes in search of less
harsh climes, carry this change virtually simultaneously into
history.

These centuries of the third millennium BC are years
of dramatic transformation. Hieratic city-states give way to
dynastic states and high civilization; wars of subjugation
become the norm; heroic mythology is born (of which the cosmic dragon-slayer motif is the prime example); and the human
ego becomes more sharply defined as *individuals* play an ever-
greater role in shaping their universe (see Chapter 19).

PATRIARCHY & THE HEROIC EGO

Of course, patriarchal mythologies don't begin with some pow-
er-mongering maniac sitting around the campfire one day, rubbing his hands together and chortling gleefully as he devises a
means to enslave and bend others to his selfish will.

No—it begins with a family's survival in a harsh, unforgiving environment.

In the matrifocal cultures settled in the fecund river valleys, the landscape—nature—is mythologized: here a sacred
peak, there a sacred spring, here a sacred grove—every element
of the geography woven into the local mythology. These agrarian economies thrive on nature's bounty—so Nature becomes

personified in the various forms of a goddess figure, supportive and nurturing—and the mythology mirrors the seasons of the year and the cycle of the heavens.

Nomadic peoples, however—again, specifically, the Indo-Europeans who overwhelm "Old Europe" and the Semitic peoples who explode out of the Arabian desert—develop a mythology centered not on any feature of landscape, which after all remains inflexible and hostile, but on elemental forces that are with them everywhere: powers of Sun and Sky and Storm and Wind and Fire. These are powerful male deities, sky gods such as Indra, Zeus, and Yahweh.

In goddess cultures the group mind prevails—all are agents of the divine, playing one's proper role, whether a peasant tilling the soil or a king who submits himself to sacrifice when Venus comes round once more. The nascent ego is not sharply defined, and the individual will is subordinate to the rhythms of nature and of society, submerged in the collective consciousness.

Out in the desert though, scrabbling among the hostile elements for scant resources, a strong decisive patriarchal ego, attuned to survival, keeps the tribe alive. Small wonder that the tribal god develops the same attributes. This shift in consciousness is apparent in the Hebrew deity, the great I AM. He identifies himself to Moses with the phrase "I Am That I Am." Though generally understood as a profound theological statement, this description can also be read as the declaration of a powerful, self-conscious Ego.

(This shift in perception isn't exclusive to nomadic patriarchs. By the end of the third millennium BC, rulers in Sumer and Egypt are asserting their individual will, stepping outside the mythological demands of their roles to find ways around their mandatory sacrifice. Whether in the role of priest-king or patriarch, the exercise of independent ego anticipates a psychological readiness for the same on the part of the larger society.)

Nomadic tribes are often patriarchal in mythology and in structure—there is no time for consensus to form when facing a sandstorm or raiding an enemy encampment— hence one ego takes precedence, one "father authority" who makes the decisions that all will obey—putting the *"patri-"* in "patriarchal."

Those groups in the deserts that didn't follow this pattern perished. Tribes whose patriarchal figures made wise decisions thrived—and those patriarchs were remembered by their descendants, who continued to worship the deity that had successfully guided their forefathers (e.g., "the God of Abraham, Isaac, and Jacob") and who commands the same fealty from these tribal elders that the elders command from their people.

Patriarchy didn't emerge purely from greed for power, but from the basic drive for survival in a hostile world. As a result, patriarchy proved a successful strategy not just for survival, but also for conquest. Though matrifocal cultures enjoyed greater wealth, vaster resources, and more manpower, they crumbled under the onslaught.

What follows, in Sumer, is the birth of something new. The mythologies of conqueror and conquered merge, meld, and morph into an uneasy marriage. The primordial goddess lives on in multiple epiphanies, each representing specific aspects of her being (e.g., Inanna and her dark sister, Ereshkigal), but the new belief system also recognizes certain political realities—particularly the assumed superiority of the masculine, patriarchal, herding structure of the invading peoples grafted onto the earlier matrifocal, agrarian society.

Though subservient to a patriarchal pantheon, the feminine, however grudgingly, is recognized and worshipped in the hybrid culture that emerges. We do see the beginnings of a taint—an association of the wild, uncontrolled, chaotic realm of the unconscious psyche with the realm of nature and of the feminine powers (whether in the form of goddess or dragon); nevertheless, even though the goddess is subdued, she remains present in nature—which is still fashioned, however violently, from the substance of the primordial goddess.

The violence of this clash of cultures is just as evident in Greek myth, where masculine gods repeatedly defeat serpentine monsters associated with female deities (from the previously cited examples of Zeus and Apollo, to baby Herakles strangling twin serpents sent by Hera to kill him in his crib, or Perseus beheading the snake-coiffed Medusa); and the same uneasy truce between masculine and feminine powers can be found.

In these cultures, however, the goddess is not completely denied.

AN ASIDE:
WHY IS THE BIBLE DIFFERENT—OR IS IT?

In Canaan, when invading Semite-speaking tribes install their patriarchal sky-god, the goddess in her several incarnations is violently opposed: her sacred "groves and high places" are razed, her priests burned alive, and her very existence denied. This is a radical solution.

Archaeological and scriptural evidence suggest this exclusive monotheism is a late development, with polytheism prevailing from the migrations of the Hebrews into Canaan on throughout the span of the kingdoms of Israel and Judah. The goddesses and gods of the Semitic Canaanites took up residence in Solomon's temple alongside Yahweh, served by sacred priestess-prostitutes during the period of the kingdoms of Israel and Judah—save for a handful of years when the Yahwist party controlled both the monarchy and high priesthood. It's only after the encounter with Zoroastrianism during the Babylonian exile and Persian restoration that the patriarchal monotheism manages to eliminate the competition.

(Joseph Campbell offers supporting evidence in *Occidental Mythology*, and anthropologist Raphael Patai's *The Hebrew Goddess* remains the pioneering study in this field.)

We find traces of Sumero-Akkadian myths not only in the tales of the Old Testament, but embedded in the language of the *Torah* itself.

Perhaps most significant, the battle between Tiamat and Marduk, appears, albeit cloaked, in the opening chapter of Genesis: "And the earth was *without form, and void*; and darkness was upon the face of *the deep*. . ."

Tiamat, her deity veiled, is etymologically the source of both *tehom* and *tohu* [in Hebrew, *tehom* = "the face of the deep," and *tohu wa bohu* = "without form, and void"], out of which God [*elohim*] shapes the physical world, creating order out of chaos as did the earlier Marduk—but with one major difference.

In the Judeo-Christian-Islamic tradition, creation is *devoid of and separate from the Divine*—which presents an unbridgeable gulf between our contemporary patriarchal faiths, and mythologies that embrace nature (examples of the latter include shamanic practices and aboriginal beliefs, the "high religions" of Hinduism, Buddhism, and Taoism, and even contemporary neo-pagan movements such as Wicca— all of which, from a strictly literal biblical interpretation, are identified with Satan . . .

. . . hence the gulf).

Thus, the ancient goddess does appear in the Old Testament, but depersonalized. In the Judeo-Christian-Islamic traditions, nature has been given a hysterectomy; no longer sacred, no longer the body of the goddess—Created and Creator exist apart.

Similarly, the serpent—which is mythologically interchangeable with the dragon and long a companion to the goddess in the garden, as evidenced in Sumerian seals that date back to 3500 BC—does not fare so well in Eden.

Why this reversal?

> [I]n the context of the Patriarchy of the Iron Age Hebrews of the first millennium BC, the mythology adopted from the earlier Neolithic and Bronze Age civilizations of the lands they occupied and for a brief time ruled became inverted, to render an argument just the opposite of its origin. And a second point, corollary to the first, is that there is consequently an ambivalence inherent in many of the symbols of the Bible that no amount of rhetorical stress on the patriarchal interpretation can express. They address a pictorial message

to the heart that exactly reverses the verbal message addressed to the brain; and this nervous discord inhabits both Christianity and Islam as well as Judaism, since they too share in the legacy of the Old Testament.

However, the Bible is not the only source in the West of such ambivalence of teaching. There is a like inversion of sense in the legacy of Greece.[5]

This "inversion," though, has never been so complete as in the biblical faiths. Why such a drastic difference between the creation stories in the Bible and what Campbell terms "the general fund of Sumero-Semitic myth, of which the Babylonian account of creation is an example?"

The Bible represents a later stage in the patriarchal development, wherein the female principle, represented in the earlier Bronze Age by the great goddess-mother of all things and in this epic by a monstrous demoness, is reduced to its elemental state, tehom, and the male deity alone creates out of himself, as the mother alone had created in the past. The Babylonian epic stands between, along a line that may be logically schematized in four steps:

1. the world born of a goddess without consort;
2. the world born of a goddess fecunded by a consort
3. the world fashioned from the body of a goddess by a male warrior-god alone; and
4. the world created by the unaided power of a male god alone.[6]

The absence of the feminine isn't simply an aberration of Judaism and Christianity, but part of an evolving continuum that reflects not only historical changes, but changes in the collective psyche. The evolution of this mythic perspective marks the origin of our contemporary Cartesian outlook. Ours is no longer a world ensouled, and subject ("me," "I"—or "ego") remains separate and distinct from everything else—from the trees, the mountains, the clouds, the chair on which one sits— none of these are experienced as conscious and alive in the sense they are in primal cultures. The Earth and all that's on it are conceived as composed of soul-less matter, created for our use.

Hence the Serpent is theologically identified with Woman, Sex, and Nature—all of which carry the taint of evil and corruption in Judeo-Christian-Islamic traditions.

Nevertheless, despite the New Testament identification of the dragon and serpent with the Christian Satan as the embodiment of evil ("And the great Dragon was cast out, that old serpent called the Devil, and Satan," Revelation 12:9), more favorable depictions of this image can be found in Hebrew mythology.

For example, Moses lets pharaoh know he is Yahweh's messenger by miraculously transforming his staff—the dead branch of a tree—into a living serpent. Similarly, when a plague of poisonous "fiery serpents" descends on the Israelites, Yahweh commands: "Make a fiery serpent and set it on a pole; and everyone who is bitten, when he sees it, shall live." It's difficult not to associate this healing image—a snake on a pole—with the serpent-entwined *caduceus* of Asklepius, Greek god of healing, or with the coiled serpent snaking up the spine in *kundalini* yoga, or even the serpent at the tree in the garden—and, indeed, this Mosaic caduceus remains as an object of worship for centuries:

Serpent gods, however, do not die, and history records that the subtle old master of the garden, recovering, took upon the newcomer an amusing and ironical revenge. For as we are told in II Kings 18: there was a brazen serpent worshipped in the very temple of Jerusalem along with the image of his spouse, the mighty goddess, known there as the Asherah. And the brazen serpent's name was Nehushtan. King Hezekiah (719– 691 BC) had them both broken up and burned, but even that was not the end; for by the period of the Maccabees (second century BC) the serpent had become attached to the image of Yahweh himself, and with that embarrassing development the question naturally arose as who, after all, was Satan, and who, or what, was God.[7]

On the same page Campbell includes drawings of seven different "Snake-footed Forms of Yahweh" that appear on coins from the Maccabee period, second to first century BC, in Judea.

Yes, the goddess is devalued in Hebrew culture, much as elsewhere in the Mediterranean world—but the exclusive and relentless monotheism associated with the nations of Israel and Judah seems a late development, projected back in time by those who compiled the Hebrew scriptures, stitching together multiple, often contrasting and competing, accounts into one monolithic, mythic narrative that, to no surprise, supported their convictions.

However, the editors of scripture were unable to erase all traces of earlier mythologies their ancestors embraced—and it's not difficult, with a little attention, to suss out these traces.

Clearly the mythological beliefs and actual practices of ancient Israelites and Jews prove far more varied, fluid, and colorful than orthodox accounts would indicate.

THAT OLD SERPENT

All dragon slayers echo that original primordial act. But why no dragon prior to this moment in time? Dragons aren't depicted in art until about four thousand years ago.

Ahh—but serpents are . . .

In most mythologies dragons and serpents are congruent symbols (even the New Testament recognizes this association in Revelations 12:9, where "the great Dragon" and "that old Serpent" are epithets for Satan, the Devil; in Estonia, on St. George's Day, it's a tradition to celebrate the famous dragon killer by killing snakes).

What characteristics are commonly ascribed to mythological serpents?

> The wonderful ability of the serpent to slough its skin and so renew its youth has earned for it throughout the world the character of the master of the mystery of rebirth . . .
>
> But the serpent, too, is a lord of waters. Dwelling in the roots of trees, frequenting springs, marshes, and water courses, it glides with a motion of waves; or it ascends like a liana into branches, there to hang like some fruit of death. The phallic suggestion is immediate, and, as swallower, the female organ is also suggested; so that a dual association of fire and water attaches to the

lightning of the strike, the forked darting of its active tongue, and the lethal burning of its poison. When imagined as biting its tail, as the mythological uroboros, it suggests the waters that in all archaic cosmologies surround—as well as lie beneath and permeate—the floating circular island Earth.[8]

The opposites—of masculine and feminine, fire and water, death and rebirth—are united in this image—and the resonance between the primordial dragon, from whose corpse the world is born, and the cosmic serpent, identified with the waters that circle the earth, rings true.

The primary difference between the pre-heroic serpent and the dragon that appears in later heroic mythologies is the act of extreme violence on the part of a masculine deity who slays the cosmic monster. Joseph Campbell suggests that there must be a psychological readiness before a mythic image can take hold in the collective psyche. The dragon emerges in tandem with the dragon slayer—there was no place for either in the pre-patriarchal, pre-heroic mythologies of earlier periods—this image did not penetrate the collective experience of the time, and so we find no dragons portrayed in Paleolithic, Neolithic, or early Bronze Age art.

The image of the serpent, on the other hand, appears as far back as the Upper Paleolithic. Marija Gimbutas, in *The Language of the Goddess*, presents an image of a snake, along with bird heads and branches, carved on an antler horn, c. 12,000 BC.

There's no way to know for sure the significance of this artifact. Anthropologist Alexander Marshack offers a plausible argument this is a ritual object related to the celebration of spring—but since we can't email anyone from the Middle Magdalenian era to settle the question, this must remain intelligent conjecture. Nevertheless, I can't help but wonder if this image doesn't point to one of the most persistent mythic patterns over time—that of the World Tree, with snake or dragon nesting among its roots, and a raptor—often eagle, hawk, or owl—perched in the uppermost branches.

Around 2000 BC we have the tale of Gilgamesh at the Huluppu tree, with the Anzu bird in the branches, and the "serpent who could not be charmed" nestled in its roots; an even earlier version has the god Shamash siding with the bird as it battles the same serpent at the base of the same tree; three thousand years later the same motif is recorded in the Norse myths of the Prose Edda, where an eagle nests atop Yggsdrasil—the immense World Tree—while a dragon gnaws at its roots and a squirrel races up and down the trunk carrying insults between the two; meanwhile, half a world away from Europe and the Near East, the sight of an eagle battling a snake atop a cactus in Mesoamerica prompts the nomadic Aztecs to settle down and found a civilization (a mythic depiction that graces Mexico's flag). Might there be a relationship between the image of the dragon, and the motif of eagle and serpent occupying opposite poles of the World Axis?

THE WINGED SNAKE

The moon hero is the tragic hero in whom darkness rests, he has his own death in him, and he sheds death as a serpent sheds skin. The moon is therefore associated with the serpent, lord of the energies of the earth, who sheds his skin to be reborn: the reborn serpent, the reborn moon.

Now the creature that pounces on the serpent is the high-flying eagle, and the bird-and-serpent conflict is a basic mythological motif. In certain mythologies they stand as enemies—as they do, for example, in biblical mythology, where serpent is cursed by the winged powers, the powers of the upper atmosphere. The bird represents the free-flying spirit (it is released from the earth) and flight . . . The serpent, however, represents the bound-to-the-earth spirit . . .

In certain mythologies where the bird and serpent symbols are mythologized, you have the image of the dragon as a winged serpent. The winged lizard is the synthesis of the two. You can have either the attack and the separation, or the synthesis; but to arrive at the synthesis, one has to go through the separation.[9]

Campbell points out that an eagle pouncing on a snake would not be an unusual sight in the ancient world. Nor would it be unusual for a sensitive, creative individual to empathize with and internalize this battle, and create a work of art that reflects the struggle in the universe and in oneself (as Joe asks of Bill Moyers, "The serpent bound to the earth, the eagle in spiritual flight—isn't that conflict something we all experience?").

> But, in fact, then, why do we not find in the Paleolithic temple caves any painting of a raptorial bird killing a serpent? Might there be required some sort of psychological readiness for the insight? And would the readiness, then, be somehow a function of the local condition?[10]

Campbell implies that the image of birds of prey attacking serpents strikes no chords in the collective psyche prior to the Bronze Age (which is about the same time dragon and slayer first appear).

Indeed, though there are plenty of images of snake-goddesses in the Neolithic periods, there is no sign of hostility between serpent and bird. Marija Gimbutas (the late professor of archaeology at UCLA who excavated several "Old Europe" sites in the Balkans) indicates the Bird Goddess and the Snake Goddess are the two primary representations of what she terms the "stiff white goddess" figurines found in graves throughout Old Europe, roughly five to seven thousand years ago. According to Gimbutas the symbols surrounding the Snake Goddess are the same as those associated with the Bird Goddess.

No enmity here.

Gimbutas tracks this theme into the classical period, where certain goddesses—all differentiated incarnations of the primordial goddess—continue to combine the same motifs (for example, Athena's attributes include the snake and the owl).

Nevertheless, by the end of the third millennium BC—as reflected in the tale of the Huluppu tree—earthbound serpent and winged raptor, who in the legend were once the closest of friends, now fight to the death—a struggle that rages as well between dragon goddess and hero god (again, hero and dragon motifs emerging together from the mythic imagination).

I have to wonder what comes first. Does a change in the collective psyche (that readiness Campbell speaks of) open the door to thinking, being, and perceiving reality differently? Did that shift in perspective prompt the revolutionary changes that forever altered the world—including the development of writing, astronomy, mathematics, statecraft—and, is the price of civilization the perpetual warfare that plagues us to this day?

Or did the change in psyche reflect societal changes already taking place—the myths of Marduk dismembering Tiamat, for example, an inner response to harsh realities in the outer world?

Many today seek to turn back the clock, return to that pre-patriarchal Eden when all lived in harmony with nature, and with each other. A laudable goal, one that speaks to my heart—though this idyllic vision strikes me as somewhat naïve, utopian, and way out of touch with the reality of Neolithic life. Yes, the oppression and devastation wrought by our patriarchal society has wreaked havoc on the planet and on each other—but I'm not sure there's a re-set button for four thousand years of human history.

> When we talk about settling the world's problems, we're barking up the wrong tree. The world is perfect. It's a mess. It's always been a mess. We are not going to change it. Our job is to straighten out our own lives.[11]

If either eagle or serpent defeats its enemy, then life is out of balance. Eliminating/ignoring the masculine energies would be as devastating and oppressive as has been the suppression of the feminine—just in a different way. Restoring the balance is what's called for, and we do that by finding the balance in ourselves. To me, this suggests enhancing the feminine aspects of the image—accord with nature, partnering with the wild, irrational energies informing the unconscious psyche.

Stepping back from the world stage, how do we engage this image?

We live heroic lives. We follow the heroic pattern when we exercise our individual will; there's no escaping that, apart from withdrawing into convent or monastery—and even then, we're still seekers, still on a quest.

We live individual lives in a heroic culture—it's hard to step outside that context and imagine pre-heroic mythologies. Peter, Paul and Mary notwithstanding, heroes don't generally make friends with the dragons they meet; they slay them—that's what makes them heroes.

But maybe there's a way *through* our hero mythology.

The battle between the serpent and eagle—the separate parts of the dragon—seems congruent to the act of slaying the dragon. As Campbell points out above, "You can have either the attack and separation, or the synthesis; but to arrive at the synthesis, one has to go through the separation."

Hmm . . . looks like we'll have to slay the dragon after all.

What's A Hero Without A Dragon?

There are so many trails one could follow from the image of the serpent-dragon—for example, a discussion of the various inflections of this image in Mesoamerica, from *Quetzalcoatl* (the feathered serpent god), who with his brother *Tezcatlipoca*, in the form of twin serpents (*coatl* meaning "twin" as well as serpent) rips asunder the fair *Tlatleutli* and fashions the earth, seas, animals, fruit, and people from her body, blood, and bones (sound familiar?), to the serpents and dragons encountered in *peyote, amanitas,* and *ayahuasca* visions by indigenous shamans and the occasional anthropologist.

But I am captured by the associations between the origins of this image and the developing ego, a relationship that not only sheds light on the past but also has practical implications for our lives today.

Shifting from macrocosm to microcosm, Campbell focuses on the significance of slaying the dragon in one's own life. We slay dragons every day—but this image points to more than just a metaphor for difficult tasks we face at work or home.

> If you have someone who can help you, that's fine too. But, ultimately, the last deed has to be done by oneself. Psychologically, the dragon is one's own binding of oneself to one's ego. We're captured in our own dragon cage. The problem of the psychiatrist is to disintegrate that dragon, break him up, so that you may expand to a larger field of relationships. The ultimate dragon is within you, it is your ego clamping you down.[12]

A personal encounter with this archetype can be shattering to the ego—and ego is simply Latin for "I" (me, my sense of myself). Anything that can smash the powerful self-image of ego as "in control" is likely to be felt as threatening and painful.

In other cultures the dragon is a benign and even boon-bestowing image, as in China (and, ultimately, it's all the same, multi-faceted image—just have to embrace the paradox), but Joseph Campbell frames this conversation in the context of dragons as they appear in European myth and faery tale, the mythic matrix out of which Western culture has emerged.

What does the dragon do in these tales?

There are differences, individual variations—but generally, dragons have a lair—a cave—and in this cave they guard one of two things: a virgin—the traditional damsel-in-distress—and/or a priceless treasure.

And usually, as they guard it, they sleep, faint tendrils of smoke unfurling from their nostrils as they snore, blissfully unconscious. . .

(Cave? Unconscious? . . .*hello*. . . Jung alert!)

Sleeping, that is, until our hero arrives, waking the ill-tempered beast from slumber with a challenge. In most tales he frees the maiden and makes off with the treasure by slaying the dragon (shades of Marduk, by St. George!).

Joe asks, "Why?"

Why does the dragon guard the girl and the gold? Neither one is of any use to him—he can't spend the cash, nor deflower the maiden (though sometimes the beast substitutes "devour" for deflower).

Campbell equates the dragon with a related image from yet another culture—that of the serpent power, asleep at the base of the spine, in *kundalini* yoga. Up the spine are seven *chakras*, or stations, through which the kundalini serpent rises once awakened, if fed and nurtured through attentive awareness.

The chakras represent the different centers of consciousness out of which we live our lives.

Campbell suggests the three lowest chakras are congruent with the dragon slumbering in the cave, hoarding the gold and imprisoning the maiden:

The first—the slumbering dragon—is at the base of the spine, where the coiled serpent sleeps—the level of mere survival, that of reptilian instincts (feed, digest, defecate, sleep, feed, etc.). We all know people whose lives are ruled by this couch potato chakra—and more than a few have been there ourselves.

Eventually, though, the serpent stirs, wakes, and is moved to do something, to attain something—inspired to get laid, so to speak—so the second chakra (the fair maiden) relates to sexual energies. The third chakra touches on economic and material realities (treasure chests of gold and jewels), or, as Campbell says, "organizing a life, building a business, learning how to master the world in terms appropriate to your condition and place."

> These three chakras are of functions that we share with the other animals. They are also clinging to life, begetting, building nests, making their way. Popular religion works on these levels, and the individual living on these levels is ego-oriented and his action must be controlled by social law.[13]

But at the fourth chakra—the Heart Chakra (called *anahata*—"no hit"—the sound that is not made by any two things striking together, that "sound of which the universe is a manifestation"), we find "the opening of the spiritual dimension: all is metaphoric of the mystery."

Campbell suggests the purpose of the slumbering dragon is to call the hero forth. In our culture, the hero goes forward to wake and slay the dragon—which doesn't mean destroying it (here Campbell alludes to the ability of serpents to shed their skin—renewal.)

We tend to think of the dragon as evil, to be overcome—whereas in India and points east, they partner with the serpent. This is all part of a cosmic passion play, repeated on the stages of our individual lives—might as well dance that dance with enthusiasm.

In Campbell's words,

> When you reach the upper chakras, you don't do without the first three: survival, sex, power. You don't destroy the first three floors of the building when you get to the fourth.[14]

Facing the dragon is intense, often painful and overwhelming—but that needn't mean evil; might be our stance towards it which lends the negative power. In other cultures the experience, though shattering, is viewed as positive—extinguishing ego's hold a threshold ordeal. . .

Bill Moyers asked Joe, "What is ego?"

> What you think you want, what you will to believe, what you decide to love, what you regard yourself as bound to. It may all be much too small, in which case it will nail you down. And if you simply do what your

neighbors tell you to do, you're certainly going to be nailed down. Your neighbors are then your dragon as it reflects from within yourself.[15]

The dragons we face outside are but reflections of the dragon inside. Facing the dragon, then, is more than just putting one foot in front of the other and getting on with the tasks of life— it requires a journey of self-reflection and inner exploration.

You can't slay what you don't seek.

"The ultimate dragon is within you." That, indeed, is a hero's quest.

NOTES

1. Joseph Campbell, The Mythic Image (Princeton: Princeton University Press, 1974; New York: MJF Books, 1996), 292.
2. Eliade, The Myth of the Eternal Return, op. cit. 39.
3. Mircea Eliade, The Sacred and the Profane New York: Harcourt, Brace, and Company, 1959; New Yor: Harper Brothers, 1961), 48.
4. Campbell, Occidental Mythology, op. cit. 22-23.
5. Ibid. 17.
6. Ibid. 85.
7. Campbell, The Mythic Image, op. cit. 294.
8. Campbell, Occidental Mythology, op. cit. 9.
9. Campbell, Mythic Worlds, Modern Words, op. cit. 31.
10. Campbell, Mythologies of the Primitive Planters –– The Middle and Southern Americas, op. cit. 378.
11. Campbell, A Joseph Campbell Companion, op. cit. 17.
12. Campbell, The Power of Myth, op. cit. 184.
13. Campbell, A Joseph Campbell Companion, op. cit. 112.
14. Ibid. 113.
15. Campbell, The Power of Myth, op. cit. 184.

TWENTY-TWO

THE MYTHOLOGIST & THE MUSES

In my writing and my thinking and my work I've thought of myself as addressing artists and poets and writers. The rest of the world can take it or leave it as far as I'm concerned.[1]

When reading Joseph Campbell, many people naturally focus on the universal motifs found in mythologies of different cultures, or find themselves taken by the parallel between mythological themes and one's own life journey—but just as significant is the central role the creative imagination plays in Campbell's world.

This was no affectation—Campbell enjoyed an intimate relationship with the arts all his life, from his college years jamming in a jazz band to receiving the National Arts Club's Gold Medal of Honor for Literature at age eighty. And though scholars such as Marija Gimbutas, Barbara Myerhoff, and David Miller admit Campbell's influence, a host of artists also acknowledge his inspiration, from Robert Bly (poet) and Richard Adams (author of *Watership Down*), to Martha Graham (choreographer), George Lucas, Steven Spielberg, George Miller (film producers/directors), and even The Grateful Dead (psychedelic rock and roll musicians).

Joseph Campbell was torn between the Way of the Scholar and the Way of the Artist much of his life. Campbell's work speaks for itself—but an understanding of Joseph's lifelong immersion in the arts underscores an intimacy with the Muses we find revealed in that work. I am drawn to explore how the creative impulse has manifested in Campbell's life and work—but first, it seems necessary to ask the nature of that creative spirit.

WHENCE CREATIVITY

The creative act is not hanging on, but yielding to new creative movement.[2]

In the creative moment we are tapped into a realm removed from intellect—what Carl Jung calls "the collective unconscious," and Rollo May refers to as a reach "beyond our own death." From this realm we bring forth forms—or rather, forms bubble up that we might capture, if we are open to them:

When you are in the act of creating, there is an implicit form that is going to be asked to be brought forth, and you have to know how to recognize it. So, they say, you are to learn all the rules and then you must forget them.

As the lyric factor is beginning to move you, the mind is supposed to watch for the emergent form,

because anything that comes out of the proper ground
is formed already. There is an implicit form intrinsic in
it, and your job is to recognize it.[3]

But to enter this realm we must find a way to disarm intellect
and sidestep the head. Our inner critic stymies creativity by
attempting to straitjacket the unconscious—apparently in fear
of impulsive, uncontrollable behavior. All too often that hesita-
tion is all that's needed to derail creative momentum.

How then do we bypass that forbidding gatekeeper?

Play is the way.

In *Primitive Mythology* (*The Masks of God*, Vol. I), Joseph
Campbell draws on historian Johann Huizenga, whose classic
work, *Homo Ludens* ("Man the Player") asserts that myth, ritual, and art have their origins in the "play-sphere" of primal
cultures. Campbell reminds us that in the world of pretend
"the whole point, at the beginning, is the fun of play, not the
rapture of seizure"—but there is indeed a "rapture of seizure"
to play, as can be seen watching children caught up in pretend
roles experiencing their play as "real."

(Campbell borrows an example from ethnologist Leo
Frobenius, who describes a four-year-old girl who is playing
Hansel, Gretel, and the Witch with three burnt matches, suddenly frightening herself and calling on her father to protect
her from the witch. Even though the little girl knows the match
is not a witch, she experiences it as such. In Frobenius's words,
"The process is creative, in the highest sense of the word; for,
as we have seen, in a little girl a match can become a witch.")

This rapture of seizure is common to myth, ritual, and art,
as well as to play:

The reader hardly need be reminded that the images
. . . when effective, are apprehended with actual
physical responses: tears, sighs, interior aches, spontaneous groans, cries, bursts of laughter, wrath, and
impulsive deeds. Human experience and human
art, that is to say, have succeeded in creating for the
human species an environment of sign stimuli that
release physical responses and direct them to ends
no less effectively than do the signs of nature the
instincts of the beasts. . .

When [British poet] A.E. Housman writes that
"poetry is not the thing said but a way of saying it," and
when he states again "that the intellect is not the fount
of poetry, that it may actually hinder its production,
and that it cannot even be trusted to recognize poetry
when it is produced," he is no more than reaffirming
and lucidly formulating the first axiom of all creative
art—whether it be in poetry, music, dance, architecture, painting, or sculpture—which is, namely, that art
is not, like science, a logic of references but a release
from reference and rendition of immediate experience;
a presentation of forms, images, or ideas in such a way
that they will communicate, not primarily a thought or
even a feeling, but an impact.[4]

In the creative act we convey an experience...

. . . from one inward world to another, in such a way that
an actual shock of recognition will have been rendered;
not a mere statement for the persuasion of the brain, but

an effective communication across the void of time and space from one center of consciousness to another. . .

The mythogenetic zone today is the individual in contact with his own interior life, communicating through his art with those "out there." But to this end communicative signs must be employed: words, images, motions, rhythms, colors, and perfumes, sensations of all kinds, which, however, come to the creative artist from without and inevitably bear associations not only colored by the past but also relevant to the commerce of the day.[5]

So communication, which takes the spontaneity of play beyond daydreaming and dabbling, is also essential to the creative process—but what is it one communicates?

In one of the Upanisads it says, when the glow of a sunset holds you and you say "Aha," that is the recognition of the divinity. And when you say "Aha" to an art object, that is a recognition of divinity. And what divinity is it? It is your divinity, which is the only divinity there is. We are all phenomenal manifestations of a divine will to live, and that will and the consciousness of life is one in all of us, and that is what artwork expresses.[6]

CAMPBELL AND THE ARTS

Joseph Campbell's own artistic pursuits began with play—playing, that is, in a seven-piece jazz band with Paul Wincoop in college. Though Joe primarily played sax (he had several different saxophones), he also played different guitars, and even a ukulele (years later he taught himself the balalaika), and helped Wincoop book "fraternity dances and junior proms."

Campbell's musical career proved profitable—according to the Larsens, ". . . most of his money during college was gotten from these engagements. His bankbook of the time shows a relatively stable balance of about $3000, not an inconsiderable sum of money in 1925."[7]

But for Campbell, music was not about money:

> Music is nothing if not rhythm. Rhythm is the instrument of art . . . It's wonderful to see a jazz group improvise: when five or six musicians are really tuned in to each other, it's all the same rhythm, and they can't go wrong, even though they never did it that way before.[8]

In 1927, after completing his M.A. at Columbia, Campbell spent two years studying in Europe on a Proudfit Scholarship. There, on the Left Bank in Paris, he discovered the world of modern art.

Through close friendships with Angela Gregory, an apprentice sculptor, and Krishnamurti (recognized by Theosophists in those years as Maitreya, the anticipated world messiah), Joseph was admitted to the inner circle of Rodin's student and successor, master sculptor Antoine Bourdelle, whose sculpture echoed powerful mythological themes—a privilege rare for the most dedicated and accomplished sculptors-in-training, and unheard of for an American who wasn't formally studying art; the master, however, recognized in

Campbell a serious student, and did not hesitate to impart cardinal artistic insights.

Fifty years later Campbell continued to cite the influence of this master artist:

> And this is the key of all art. This is the key of form. The rhythm is implicit in your own body. It is implicit in your expression. And when the rhythm is properly, fortunately achieved, the result is radiance, rapture, beholding it. Why? Because the rhythm before you is the rhythm of nature. It is the rhythm of your nature. Cezanne says somewhere, "Art is a harmony parallel to nature." Art is the rendition of the interface between your nature and the nature out there.
>
> . . . When I was a student in Paris, back in the 1920s, I knew a sculptor, a very great sculptor, Antoine Bourdelle, who used to say, *"L'art fait ressortir les grandes lignes de la nature"* [Art vividly brings out the grand lines of nature]. And that is all it does. And why is it that you are held in aesthetic arrest? It is because the nature you are looking at is your nature. There is an accord between you and the object, and that is why you say, "Aha!"[9]

Campbell spent much of his free time after returning to New York at the studio of his sister's teacher, Cubist sculptor Alexander Archipenko (where he met Isamu Noguchi, noted Japanese-American sculptor and landscape artist, who became a lifelong friend), fitting comfortably into the artistic milieu there.

At the same time Joe made a personal decision to give up the academic paper chase as life took a decidedly bohemian turn.

So I came back to New York in 1929 and Booommm! I didn't have a job for five years. My father's hosiery business was in very bad condition in the Crash. I didn't know where I was. The world had blown open. I'm no longer in the Ph.D. bottle. I don't want to go on with my little Arthurian pieces. I had much more exciting things to do—and I didn't know what they were.

I wanted to write, I wanted to be an anthropologist—I didn't know what! A new world was around. So I said, "To hell with it, Columbia!"

I'm writing short stories. I discover American literature, Hemingway, Sinclair Lewis, the whole bunch. Hemingway just knocks me over, those early things of his—*In Our Time, Men Without Women, The Sun Also Rises*. Like every callow young author, I wanted to write like him; meanwhile Joyce was interesting.

Five years, no job! . . . Writing stories nobody would buy.[10]

Campbell spent most of those five years living simply in Woodstock, mainly reading and writing, and sharing meals, conversation, and much laughter with members of the thriving local art colony. He did take time out from his retreat to Woodstock to travel across country to the Pacific Coast, where, on Monterey's Cannery Row, he fell in with a group of bohemian spirits that included biologist Ed Ricketts and author John Steinbeck, well before their reputations had solidified.

This was a period of tremendous creative ferment for all three men, described in detail in *The Fire in the Mind* (traces of their collective adventures appear in disguised form in two of Steinbeck's novels, *Cannery Row* and *Tortilla Flats*). Campbell and Steinbeck passed many hours together discussing the nature of writing, while Ricketts and Campbell soon found themselves writing *about* nature (see Chapter 15). Campbell's interest in writing proved more than just a passing fancy.

In New York he had sought guidance and instruction from author John Gallishaw, who agreed to serve as his literary agent. Campbell wrote several short stories intended for publication as early as 1929—"The Semple Way" in March of 1929, "The Love Curve," "Sailor Alone," and "Protest" in the summer of 1929—and continued all the way through "Voracious" in 1948—almost 20 years writing short stories . . . no passing flirtation that!

Many of the early stories have disappeared. Joe sold only one—"Strictly Platonic," in 1932, to Liberty—for $350 dollars, a sizable figure at the height of the Depression. (Joseph Campbell Foundation has since collected and published several of Joseph Campbell's extant short stories in *Mythic Imagination*.)

(Interesting that, even though we think of Campbell as more teacher than artist, between his substantial earnings playing jazz in college and the fee for "Strictly Platonic," it could be argued that the bulk of Campbell's income, up until he accepted his teaching position at Sarah Lawrence College, derived from the arts.)

The Larsens include synopses of "Strictly Platonic" and several other stories. They describe two short stories from 1945—"The Maimed King" and "The Belly of the Shark"—with the following:

> These stories were never published, but they bristle
> with powerful images, and suggest a consciousness
> in love with its own metamorphic capabilities. These
> stories fall somewhere between the surreal parables of
> Franz Kafka, the coolly uncompromising depictions
> of O. Henry, and the interesting possibilities of Ray
> Bradbury's fantasies.[11]

Makes one curious. They do, though, offer less flattering cri-
tiques of other stories.

Campbell also penned a couple of novel-length works—
including "The Mavericks," a treatment of his encounters with
Adelle Davis and John and Carol Steinbeck, and "A School for
Witches," based on his summer adventure with Ed Ricketts
collecting tide pool specimens from Seattle to Sitka, aboard
the *Grampus*.

In his later years, Campbell downplayed those early literary
efforts:

> I wrote a detective story, which a cleaning woman threw
> out—thank God! And a novel. The novel was contrived
> and stupid. You know, a novelist has to be interested in
> the way things look, in the way the light falls on your
> sleeves and that kind of thing. That's not my talent and
> I found that everything I did was stiff and I quit.[12]

Though Joseph Campbell published no fiction apart from that
one short story, he was generally involved in one creative project after another throughout his life.

Back in New York, Joe and his wife, dancer/choreographer Jean Erdman, were part of a circle of young artists, composers, filmmakers, writers, and other eclectic figures. In the mid-1940s, Campbell and the avant-garde composer John Cage partnered on a modern opera, titled "Perseus and Andromeda" (the opening scene, fragmentary outlines, annotated scores, dialogues, etc., have been found among Joe's papers, though the opera was never completed); Maya Deren counted on Campbell's help in forming the Creative Film Foundation to nurture independent film artists – he eventually became president of the nonprofit; after retiring from Sarah Lawrence, he collaborated with his wife, Jean, in projects at her Theater of the Open Eye . . . just a few highlights from decades of active participation in and support of the arts.

THE ART OF NONFICTION

> I have two ways of writing. One is a programmed way: I know what I'm going to say and I write it and that's third-rate stuff. The wonderful thing is when I get on a certain beam that hits the level of mythic inspiration. From there on I know about three words ahead what I'm going to say. When the writing's going like that I know I'm in the groove . . . it feels like riding a wonderful wave . . .[13]

The Larsens describe a major lesson Campbell learned from Gallishaw, his literary agent and short story Yoda:

> In effect, the writer is like a magician, an illusionist,
> who provides a scaffold of experiences or images, and
> the active mind of the beholder—the reader—fills in,
> producing the illusion of experiencing a "slice of life" or
> "a dramatic event."[14]

This strikes me as very much the same approach Campbell applied to his great works, whether *The Hero with a Thousand Faces*, *The Masks of God*, or others: he dances beautifully, drawing on this image here, a snatch of myth there, but often only suggesting, allowing "the active mind of the beholder—the reader [to] fill in." I am reminded of an artist who uses the fan brush not to draw a figure, but to create wavy, fuzzy, feathery, "maybe" outlines that suggest an image to the viewer, who then in effect becomes co-creator with the artist by applying their own imagination to the painting.

Many is the time I've read Joseph Campbell not noticing all the skillfully couched caveats that allow more than one interpretation, which can sometimes lead to seemingly contradictory conclusions if one tries to nail Campbell down to a single line of thought that follows a logical, linear, "scientific" rendering—but actually serve to enlarge each thought and image presented, adding depth and dimension, if seen with an artistic (or mythic) eye.

When traversing a myth-scape populated with symbolic imagery, it helps to remain open to paradox.

It's not that Campbell is fuzzy. Picasso is no fuzzier; each image Picasso employs opens out to a multitude of possibilities, just as with myth. Any perceived vagueness in Campbell is not because of a lack of clarity to the concepts and images presented, but rather a result of the array of possibilities and associations, personal and collective, that each image opens out to—which can be annoying, at the very least, for those who expect truth to be rendered in one simple, straightforward formulation.

Such symbols and images are the raw material of art as well as myth, so it is no surprise that Campbell admits the visionary artist is his primary audience—which may explain why his work often plays better in Hollywood than in the halls of academia. He says, concerning George Lucas's famous use of *The Hero with a Thousand Faces* as a source of inspiration for his *Star Wars* films:

> It's very gratifying to know that this little book of mine is doing what I wanted it to do, namely to inspire an artist whose work is actually moving in the world. *The Hero with a Thousand Faces* was refused by two publishers; the second one asked me, "Well, who will read it?" Now we know.[15]

Ultimately, Joe's gift was teaching that which is unteachable—and his writing approaches art, in the best Joycean sense, in the amalgamation and assimilation of traditional archetypal images into an opus that draws on ancient mythic themes, yet feels grand and fresh and new.

At some point along the way Campbell let go the Way of Art and closed the door on "creative writing"—opting, instead, to write creatively for the artist.

Joseph Campbell's short stories may not have enjoyed popular success, but Joseph Campbell's projects, whether writing, lecturing, or teaching, have been grounded in the creative imagination. Whether discussing art or myth or literature, the *image* is primary for Campbell, and mystical experience cognate with aesthetic arrest.

The goal of life is rapture. Art is the way we experience it.[16]

A case could be made that Campbell is an artist's artist—he immersed himself in the raw material of art, in archetype and image, his work appealing to and inspiring generations of artists in every genre.

A PRACTICAL CONCLUSION?

An artist is not in the field to achieve, to realize, but to become fulfilled. It's a life-fulfilling, totally different structure . . . And it doesn't matter whether you're first-, second-, or third-rate in the public eye. Each artist, as I know them, is in fulfillment in his or her own way. It's not a competitive field.[17]

Perhaps the chief practical conclusion that comes to mind is that creativity does not concern itself with practical conclusions. No one who follows the creative path is guaranteed prosperity, or even security. Campbell pointed out that most artists he had known lived "without knowing how their life is going or how it's going to be." That path takes commitment and courage.

But does creativity remain the domain of artists alone, or is access open to all? For those of us who are not artists, how do we find our way into this realm?

> Life as an art and art as a game—as action for its own sake, without thought of gain or loss, of praise or blame—is the key, then, to the turning of living itself into a yoga, and art is the means to such a life.[18]

Play is the Way.

NOTES

1. Larsens, A Fire in the Mind, op. cit. 556.
2. Campbell, A Joseph Campbell Companion, op. cit. 262.
3. Campbell, Mythic Dimension, op. cit. 183.
4. Campbell, Primitive Mythology, op. cit. 39.
5. Campbell, Creative Mythology, op. cit. 92, 93.
6. Campbell, Mythic Dimension, op. cit. 187.
7. Larsens, A Fire in the Mind, op. cit. 50.
8. Campbell, A Joseph Campbell Companion, op. cit. 249.
9. Campbell, Mythic Dimension, op. cit. 187.
10. Campbell, "The Professor with a Thousand Faces," op. cit.
11. Larsens, A Fire in the Mind, op. cit. 313.
12. Campbell, "Seventy Years of Making Connections," op. cit.
13. Campbell, "Mythic Reflections," op. cit.
14. Larsens, A Fire in the Mind, op. cit. 128.
15. Campbell, Pathways to Bliss, op. cit. 132.
16. Campbell, A Joseph Campbell Companion, op. cit. 245.
17. Campbell, Hero's Journey, op. cit. 94.
18. Campbell, Myths To Live By, op. cit. 124.

TWENTY-THREE

MYSTERIES SACRED & PROFANE

Aldous Huxley's *The Doors of Perception* (1954), describing his own visionary experiences under the influence of mescaline, opened the way to a popular appreciation of the ability of hallucinogens to render perceptions of a quasi, or even truly, mystical profundity. There can be no doubt today that through the use of such sacramentals revelations indistinguishable from some of those reported of yoga have been experienced.[1]

In the mid-1960s, Joseph Campbell was shocked to see royalties from *The Hero with a Thousand Faces* jump up "one full decimal point." This happy mystery was solved when he learned that his classic work on the hero's quest had become "a kind of TripTik®" for the LSD experience!

For the benefit of younger readers, before GPS navigation a TripTik® was a planning tool booklet provided by AAA to its members, in conjunction with paper

road maps, that broke long automobile trips down into
stages and served as a guide to sights encountered along
the way – SG.

Campbell seems an unlikely candidate for hippie patron saint
(Robin Larsen, in *A Fire in the Mind*, recalls Joe complaining
about "hippies and liberals" during the Vietnam War); even
more surprising is the thought that this dignified, dedicated
scholar might somehow be associated with the drug culture.

At the same time, Campbell enjoyed friendships with
Albert Hofmann, the Swiss chemist who first synthesized LSD
in 1938 (and just celebrated his 101st birthday last month
[January 11, 2007 – SG], still going strong); Huston Smith,
a noted religious studies scholar involved in early psychedelic
research at Harvard; Alan Watts, celebrated author and mystic who was no stranger to LSD; Stanislav Grof, a frequent
collaborator with Campbell at Esalen seminars known for his
research into the nature of consciousness (including observation and documentation of thousands of legal LSD research
sessions at the Psychiatric Research Institute in Prague and the
Maryland Psychiatric Research Center in Baltimore); and, the
last years of Joe's life, the Grateful Dead, who occupied the
epicenter of psychedelic counterculture for over three decades.

Joseph Campbell seems one of the few in his circle who
didn't partake of psychedelics at some point—a conscious
choice on his part—but he remained open minded, not at all
inclined to discount the experiences of those who did.

Of course, the drug culture of the sixties eventually faded
into oblivion. Campbell's encounters through the seventies
and eighties were with serious practitioners in psychology,

anthropology, biology, and other fields who approached the subject of psychedelics not as a lark, but as one tool among many that expand our understanding of the nature of consciousness. Campbell certainly valued the research and insights of these recognized experts, whose observations often paralleled his own.

But what might those parallels be? Perhaps a case could be made regarding insights into the nature of human consciousness, but what possible light could the study of hallucinogens shed on mythology?

That question can't properly be answered without a brief survey of the role sacred plants have played in human culture. Then, examining the archetypal elements, we'll recognize a form emerging from this seemingly formless experience; that shape should lead us to the contemporary resurgence of interest in shamanism, and, finally, to the familiar motif Joseph Campbell sees in this turn toward psychoactive substances— part of a larger pattern reflecting a shift in Western culture of mythic proportions.

> Just a note about terminology: many researchers (R. Gordon Wasson, Richard Evans Shultes, Huston Smith, etc.) prefer *entheogen* ("God-containing" or "God-enabling") over *psychedelic* ("mind-manifesting"), which is accurate but carries baggage from the sixties – or worse, *hallucinogen*, which inaccurately portrays the experience as hallucination alone. I tend towards psychedelic, as it's the most familiar term, and entheogen, for variety's sake (usually when emphasizing mystical aspects), using hallucinogen only when discussing common perceptions.

What a Long Strange Trip It's Been

Psychoactive plants were already entwined with the family tree well before the bifurcation of our particular branch (*Homo sapiens*). Terence McKenna, in *The Food of the Gods,* points out the psychoactive mushroom *Stropharia cubensis* appears to have been part of our ancestors' diet in East Africa over a million years ago. In low doses this mushroom increases visual acuity, which could prove a crucial advantage when hunting, enhancing the ability to track prey over vast vistas of veldt—a "competitive edge," in Darwinian terms.

In higher doses, however, *Stropharia cubensis* alters consciousness—leaving open the possibility that sacred mushrooms played a role in the evolution of human consciousness.

Hippie sapiens?

Open to question as that may be, we do know teacher plants have long been associated with shamanic rites, particularly vision quests. Shamans access transcendent realms via altered states of consciousness occasioned by one of several "techniques of ecstasy" (subtitle to Mircea Eliade's classic study of *Shamanism*), which may include any combination of physical ordeals, fasting, sex, dancing, drumming, and drugs.

Many scholars, Eliade included, once assumed the ingestion of hallucinogens an inferior path reflecting a later decadent phase in shamanic cultures; a growing body of research, including anthropological finds and contemporary fieldwork, belies that assumption. (Daniel Pinchbeck, author of *Breaking Open the Head*, an examination of contemporary shamanism, asserts Eliade eventually reversed his position.)

Over 50 species of psychoactive plants have been used by tribes on the African continent—such as *iboga* among the Bwiti of Gabon and the Congo. Similarly, *datura* midwifes the vision quests and healing rites of shamans from New Guinea to New Mexico. Shamans in Siberia rely on fly agaric (*Amanita muscaria*), while *psilocybin* mushrooms perform the same function for several North American tribes.

Archaeology has unearthed evidence of ritual *peyote* use back to seven thousand years ago. Joseph Campbell speaks highly of the peyote-influenced mythology of the Huichol Indians in Mexico (for whom this powerful psychedelic cactus is a Sacred Being ingested in regular rituals), declaring their "pattern is exactly that of the visionary journey which I have designated the 'Monomyth' in *The Hero with a Thousand Faces* . . ." (Joseph Campbell, *Mythologies of the Primitive Planters: The Middle and Southern Americas*, 302)

Meanwhile, in the 1950s, R. Gordon Wasson discovered *teonanacatl*—"the flesh of the gods"—a sacred psilocybin mushroom still used among tribal shamans in the highlands around Oaxaca, Mexico. Campbell points to the continuity of this cult in the discovery of 2,300-year-old stone images of the same sacred mushroom found in burial sites along Guatemala's Pacific coast.

In fact, 130 different species of psychoactive plants have been used in tribal societies throughout the Americas (inspiring a tongue-in-cheek reference by Campbell in *The Hero's Journey* to pre-Columbian Mesoamerica: "Now that's a drug culture!")

In the tropical rainforests the Yanamamo brew *yage*, the Quechua *ayahuasca* —perhaps the most powerful teacher plant in use today, a liana through which shamans receive visions that offer knowledge about the ways of the creatures and spirits of the rainforest—and not just esoteric wisdom, but information immediately applicable to daily life (like which plants are poisonous, which beneficial, how they should be prepared, etc.).

That might seem difficult to reconcile with our contemporary Cartesian perspective, but Western science is able to live with the dichotomy if there's a benefit to be had—and there is.

Richard Evans Shultes (1915–2001), Jeffrey Professor of Biology and Director of the Botanical Museum at Harvard, discovered thousands of plants in the Amazon basin over his lifetime that have added hundreds of beneficial drugs and medicines to the modern pharmacopoeia—but he acknowledges much of this information came from the consumption of ayahuasca with shamans who were able to guide him to crucial plants revealed by the spirits ayahuasca provides access to—which means that hundreds of thousands of people are alive today, and millions more have had their quality of life improved, thanks to shamans (and the occasional biologist) "tripping" in the jungle!

One doesn't hear that in the television advertising.

In recent decades, anthropological fieldwork (like that of Michael Harner and Jeremy Narby) has helped document the often-astonishing characteristics of such rituals, as well as located the source of several tribal mythologies in the visions inspired by these plants. And, as Richard Evans Shultes, Albert Hofmann, and Christian Ratsch observe in their comprehensive survey, *The Plants of the Gods,* "there is hardly an aboriginal culture without at least one psychoactive plant."

HIGH CULTURES AND SACRED PLANTS

> Ecstasy! In common parlance ecstasy is fun. But ecstasy
> is not fun. Your very soul is seized and shaken until it
> tingles. After all, who will choose to feel undiluted awe?[2]

General use of psychedelics fell out of favor with the advent of agriculture, roughly eight to ten thousand years ago—difficult to get up and plow the south forty at dawn if you've been communing with God all night! As tribal cultures gave way to civilization, the use of sacred plants fell to an elite and influential minority—primarily priests and priestesses, initiates into mystery cults, and, the last few centuries, artists, poets, mystics, philosophers, and other bohemian spirits in Western culture.

In 1969, R. Gordon Wasson identified Amanita muscaria—or fly agaric—as the *Soma* of India's Rig-Vedas. According to Wendy Doniger (who assisted Wasson with the translation of Sanskrit texts and currently occupies the Mircea Eliade Chair of Religious Studies at the University of Chicago), both the Upaniṣads and the techniques of yoga can be viewed as an attempt to recapture the vision granted by the *Soma* plant that "underlies the whole of Indian religion and everything of a mystical nature within that religion is pertinent to the identity of that plant" (cited by Huston Smith in *Cleansing the Doors of Perception*, 49).

The question of *Soma*'s identity is not settled to everyone's satisfaction (the argument isn't over whether *Soma* refers to an entheogen, but to which one; Wasson's thesis has been embraced by Doniger, Huston Smith, Claude Levi-Strauss, Richard Shultes,

Robert Graves, and Joseph Campbell, among others); but there's no question that the Amanita mushroom was in use in the Indus Valley at least 3,500 years ago, and a number of psychoactive plants remain central to the Indian mythos—particularly cannabis (for example, at one point while seeking enlightenment Buddha is said to have survived on one hemp seed a day), and *datura*, which in India is called "tuft of Shiva" (*datura* blossoms are woven into the flying locks of the famous image of Shiva Nataraja—"the Lord of the Cosmic Dance"—and when Buddha was preaching, heaven was said to sprinkle the *datura* with dew).

And then there are the Greek mystery cults:

> Some very interesting research concerning the plants associated with these cults has shown that the people who were going to go through the great ceremony consumed a barley drink before attending the rites. One of the historically important hallucinogens is ergot, which is produced by a fungus that grows parasitically on barley. Since one family was for centuries in charge of the rites, many now believe that this barley broth contained a bit of the ergot. There is a very fine study called *The Road to Eleusis*, written by Albert Hofmann, who discovered LSD; R. Gordon Wasson; and classical scholar Carl A. Ruck. This book deals with the entire ritual of Eleusis in detail as a ceremonial matching of the rapturous state of the people who have taken the drink with a theatrical performance that is rendered as an epiphany. So there is an inward readiness to an outer fulfillment.[3]

Campbell has playfully noted parallels between these ancient mystery rituals and the celebratory bacchanalian pageantry of the Grateful Dead (which prompted guitarist/songwriter Jerry Garcia to respond, "They didn't know what they were saying, and we don't know what we're saying, but we think we're saying the same thing"). Whether or not the comparison holds, it nevertheless appears that an ergot compound—precursor to LSD—inspired the mystery rites of this influential sacred cult that endured nearly a thousand years and included participants ranging from Socrates and Plato to Aristophanes and, quite possibly, St. Paul (much of Pauline theology detailed in the New Testament parallels imagery associated with the mystery cults). These initiation rites contributed to a beautiful, elegant mythology whose echoes are still heard today.

Even in Christianized Europe of the Middle Ages the ritual use of Amanita muscaria, nightshade, witch bane, and other psychedelics were often part of sacred ceremonies celebrating the turn of seasons, cross-quarter days, and full moons—those "riotous *sabbats*" that brought charges of witchcraft and satanism during the period of the Inquisition. (Michael Harner points out the common image of the witch riding her broomstick to the sabbat has an origin in the traditional means used to apply ointments of belladonna, hemlock, and henbane to vaginal membranes, thus triggering the ecstatic visionary experience—a wild ride indeed!)

Meanwhile, in the eleventh century Avicenna, celebrated Islamic physician and philosopher, recommended *datura*—which is coincidentally congruent with the appearance of the arabesque (an intricate visual pattern *datura* users often report) as a mystical, unifying theme in Islamic art and architecture.

These examples barely scratch the surface. Traditional cultures have generally considered sacred the altered states these substances occasion. Alan Watts, Robert Graves, R. Gordon Wasson and others have even suggested religion itself may have its source in "such chemically-induced theophanies."

What, then, do these theophanies contain?

The mythic image.

SWIMMING WITH ARCHETYPES

> Let us first ask about the waters into which he has descended. They are the same, we have said, as those of the mystical experience. What, then, is their character? What are their properties and what does it take to swim?
>
> They are all the waters of the universal archetypes of mythology. All my life, as a student of mythologies, I have been working with these archetypes, and I can tell you, they do exist . . .[4]

(Joseph Campbell, *Myths to Live By,* 209)

After the end of the turbulent sixties Joseph Campbell confessed to Sam Keen that, while psychedelics had "uncovered the unconscious depths in a society that is lopsidedly rational and evaluative"—thus demonstrating that the archetypes of the unconscious "are as real as tables and chairs"—he nevertheless feared the drug culture had been "caught in the fuzzy end of things":

> The young seem bewildered by the world of the psyche. They came into it too fast. It is like the situation in

Greek mythology where a person says to a god, "Show me yourself in your full power." And the god does, and the person is blown to bits.[5]

While decrying both the fuzziness and the frenzied extremes of the period, Campbell acknowledged that many had nevertheless experienced "a more serious encounter with the religious practices and myths of the East—Zen, meditation, yoga, etc."

In the pages of *Life* magazine in the 1960s, the lack of purpose to the hippie lifestyle seemed obvious: hordes of barefoot, bedraggled, yet colorfully clad adolescents milling about the corner of Haight and Ashbury getting high, then wandering over to Golden Gate Park to get high, have sex, eat free food, get high, dance to free music, find a crash pad and have more sex and drugs. No aims, no ambitions—a generation lost and adrift.

Given the media hype, it's easy to understand how Joseph Campbell sometimes lumped LSD users in with schizophrenics, whom he describes as drowning in the same waters in which mystics swim. That may indeed have been the experience of some; though LSD has never been demonstrated to be the source of mental illness, it can unmask underlying disturbances in those already psychologically fragile—a risk too great to rationalize casual recreational use.

But it turns out that not all who wander are lost.

Vision Quest

In principle, every individual seems to have experiential access to mythological themes of all times and all cultures. On many occasions, unsophisticated subjects have described in detail complex mythological images and even entire scenes from Central or South America, Polynesia, Mesopotamia, India, Egypt, Japan, and other areas that they definitely did not know about intellectually. These observations clearly support Carl Gustav Jung's concept of the collective unconscious ... [6]

Huston Smith points out that Stanislav Grof has logged over twelve thousand clinical hours monitoring legal LSD sessions (and draws on another eight hundred case studies conducted by his colleagues). After legal research on LSD and other psychedelic substances was suspended in the wake of the youth revolt of the sixties, Grof developed a technique he calls Holotropic Breathwork™ (akin to a Hindu breathing practice used in rebirthing sessions) to induce altered states of consciousness, thus allowing research to continue.

A surprising number of patients identified with mythic imagery, familiar and foreign, during psychedelic sessions:

> The subject can witness numerous scenes from the mythology and folklore of any culture in the world and visit any number of mythical landscapes. He or she can also experientially identify with legendary and mythical heroes and heroines, or fantastic mythological creatures. It is possible to experience the labors of Hercules or the adventures of Theseus and Jason. One can become the legendary Polynesian hero Maui, or suffer through the ordeal of the twins in the Mayan *Popul Vuh*. Among the archetypal creatures that subjects have identified with

in psychedelic sessions and during holotropic breathing were Uroboros, Typhon, Centaurs, Cerberus, Sphinx, various European, oriental, and pre-Columbian dragons, Snow White, legendary knights, mermaids, fairies, elves, gnomes, Scandinavian trolls, and others.[7]

These observations echo ancient as well as contemporary accounts of those who have ingested sacred plants. Grof's follow-up research indicated subjects found themselves drawn to beliefs and practices they had previously ridiculed—including astrology, alchemy, Tarot, the I Ching, gnostic teachings, and Eastern disciplines—and developed "a deep interest in the spiritual path."

Whether LSD in the laboratory, or ayahuasca in a tribal rite, all subjective accounts suggest the psychedelic experience is of the same order and shares the same source as myth and dream—so no surprise they share the same structure as well.

> [Campbell & Jung] have demonstrated that true myths are manifestations of fundamental organizing principles that exist within the cosmos, affecting all our lives. Jung called them archetypes.
>
> These archetypes express themselves through our individual psyches, but they are not human creations. In a sense archetypes are supraordinated to our psyches and represent universal governing principles at work within our individual lives. Archetypes are universal and they cross historical, geographical, and cultural boundaries, though they may appear under different names or show variation from culture to culture. Since

myths involve archetypes, they can truly be said to have autonomy, and they are in no way dependent on us to create them. They exist in that vast sea of human knowledge that Jung referred to as the "collective unconscious," as real as the birds that fly in the sky or the marine life that lives in the ocean.[8]

Grof found the imagery of death-and-rebirth central to a stage of the LSD experience that not everyone reaches. The subject finds him or herself awash in the contents of the personal unconscious, confronting everything from sexual and religious taboos to childhood fears and family relationships. Often this involves consciously re-experiencing one's own birth trauma (even details previously unknown to the subject), followed by catharsis—a release or breakthrough into transpersonal realms:

> Dr. Grof has found (and I find this extremely interesting) that the differing imageries of the various world religions tend to appear and to support his patients variously during the successive stages of their session. In immediate association with the birth trauma, the usual imagery brought to mind is of the Old and New Testaments, together with (occasionally) certain Greek, Egyptian, or other pagan counterparts. However, when the agony has been accomplished and the release experienced of "birth"—actually a "second" or "spiritual" birth, released from the unconscious fears of the former, "once born" personal condition—the symbology radically changes. Instead of mainly Biblical, Greek, and Christian themes, the analogies now point toward the

great Orient, chiefly India. "The source of these experiences," says Dr. Grof, "is obscure, and their resemblance to the Indian descriptions flabbergasting."[9]

Joseph Campbell met Stanislav Grof in the early seventies—but it was Grof's meticulous research into LSD and other entheogens in the fifties and sixties that first documented mythological imagery revealing the contents and structure of the unconscious psyche, thus providing independent scientific confirmation of many of Campbell's insights and observations. It turns out the psychedelic experience mirrors the hero's quest—*departure* from the world of everyday experience, followed by a crisis of *initiation* (death/rebirth), and a *return*—and not just in the broad outline, but in exquisite detail.

No wonder *The Hero with a Thousand Faces* was adopted as a guide to the LSD experience; the book embraces the entire cast of characters across mythologies, mapping the multiple expressions of the hero motif as it unfolds across cultures, and in the individual life. Trippers in the sixties turned to *Hero* not because it imposes structure on a formless experience, but because the myths and rituals Campbell describes therein correspond with the inherent nature of the psychedelic experience.

> That was the era of inward discovery in its LSD phase. Suddenly, *The Hero with a Thousand Faces* became a kind of TripTik® for the inward journey, and people were finding something in that book that could help them interpret their own experience. The book is the presentation of the one great mythic theme—that of the journey, of the quest, and of the finding, and the

return. Anyone going on a journey inward or outward to find values will be on a journey that has been
described many times in the myths of mankind, and I
simply put them all together in that book.[10]

THE QUALITY OF ILLUSION

Considering the intensity of immersion in the symbolic realm,
it's no surprise that many psychedelic explorers in the fifties
and sixties became seekers, turning to mythological structures
to provide a framework within which they could process and
explore the insights and imagery of what might otherwise have
been a life-shattering experience.

Alan Watts offered Buddhism as a model, leaning toward
the elegant simplicity of Zen; Aldous Huxley and Richard Alpert
(Ram Dass) embraced Hindu traditions; Carlos Castenada
espoused the shamanic model; and the Grateful Dead evolved
a spontaneous structure that contained and nurtured the psychedelic experience—a potent traveling circus centered on
Dionysian dancing and shamanic soundscapes, that allowed the
time and space for visionary states to safely unfold.

Many in traditional disciplines across the spectrum automatically discount the validity of "instant enlightenment,"
claiming realization must be earned and maintained through
commitment and hard work, not chemistry. This objection mistakes collective stereotypes shaped by the media-fueled frenzy
of the sixties ("hedonistic adolescents catching a momentary
buzz") with actual experience.

Forty years after the Summer of Love we are better able

to chart the aftermath of the psychedelic explosion. Multiple studies have, for example, demonstrated a common trajectory to LSD experimentation: Addiction is not a problem; with some exceptions, the standard rhythm with psychedelics is one of intense use over a limited period of time, followed by a tapering off and eventual discontinuation, as if the entheogen had served its purpose. This pattern is the direct antithesis of every other class of psychoactive substances (including alcohol, tobacco, opiates, and stimulants). Apparently, the experience of that overwhelming, soul-shaking, undiluted awe Wasson describes, coupled with the confrontation with one's shadow *and* the dissolution of the ego, is not easy to endure on any regular basis . . . so the tendency is to move on to less intense means of accessing the inaccessible (yoga, fasting, meditation, initiation rituals, etc.).

Alan Watts succinctly summed up this dynamic: "Once the call goes through, you hang up the phone."

Several studies have explored the spiritual nature of the psychedelic state, but one of the best documented is described by Huston Smith:

> In his doctoral study at Harvard University, Walter Pahnke worked out a typology of religious experience (in this instance, mystical experience) based on classic reports that Wallace Stace included in his *Mysticism and Philosophy*. Pahnke then administered psilocybin to fifteen theology professors and students (half the total population of thirty) in the setting of a Good Friday service. The drug was given in a "double-blind" experiment, meaning that neither Dr. Pahnke nor his

subjects knew which were getting psilocybin and which fifteen received placebos to constitute a control group. Subsequently the subjects' reports of their experiences were rated independently by three former schoolteachers on the degree (strong, moderate, slight, or none) to which each report evinced the nine traits of mystical experience that Stace enumerates. The results showed that "those subjects who received psilocybin experienced phenomena which were indistinguishable from, if not identical with, the categories defined by our typology of mysticism."[11]

Far from a fleeting illumination, this mystical experience proved significant and life lasting for the seminarians and theologians involved (Smith, one of the original participants, is today a widely- respected religious scholar whose volume, *The World's Religions*—originally published as *The Religions of Man*—remains a standard college text).

Whether entheogen-induced altered states are *similar* to mystical experience, or rather they *are* mystical experience, seems a moot point (especially to many who have experienced psychedelics). Considering a key illumination of mystical experience is the realization that "All is Illusion," there's a certain irony in maintaining an exclusive belief that there is a "real" realization of the illusory nature of all reality (including the realization itself) through, say, sitting zazen, while the identical experience of the *same* underlying truth achieved through the ritual ingestion of a mushroom or cactus must be illusory—a line of reasoning that paints itself into an imaginary corner.

What we do know is that psychedelic experimentation for

many individuals opened the door to a deeper exploration of their own spirituality, often in conjunction with a recognized religious tradition (Yoga, Vedanta, Zen, Christianity, etc.), and, just as often, through a self-created path.

This isn't to suggest that Joseph Campbell advocated indiscriminate use of psychedelics to "find God"—there are so many other paths to the Transcendent that are less hard on the body, have less in the way of distracting fireworks, and are legal almost everywhere—but psychedelics do represent one portal that has proven significant in the lives of many.

For a few hardy adventurers, though, spiritual exploration through the use of sacred plants has become a discipline all its own.

PSYCHEDELIC SHAMANS

Psychedelic shamanism strikes some as a trendy term to justify the self-indulgence of dotcom druggies and sixties burnouts; practitioners, on the other hand, maintain the inward turn midwifed by psychoactive plants is a legitimate realization of the mythic vision quest.

Though off the radar of most First World peoples, the study (and practice) of shamanism is a serious and growing discipline—one that includes an expanding interest, among scientists *and* seekers, in psychedelic shamanism. Mainstream critics discount this movement, either ignoring it completely, or assuming proponents are simply drug-addled hippie-wannabes.

Nevertheless, this theme has been picked up by a new generation. Committed practitioners—such as journalist Daniel Pinchbeck, anthropologist Jeremy Narby, and the late, legendary

Terence McKenna—are identified with contemporary shamanism, a movement that stretches from the rainforests of Mesoamerica, the plains of Africa, and the remote reaches of Nepal, to Europe and the United States, where this decidedly individual practice finds collective expression in events like the counterculture's Rainbow Family gatherings and the annual Burning Man festival.

Of course, not all shamanic practices involve the use of psycho-active plants—but those that do have been discussed in detail at the Visionary Etheobotany Conference, an annual weeklong event held over thirteen years that drew biologists, botanists, chemists, psychiatrists, anthropologists, and shamans (both tribal and self-proclaimed) to Palenque, Mexico (discontinued, unfortunately, after McKenna's passing). Similar events are held annually in Hawaii, Jamaica, and elsewhere. These aren't the party sessions that the common stereotype assumes, but opportunities for the presentation of serious research and the exchange of information between members of different disciplines.

Is this simply a cultural hiccup, intriguing, but insignificant—an aberration with less impact in the long run than a Trekkie convention? Or might the resurgence of interest in psychedelic shamanism be the canary in the coal mine, portending a shift of mythic proportions rumbling up from the bowels of contemporary culture?

THE INWARD TURN

Joseph Campbell noted congruencies between our period and two previous episodes when the ritual use of sacred plants emerged as a response to the breakdown of a prevailing mythology.

One ran concurrent with the Indo-European subjugation of the Achaean peninsula, culminating centuries later in Alexander's conquest of Asia Minor, the Fertile Crescent, and northern India, followed by Roman domination of the Mediterranean world. Local mythologies were threatened by the new and pervasive cosmopolitan culture of the Hellenistic and Roman worlds—what had held true seemed in dissolution. As the discredited local cults languished, the mystery cults emerged, compensating this loss of the sacred with an inward experience of the universal divine (often precipitated by consumption of a sacred plant).

Campbell also finds a parallel in American history, in the aftermath of the tragic slaughter of the buffalo in the decade between 1870 and 1880. The buffalo was not only the chief food animal of the Plains tribes (and chief source of clothing, blankets, dwellings, etc.), but also their primary spiritual symbol. As Campbell points out in *An Open Life* (with Michael Toms), "It was when the social religion dissolved and the object of the cult disappeared that the peyote cult came up from Mexico and overwhelmed the Plains cultures" (104).

> What does peyote do? It gives you visions from inside. So the outside social structure is no longer sanctified through rites. The rite has been taken away, the object of the ritual no longer exists, nor does the manner of life that made it relevant. An inward turn, then, is the only resort for the individual—he finds his religion inside—and that's what's happening to ourselves right now. The authority of the inherited religions is in question. Christianity and Judaism are on the rocks, at least for many of the young people in our

culture. So along comes the peyote and LSD fad of the 60s—inward turning. And today it's no longer LSD so much, but meditation.[12]

Joseph Campbell isn't recommending we turn to psychoactive drugs—indeed, he never indulged himself, despite the opportunity:

> I prefer the gradual path . . . My feeling is that mythic forms reveal themselves gradually in the course of your life if you know what they are and how to pay attention to their emergence. My own initiation into the mythic depths of the unconscious has been through the mind, through the books that surround me in this library. I have recognized in my quest all the stages of the hero's journey. I had my calls to adventure, my guides, demons, and illuminations.[13]

Nevertheless, Campbell notes the spontaneous reappearance of this psychedelic motif in society suggests the tip of an iceberg, signaling a shift from faith in authority to reliance on an authentic and individual inward experience. "The Shaman," as Campbell writes in *Primitive Mythology* (213), "is one who, as a consequence of a personal psychological crisis, has gained a certain power of his own."

WAKING THE SHAMAN

Though LSD as a social issue has faded away, the spiritual use of psychedelics continues—and is even legally protected in some forms. As recently as 1993 the United States Congress passed legislation ensuring the right of the members of the Native American Church to use peyote—and, in 2005, the Supreme Court unanimously ruled in favor of a small religious group that imports ayahuasca from the rainforest for religious ceremonies (Ashcroft v. Uniao Do Vegetal).

Of course, despite the growing interest, only a small minority of the public has any experience with psychedelics. Even though I imagine Joseph Campbell would be pleased to see scientific research allowed, believing there's so much yet to be learned, and would certainly support the protection of indigenous traditions, I can't imagine him advocating the wholesale indiscriminate use of psychedelics.

However, as he notes, meditation and other expressions of this inward turn are also more widespread and on the rise, a further response to the absence of the sacred in our society.

The loss of faith in the dominant mythological paradigm doesn't represent a social failure so much as it anticipates a cultural shift every bit as significant as the emergence of agriculture ten thousand years ago. Accompanying this transition, Campbell sees the archetype of the shaman resurfacing:

> The binding of the shamans . . . by the gods and their priests, which commenced with the victory of the Neolithic over the Paleolithic way of life, may perhaps already be terminating—today—in this period of the irreversible transition of society from an agricultural to an industrial base, when not the piety of the planter, bowing humbly before the will of the calendar and the gods of rain and sun, but the magic of the laboratory,

flying rocket ships where the gods once sat, holds the
promise of the boons of the future.[14]

We are passing from an agricultural phase that has provided
the context of life for ten thousand years, zipping through the
industrial and into the information age at breakneck speed.
Indeed, as in the period of the Mediterranean mystery cults,
what had held true seems in dissolution.

Joseph Campbell would not be surprised by the spontaneous resurgence of shamanism (psychedelic or otherwise)
we're seeing today—it's the harbinger of broad change to come.

But there's a personal and practical aspect to the motif as
well. Though he is hardly recommending we all drop acid or
jaunt off to Gabon to eat iboga with the Bwiti, Joseph Campbell
nevertheless affirms the increasing relevance of the shaman
archetype in an age that has lost its mythic moorings:

> The Shaman goes off on his own flight. The priest is the
> agent of a village system of gods. There is a pantheon
> of which he is the ordained minister. But the Shaman
> goes off to have his own experience, his own familiars,
> his own personal guardians, and they are the ones that
> carry him into these distances.[15]

We can no longer rely on a dynamic collective tradition to point
the way. Each must follow one's own path, forge one's own myth.

Anyone know where to find a good roadmap for the journey?

[ADDENDUM: Tempting to claim the above, written 15
years ago, is eerily prescient—but it does seem to foreshadow
a greater acceptance among the public today, coupled with

the relaxation of legal restrictions and an increase in scientific research, as documented in science and nature writer Michael Pollan's *How to Change Your Mind: What the New Science of Psychedelics Teaches Us About Consciousness, Dying, Addiction, Depression, and Transcendence.*]

NOTES

1. Campbell, Inner Reaches of Outer Space, op. cit. 61.
2. R. Gordon Wasson, quoted in Huston Smith, Cleansing the Doors of Perception (New York: Jeremy P. Tarcher/Putnam,2000; Boulder, CO: Sentient Publications, 2003), viii.
3. Joseph Campbell, Mythos, Vol. 1: The Shaping of Our Mythic Tradition, Episode 5: "The Mystical Life" (New York: Unapix, 1999; London: Acorn Media, 2007).
4. Campbell, Myths To Live By, op. cit. 209.
5. Joseph Campbell, "Mythic Reflections," interview by Sam Keen, Psychology Today (July 1971).
6. Stanislav Grof, The Adventure of Self-Discovery (Albany: State University of New York Press, 1988), 127.
7. Ibid. 126.
8. Grof, The Holotropic Mind, op. cit. 156.
9. Campbell, Myths To Live By, op. cit. 262.
10. Campbell, "Living Myths" interview op. cit.
11. Smith, Cleansing the Doors of Perception, op. cit. 22.
12. Campbell, "Living Myths" interview, op.cit.
13. Campbell, "Man and Myth" interview, op. cit.
14. Campbell, Primitive Mythology, op. cit. 258.
15. Joseph Campbell, "Interview with Joseph Campbell," interview by John Lobell, Natural Living with Gary Null, WBAI Radio (December 28, 1983)

TWENTY-FOUR

SPIRIT WIND

> The wind is air, the highest holy power of the universe,
> Brahman, the life-force of the world; for the wind per-
> sists in its blowing when all the other powers of the body
> of the universe have temporarily ceased to exist ... [1]

One might live a celibate life, forego the comforts of home and
family, maybe even go a few days without food or water—but I
have yet to meet anyone who can pass an hour without taking
a breath. Earth's atmosphere provides the context for all life.
The air we breathe is the same air our fellow creatures breathe.
Even the plants and trees mirror this dance, breathing out as
we breathe in.

> Nothing is more common to the diverse indigenous
> cultures of the earth than a recognition of the air, the
> wind, and the breath, as aspects of a singularly sacred
> power. By virtue of its pervading presence, its utter
> invisibility, and its manifest influence on all manner

of visible phenomena, the air, for oral peoples, is the archetype of all that is ineffable, unknowable, yet undeniably real and efficacious.[2]

Air, wind, and breath are subtle expressions of a universal archetypal experience common not just to pre-literate cultures, but a source of exquisite imagery found in all mythologies, mystical traditions, and metaphysical systems.

Joseph Campbell associates such mythological archetypes with the Indian concept of *mārga*:

> *Mārga* comes from a root that has to do with an animal trail; it means "the path." By this, Indians mean the path by which the particular aspect of a symbol leads you to personal illumination; it is the path to enlightenment.[3]

Is it all in the imagination, or do mythological images reference real experiences, available and accessible to real people in the real world?

We'll explore this question by taking a cue from Campbell's description of *mārga*—pick up the traces of a single universal motif at its source in collective human experience, and follow its trail through a variety of languages, cultures, and mythological systems to see if this path might indeed point to personal illumination.

Where does our journey begin?

With a deep breath . . .

THE BIG GULP

It's no surprise that creation myths often open with the wind stirring the waters. In Genesis 1:2 we read that, "the Wind (or Spirit) of God moved across the face of the waters"; among the Diné (or Navajo), *n'ilch'i*—the Holy Wind—existed first; in Babylonian myth *Anu* begets the four winds on the surface waters of *Tiamat*, disturbing the dragon goddess of chaos whose being forms the substance of all that is; and then Joseph Campbell often points to Patanjali's *Yoga Sutra*, which likens the phenomenal world (as experienced through the organs of mind and senses) to the surface of a pond rippled by the breeze.

No humans existed at the beginning of time to witness these miracles—but the mythological act that gives life to mankind is rooted in human experience.

Life outside the womb for every human begins with that first breath. Every breath thereafter marks our existence as a separate, individual being growing into its own conscious awareness of the world around itself—until our final breath, when consciousness recedes, to we know not where.

Consciousness washes in, consciousness washes out—but whence the source of consciousness, and where does it go? Mythology associates consciousness with breath—so what, then, is the source of breath?

> And the Lord God formed man of the dust of the ground, and breathed into his nostrils the breath of life, and man became a living soul.
>
> (Genesis 2:7)

The Hebrew word for "soul" in this passage is *naphesh*—"a breathing creature." Corresponding terms in Indo-European languages parallel Semitic derivations. In Latin, for example, *anima* means "breath" AND "soul" (etymologically then, an animal is "a being which breathes," or "a being having a soul," congruent to the Hebrew *naphesh*). Similarly, *atman*, in Sanskrit, often translated "soul" or the "divine Self," comes from the root *an* ("to breathe"), and is related to the German *Atmen* ("breath") and the English "atmosphere."

Though these terms clearly resonate with the biblical image, there do seem to be significant differences, particularly in the extension of consciousness and soul beyond the confines of the human mind.

Another variance would appear to be in contrasting mythological perceptions of the Creator:

> He [the Divine Self] dwells in the breath, He is within the breath; the breath, however, does not know Him: the breath is His body, He controls the breath from within. He dwells in the mind, He is within the mind; the mind does not know Him: the mind is His body, He controls the mind from within. (*Brhadaranyaka Upaniṣad* 3.7.1)[4]

A far cry from the cosmic mouth-to-mouth resuscitation described in Genesis! God isn't just the source of breath in Hindu mythology, but *inhabits* the breath and *is* the breath (and, by extension, inhabits and is the mind—consciousness—as well). That's somewhat abstract and vaporous compared to the robust, vigorous God of Judeo-Christo-Islamic mythologies, who projects a sharply-defined muscular ego ("I Am That I Am") more clearly in tune with Western sensibilities. The God of scripture might be the *source* of breath, the *source* of human consciousness, but he doesn't *identify* with either...

. . . or does He?

A WIND DIVINE

Recall the passage from Genesis 1:2, which the King James version translates as the "Spirit" of God moving over the face of the waters. The Hebrew word translated "spirit" is *ruach*, which also means "wind," "blow," or "breathe." Joseph Campbell adds another layer to this association, citing Professor T.J. Meek's discussion of the origin of Yahweh (the "unpronounceable" name of God, spelled in Hebrew with just the consonants YHWH):

> "The name [states Professor Meek] . . . was foreign to the Hebrews, and in their attempted explanation of it they connected it with the word *hayah*, 'to be,' just as the Greeks, who did not know the origin and exact meaning of "Zeus," connected the name with 'to live,' whereas it is derived from the Indo-European *dyu*, 'to shine.' The contention that Yahweh was of Arabian origin is clearly in accord with the Old Testament records, which connect him with the Negeb and with southern sanctuaries like Sinai-Horeb and Kadesh . . . The most probable [origin of the name] in our opinion is from the Arabic root *hwy*, 'to blow.'"[5]

David Abram, who explores the origin of language in the animate natural world in *The Spell of the Sensuous* (an exquisite, elegant volume I cannot recommend highly enough), points out that some scribes, to compensate for Hebrew's lack of written vowels, adopted the Aramaean practice of using the consonants H, W, and Y to note vowel sounds. Abram then offers a brilliant observation as to why vowels are missing in Hebrew texts, shedding further light on the relationship of Yahweh (YHWH) to Breath:

> While consonants are those shapes, made by the lips, teeth, tongue, palate, or throat, that momentarily obstruct the flow of breath and so give form to our words and phrases, the vowels are those sounds that are made by the unimpeded breath itself. The vowels, that is to say, are nothing other than sounded breath. And the breath, for the ancient Semites, was the very mystery of life and awareness, a mystery inseparable from the invisible *ruach*—the holy wind or spirit. The breath, as we have noted, was the vital substance blown into Adam's nostrils by God himself, who thereby granted life and consciousness to humankind. It is possible, then, that the Hebrew scribes refrained from creating distinct letters for the vowel-sounds in order to avoid making a visible representation of the invisible. To fashion a visible representation of the vowels, of the sounded breath, would have been to concretize the ineffable, to make a visible likeness of the divine. It would have been to make a visible representation of a mystery whose very essence was to be invisible and hence unknowable—the

sacred breath, the holy wind. And thus it was not done.[6]

Different language groups, different geographical regions, vastly different cultures—yet whether *Brahman*, *YHWH*, or *n'ilch'i* of the Diné, the Name of God is written in the Wind.

THE AIR WE BREATHE

But what is the individual to God?

> [B]reath, as we learn in the next section of Genesis, is the most innocent and elemental bond linking humans to the divine; it is that which flows most directly between God and man. For after God forms an earth-ling (adamah), He blows into the earthling's nostrils the breath of life, and the human awakens. Although ruach may be used to refer to the breath, the Hebrew term used here is *neshamah*, which denotes both the breath and soul. While ruach generally refers to the wind, or spirit, at large, neshamah commonly signifies the more personal, individualized aspect of wind, the wind or breath of a particular body—like the "wind within one" of a Navajo person. In this sense, neshamah is used to signify conscious awareness.[7]

The relationship of the individual soul to God in early Hebraic mythology seems little different from that of *atman* to *Brahman* in Hindu mythology—the same as breath to wind, or individual consciousness to spirit.

The association of breath to spirit is reflected in our language as well as our myths. The afore-mentioned *nephesh*, *ruach*, and *neshamah* are related to breath, wind, spirit, and soul. *Pneuma* (Greek for spirit), *psyche* (soul, mind) and *anima* (soul) are also related to wind or breath, as are *atman* and *Brahman*; similarly, prana, *chi,* and *ki* are Sanskrit, Chinese, and Japanese terms for the subtle breath, spirit, or energy that infuses the universe. In English we find *spirit* itself embedded in re*spir*ation, in*spir*ation, e*xpir*ation, and other breath-related terms—clearly a common thread, no matter the language or culture.

This mythic motif conveys a subtle and sublime metaphysical realization—an illumination arrived at not through abstract theological reasoning, but rather flowing directly from subjective experience.

Engaging the Metaphor

Normally, my heart beats on its own: "I" don't exert direct conscious control over the frequency or intensity. All other bodily processes—circulation, perspiration, metabolism, etc.—are similarly autonomic, or "unconscious." Obviously, I *am* beating my heart, modulating my internal body temperature, secreting necessary hormones – but not the conscious, waking me.

Breathing also occurs without conscious direction or intervention—yet it is different from other involuntary processes in that we *can* consciously control our breath with intention. Hence, breathing is that act where consciousness and the unconscious most clearly come together, and so has long served as a launching pad for subjective explorations of the mystery of Being.

Joseph Campbell charts this development as starting roughly five thousand years ago, once someone in India noticed that we breathe differently when being chased by a tiger than when lounging on the lush green banks of a river skipping stones across the water.

In the first circumstance, one is in an agitated state of mind; in the second, one is peaceful, calm and serene. Naturally we believe it's the circumstances that trigger the breathing **and** the state of mind (who isn't agitated when chased by a tiger?), but what if we turn it around, and put the breathing first?

> You begin by breath control, by breathing to a certain pace, and the breath is very curious . . . The notion is that emotion and feeling and state of mind is related to breath. When you are at rest, the breathing is in a nice, even order. When you are stirred with shock, the breathing changes. With passion the breathing changes. Change the breathing, and you change the state.[8]

Sure enough, hyperventilating can leave us anxious and agitated, even if there are no tigers in the immediate vicinity, while a focus on steadying the breath induces tranquility and equanimity, leaving us open to stillness—the silence beneath the rush of reality.

BREATH WORK

The practical method employed to this end is indeed strange. It is known as *pranayama,* "disciplined control

(*yama*) of the breath (*prana;* Latin, *spiritus*)" . . . This
continuing through hours without end for days, for
months, or for years, at some point the body and mind
together become fundamentally aware and convinced
that the energy by which the body is pervaded is the
same as that which illuminates the world and maintains
alive all beings, the two breaths being the same: which
is the awakening of the body to its inherent spirituality.[9]

There are many different breathwork techniques, from simply
observing one's breath (a long-term process of regular meditation requiring discipline and commitment) to much more dramatic, even explosive, practices, like the *prañic* breathing central
to tantric traditions that resurfaces in contemporary Western
approaches (such as Rebirthing Breathwork, as practiced by
Leonard Orr and Sondra Ray, or the Holotropic Breathwork™
technique pioneered by Stan and Christina Grof). Eastern
practices once considered foreign and exotic are far more common in the West today—hence the value of seemingly archaic
mythological imagery in processing those experiences.

As a regular practice I am drawn to the sitting meditation of
zazen. Through this ritual I observe breath flow in, and breath
flow out, like the tide—and so recognize I am not the source
of my breath; at the same time, I watch thoughts flow in and
thoughts flow out, independent of conscious intention, and so
recognize that I am also not the source of my thoughts, not the
source of consciousness—an embodied "knowing" that grows
out of practice, mirroring the mythic motifs discussed above.

Other techniques trigger different, more spectacular experiences, but these, too, reflect the mythology of Breath.

For example, I have participated in rebirthing rituals on several occasions. No past-life memories have surfaced, nor did I re-experience my birth trauma, but there were a few mind-boggling moments that seem somehow to have slipped the bonds of time. I offer this personal example to indicate one role a mythic image can play in individual experience today:

The guide for my first rebirthing experience was a good friend thoroughly trained in the technique. At his instruction I lay down on a bed and performed rapid, shallow, circular breathing—not easy to maintain for an extended period, so his coaching helped keep me focused and on track the next two hours.

Intriguing process—monotonous at first, interminably so—but then I noticed a tingling in fingers and toes, a metallic taste in the mouth, and a heavy coldness—not shivery, but oddly refreshing, starting in the extremities and slowly moving up my limbs.

No need to bore everyone with the details, but I'll mention one tangible tidbit. Halfway through I needed to heed nature's call, so my coach allowed the necessary break, encouraging me to maintain the circular rhythm of my breath while away. I slowly shuffled down the hall to the bathroom—and shuffle is the right word, for that's all I could do.

When I looked in the mirror, my face appeared different, the fingers of my hands were scrunched together in a tight little wedge (like a newborn babe?) with my body drawn up so that I appeared smaller—and I could not, voluntarily, release my fingers or unclench my hands, which made taking care of business a touch more challenging than usual . . .

. . . and then, back to the bed, breathing, breathing . . .

At one point I recall thinking I had drifted off, for I heard my guide's voice somewhere in the distance, calling me back, urging me to breathe—and I felt a little disappointed in myself, assuming I had simply fallen asleep.

This happened twice more.

With the process complete I finally surfaced, feeling peaceful and relaxed. That's when my guide informed me that on the three occasions when I thought I had drifted off, I actually stopped breathing. Aaron had timed each occurrence; the last was the longest—*after* exhaling, I did not breathe in for a full five minutes and thirty-seven seconds!

Aaron finally called me back when my lips turned blue.

He asked where I had gone that last time the breath had left.

I recounted moving through a passageway of red rock, similar to the Siq, the entry to the ancient Nabatean city of Petra (the setting of the final scene in *Indiana Jones and the Holy Grail*), toward a warm, welcoming, bright, loving light—not exactly white, but an ivory hue—where, at some sort of rustic cabin that proved larger on the inside than the outside, I was welcomed by my deceased father, and surrounded by a supportive crowd of friends and relatives long gone. I recall a warm, intimate, somewhat lengthy exchange with my father, though I'm not sure if words were involved; everyone else seemed somewhat amorphous and vague.

In fact, I had a sense that the deeper I journeyed into this realm, the more vague it becomes—as if I and the world were slowly dissolving—yet I felt no anxiety about this possibility

. . . and then I heard Aaron's voice, faint, but growing stronger: ". . . breathe . . . Breathe . . ."

It's a sweet memory I treasure today.

True, there could be many explanations. It might be no
more than the nitrogen "high" affecting my brain in the
absence of oxygen, a hallucination triggered by self-induced
hyperventilation—or it might be the dying flickers of the elec-
trons in my brain building a pleasant image, a compensatory
metaphor for the most unpleasant process (to waking ego) of
the body dying.

Yes, it could all be hallucination—but there's one other
element in the adventure where the dream intersects waking
reality.

During one of the other episodes when I stopped breathing,
I recall attending a party, meeting a cute girl, talking to her for
hours on a front porch, and then, as rain descends, retreating to
a hippie van parked in front of the house and, well, everything
kind of faded out from there . . .

I shared this . . . what?—memory? dream? wishful thinking?—with my guide.

The other image, of the long passage with the light at
the end and the meeting with my father, seemed archetypal
enough—but we could make neither heads nor tales out of this
image, no matter what symbols we tried to see . . .

. . . until that evening, when I pedaled a borrowed bicycle
seven miles across Portland to a party I had been invited to that
afternoon, *after* the rebirthing, where I talked for hours with a
now familiar girl on the front porch, until it started storming
and we had to take shelter inside a Volkswagen van.

(Is that a Rod Serling voice-over in the background?)

Though a part of me remains inclined to write off the
encounter with my father as self-induced hallucination, the pre-
cognitive nature of the vision of the girl-on-the-porch makes it

difficult for me to simply dismiss either episode.

I don't know what to make of it all, so I treat this as an experience of metaphor: true on the inside, not sure what on the outside.

The way I process this memory is through the mythological complex of wind and spirit and breath and soul. Consciousness seems to have left my body with my breath—and consciousness returned when breath returned.

Sound familiar?

Archetypal imagery provides a context within which to place this and similar experiences; conversely, my personal experience allows a greater appreciation of the depth and profundity of the many mythic variations on this universal motif, and I am thrilled to find echoes of this theme underlying my own Judeo-Christian tradition.

If these are my thoughts after but a brief immersion, what of someone whose whole life is devoted to such rituals, one who regularly ventures forth into the Otherworld—a mystic, or a shaman? Perhaps we catch a glimpse of how myths might have emerged—as "found" truths, conveyed to the outer world through the power of the poetic image.

Of course, one needn't have a full-fledged mystical vision to connect with a mythic symbol.

TAKING FLIGHT

A wandering monk in India is often referred to as *hamsa* ("gander" or "swan") or *paramahamsa* ("supreme gander"):

The wild gander (*hamsa*) strikingly exhibits in its mode of life the twofold nature of all beings. It swims on the surface of the water, but is not bound to it. Withdrawing from the watery realm, it wings into the pure and stainless air, where it is as much at home as in the world below . . .

On the one hand earth-bound, limited in life-strength, in virtues, and in consciousness, but on the other hand a manifestation of the divine essence, which is unlimited, immortal, virtually omniscient and all-powerful, we, like the wild goose, are citizens of the two spheres. We are mortal individuals bearing within ourselves an immortal, supra- individual nucleus . . .

The macrocosmic gander, the Divine Self in the body of the universe, manifests itself through a song.[10]

This is a song we all sing, though few actually hear it. However, if you focus on your breath, you'll hear the sound *ham*, just barely audible, every time you inhale—and the syllable *sa* sounds with every exhale. *"Ham-sa, ham-sa,"* sings our breath all day, all night, all one's life, making known the inner presence of this wild gander to all with the ears to hear.

But the song, like the image of the wild gander, is twofold. Not only does our breath sing *"Hamsa, hamsa"* but also *"sa-' ham, sa-' ham."*

> *Sa* means 'this' and *ham* means 'I'; the lesson is, 'This am I.' I, the human individual of limited consciousness, steeped in delusion, spellbound by Maya, actually and fundamentally am This, or He, namely the Atman or Self, the Highest Being of unlimited consciousness and existence.

I am not to be identified with the perishable individual, who accepts as utterly real and fatal the processes and happenings of the psyche and the body. 'I am He who is free and divine.' That is the lesson sung to every man by every movement of inhalation and exhalation, asserting the divine nature of Him in whom breath abides.[11]

One needn't adopt a mendicant lifestyle, indulge in tantric practices, or even meditate, to appreciate and be inspired by the profound poetic image evoked in the whisper of one's own breath,
    . . . but a deep breath is, indeed, the perfect place to start.

NOTES

1. Heinrich Zimmer, Philosophies of India, ed. Joseph Campbell (Princeton: Bollingen Foundation / Princeton University Press, 1951; Princeton: Princeton University Press, 1989), 171. Citations are from the 1985 printing.
2. Abram, The Spell of the Sensuous, op. cit. 226.
3. Campbell, Pathways to Bliss, op. cit. 96.
4. Zimmer, Philosophies of India, op. cit. 366.
5. T.J. Meek, Hebrew Origins, cited in Campbell, Occidental Mythology, op. cit. 132-131.
6. Abram, The Spell of the Sensuous, op. cit. 241-242.
7. Ibid. 239.
8. Joseph Campbell, Mythos, Vol. 2: The Shaping of the Eastern Tradition, Episode 3: "Our Eternal Selves" (New York: Unapix, 2000; London: Acorn Media, 2008).
9. Campbell, The Inner Reaches of Outer Space, op. cit. 44.
10. Heinrich Zimmer, Myth & Symbols in Indian Art and Civilization, ed. Joseph Campbell (Princeton: Bollingen Foundation / Princeton University Press, 1946; second Princeton / Bollingen paperback printing, 1974), 48. Citations are from paperback edition.
11. Ibid. 49-50.

ABOUT THE
JOSEPH CAMPBELL FOUNDATION

JOSEPH CAMPBELL FOUNDATION (JCF)
is a not-for-profit organization founded to:

1. Preserve, protect, and perpetuate the work of Joseph Campbell by:
   - Cataloging and archiving his works
   - Developing new publications based on his work
   - Directing the sale and distribution of his published works
   - Protecting copyrights to his works
   - Increasing awareness of his works by making them available in multiple digital & analog formats

2. Further Campbell's pioneering work in comparative mythology and religion by:
   - Promoting the study of mythology and comparative religion
   - Implementing and/or supporting diverse mythological education programs
   - Supporting and/or sponsoring events designed to increase public awareness
   - Donating Campbell's papers to the New York Public

Library and his personal library to OPUS Archive &
Research Center
- Making JCF's website (jcf.org) a forum for mythological-
ly-informed cross-cultural dialogue

3. Help individuals enrich their lives by:
- Receiving JCF's Weekly Digest, "MythBlast,"
and related offerings
- Exploring and utilizing some of the many mythological
resources available at www.jcf.org
- Joining in one of the various mythologically-related activities that JCF periodically undertakes

For more information on
Joseph Campbell
and Joseph Campbell Foundation
visit

www.jcf.org

ABOUT STEPHEN GERRINGER

Stephen Gerringer and his wife Destiny live in Modesto, California. After 9/11, Stephen stepped away from teaching English and literature in junior high to pursue his interest in the mythic imagination. He has been a Working Associate of Joseph Campbell Foundation since 2003, where Stephen's responsibilities have included serving as the author of JCF's Practical Campbell essay series, facilitating collaborations with other institutions, speaking on mythic themes to JCF Mythological RoundTable® groups, outside organizations, and college and high school audiences, and editing a soon-to-be-published volume compiled from interviews and post-lecture Q & A sessions with Joseph Campbell.

BIBLIOGRAPHY

Abram, David. *The Spell of the Sensuous: Perception and Language in a More-Than-Human World.* New York: Pantheon Books, 1996.

Bair, Deirdre. *Jung: A Biography.* Boston: Little, Brown, and Company, 2002.

Baring, Anne and Jules Cashford. *The Myth of the Goddess: Evolution of an Image.* New York: Penguin Arkana, 1993. First published 1991 by Viking.

Cammerloher, M.C. "The Position of Art in the Psychology of Our Time." In *Spiritual Disciplines: Papers from the Eranos Yearbooks,* edited by Joseph Campbell, 424-447. Princeton: Princeton University Press, 1985. First published 1960 by Princeton University Press.

Campbell, Joseph. *A Joseph Campbell Companion.* Edited by Diane K. Osbon. New York: Harper Collins Publisher, 1991.

_____. "An Interview with Joseph Campbell." Interview by John Lobell. *Natural Living with Gary Null,* WBAI Radio, December 28, 1983.

_____. "An Interview with Joseph Campbell." Interview by Gerald McDermott. *New Boston Review,* Vol. I No. 2, Fall 1975,

_____. "An Interview with the Master of Mythology." Interview by Joe Nigg. *The Bloomsbury Review*, April/May, 1984, 21-23.

_____. *Asian Journals*. Edited by David Kudler. Novato: New World Library, 2017. Originally published in 2002 as two volumes: *Baksheesh & Brahman: Asian Journals—India,* and *Sake & Satori: Asian Journals*, by New World Library.

_____. *Correspondence: 1927 – 1987*. Edited by Evans Lansing Smith, Ph.D. and Dennis Patrick Slattery, Ph.D. Novato: New World Library, 2019.

_____. "Elders and Guides." Interview by Michael McKnight. *Parabola*, Vol. V No. 1, February 1980, 57-65.

_____. *Historical Atlas of World Mythology*. Vol. 1, *The Way of the Animal Powers*. Part 1, *Mythologies of the Primitive Hunters and Gatherers*. New York: Harper & Row, 1988.

_____. *Historical Atlas of World Mythology*. Vol. 2, *The Way of the Seeded Earth*. Part 1, *The Sacrifice*. New York: Harper & Row, 1988.

_____. *Historical Atlas of World Mythology*. Vol. 2, *The Way of the Seeded Earth*. Part 3, *Mythologies of the Primitive Planters — The Middle and Southern Americas*. New York: Harper & Row, 1989.

_____. Unpublished interview with Joseph Campbell by Costis Ballas. 9-27-85. Box 93, Folder 24, Joseph Campbell Papers. Manuscripts and Archives Division, The New York Public Library.

_____. Unpublished interview with Joseph Campbell by E. Bouratinos. 9-30-85. Box 93, Folder 25, Joseph Campbell Papers. Manuscripts and Archives Division, The New York Public Library.

_____. "Joseph Campbell, Mythologist: Seventy Years of Making Connections." Interview by D.J.R. Bruckner. *New York Times Book Review*, December 18, 1983.

_____. "Joseph Campbell: The Mythic Journey." Interview by Joan Marler. *The Yoga Journal*, Nov./Dec. 1987.

_____. "Living Myths: A Conversation with Joseph Campbell." Interview by Lorraine Kisly. *Parabola*, Volume I Issue 2, Spring 1976, 70-81.

_____. "Man & Myth: A Conversation with Joseph Campbell." Interview by Sam Keen. *Psychology Today*, July 1971.

_____. "Mythic Reflections." Interview by Tom Collins. *In Context: A Quarterly of Humane Sustainable Culture*, Vol. 12, Winter 1985/1986, p. 52

_____. *Mythic Worlds, Modern Words*. Edited by Edmund L. Epstein, Ph.D. Novato: New World Library, 2003. First published 1993 by HarperCollins.

_____. *Mythos*, Vol. 1, *The Shaping of Our Mythic Tradition*, Episode 3, "On Being Human." Acorn Media, 2007. Originally distributed by Unapix, 1999.

_____. *Mythos*, Vol. 2, *The Shaping of the Eastern Tradition*, Episode 1, "The Inward Path." Acorn Media, 2008. Originally distributed by Unapix, 2000.

_____. *Myths of Light*. Edited by David Kudler. Novato: New World Library, 2002.

_____. "Myths of the Universe: The Earth Spirit and the Coming of the New Age — an Interview with Joseph Campbell." Interview by Cate Miodini. *Anima: An Experiential Journal,* Vol. 13, no. 1, Fall 1986 29-36.

_____. *Myths to Live By.* New York: Penguin Compass, 1993. First published by Viking Press, 1972.

_____. "Out of Our Own Center." Interview by Michael Toms. *Sunrise,* Aug-Sept. 1979, 324-332.

_____. "PW Interviews Joseph Campbell." Interview by Chris Goodrich. *Publisher's Weekly Review,* 8-23-85.

_____. *The Flight of the Wild Gander.* Novato: New World Library, 2002. First published by Viking Press, 1969.

_____. *The Hero's Journey: Joseph Campbell on His Life and Work.* Edited by Phil Cousineau. Novato: New World Library, 2003. First published by Harper & Row, 1990.

_____. *The Hero with a Thousand Faces.* 3rd edition (with revisions). Novato: New World Library, 2008. First published by Bollingen / Princeton University Press, 1949.

_____. *The Inner Reaches of Outer Space.* Novato: New World Library, 2002. First published by A. van der Marck, 1986.

_____. *The Masks of God.* Vol. 1, *Primitive Mythology.* Collected Works of Joseph Campbell edition (with revisions). Novato: New World Library, 2022. First published 1959 by Viking Penguin, Inc.

_____. *The Masks of God.* Vol. 2, *Oriental Mythology.* Collected Works of Joseph Campbell edition (with revisions). Novato: New World Library, 2021. First published 1962 by Viking Penguin, Inc.

_____. *The Masks of God.* Vol. 3, *Occidental Mythology.* Collected Works of Joseph Campbell edition (with revisions). Novato: New World Library, 2021. First published 1964 by Viking Penguin, Inc.

_____. *The Masks of God.* Vol. 4, *Creative Mythology.* New York: Penguin Books 1976. First published 1968 by Viking Penguin.

_____. *The Mythic Dimension.* Edited by Antony Van Couvering. Novato: New World Library, 2007. First published by HarperSanFrancisco, 1997.

_____. *The Mythic Image.* New York: MJF Books, 1996. First published by Princeton University Press, 1974.

_____. "The Mythic Journey." Interview by Joan Marler. *Yoga Journal,* Nov./Dec/ 1987.

_____. *The Power of Myth with Bill Moyers.* New York: Anchor Books, 1991. First published by Doubleday, 1988.

_____. "The Professor with a Thousand Faces." Interview by Donald Newlove. *Esquire Magazine,* Vol. 88, no. 3, Sept. 1977.

_____. "The Wisdom of Joseph Campbell. Interview by Michael Toms. *The Wisdom of Joseph Campbell.* Hayes House Productions, 1997.

_____. *Pathways to Bliss.* Edited by David Kudler. Novato: New World Library, 2004.

_____. *Thou Art That.* Edited by Edmund L. Epstein, Ph.D. Novato: New World Library, 2001.

Cooper, Kenneth H. *Aerobics.* New York: Bantam Books, 1969.

Csikszentmihalyi, Mihalyi. *Finding Flow: The Psychology of Engagement with Everyday Life.* New York: Basic Books / Perseus Books, 1992.

Eliade, Mircea. *The Myth of the Eternal Return.* Princeton: Princeton University Press, 1954.

_____. *The Sacred and the Profane.* New York: Harper Brothers, 1961. First published by Harcourt, Brace, and Company, 1959.

Eliot, Alexander, with Joseph Campbell and Mircea Eliade. *Myths.* Maidenhead, England: McGraw Hill, 1976.

Gimbutas, Marija. *The Living Goddesses.* Berkeley and Los Angeles: University of California Press, 1999.

Grof, Stanislav. *The Adventure of Self-Discovery.* Albany: State University of New York (SUNY) Press, 1988.

_____. with Hal Zina Bennett. *The Holotropic Mind.* San Francisco: HarperSanFrancisco, 1993.

Harpur, Patrick. *Daimonic Reality: A Field Guide to the Other World.* Grand Rapids: Pine Woods Press, 2003. First published by Viking Press, 1994.

Hillman, James. "This Question of Images." In *Saga: Best New Writings on Mythology*, Vol. 1, edited by Jonathan Young. Ashland: White Cloud Press, 1996.

Hyde, Lewis. *Trickster Makes This World.* New York: Farrar, Strauss, and Giroux, 1988.

Jung, C.G. *Dream Analysis: Notes of the Seminar Given in 1928–1930.* Princeton: Princeton University Press, 1984.

_____. *Man and His Symbols*. New York: Dell Publishing, 1968. First published by Aldus Books, 1964.

_____. *Memories, Dreams, Reflections*. New York: Vintage Books / Random House, 1963.

_____. *The Archetypes and the Collective Unconscious*. 2nd edition. Princeton: Princeton University Press, 1968.

Larsen, Stephen, Ph.D. and Larsen, Robin. *A Fire in the Mind*. Rochester, Vermont: Inner Traditions International and Bear & Company, 2002, All rights reserved. Reprinted with permission of the publisher. First published 1991 by Doubleday.

Kerenyi, Carl. "Man and Mask." In *Spiritual Disciplines: Papers from the Eranos Yearbooks*, edited by Joseph Campbell, 151-167. Princeton: Princeton University Press, 1985. First published 1960 by Princeton University Press.

Maher, John M. and Dennis Briggs, ed. *An Open Life: Joseph Campbell in Conversation with Michael Toms*. New York: Harper & Row, 1989.

Markley, O.W., ed. *Changing Images of Man*. Oxford: Pergamon Press, 1982.

Murphy, Michael. *The Future of the Human Body: Explorations Into the Further Evolution of Human Nature*. Los Angeles: Jeremy P. Tarcher, Inc., 1992.

Pagels, Elaine. *The Gnostic Gospels*, © 1979, Vintage Books Edition 1989. First published by Random House, 1979.

Platania, Jon, Ph.D. *Jung for Beginners*. New York: Writers and Readers Publishing, Inc., 1997.

Polak, Fred. *The Image of the Future*. Translated by Elise Boulding. Amsterdam: Elsevier Scientific Publishing Company, 1973.

Segal, Robert. *Joseph Campbell: An Introduction*. New York: Penguin Books, 1997. First published by Garland Publishing, Inc., 1987.

Singer, June. *Boundaries of the Soul*. New York: Anchor Books, 1973.

Skafte, Diane, Ph.D. "The Sibyls." In *Saga, Best New Writings on Mythology*, Vol. 2, edited by Jonathan Young. Ashland: White Cloud Press, 2001.

Smith, Huston. *Cleansing the Doors of Perception*, Boulder, CO: Sentient Publications, 2003. First published by Jeremy P. Tarcher/ Putnam, 2000.

Spence, Lewis, tr. *The Popol Vuh: The Mythic and Heroic Sagas of the Kiches of Central America*. London: David Nutt, 1908.

Steinbeck, John, *The Log from the Sea of Cortez*. New York: Penguin Classics, 1995. Originally published by Viking Press, 1951.

Tam, Eric Enno. *Beyond the Outer Shores*. New York: Four Walls Eight Windows, 2004.

Vogler, Chris. *The Writer's Journey: Mythic Structure for Writers*. 3rd edition. Studio City, California: Michael Wiese Productions, 2007; 25th Anniversary edition 2020. Excerpts reprinted with permission from Michael Wiese Productions (www.mwp.com).

Watts, Alan. *In My Own Way*, New York: Vintage, 1973. First published by Pantheon Books, 1973.
_____. *Myth and Ritual in Christianity*, New York: Vanguard Press 1953

Zimmer, Heinrich. *Myth & Symbols in Indian Art and Civilization.* Edited by Joseph Campbell, Princeton: Princeton University Press, First published by Bollingen Foundation / Princeton University Press, 1946.

_____. "On the Significance of the Indian Tantric Yoga." In *Spiritual Disciplines*, edited by Joseph Campbell, 3-58. Princeton: Princeton University Press, 1985. First published by Bollingen Foundation / Princeton University Press, 1960.

_____. *Philosophies of India.* Edited by Joseph Campbell. Princeton: Princeton University Press, 1989. First published by by Bollingen Foundation, Princeton University Press, 1951.

_____. *The King and the Corpse.* Edited by Joseph Campbell. 2nd edition. Princeton University Press, 1956. First published by Bollingen Foundation / Princeton University Press, 1948.

PERMISSION ACKNOWLEDGMENTS

The author is grateful to all publishing companies that have provided permission to quote passages from the works they have printed, and would like to single out for special acknowledgment the following small, independent publishers and individual authors for their assistance:

Jules Cashford, co-author (with Anne Baring) of The Myth of the Goddess: Evolution of an Image

Robert Segal, author of Joseph Campbell: An Introduction

A Fire in the Mind: The Life of Joseph Campbell
By Stephen Larsen, Ph.D. and Robin Larsen
Published by Inner Traditions International and Bear & Company

Cleansing the Doors of Perception
by Huston Smith
Published by Sentient Publications

Daimonic Reality: A Field Guide to the Otherworld
by Patrick Harpur
Published by Pine Woods.

The Writer's Journey (25th Anniversary edition)
by Chris Vogler

Printed in the USA
CPSIA information can be obtained
at www.ICGtesting.com
LVHW071204190923
758613LV00015B/646/J

9 781611 780352